The Internet Society
Advances in Learning, Commerce and Society

WITPRESS

WIT Press publishes leading books in Science and Technology.
Visit our website for the current list of titles.
www.witpress.com

WITeLibrary

Making the latest research accessible, the WIT electronic-library features papers presented at Wessex Institute of Technology's prestigious international conferences.
To access the library please visit www.witpress.com

FIRST INTERNATIONAL CONFERENCE ON
THE INTERNET SOCIETY
ADVANCES IN LEARNING, COMMERCE AND SECURITY

THE INTERNET SOCIETY 2004

CONFERENCE CHAIRMEN

K. Morgan
University of Bergen, Norway

C.A. Brebbia
Wessex Institute of Technology, UK

J.M. Spector
Syracuse University, USA

INTERNATIONAL SCIENTIFIC ADVISORY COMMITTEE

D Champion
D Feng
N Karmakar
Y Khmelevsky
T Koehler
G Kotsis

S Lal
S Mecca
F Stowell
A Szabo
V Ustymenko

Organised by
Wessex Institute of Technology, UK
and
The University of Bergen, Norway

Preface

Although many people think of the developments within Information and Communications Technology (ICT) as being purely computational and mathematically based in reality it is the human and social changes that are the most dramatic and far reaching.

This book provides an overview of some of the most important aspects of human experience that have been impacted by this developing technology, namely education, commerce and security. ICT has dramatically altered the ways in which we view education and commerce, providing not only new academic sub-disciplines but also substantial changes to society as a whole. Included within this book are contributions that document these changes, the reasons for them and how they will develop in the future. Leading authorities from around the world describe their research in papers that cover the full range of theoretical and practical implications for this new technology. These range from strategic issues in deciding how a new technology can aid a nation's educational, intellectual and commercial development, through to extremely detailed coverage of the very latest developments in security for mobile devices.

It is our hope that readers of this book will not only find in depth information about the latest scientific developments in the field but also a perspective that shows how these new technologies and techniques directly impact our lives and our common futures. It is this image of a common future that is increasingly important because the Internet Society is a global society that touches and affects us all.

Konrad Morgan & Mike Spector
2004

K. Morgan
University of Bergen, Norway

J.M. Spector
Syracuse University, USA

Published by

WIT Press
Ashurst Lodge, Ashurst, Southampton, SO40 7AA, UK
Tel: 44 (0) 238 029 3223; Fax: 44 (0) 238 029 2853
E-Mail: witpress@witpress.com
http://www.witpress.com

For USA, Canada and Mexico

Computational Mechanics Inc
25 Bridge Street, Billerica, MA 01821, USA
Tel: 978 667 5841; Fax: 978 667 7582
E-Mail: infousa@witpress.com
http://www.witpress.com

British Library Cataloguing-in-Publication Data

A Catalogue record for this book is available
from the British Library

ISBN: 1-85312-712-4
ISSN: 1742-5069

> *The texts of the papers in this volume were set
> individually by the authors or under their supervision.
> Only minor corrections to the text may have been carried
> out by the publisher.*

No responsibility is assumed by the Publisher, the Editors and Authors for any injury and/or damage to persons or property as a matter of products liability, negligence or otherwise, or from any use or operation of any methods, products, instructions or ideas contained in the material herein.

© WIT Press 2004.

Printed in Great Britain by The MFK Group, Stevenage.

All rights reserved. No part of this publication may be reproduced, stored in a retrieval system, or transmitted in any form or by any means, electronic, mechanical, photocopying, recording, or otherwise, without the prior written permission of the Publisher.

The Internet Society
Advances in Learning, Commerce and Society

Editors

K. Morgan
University of Bergen, Norway

J.M. Spector
Syracuse University, USA

Contents

Section 1: Computer supported collaborative learning

The development of a collaborative learning framework to support sustainable development
P. Mangan, L. Doherty & M. Layden 3

Remote operational medical assessment and management
H. B. Sorensen & J. S. Riess 13

Developing digital portfolios: how ICT can facilitate pupil talk about learning
K. Wall, S. Higgins, J. Miller & N. Packard 27

A model for collaboration: integrating technology into the elementary media arts and studies curriculum
S. Nuss & K. Conely 37

Section 2: Strategic issues for the design of new learning systems

Curriculum design and management: a systems view
S. Mecca 49

Learning objects in use
J. Bennedsen 61

Modularization of learning outcomes: a "design-down" competency driven instructional design approach
T. M. Stavredes & S. Clawson 69

Work-centred design and decision support in an Adaptive Decision-Enabling and Proficiency Toolkit (ADEPT)
A. Hafich, H. B. Sorensen & J. Owens 79

Section 3: The evaluation of new learning systems

Privacy and security in digital environments: the psychological issues
K. Morgan 89

Evaluation of learning material in PORTAL project:
the case of quality management and benchmarking in public transport
C. Taxiltaris, P. Papaioannou & S. Basbas 99

Biological science misconceptions amongst teachers and primary students
in Jordan: diagnosis and treatment
I. Abu-Hola 109

Expanding online learning exam options with computer-based assessment
E. M. Weeden 119

Preliminary results exploring the use of alternate instructional methods
in mathematics
D. Bond-Hu 131

Tools for teaching molecular spectroscopy
M. Dalibart 139

Evaluation of CBT for increasing threat detection performance
in X-ray screening
A. Schwaninger & F. Hofer 147

The training environment support system: a system designed to enhance
dynamic satellite operator training
H. B. Sorensen, K. Neville, C. Barba, R. Kellermann & R. Andrade 157

Content management systems for e-learning: an application
A. Cucchiarelli & S. Valenti 165

Section 4: Identification and verification

Identification of parts in identity-based encryption
G. Stephanides & N. Constantinescu 177

Authenticating mobile device users through image selection
W. Jansen 183

Section 5: Interface design issues

Cognitive style and interface design: findings from
the HomeNetToo project
L. A. Jackson, F. Biocca, A. von Eye, Y. Zhao & H. Fitzgerald 195

A learning tool for the visualization of general directed
or undirected rooted trees
K. Paparrizos, N. Samaras & A. Sifaleras 205

Contributions of an electronic performance support system to learning
a complex cognitive skill
A. Darabi 215

Metacognitive questions to improve surfing and learning activities
on the Web
G. Chiazzese, A. Chifari, S. Ottaviano, L. Seta & M. Allegra 227

Section 6: Security in e-commerce settings

Cryptography as a formal method and model for security
in electronic payments
T. Tsiakis, G. Stephanides & G. Pekos 235

MARAH: an RBAC model and its integration in a Web server
P. Díaz, D. Sanz & I. Aedo 243

Forced encryption solutions
H. B. Wolfe 253

Section 7: Strategic issues

Legal and policy challenges facing electronic commercial marketplaces
and trading exchanges
J. Matsuura 263

Developing competitive advantages through e-business
of Lithuania's SMEs
R. Gatautis 269

E-business technology education: a preliminary model
S. Dhanjal & Y. Khmelevsky 279

How can the private sector benefit from the public sector's
e-procurement experiences?
H. Lindskog 289

E-procurement: 'supporting opportunities'
J. W. ten Berge, J. H. R. van Duin & P. H. M. Jacobs 299

Knowledge management in higher education:
the business-side performance
L. C. Rodrigues, E. A. Maccari & M. I. R. de Almeida 309

Author Index 319

Section 1
Computer supported collaborative learning

The development of a collaborative learning framework to support sustainable development

P. Mangan[1], L. Doherty[2] & M. Layden[3]
[1]School of Engineering, Letterkenny Institute of Technology, Ireland
[2]Western Health and Social Services Board, Ireland
[3]HEAT Energy and Development Consultants, Ireland

Abstract

Traditional education has generally not effectively supported local communities. This has resulted in graduates not possessing the relevant skills to allow the development of sustainable community structures. The development of more effective learning approaches, which include collaborative learning, greatly assists the process of sustainable development.

Good decisions come from good information, however determining the quality of information may be difficult. Educations aims to provide students with the ability to make good decisions based on available information. Scientific and technical information tends to dominate decision-making, however it often ignores the values, knowledge and expertise of other groups. This limits the range of development options and often results in inappropriate solutions being adapted. The design of an effective collaborative learning and planning process aims to address this difficulty and incorporate different knowledge sources as well as the values and ethics of those the process is designed to help, which is generally the community.

This study identifies the basic elements of collaborative-based learning and decision making through the analysis of a number of case studies. Based on the findings, a novel collaboration based learning framework is developed. This framework is supported through the development of an implementation process, which facilitates sustainable development through social learning and the building of social capital.

Keywords: collaboration, decision-making, sustainable development, social learning, social capital.

 The Internet Society: Advances in Learning, Commerce and Security, K. Morgan & M. J. Spector (Editors)
© 2004 WIT Press, www.witpress.com, ISBN 1-85312-712-4

1 Introduction

Traditional education aims to allow the integration of students into traditional social and economic structures. The formal paternalistic education model, which is generally used in Western society, is based on experts providing correct and value neutral information which the student is expected to learn and internalise.

All education is value based so educators are effectively instilling their own values through the learning process. These practices hinder the development of value systems, which are ecologically rather than technologically orientated. Other models of education, which facilitate internalisation of the principles and values associated with sustainable development, are more democratic and responsive to the needs of the participants. New forms of education such as those that build on the values of the students rather than the educator, can provide the necessary skills for students to deal effectively with the challenges facing society due to unsustainable practices. Without providing these skills at an early stage to future decision-makers, it is unlikely that significant, rapid and sustainable development can take place.

Many educational studies have shown that people judge their most significant learning experiences to come from everyday life rather than from formal learning Henry [1]. Studies of well-being suggest that happy, contented people are those that are actively absorbed in challenges which they can complete successfully, where they get feedback on progress and are supported by a social network to which they feel they belong Haworth [2]. The concept of learning through experience is perhaps a more appropriate model for learning than traditional lectures Kolb [3]. This learning process entails successive rounds of experience, reflection, re-conceptualising and testing which builds skills through learning from experience, rather than from theory.

1.1 Background

1.1.1 Sustainable development
Sustainable Development according to Norton et al involves three economics related issues Norton *et al* [4]; an economy which is active on a sustainable scale relative to its ecological support system, a fair distribution of resources, among human and other species and the efficient allocation of resources. Over time, as the economy expands, due to population growth and increasing consumer expectations, there is also a corresponding increase in the impact of these economic activities on the environment Arrow *et al* [5]. Efforts to limit increases in consumption and ensure fair distribution of resources are extremely complicated and difficult to accomplish. Any attempt to understand problems of this scale must address the fundamental issue of personal preference and values.

1.1.2 Education and values
The values and preferences of children are learned and taught so the preferences of future generations are dependant on the preferences of present generations Mainwaring [6], Norton *et al* [4]. Learned values evolve through a process of

decision-making therefore learned and inherited values and preferences can change provided that these preferences are challenged by making difficult decisions. Attempting to influence society's values therefore appears to be beneficial and necessary to achieve sustainable development. It has been questioned whether it is ethical to seek to influence preferences and values. Influencing people is not however inconsistent with a functioning democratic society. For a democracy to function effectively, it is necessary for structured decision-making, learning and value change to occur.

2 Method

The methodology on which this study is based is primarily a review of literature relating to collaborative learning and planning processes. Based on the results of this literature review, a theoretical collaborative learning and planning framework was developed. This framework assists in the process of sustainable development through the development of social capital, decision-making ability and self-sufficiency. A creative problem-solving workshop was undertaken to develop a suitable implementation mechanism and a consultation process was undertaken to obtain the views of relevant stakeholders. This consultation was carried out using focus groups and stakeholder semi-structured interviews.

3 Results

3.1 Stakeholder participation and learning

The development of new values systems is a necessary precondition for sustainable development to advance. Developing appropriate values can be achieved if stakeholders are engaged in decision-making regarding issues that affect them. Habermas has suggested that when a collective course of action is taken, individuals can put forth proposals that are critiqued through public discourse Habermas [7]. This discourse enables people to compile information in a coherent manner and examine new ideas, claims, beliefs and values Forester [8]. Through communicative action, this process creates legitimacy by building consensus and mutual understanding and the integration of different beliefs and knowledge types Forester [8]. Without such a dialogue, those in power can make unsupported claims and avoid criticism and debate through sanctions, strategic exclusion or threat, thereby hindering learning and development Forester [8].

A collaborative dialogue supports learning and understanding in a personal manner that speeches and oral hearings are incapable of accomplishing Daniels and Walker [9]. Opinions are examined, assumptions questioned, and common interests determined through constructive public consideration Reich [10]. An active dialogue that respects the interests of all individuals and groups and provides for their participation in a planning or decision-making process creates an atmosphere conducive to the understanding of each party's values, interests, and concerns. A free exchange of information facilitates the perception and development of empathy with the various values and interests expressed Moote and McClaren [11]. This can lead to the revision of the participant's own values and interests, which is in the public interest Moote *et al* [12]. This process in effect stimulates effective group learning and decision-making and the internalisation of knowledge.

In a group decision-making and learning process, the degree of participation of stakeholders depends on a large number of factors including: degree of freedom allowed, commitment to the process, resources available, level of knowledge, benefits accruing etc. The knowledge and skills of the participants however improve over time, through the constant re-evaluation of previous decisions. The level of participation varies from person to person and from process to process however a number of stages of participation are to be expected. As the participants gain knowledge, experience and earn additional freedoms they are able to contribute more fully to decision-making. A model of stakeholder participation, based on the work of the UNDP is represented graphically in Figure 1 [13]. In this diagram, the stakeholders gradually develop from being manipulated to a situation where they can effectively manage and make all relevant decisions. During this learning process, expert support diminishes as skills improve and social capital increases.

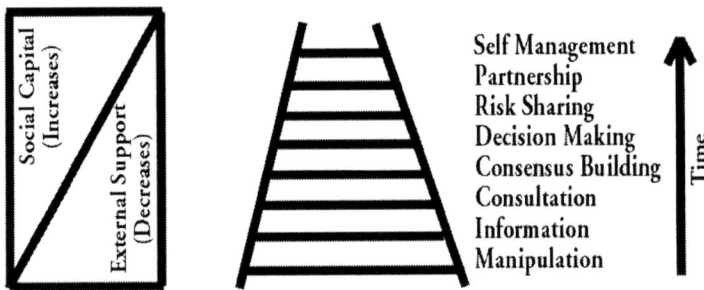

Figure 1: United Nations Development Programme [13].

3.2 Collaborative learning

A literature review of participative processes and collaborative learning identified several basic principles, which should be applied to collaborative learning processes. A synthesis of these basic principles, may be summarised as:
- Ensure democratically inclusive processes.
- Careful boundary definition.
- The use of participative methodologies.
- Aim to improve social capital.
- Provide adequate resources.
- Ensure double-loop learning.

3.3 Learning framework

Based on the work of Beierle and Cayford and these principles, a six step collaborative learning framework has been developed which facilitates the building of stakeholder knowledge, skills and expertise Beierle and Cayford [14]. The key steps involved in setting up this process are as follows:

Step 1: Determine the need for Public Participation and Learning

Three kinds of rationale for public participation and learning are useful in determining whether this approach should be used Fiorino [15], Perhac [16]. The acceptance of one or all of these rationales are a necessary first step in the process of designing a collaborative public participation based learning framework. If it is decided that all or some are necessary for success then collaborative processes should be used. These three rationales are as follows:
1. Instrumental rationale argues that public participation facilitates public policy formulation and implementation.
2. Substantive rationale argues that public participation leads to better decisions.
3. Normative rationale argues that public participation is a right of citizens and is a route to a healthy democratic society.

Even if it is decided that one or more of these rationales is appropriate then the local or state agencies must consider whether they are willing to:
1. Agree to flexibility and open-mindedness regarding the design of the process and its outcomes.
2. Accept the legitimacy of public values and recognise that this may lead to the setting of priorities, which the agency believes are wrong.

Step 2 Identify the goals and boundaries

The specific project goals along with the social and learning goals and boundaries must be clearly defined. These goals will dictate many of the design features of the process. Each goal should be examined to identify any critical assumptions. In addition a methodology needs to be developed to verify whether these goals have been met, within the given project limitations.

Step 3 Answer key design questions

There are four key questions, which must be addressed. These are:
1. Who should participate? In answering this question an assessment must be made regarding the number of people who will be affected by the decisions.
2. What degree of public participation is appropriate?
3. How much influence should the participants have? The more influence participants have in the design of the process, the more responsive it will be to their needs. This should result in a more effective decision-making process as one of the few mechanisms for building trust is through increasing public influence in the process Schneider et al [17].

4. What role will the sponsoring agency have? The agency will have to balance responsiveness against control of the process and outcomes. The building of trust will result in the gradual shifting of control towards the other participants and the creation of a more responsive process.

Step 4 Select and modify a framework, which will develop social capital
The above design questions can be reformulated into a series of operational questions. These are:
1. Is the scope of inclusion to be narrow or broad?
2. Will representation of stakeholder interests be based on socio-economic or interest group criteria?
3. Will the engagement be information sharing or strategic decision-making?
4. Will the level of public influence be limited or high?
5. Will the role of the sponsoring agency be passive or active?

Each of these operational issues may be answered by selecting an intermediate answer to each one of these issues. The balance of answers when incorporated in a framework, should attempt to increase rather than decrease social capital and learning.

Step 5 Determine the resource requirements
Resource limitations hamper the development of any process. The careful assessment of the resource requirements and the availability of resources will determine whether the goals are achievable. More modest goals may have to be set to match available resources, or additional resources may need to be sought.

Step 6 Learning through a process of evaluation
A well-designed framework is theoretically easy to evaluate, however in practice it is difficult. The goals identified in step two can be converted into evaluation criteria. The evaluation can then consist of the testing of assumptions, which set the design choices of step three. The regular evaluation of the framework and process using summative and formative methods should lead to the gaining of new insight which when applied, should lead to a gradual improvement of the framework and practices.

3.4 Integration framework

The structure, which has been developed in order to support the practical implementation of the six-step social learning and planning framework, is based on the output from the creative problem-solving workshop, consisting of individuals from technical and non-technical backgrounds. The structure consists of four main elements, stakeholders, project management team, technical support team and also the output of the process, which consists of policies, programmes and projects. The role of the project management team is to facilitate the process and ensure that the framework principles are applied. In addition they ensure that the decision-making process is carried out in a rigorous manner. They also ensure that the power relations between all participants are effectively managed and that personal and organisational learning takes place. The role of the technical support team is to ensure that the data and information requirements of the stakeholders are met. This may be achieved by carrying out research, developing models or technical expertise which will assist the stakeholders in making well-informed decisions. A diagrammatic representation of the structure of the collaborative learning and planning framework is shown in Figure 2.

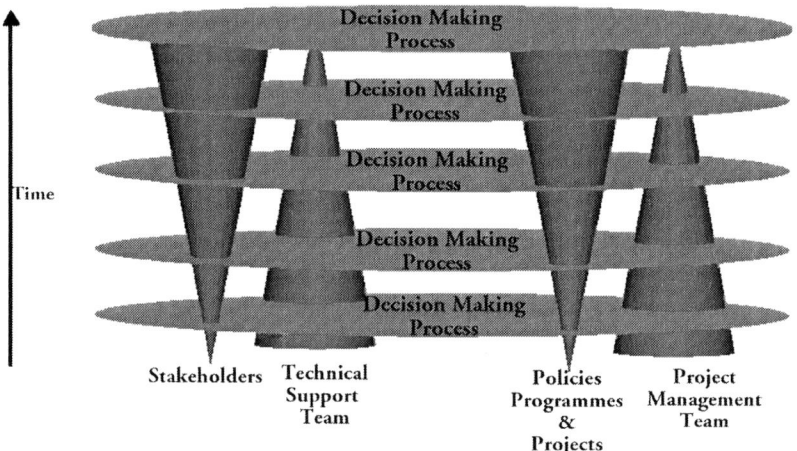

Figure 2:   Structure and development of the collaborative learning and planning framework over time.

The three participant groups interact while using a formal decision-making process, through which decisions are made and action is taken. The degree of involvement of the participants varies over time, with stakeholder participation increasing while technical support and project management roles gradually decrease and are transferred to the stakeholders. From an initial start position where the technical support team and project management team effectively control the process, this evolves to a situation where the stakeholders have the necessary expertise to undertake both of these functions independently. At this stage the project management team and technical support team functions have been taken over by the stakeholders and they fully withdraw from the process. As the stakeholder's expertise grows the number, complexity and size of projects, which they undertake, grows.

3.5 Decision making process

The decision making process is a key element of the process of collaborative decision-making and learning. The development of decision-making skills is a key component of sustainable development, as is the development of a community's ability to manage their own affairs in an environmentally responsible manner. By building on the experience gained from previous decision-making the participants can improve the effectiveness of their decision-making.

The stakeholders involved in the planning process are the decision makers. It is their role to ensure that effective policies, programmes and plans are developed to ensure that environmental, social, economic, cultural and political concerns are met. This cyclical process consists of six main steps along with a continuous process of monitoring and evaluating the information and decisions.

3.5.1 Description of the decision making process

The decision making process has been selected from a range of models as it was initially developed to assist in decision-making in contested environments. The steps are:

1. Explore the context of the issues. This involves exploring the needs and wants of the participants and the characteristics of the situation. It also explores and judges the relationships, which exist within a given framework.
2. Formulate problems and opportunities. In order to address the issues identified in stage one, a number of problems and opportunities are identified using a range of techniques such as "Potential Problem Analysis", "Conventional Brainstorming", Martin *et al* [18] and others.
3. Create a model. A model or series of models of the given situation are created in order to determine the likely outcomes of a range of actions or scenarios.
4. Carry out analysis. The results of the models are combined with a wide range of information sources to obtain as accurate a representation of the situation as possible.
5. Interpret results. Based on the insights gained from the modelling and analysis processes, decisions are made regarding the best course of action to take.
6. Take action. Once a decision has been made it is implemented through a range of policies, programmes and projects in order to achieve the required objectives.

4 Discussion

The lack of appropriate learning frameworks hinders the process of sustainable development and also limits the success of decision-making. Environmental problems and opportunities are not single, unique events but are constantly evolving, as society develops. In order to adequately address environmental issues and sustainable development, planning should be seen as a continuous process and not as an output. Sustainable learning strategies therefore should consist of a cyclical decision-making process, which is constantly modifying its planned actions in light of new information, and changing circumstances.

Collaborative learning processes take much more time to carry out than conventional educational programmes and they can be more resource intensive. They can however capitalise on stakeholder resources and have the potential to be more cost effective in the long-term than conventional planning systems, as they help to avoid major conflicts, litigation, project abandonment, and policy reversal.

Collaboration facilitates the sharing of power and expertise among specialists and the public and allows the transfer of knowledge. This greatly assists in the building of trust and allows the integration of local knowledge, values and beliefs into decisions, which will leads to the development of more appropriate solutions for local problems.

Overall the collaborative decision-making and learning framework, which has been developed, is an appropriate solution for the effective planning of sustainable development and for the education of its participants. It incorporates a number of improvements on traditional educational processes, as it is participation based. It adds to the body of knowledge in relation to the role which education can play in the area of development planning and provides a challenging way of thinking about the role of education. It combines community development and the building of social capital, which is a relatively new aspect of learning. It also involves the community in a practical way in all aspects of decision-making, which facilitates the process of sustainable development.

References

[1] Henry, J. 2001. Creativity and Perception in Management. London: Sage.
[2] Haworth, J. 1997. Work, Leisure and Wellbeing. London: Routledge.
[3] Kolb, D. 1984. Experiential Learning. Englewood Cliffs, N.J.: Prentice-Hall.
[4] Norton, B., R. Costanza, and R.C. Bishop,. 1998. The evolution of preferences, Why "sovereign" preferences may not lead to sustainable policies and what to do about it. Ecological Economics 24: 193-211.
[5] Arrow, K., Bolin, B., Costanza, R. et al. 1995. Economic growth, carrying capacity, and the environment. Science, no. 268: 520-521.
[6] Mainwaring, L. 2001. Environmental values and the frame of reference. Ecological Economics 38: 391-402.
[7] Habermas, J. 1984. The theory of communicative action 1: Reason and the rationalisation of society. Boston: Beacon.
[8] Forester, J. 1993. Critical Theory, Public Policy, and Planning Practice: Towards a Critical Pragmatism. Albany, NY: State of New York Press.
[9] Daniels, S., and G. Walker. 1996. Collaborative learning: improving public deliberations in ecosystem-based management. Environmental Impact assessment 16: 71-102.
[10] Reich, R. 1988. Policy making in a democracy. In The Power of Public Ideas. Reich, R. Ed. Cambridge, MA: Harvard University Press.

[11] Moote, M., and M. McClaren,. 1997a. Implications of participatory democracy for public land planning. Journal of Range Management 50: 473-481.
[12] Moote, M., M. McClaren, and D. Chickering,. 1997b. Theory in Practice: Applying participatory democracy theory to public land planning. environmental Management 21, no. 6: 877-889.
[13] United Nations Development Programme. 2000. Empowering People: A guide to participation. New York: The United Nations.
[14] Beierle, T.C., and J. Cayford. 2002. Democracy in practice: Public participation in environmental decisions. Resources for the Future.
[15] Fiorino, D. 1990. Public participation and environmental risks: A survey of Institutional Mechanisms. Science, Technology and Human Values 152: 226-243.
[16] Perhac, R. 1996. Defining risk: Normative considerations. Human and Ecological Risk Assessment 2, no. 2.
[17] Schneider, M., P. Teske, M. Marschall, M. Mintrom and C. Roch. 1997. Institutional arrangements and the creation of social capital: The effects of public school choice. American Political Science Review March: 82-93.
[18] Martin, J., R. Bell, and E. Farmer,. 2000. Technique Library: Creativity, Innovation and Change. B822: M.B.A. Programme. Milton Keynes: The Open University.

Remote operational medical assessment and management

H. B. Sorensen[1] & J. S. Riess[2]
[1]US Air Force Research Laboratory, USA
[2]Education and Training Solutions, USA

Abstract

Serious voids exist in remote operational health care management creating an active global search for solutions to pressing medical readiness issues. Chemical and biological agents and new operational threat environments combined with a rapidly changing scientific database and scarce medical resources accelerate the demand for new tools and methods to enhance and strengthen remote medical management capabilities. Tools that distribute knowledge and capabilities to aid a range of first-responders in comprehensively evaluating a medical situation, guide the uniform collection and reporting of critical information, and provide a telemedicine clinical reach-back to medical experts for rapid point-of-care evidenced-based guidance are essential components of today's medical preparedness and response plans. Medical and non-medical first-responders are required to work closely with other types agencies and effectively respond in a coordinated fashion to a wide range of situations. Because of technical, management, organizational and cultural differences, there is little sharing between first-responder communities of training formats, techniques, curricula or standard operating procedures critical to providing a high-quality response.

This paper will describe a framework and methodology being developed for a distributive, deployable, protocol-driven training system with integrated telemedicine capabilities to enhance and streamline the assessment and management of remote medical situations across military and civilian environments, nationally and internationally. This system could enhance the efficient and effective transfer of remote clinical and logistical information, expedite appropriate medical intervention, significantly leverage available medical resources and knowledge, reduce mortality, morbidity and the incidence of medical errors and reduce long-term injury related disabilities through rapid remote management of medical conditions. The developing system will assist in managing and responding to a range of foreign and domestic crisis situations by providing a highly coordinated and streamlined system for effectively orienting and training while functionally and culturally integrating the full range of first-responder skill sets towards an international agenda.

Keywords: treatment protocols, medical assessment, first responder, medical skills training, training management, standardized protocols, remote treatment.

The Internet Society: Advances in Learning, Commerce and Security, K. Morgan & M. J. Spector (Editors)
© 2004 WIT Press, www.witpress.com, ISBN 1-85312-712-4

1 Introduction

Standardization of first-responder training – in both military and civilian communities is extremely limited. While there is some overlap in core content being taught, there are wide variations between training programs in overall content, methodologies, terminologies, systems and environmental assumptions. Without higher-level standards and guidelines, first-responders find it difficult to rapidly locate, acquire, share, distribute and deliver training information. In addition, they are unable to determine either state of readiness or time relevance of the information accessed. Unfortunately, the lack of standards in the first-responder community includes *treatment protocols*. This lack of standards severely impacts interoperability on a scene where first-responders come from different agencies and may have been trained to a different protocol.

The United States is expanding its capacity to manage and respond to a range of foreign and domestic crisis situations by increasing and/or modifying its emergency response and management capabilities, as well as manpower requirements. One of the biggest priorities across federal (military and non-military), state and local governments, private health systems, and academic medical centers is the development and training of first-responders. Post-9/11, the classification, mission and educational requirement content of the "first-responder" has expanded and is increasingly becoming more complex and somewhat fragmented in its orientation. Historically rooted in fire rescue and law enforcement (non-medical) prior to the development of emergency medical systems (EMS), the first response role has been adapted by a range of medical (civilian and military) and most recently the public health communities. This first response role incorporates a broad array of individuals providing field-based emergency medical services. From the average citizen by-stander to trained personnel, both medical and non-medical, to expert diagnostic response teams at the Centers for Disease Control etc., first-responders are one of the fastest growing components of the expanding US emergency response system.

Both medical and non-medical first-responders are required to work closely with other types of responder communities and effectively respond in a coordinated fashion to a wide range of different situations. Because of technical, management, organizational and cultural differences there is little sharing between first-responder communities regarding training formats, techniques, curricula or standard operating procedures critical to providing a high-quality response. Conferences, periodic joint mass-casualty exercises with mock scenarios and protocols, and information or courses posted on-line or in manuals tend to be useful. However, they fall short of a proactive, highly-coordinated streamlined system for effectively orienting, training, and functionally and culturally integrating the full range of first-responders skill sets towards a national agenda.

The Gilmore Commission's Report on combating terrorism emphasized the need to improve medical health care programs to include:

- Initial and continuing education training on medical response to terrorist attacks and ensure the implementation of that training by making it part of the professional licensing and certification process.
- Establish standards and protocols for the dissemination of critical information as well as simplify and standardize mandatory reporting procedures
- To complete coordination requirements among public health officials, public and private hospitals, EMS services, law enforcement, fire services, and the emergency management community.

2 Protocol driven training system

There are few centralized medical controls governing the development and delivery of first-responder training or response. The United States federal, state and local governments and the Uniformed Services are investing untolled amounts of time and money in the development of first-responder skill sets. However, this approach provides limited focus on curricula development, evaluation of work performance and sustainment training. Due to limited strategic planning and coordination across agencies relative to training, there is no established operating framework.

2.1 Common responder skills

Research indicates that approximately 75% of basic medical first-responder skills and knowledge are shared or "common" across medical specialties while perhaps 25% are highly unique depending on the mission and assigned organization. The unique skills that are attained tend to cross all responder domains. For example, the Army medic (91W) is trained predominantly to assess and manage remote adult trauma and war-related injuries. In contrast, the Coast Guard personnel focus more on search and rescue cases at sea. In addition, within the US the local community-based EMT and paramedics focus on different types of medical emergencies relating to cardiac and pulmonary disease, diabetes and different populations (elderly, children etc). In the civilian setting hospitals, flight teams are generally close-by, long-term sustainment of trauma patients is generally unnecessary, and remote care is not remote compared to military environments. Although patient population roles and responsibilities may differ across medical first responders, most of the required skills are described as shared skills. These shared skills include performance of airway management, control of bleeding etc., and therefore can benefit from shared curricula.

A framework and methodology for achieving and implementing a core curriculum for EMS in the private sector is underway. A standardized core curriculum for emergency medical personnel has been funded by the National Highway Transportation and Safety Agency (NHTSA) and is a part of the National Education Agenda for EMS.

2.2 Integrity of courseware

There are many overlapping sets of first-responder training courses. Training content for most courses (military and civilian) tends to be organized around body systems, medical conditions or events (chemical or biological attack) but not always in a standardized format or vocabulary. While there are updates implemented periodically, the data is not always quality controlled, evaluated or linked real-time to the latest scientific research. With the emergence of new wireless technologies, all sorts of medical information is now being placed on Personal Digital Assistants (PDA) and fielded without validation or the ability to dynamically refresh. This calls into question the reliability, quality and control of that information as many are stove-piped solutions which are not being adequately monitored and maintained.

2.3 Training variation

There are many overlapping sets of first-responder training courses. Training content for most courses (military and civilian) tends to be organized around body systems, medical conditions or events (chemical or biological attack) but not always in a standardized format or vocabulary. While there are updates implemented periodically, the data is not always quality controlled, evaluated or linked real-time to the latest scientific research. With the emergence of new wireless technologies, all sorts of medical information is now being placed on Personal Digital Assistants (PDA) and fielded without validation or the ability to dynamically refresh. This calls into question the reliability, quality and control of that information as many are stove-piped solutions which are not being adequately monitored and maintained.

2.4 Medical training delivery

Most courses are still delivered to students in paper/textbook format. Courses are presented using electronic files which are developed in MS Word, PowerPoint or PDF format, posted for instructor use on Local Area Networks. Some courses are available on-line for access and review via a Website on the Internet. For Example, Army Medical Department (AMEDD) through its Department of Distance Learning offers a variety of refresher courses for the (91W) Health Care Specialist which are used to provide a portion of the continuing education units (CEU) required to satisfy the National Registry of Emergency Medical Technicians (NREMT) registration requirements. Specialized procedures are being taught using computer-based training tools provided by medical training companies. Human patient simulators or mannequins are also being used to train specific skills.

According to the Office of Management and Budget, the 2004 Budget proposes $3.5 billion to ensure that first-responders are properly trained and equipped. This includes funds to purchase protective gear for working in hazardous environments and devices for detecting and disarming explosives and other dangerous materials. Out of this amount, $500 million will support assistance to firefighters, particularly for terrorism preparedness, and $500 million will support state and local law enforcement's anti-terrorism efforts, $1.1 billion is to train first-responders at the federal, state, and local level.

First-responder initiatives provide an incentive to develop mutually supportive programs that maximize effective response capability. Only through joint planning, clear communication, comprehensive coordination at all levels and increased information sharing, will America's first-responders be sufficiently trained and equipped.

There are many strong regional efforts underway and consortiums are forming rapidly, however there is still a missing attribute of the system, and that is an advanced infrastructure to support the complex collaborative training that the first-responder community requires.

3 DMCA and the web services architecture

A Distributed Medical Curricula Architecture (DMCA)™ that can support the first-responder community is needed. The construction of the DMCA using the emerging methods of Web Services architecture is currently in the initial stages of development. While other methods have been proposed and successfully implemented to improve integration in the training community, they do not address the full scope of the problems facing the first-responder community. The DMCA is not meant to replace these previous efforts but to expand on and strengthen existing capabilities by creating a dynamic, interactive, distributed architecture that takes full advantage of current best practices in information sciences.

Web Services architectures are built on XML technologies and are the main way that businesses will interact in the future to transfer data and conduct transactions across disparate architectures, programming constructs, and paradigms. The use of Web Services is expanding rapidly as the need for application-to-application communication and interoperability grows. Web Services reflect a new service-oriented environment that offers a standard means of communication among different software applications, running on a variety of platforms and/or frameworks.

Web Services have characteristics valuable in supporting the first-responder community. By creating the methods necessary for the DMCA we will provide the foundation for others in the first-responder community to build, publish and share a wide variety of internet-based information services.

3.1 Key characteristics of web services

Web services are self-describing When creating a web service, one also creates an interface to the service. The service description includes human-readable documentation so that other developers and users can easily integrate the service. The service description identifies methods, method arguments, and return values necessary for computer interface with the service. Such self-describing services make it easier for first-responders to integrate various resources to support their specific, local needs.

Web services are discoverable When creating a web service, one publishes a description to a discovery agent so that interested parties can find the service and locate its public interface. Users can search for services using human-readable descriptions and when they find a service that provides the information or resources they need, the instructions for access are included. A single search could return a wide variety of services related to a problem. As an example, first-responders could search for services related to the management of biological incidents and "discover" services ranging from pre-incident training and evaluation to real-time operational support.

Web Services can provide an architecture supporting a wide range of training and operational resources. The developing architecture should solve both the mundane problems of the training community as well as offering new, sophisticated capabilities that will transform the existing training paradigm. By creating the DMCA, a broad range of users within the first-responder community will more easily interact, collaborate, jointly develop, plan and deliver first-responder training using a standard architecture. Such systems will provide real-time information relative to first-responder manpower, distribution and tracking of skill-sets and job descriptions for both peacetime and wartime configurations.

Web Services are the next stage of evolution for e-business -- the result of viewing systems from a perspective that everything is a service, dynamically discovered and orchestrated, using messaging on the network. In the Web Services architecture, each component is regarded as a service, encapsulating behavior and providing the behavior through an API available for invocation over a network. This is the logical evolution of object-oriented techniques (encapsulation, messaging, dynamic binding, and reflection) to e-business. The developing DMCA will ultimately addresses the problems identified above.

3.2 DMCA's roles and operations

DMCA is described from a service-oriented architecture perspective. As depicted in Figure 1, this architecture sets forth three roles and three operations.

The fundamental roles in DMCA are service providers, service requesters, and service brokers. A DMCA architecture requires three fundamental operations: *publish, find, and bind*. Service providers *publish* services to a service broker. Service requesters *find* required services using a service broker and *bind* to them. These ideas are shown in the following figure 1.

- **Service Provider**, the service provider implements the service and makes it available on the Internet (or Intranet in the case of complete control and security)
- **Service Requestor**, any consumer of a web service, who opens up a network connection and sends a message to a service provider
- **Service Registry**, a centralized directory of services; the registry provides a central place where data producers and developers can publish new services or find existing one

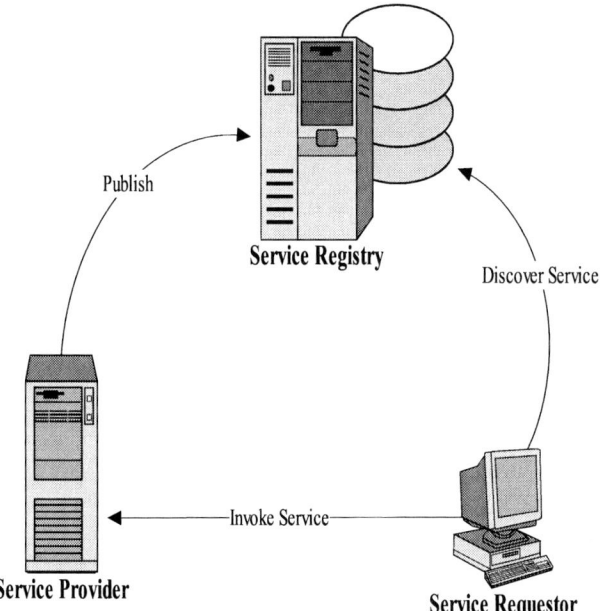

Figure 1: Web service roles.

3.2.1 Service provider perspective
1. First, the publisher would identify the data or service to be provided.
2. Second, prepare the data or service for publication; this would involve the steps already described above:
    a. standardizing the data using existing standard data dictionaries to maximize interoperability
    b. adding meta-data so that the data/service is self-describing
3. Third, the publisher would provide a service description, including an interface that explains how requestors are to connect to the service, and make requests.
4. Forth, the publisher would deploy the service to a publicly accessible (or possible secure) server.
5. And finally, the publisher would submit the service description to a central registry.

3.2.2 Service requestor perspective
First, the requestor must find (discover) the service of interest. This first step would involve searching or browsing a central registry for the data and/or services of interest. The registry should contain human-readable descriptions of the data and/or service.
1. Second, after discovering the service, the user would retrieve a service description. This could be a human-readable instruction, or application

programming interface (API) for connecting to the service, submitting a request, and listening for a response.
2. Third, a client-side application would then invoke the service. Custom client-side applications could be built to support specific types of web services, e.g., data requests.
3. Lastly, the service requestor would actually invoke the web service.

3.2.3 Communication protocol in DMCA architecture

The basic, high-level web services communication protocol is used to illustrate this DMCA architecture, its generality and potential applicability to the medical educational communities, and its eventual developers. The web services communication protocol demonstrates how a DMCA uses network communications, the HTTP/HTTPS transport protocols, the SOAP messaging protocol, and the XML language. UDDI and WSDL can help complete the connection between applications. To help you better understand how this architecture interoperates using UDDI, a diagram (Figure 2) was constructed of an informal "protocol stack." The protocol stack has four main layers and each has been briefly described as follows:

- **Service Transport**: this layer is responsible for transporting messages between the different roles, e.g., between a service requestor and service provider. Example implementation: Hyper Text Transport Protocol (HTTP)
- **XML Messaging**: this layer is responsible for encoding messages in a common format so that messages can be understood at both ends of the connection. Example implementations: XML-Remote Procedure Call (RPC), and Simple Object Access Protocol (SOAP)
- **Service Description**: this layer is responsible for describing the public interface to a specific web service. Example implementation: Web Service Descriptive Language (WSDL)
- **Service Discovery**: this layer is responsible for centralizing services into a common registry, and providing easy publish and find functionality. Example implementation: Universal Description, Discovery, and Integration (UDDI)

4 Architectural representation

Designing, developing, deploying, executing, and maintaining a Web service can require many different tools and technologies. While working on this proposed web services architecture, emerging technology development standards and techniques will be applied including standard J2EE components, W3C standards, and security standards. The proposed web services will be based on the J2EE platform, which automatically inherit all the standard J2EE benefits. These benefits include a simple and familiar component-based development model, scalability, support for transactions, life-cycle management, easy access to existing enterprise systems through the use of J2EE APIs (such as JDBC and

JTA), Microsoft Common Object Model (COM) protocol, CORBA (Common Request Broker Architecture) and a simple and unified security model.

In addition, object oriented methodologies and unified modeling languages (UML) will be considered which will allow the DMCA to fully capture the requirements and directly transfer them into the design and development phases for distributive, deployable, protocol-driven, and training systems with integrated telemedicine capabilities. These capabilities will enhance and streamline the assessment and management of remote medical situations across military and civilian settings. In addition, during the development process this approach will allow one to visualize, understand and reason about the architecturally significant elements and identify areas of risk that require more detailed elaboration and attention.

The service-oriented DMCA will provide an infrastructure capable of supporting a wide range of functions including;

1. Collaboration and member management system
2. Medical curricula development system
3. Content management
4. Continuing Medical Education Training and Management
5. Web Semantic Meta database from NLMS
6. Artificial Intelligence/decision support systems (can be imbedded inside the system for recommendations and error handling and quicker information retrieval)
7. CME Certification management
8. Meta Data search and Discovery Agents

The proposed DMCA can create a common network for medical professionals.

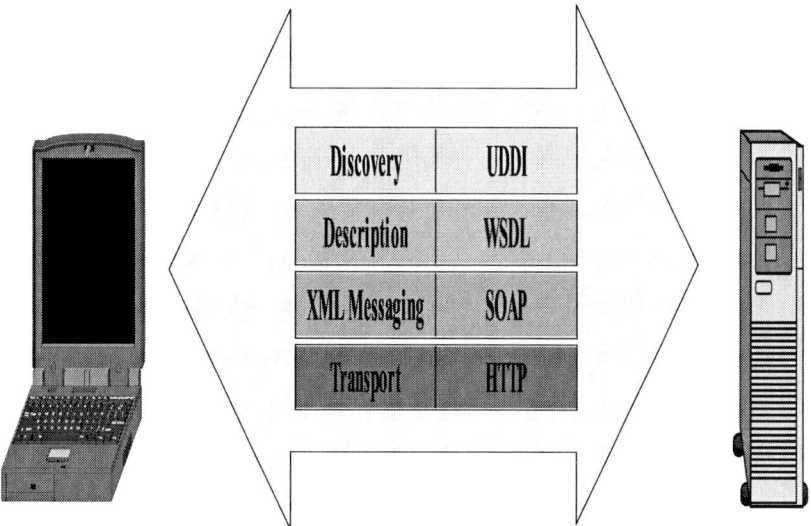

Figure 2: DMCA's web service protocol stack.

5 Medical readiness initiatives

5.1 Emergency medical systems

The *Education Agenda* is a vision for the future of EMS education. It was developed by a task force representing the full range of professions involved in EMS education, including EMS administrators, physicians, regulators, educators, and providers. The *Agenda* proposes an education system with five integrated primary components:

- National EMS Core Content
- National EMS Scope of Practice Model
- National EMS Education Standards
- National EMS Education Program Accreditation
- National EMS Certification

A key benefit of this system's approach will be an enhancement of the consistency of instructional quality achieved through an interaction among three system components, the National EMS Education Standards, National EMS Education Program Accreditation, and National EMS Certification. At the higher levels of education, this strategy for ensuring consistency allows the use of less prescriptive National EMS Education Standards in place of the current National Standard Curricula (NSC). With less dependence on a prescriptive NSC, instructors will have greater flexibility for targeting instruction to specific audiences, resulting in enhanced comprehension and improved student competence.

- The National EMS Core Content is a comprehensive list of skills and knowledge needed for out-of-hospital emergency care. Specification of the Core Content is primarily a medical concern and will be led by the medical community
- The National EMS Scope of Practice Model divides the National EMS Core Content into levels of practice, defining minimum knowledge and skills for each level. Since this determination is fundamentally a system issue, the system regulators will have the lead in its development.
- The National EMS Education Standards take the place of the current National Standard Curricula, specifying minimum terminal learning objectives for each level of practice. Being basically an educational task, the development of the National EMS Education Standards will be led by educators.

National EMS Education Program Accreditation is applied to all nationally recognized provider levels and is universal. Accreditation is the major mechanism for verifying educational program quality for the protection of students and the public.

National EMS Certification is available for all nationally recognized provider levels and is universal. Certification involves a standardized examination process and contributes to the protection of the public by ensuring the entry-level competence of EMS providers.

5.2 Tactical medical coordination system

TacMedCS (Tactical Medical Coordination System) is a wireless communication system that uses radio frequency (RF) technology to capture and display real-time casualty data in the field. The collected data is used to identify, locate, and track casualties and medical resources. TacMedCS users include both military medical personnel and civilian emergency responders. TacMedCS is applicable in conventional warfare, humanitarian assistance, peacekeeping, disaster relief, and homeland defense settings.

The 'intelligent' ID Tags facilitate accurate casualty tracking and recorded medical history. This provides the TacMedCS system with the robust capability of information storage. Casualty data is not lost because the data is always available on the ID tag.

The Navy's Fleet Hospitals are currently integrating the hardware and software to support a field hospital with operating rooms, ancillary services and up to 500 beds. The mobile system fits into four rugged cases, and supported the war in Iraq. X-rays can be sent anywhere in the world to be read and are turned around in an hour around the clock. This is possible because the system comes equipped with a satellite dish, folded into one of the heavy-duty cases, which allows the field hospitals to communicate with other military medical facilities in real time.

The new technology is part of a proven strategy to treat the injured outside a traditional hospital setting during the "golden hour" when quick medical care may save a life. Twenty-eight vendors have provided software and hardware for the system. For the military, the compact system is a vast improvement from past methods, which required truckloads of equipment to set up a frontline hospital in a "M*A*S*H"-like setting. Once operational, the Fleet Hospitals will be able to abandon paper in favor of electronic communications and records.

In March 2003, Health and Human Services (HHS) Secretary Tommy G. Thompson announced that HHS began testing a system using handheld personal digital assistants (PDAs) for transmitting urgent information about biological agents to clinicians. The three-month pilot test of the PDA network was designed to gauge the best ways for federal officials to communicate effectively with front-line clinicians in the event of a bioterrorist attack. The project will evaluate how and when clinicians download this urgent information and whether they find it useful to receive it via their PDAs.

"This important new project will allow us to harness the power of technology to communicate with many of the doctors, nurses, and other clinicians who will be called on to diagnose and treat patients quickly in the event of a bioterrorist attack," Secretary Thompson said. "This will literally allow them to have critical information at their fingertips when they need it most."

The project evaluates the use of a system created by ePocrates, the nation's largest physicians' handheld network, for sending an urgent "Doc Alert" message to more than 700,000 front-line clinicians, including more than 250,000 physicians -- more than 40 percent of the practicing physicians in the United States. The test message will contain a special memo on the highest threat (category A) biological diseases/agents, which include anthrax, botulism, plague, smallpox, tularemia and viral hemorrhagic fevers, including Ebola. The message will also include Web links for clinicians to go to for additional information about diagnosing and treating the conditions caused by the biological agents. Clinicians will be able to save this information to their PDAs for future reference.

The pilot project is being managed by HHS' Agency for Healthcare Research and Quality (AHRQ) and is designed to complement the Centers for Disease Control and Prevention's existing Health Alert Network, which was created in 1998 and is used by the Department to communicate directly with more than 25,000 public health officials in the 50 states, eight U.S. territories and seven large cities.

6 Conclusions

There are a broad range of stakeholders and first-responder groups across military and civilian organizations that share a common problem, even within each agency i.e., Army, Navy etc. The lack of a technical architecture that provides an end-to-end solution for training as well as an intelligent knowledge repository which can be leveraged and mined across multidisciplinary domains by medical planners, analysts and researchers. Study results confirmed the value of developing an infrastructure which facilitates the development, sharing and real-time updating of curricula, best practices, lessons learned and outcomes.

Most healthcare teaching/learning platforms, where available, are usually stand-alone systems. They basically provide only one service (teaching/learning) for a given set of units (courses) which are stored within a single system generally as a PowerPoint, MS Word or PDF file. Some are made available for course presentation or for posting on a website. Sharing course materials and other training resources in a distributed environment is not a common occurrence. Existing platforms find it difficult to share data with other platforms, even when the units follow the Shareable Content Object Reference Model (SCORM) standard, since there is no standardized way of exchanging various course units and training resources. In addition, integration of such platforms in a distributed environment across military and civilian contexts is even more challenging and complicated.

Building the DMCA will present challenges. Standard nomenclatures will need to be adopted, as will standard descriptions for critical knowledge and skills. This initial study has directed the inclusion of specific use cases that will help test the process and to initial products and services for the DMCA.

References

[1] Department of Defense. Military medical readiness skills training. (DoDI 1322.24). Department of Defense, 1995.
[2] Grisanti, Ronald J. Medical mistakes kill 100,000+ Americans a year, http://www.dtrgrisanti.com/dangerous_medicine.htm
[3] Headquarters, United States Air Force. Aerospace medical service specialty, AFSC 4N0X1, Career field education and training plan. (CFETP 4N0X1, pts. I and II). Washington, DC: Department of the Air Force, 2002.
[4] Headquarters, Department of the Army. Soldiers manual and trainer's guide, health care specialist, Skill levels 1/2/3/4/5, MOS 91W. (STP 8-91W15-SM-TG). Department of the Army, 2001.
[5] Office of Management and Budget website, http://www.whitehouse.gov/omb/budget/fy2004/winning.html
[6] Second Annual Report to The President and the Congress. Advisory Panel to Assess Domestic Response Capabilities for Terrorism Involving Weapons of Mass Destruction, 15 December 2000.

Developing digital portfolios: how ICT can facilitate pupil talk about learning

K. Wall, S. Higgins, J. Miller & N. Packard
Centre for Learning and Teaching, University of Newcastle, UK

Abstract

The Digital Portfolio Project at Newcastle University aimed over one year (2002/2003) to support teachers in producing, storing and accessing assessment portfolios of learner's work using ICT. A major element of this was the investigation of the impact that these portfolios had on teachers and learners, particularly focusing on how they could be used to facilitate pupil talk about the learning process and metacognition. This paper draws on evidence of pupil views collected as part of 14 teacher-led case studies exploring digital portfolio development in classrooms across the primary age phase (3-11 years). The teachers all approached the task in different ways and the variety of end products was large; however, the common result was the value placed on using the portfolio as a tool of reflection and celebration of children's learning. As part of the data collection teachers were encouraged to gather pupil views about the digital portfolio learning process. These comments provide an interesting and surprisingly analytical perspective of the research and learning process not commonly considered in the academic community. They reveal astute comprehension regarding the possible implications of using ICT to document achievements, the positive effects of recording classroom activities using digital media and how using this evidence to reflect on the activities can be a meaningful and worthwhile process. The pupils recognise the important role that ICT takes in this process and also appreciated the possibilities for themselves and their peers as learners. This paper documents the pupils' views and uses them to review the strength of the Digital Portfolio process and the benefits of using it in the primary classroom.

Keywords: collaborative learning, innovative use of ICT, pupil views, digital portfolio, formative assessment.

1 Developing thinking and learning through metacognition

The project drew on a number of strands of educational research, in particular developing thinking and learning through thinking skills approaches and metacognition [1, 2] improving learning through formative assessment [3] and the development of self-regulated learning [4]. There is also a wealth of literature into the effective use of ICT in schools (see, for example the British Educational Research Association 'professional user review' [5]) and the use of digital portfolios in particular. Some key influences from each of these areas are outlined below. The literature also suggested that an action research approach was likely to be an effective means to support development in schools as such approaches had already been tried and evaluated in the area of formative assessment [6], ICT generally [7] as well as with digital portfolios in particular [8].

There has been considerable research into metacognition or 'thinking about thinking' which suggests that teaching needs to make explicit the process of learning as well as the curriculum content [9]. The goal of such approaches is to develop positive dispositions towards learning so that learners believe that, with sufficient effort and effective strategies, they can learn and understand challenging material [10, 11]. One way of doing this is to review learning and help pupils to see their successes. A number of thinking skills approaches have demonstrated impact on learners' attainment drawing on this theoretical background [12].

The potential of formative assessment in schools has been heralded as offering an effective means to improve learning and raise standards by developing more effective feedback to learners in order to help them understand and apply assessment criteria to their own work [3]. In the forefront of development in schools were Torrance and Pryor [13] who identified the importance of paying close attention to verbal interaction in classrooms and teachers' changing thinking about events in the classroom. Clarke's work has also had significant impact [14, 15]. She has shown how collaborative work between pupils can enhance learning through making learning objectives and success criteria explicit as well as indicating the support possible from a range of people in giving assessment feedback.

However, it also has to be acknowledged that the impact of ICT on teaching and assessment practices is complex [16] as it is challenging for teachers to develop new pedagogical approaches at the same time as developing new ICT skills [17]. Our view in this project was that the integration of new equipment and tools may provide a window for change that can support professional development.

Overall the impact of ICT on standards of attainment is perhaps somewhat disappointing considering the enthusiasm and expense that has been invested in this area [5]. Our premise was that ICT on its own would not have an impact on teaching and learning, but that its use would need to be integrated effectively into teaching and learning in classrooms and that this would involve teachers in making complex choices about when and where to use ICT [17]. This, in turn, would be influenced by their skills and confidence in using ICT and by their beliefs and thinking about teaching and learning more broadly [18].

The idea of digital portfolios in education is not new. Early work tended to focus on the potential record keeping aspects of portfolios or on the benefits of multimedia to record aspects of learning. There have been few evaluations of impact on learners' attainment or research into the effects of using portfolios on teachers, pupils or the curriculum. Positive benefits are usually reported for the development of skills and attitudes [19]. There is some evidence that learners benefit from collaborative use of web-based portfolios [20] and that pupils of primary age in particular may need teacher and peer support to make the most of the opportunities offered by digital media [21]. Other benefits include learners reporting better understanding of assessment as well as developing understanding of how to manage their own learning [22].

One project in the Washington DC area of the United States examined the use of digital student portfolios as an instructional, assessment and evaluation tool. The project illustrated the processes by which pre-service and in-service teachers were able to work with primary age pupils to create their own digital portfolios using the HyperStudio authoring program. Evaluation of these portfolios showed a significant improvement in student achievement, and teachers reported these portfolios to be a valuable tool in monitoring student behaviour and communicating future educational goals to parents, administrators, and other teachers [23]. Most studies also highlight the need for support to be available for teachers to develop their ICT skills as well as support for technical issues which will inevitably arise [8].

This analysis of the research literature suggested that digital portfolios have the potential to support formative assessment in primary classrooms and that this might develop pupils' awareness and understanding of their own learning. This process was also likely to support the development of pupils' ICT skills and, if an action research approach was used, it should support the professional development of the teachers involved, both in terms of their ICT skills and confidence as well as broader impact on teaching and learning. However, there were also a number of studies that suggested there might be some challenges in terms of the existing skills of both pupils and teachers which would need support in order to ensure that the potential of such an approach was achieved.

2 An overview of the project

The main objective of the project was to explore the feasibility of using ICT, particularly digital images, video and voice recordings, to capture assessment information which would help learners reflect on their learning and that would help teachers record and store aspects of learning which might otherwise be difficult to collect. The key task was to identify and to try out activities or 'snapshots' of learning that could support the development of metacognitive talk in the classroom through the use of ICT. The main intention was that this information could be used as part of the process of teaching and learning in the classroom to help learners review and identify their learning. The broad aims were to support teachers in producing, storing and accessing assessment portfolios of learners' work in order to develop practical approaches to formative assessment with teachers.

A secondary and longer term aim of the project was to investigate the practicality of collecting and storing such information in a database or 'electronic album' to store samples of formative and summative assessment. Views might then be available for different users such as learners who could see their own work and the teacher's feedback, class teachers who would need to see the work of all of the pupils in their class, subject co-ordinators and managers in the schools (e.g. head teachers and deputy heads) who might want to review summaries by class and National Curriculum level, and parents who might see the work of their own child, the child's comments and the teacher's evaluation of how their child was progressing.

An important part of the project was engaging with the participants' perspectives on the learning which was enhanced or supported by the use of digital technologies. At the core of the project are case studies undertaken by the teachers themselves. To extend the research and evaluation of the potential impact of digital tools to support learning, information was also collected from pupils as a way of identifying what impact the development work was having on their thinking as learners. Some of the schools involved also involved or informed parents about the work that was being undertaken and this provides an additional perspective.

3 Pupils' views on their learning and the value of the digital portfolio work

This paper focuses on pupils' views which emerged as an interesting and valuable aspect of the evaluation. Blanchard [24] recently observed:

> "Whenever one tries to find out and understand pupils' perceptions, there is an implicit message that their views count and that they have a valued role to play in deciding how to organise things. When such communication takes place within the curriculum, as part of the teaching and learning, it is all the more powerful in building pupils' confidence to express themselves and pursue what they want to achieve." (p.265)

This quotation summarises the vision of the Digital Portfolio Project with regard to the importance placed on the pupils' perspectives, not only in the learning process, but also as part of the research. It was felt that the pupils provided an interesting and analytical view of the research and learning process; one that is not commonly considered in the academic community, although it is an increasingly popular research strand in the UK [25, 26]. This is an important perspective because it is so closely associated with the underpinning philosophy of the project.

When their comments are summarised they reveal astute understanding regarding the possible implications of ICT to document their achievements, the positive effects of recording classroom activities using digital media and how using this evidence to reflect on activities can be a meaningful and worthwhile process. Pupil views document a critical part of this investigation: the process of and the learning outcomes which the digital portfolios facilitated.

Most research into pupil views has been completed by undertaking interviews with children either individually or as groups (focus group), this can be problematic as pupils, and young children in particular are usually eager to please and will therefore answer questions, especially from a teacher, in a way that they think will please them. Interviewing pupils is also time consuming and difficult to manage in lesson time. As this project was teacher-led the collection of pupil views needed to be structured in such a way that could be implemented by teachers in their classrooms.

The data collection method that was used had its foundation in a piece of research done by Hanke [27], where the perceptions of Year 1 children towards the Literacy Hour were investigated through the use of response templates. These templates represented the 4 sections of the Hour and required the children to draw in the faces of the pupils, with emphasis put on the expression which was chosen, with added speech/thought bubbles to provide an explanation for their interpretations. The findings of Hanke's research show pupils, even at this young age, have great empathy with other children in the class and a well-developed perception of the processes involved in the Literacy Hour.

The idea of response templates was adapted to incorporate the different learning and/or ICT-based activities that might be associated with the Digital Portfolio process. A key idea was that of reflection with an emphasis on the learning process that was closely associated.

Figure 1: One example of the response templates used in the project.

The templates were designed to promote and capture the elements of reflection on learning or metacognition in particular both the internal elements (what the child feels is going on inside his or her head; what they think they have learnt, what skills they have achieved, and, importantly, how they have achieved their goals) and the external elements (what they think the benefits are more generally and what they would tell other children about the activity).

The templates had to find a balance between being specific enough to support pupils' thinking and reflection on their learning during particular tasks and general enough to be used across the great variety of work going on in classroom under the auspices of the Digital Portfolio Project. The common feature of all of the templates that were designed was the use of a speech bubble to express external elements and the thought bubble to express internal elements. These cartoon-like icons were kept constant, even though the particular scenario shown might be different (such as working with a video camera or on a computer). The intention was to make the data collection as comparable across situations as possible, but whilst offering support (in the form of pictures) to remind the pupils about the specific digital tools that they had used.

A key theme from the pupil comments is the recognition that the process of creating a Digital Portfolio and the final end product are equally important as part of the learning process. With regards to the process, many of the children commented on the importance of reflection and how the collection of evidence using digital media was beneficial.

> "Using the video made us look back and check our work"
> "You can see what you are doing and it helps me to see mistakes. If I didn't use the video I couldn't see the mistakes I was doing"

This was particularly the case in subjects of a more practical nature, such as design and technology, where this evidence collected became central to the 'do and review' process.

> "Photographs helped us with the designing of the Scilliewiggle."
> "I think you should use digital blues because you can look back and see what the next step is and to remember things."

In these more practical subjects the children also recognised the advantages of having a digital record of their work, images of the product at different stages during its creation and the finished result. These might have been lost or damaged if more traditional methods had been relied upon.

> "At the end you see all the different bits and how they make a finished product."

The pupils observed that reflection could help learning in a number of ways, such as supporting discussions between themselves and their teacher:

> "It was good checking the learning objectives and when your teacher told you that you had got them"

It can support discussions with their peers as part of group work:

> *"I have learned that working in a group you work together to reach what you are achieving."*
> *"It was good working with different people. My partner that I worked with was someone that I didn't know but because we were helping each other with recording video, I got to know him really well."*

It can be used as evidence to support the achievement of attainment targets and learning objects for assessment purposes:

> *"It was good that we got to show where we met the learning objectives. It was like a success criteria."*

The children also acknowledged that it could help them reflect on their skills, whether ICT, subject related or more general:

> *"It's a great way to learn and to look back on your work. You can look back at methods you've used, for example in maths. It also helps you to learn a lot about computers and that's good because computers are needed."*

Or sometimes awareness at a more personal level about their confidence and sense of achievements:

> *"I've done something that I have acquired myself"*
> *"I'd like to show it to my teacher at Middle School but just the teacher and me. She can tell me how I can improve then."*
> *"To learn more. To enjoy and have fun. To show your skills to everyone and not be shy. Help people to learn new things."*

As the children learnt and mastered these skills there was also an element of independent learning and achievement which was recognised by the children as important. The pupil-led focus of the digital portfolios that many of the participant teachers wished to work towards and aimed to achieve was obviously something that the pupils valued.

> *"It was good because the children did it not the teachers"*

As well as benefiting the reflection process, the pupils identified that the use of ICT meant that their work could be easily shared with others. This was a frequent comment, particularly with reference to involving parents and sharing with the wider school community.

> *"This is me and mum and dad watching me on the computer. We are smiling"*
> *"On computers you can put it on a floppy disc and use it at home and show your family."*

"I'm going to tell my mam, I've got something really special for you, you can see me at school."

On occasions pupils showed remarkable empathy in making observations regarding the suitability of using ICT as a method of recording achievement for pupils who find writing difficult and with special educational needs.

"It is easier on the computer than on a display because you can listen rather than read. It is useful for disabled people."

Although the learning of ICT skills was not a focus of the project it is obvious from the comments made by pupils that this has been an important outcome. Many remarked on the different hardware and software that they had used and the new things associated with them that they had learnt.

"I have learnt how to edit and think about not to delete things that you want. To think about putting clips in order."

"As well as things I have learnt in the lessons, I have learnt how to work the video camera, use the sound recorder and PowerPoint."

Finally many of the comments relate to their enjoyment of the project:

"I would tell children that this project is great fun and you will learn a lot."

4 Conclusions

This aspect of the Digital Portfolio Project has meant a number of important conclusions can be made. Firstly, asking pupils about how they learn and how a process of developing learning tools affects them is a valuable activity. The comments they have made are both informative and astute. The research has shown that pupils' views can provide influential insight into the processes involved in learning and, more specifically, how ICT can facilitate this.

Secondly, the Digital Portfolio Project has demonstrated the way in which multi-media can be used to facilitate children's talk about their learning. The combination of a digital portfolio and thinking skills has been revealed to be a powerful one with plenty of scope for development in the primary classroom. The reflective nature of the pupils' comments regarding their learning and achievement as part of the digital portfolio give valuable evidence to support formative assessment theory [3, 14]. The role of ICT in this assessment adds an interesting new development.

Thirdly, a digital portfolio has the potential to create independent learners who are responsible for the collection of their own evidence of achievements across the curriculum and that this process has an impact on the pupils and how they perceive themselves and their learning. Evidence from the project indicates how ICT can be used effectively to support the learning of pupils and help to enhance their autonomy [22].

References

[1] Biggs J.B. (1988) The role of meta-cognition in enhancing learning. *Australian Journal of Education* **32(2)**, pp. 127-138.
[2] Higgins, S. (2001) *Thinking Through Primary Teaching* Cambridge: Chris Kington Publishing
[3] Black, P. and Wiliam, D. (2003) 'In Praise of Educational Research': formative assessment *British Educational Research Journal* **29(5)**, pp. 623-637.
[4] Zimmerman, B. J. (1989). Models of self-regulated learning and academic achievement. In B.J. Zimmerman & D.H. Schunk (Eds.), *Self-regulated learning and academic achievement: Theory, research, and practice*. New York: Springer-Verlag.
[5] Higgins, S. (2003) *Does ICT Improve Learning and Teaching in Schools?* Nottingham: British Educational Research Association
[6] Torrance, H. & Pryor, J. (2001) Developing Formative Assessment in the Classroom: using action research to explore and modify theory, *British Educational Research Journal*, 27(5), pp. 615 - 631.
[7] Somekh, B. & Davis, N. (Eds.) (1997) *Using Information Technology Effectively in Teaching and Learning: Studies in pre-service and in-service teacher education* (London & New York, Routledge).
[8] Kankaanranta, M. (2001) Constructing digital portfolios: teachers evolving capabilities in the use of information and communications technology, *Teacher Development*, **5(2)**, pp. 259-275.
[9] Berardi-Coletta, B., Buyer, L. S., & Dominowski, R. L. (1995). Metacognition and problem-solving: A process oriented approach. *Journal of Experimental Psychology--Learning, Memory, and Cognition*, 21, pp. 205-223.
[10] Pressley, M., El-Dinary, P.B., Marks, M.B., Brown, R. & Stein, S. (1992). Good strategy instruction is motivating and interesting. In K.A. Renninger, S. Hidi, & A. Krapp (Eds.), *The role of interest in learning and development*. Hillsdale, NJ: Erlbaum.
[11] Jausovec, N. (1994). Can giftedness be taught? *Roeper Review*, 16, pp. 210-214.
[12] Higgins S, Baumfield V, Lin M, Moseley D, Butterworth M, Downey G, Gregson M, Oberski I, Rockett M and Thacker D (2004) *Thinking skills approaches to effective teaching and learning*. Research Evidence in Education Library. London: EPPI-Centre, Social Science Research Unit, Institute of Education.
[13] Torrance, H. & Pryor, J. (1998) *Investigating Formative Assessment: teaching, learning and assessment in the classroom* Buckingham: Open University Press.
[14] Clarke, S. (1998) *Targeting Assessment in the Primary Classroom: strategies for planning, assessment, pupil feedback and target setting* London: Hodder & Stoughton.

[15] Clarke, S. (2001) *Unlocking Formative Assessment: practical strategies for enhancing pupils' learning in the primary classroom* London: Hodder & Stoughton.

[16] Moseley, D., Higgins, S., Bramald, R. Hardman, F., Miller, J., Mroz, M., Tse, H., Newton, D., Thompson, I., Williamson, J., Halligan, J., Bramald, S., Newton, L., Tymms, P. Henderson, B. and Stout, J. (1999) *Ways Forward with ICT: Effective Pedagogy using Information and Communications Technology in Literacy and Numeracy in Primary Schools* Newcastle upon Tyne: University of Newcastle upon Tyne.

[17] Moreland, J., Jones. & Northover, A. (2001) Enhancing Teachers' Technical Knowledge and Assessment Practices to Enhance Student Learning in Technology: A Two Year Classroom Study, *Research in Science Education*, **31**, pp. 155 - 176.

[18] Higgins, S. and Moseley, D. (2001) Teachers' thinking about ICT and learning: beliefs and outcomes, *Teacher Development* **5(2)**, pp. 191-210.

[19] Chang, C. (2001) Refining Collaborative Learning Strategies for Reducing the Technical Requirements of Web Based Classroom Management, Innovations in Education & Teaching International., **38(2)**, pp. 133 - 143.

[20] Chang, C. (2001) A study on the evaluation and effectiveness analysis of web - based learning portfolio (WBLP), British Journal of Educational Technology, **32(4)**, pp. 435 - 458.

[21] Frank, M., Reich, N. & Humphreys, k. (2003) Respecting the human needs of students in the development of e-learning, *Computers and Education*, **40**, pp. 57 - 70.

[22] Chen, G., Liu, C., Ou, K. & Lin, M. (2000) Web Learning Portfolios: A Tool For Supporting Performance Awareness, Innovations in Education & Teaching International., **38(1)**, pp. 19 - 30.

[23] Irvine, S.E. & Barlow, J. (1998) The digital portfolio in education: an innovative learning and assessment tool, *Journal of Information Technology for Teacher Education*, **7(3)**, pp. 321-330.

[24] Blanchard, J. (2003) "Targets, Assessment for Learning and Whole School Improvement." *Cambridge Journal of Education.* **33(2)**, pp.257-271

[25] MacBeath, J., Demetriou, H., Rudduck, J. and Myers, K. (2003) *Consulting Pupils: A Toolkit for Teachers.* Cambridge: Pearson Publishing

[26] Clarke, A., McQuail & Moss, P. (2003) *Exploring the Field of Listening to and Consulting with Young Children.* London: DfES Publications

[27] Hanke, V. (2000) "Learning about Literacy: children's versions of the Literacy Hour." *Journal of Research in Reading.* **23(3)**, pp.287-297.

A model for collaboration: integrating technology into the elementary media arts and studies curriculum

S. Nuss & K. Conely
Brookside Elementary School, Cranbrook Educational Community

Abstract

The model for technology integration at Cranbrook Schools Brookside, the elementary division of Cranbrook Educational Community Schools (www.cranbrook.edu), a private college preparatory day and boarding school in Bloomfield Hills, MI has been developed by the media arts and studies faculty, Dr. Shirley Nuss and Kimberly Conely, Ph.D., candidate. In addition to providing students with a broad and challenging academic environment, Cranbrook is world renown for its comprehensive integration of the arts into the overall elementary and secondary school curriculum. Using Cranbrook's well-established, art-based curricular framework as their impetus, the instructors created an interdisciplinary teaching model that would complement and enhance Cranbrook's philosophy and also address and help mitigate some of the disturbing trends in education perpetuated by the ongoing 'digital revolution.' The professor's approach to the overall integration of Cranbrook's philosophy with state-of-the-art technology in the media arts and studies class is based upon multiple methodologies and technologies including cinema studies, art history, analogue and digital photography, and computer visualization and enhancement. Their unique model utilizes three basic, grade appropriate, instructional components. The first focuses on the ideation-conceptualization process. The second phase incorporates technological instruction and execution. The third step is total integration of components one and two supplemented by further exploration and development of creative thought processes resulting in a comprehensive, multi-disciplinary student production project. For the purposes of illustration, samples of students' work (grades 3, 4, and 5) will appear throughout the following discussion.
Keywords: interdisciplinary, digital revolution, emotional connectivity, meta-cognitive, ideation-conceptualization, hegemonic, cognitive development, coded-language.

1 Introduction

This media arts and studies interdisciplinary technology instructional model was developed as a flexible platform for meta-cognitive planning strategies that incorporate the latest age-appropriate technology and visual enhancement software into their evolving curriculum goals and objectives. The following discussion will illustrate how the use of technology, including analogue and digital cameras, desktop and laptop computers, and various age-appropriate visual enhancement software can be appropriated as tools to enhance and expand, rather than provide the basis for, the learning strategies developed in a media arts and studies classroom. There are three basic student-learning objectives of this approach; the first is to provide the students with an opportunity to acquire the skills necessary to use technology as a means of expression and communication. The second, and most critical goal of this strategy is to familiarize students with the coded language of media producers and help them learn to use this knowledge as a basis for making informed decisions regarding the media's objectives and their specific media choices from internet gaming to television programming. Ultimately, we are trying to help students make and develop emotional connections to each other and their learning environments. As educators we are using technology to train the student to simultaneously see, conceive, create, connect with, and interpret his/her surroundings and experiences.

2 Counteracting a disturbing trend

The professors have created this model for technology in the media arts and studies classroom as an attempt to help balance a disturbing trend that has broad reaching ramifications regarding the overall education of the 21st century elementary student. In general the trend begins in infancy, when many of America's children are exposed to a wide range of uncensored media products in their homes including newspapers, magazines, video games, televisions with one hundred plus channels, on-demand cinema, and computers with 'always on' Internet access. Outside of the home, children are also unwittingly exposed to, and manipulated by multifarious forms of media including graphic signage of all types decorating billboards, buses, and storefronts, and video kiosks strategically stationed in every available superstore corner. Educators must begin to not only acknowledge the consequences of the 'digital revolution' and the ways it will affect a child's cognitive and cultural development in and outside of the classroom, but devise strategies that counterbalance the potential negative effects.

- Children spend more time watching television (on average more than 25 hours per week) than any other activity except sleeping.
- For every hour of regular programming a child may be exposed to more than 25 television commercials, which means they view as many as 40,000 television commercials every year.

Research suggests that young children may actually be unable to distinguish between programming and commercials. Whether at home or in school, children are not generally taught to recognize that commercials and most media are purposefully designed to sell them a product, service, and/or way of thinking.

- 78.9% of households with children in the United States own a computer.
- 53% of the teens surveyed report they use the Internet to browse, 51% to study or do research, 51% use it to send and receive email, and 32% use it to play games.

According to the National Institute on Media and the Family, "children between the ages of 3 and 5 are at a critical stage in brain development, specifically for the development of language and other cognitive skills." Based upon the above data, educators can conclude that the combined average television viewing and computer/video game use is higher in actual hours of passive participation than normal family interaction and any regularly scheduled student teacher contact time. In the 21st century, media in all of its forms actually becomes the overall dominant influence on the development of brain neural networks because it displaces the time a child would spend doing activities that include primary verbal interactions deemed absolutely necessary for early, successful cognitive development.

Despite the results of this research, most media producers that focus on creating content for our youth readily acknowledge that they are accountable first and foremost to the advertisers, rather than the children and teenagers consuming their product. What has become the "teacher" or rather *'in loco parentis'* in the home environment is primarily focused on pleasing the financial sponsor of the program. Current studies though informative, fail to reflect the actual media-initiated and cultivated simulacrum "culture" continually represented and ultimately perpetuated to undiscerning children, teenagers, and their parents. The reality represented in popular media is often based upon fabricated ideas and concepts. The consequence of this anomaly is that many of the dominant media initiated hegemonic ideas and images seem to go unquestioned and are readily adopted by children and their parents. In subtle, yet often frequent occurrences within programming and commercials, the so-called ideal body type is consistently shown, violence as a means of problem solving is perpetuated, and stereotypes are reinforced. Some researchers argue that the current epidemic of eating disorders, anxiety, and depression plaguing our nation's children as they either strive to integrate and/or meet these unattainable images are a direct result of this unrealistic representation of reality. According to David Walsh, this deluge of sexually explicit, violence-centered media de-sensitizes and ultimately replaces the child's ability to make the emotional connections necessary for successful learning, growth, and maturity. To counteract this desensitization, we recommend media arts and studies instructors create projects for students that stimulate emotional involvement.

3 The model – three instructional components

3.1 Ideation-conceptualization process

Each grade level project idea is conceptualised using a visual tool (figure 1) that is consistent with a students' grade level curriculum, and developmental skills (emotional maturity, small and gross motor skills, visual recognition skills, and tested sequential learning capabilities). The ideation-conceptualization step is grounded in current research pertaining to brain development and learning. Research shows that long-term memory, which often involves factual/label and location components, should be supplemented by an emotional component that binds and contributes to the overall learning experience. It is important to note that a 10-year-old can readily remember the words to a commercial jingle and/or a sitcom theme song, but often has difficulty remembering a short poem or the basic multiplication tables he /she was asked to memorize. The emotional connections caused by continual exposure to commercials and sitcoms seem to trigger a memory response that is not consistent with the rote memorization practices indigenous to the educational setting. Robert Sylwester encourages educators to "help students begin to find relationships between the somewhat random, often trivial fact filled experiences of everyday life and the few enduring principles that define life-and then to help them create and constantly test the memory networks that solidify those relationships" (102). We have found that when developing a project that uses pre-visualization techniques and technology it is paramount to include an emotional connection experience to encourage and promote the development of the imprinted brain pathways.

Ideation Conceptualization Model

Coded Media Language ↔ Ideation Conceptualization ↔ Technology Tools

Visual Technological Emotional Connections

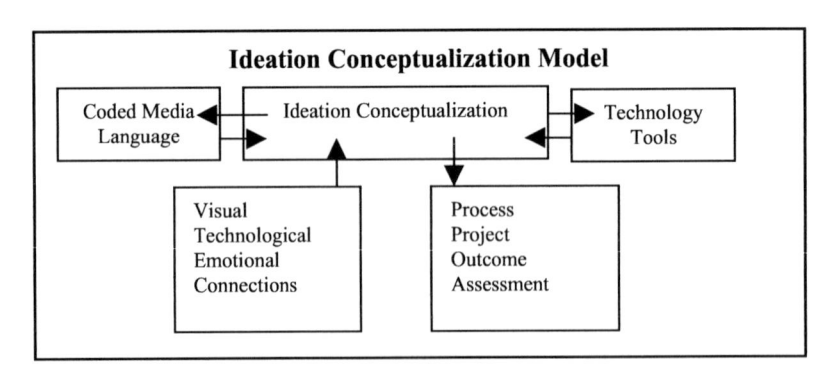

Process Project Outcome Assessment

Figure 1.

3.2 Technology tools

The second phase of our program incorporates comprehensive technological instruction with consideration of age appropriate fine and gross motor skills as well as maturation level ranges for the purposes of successfully executing grade specific projects. This includes all applicable media related terminology from cinema studies, photography, art history, television, radio, print, and computers. Students are given multiple opportunities for hands-on experimentation with image capturing mechanisms and exposure to a wide variety of computer software applications. During this phase of instruction we have noticed that male students are more apt to easily gravitate toward, and master the equipment quicker, while some of our female students initially hesitate before they begin to experiment. We have also noticed that with a gentle nudge of encouragement and additional hands-on instruction, the female students will quickly address their fears and readily embrace the technology as a new form of personal expression.

3.3 Project process, integration and outcome

The third step is total integration of phases one and two (listed above) supplemented by further exploration and development of creative thought processes resulting in a comprehensive, multi-disciplinary project. To effectively meet the stated goals, students are provided with the opportunity to create individualized projects that they can claim ownership of, and share with their classmates. To help students learn to self-evaluate and edit, progress and project critiques are scheduled on a regular basis using the SmartBoard technology. There is no doubt that students seem genuinely captivated and motivated when they have the opportunity to create an original expression.

4 The projects

4.1 3rd, 4th and 5th grade media arts and studies projects

In addition to building upon age-appropriate cognitive skill levels, our goals for student learning and enrichment cover three basic developmental and learning areas. First, we want to provide a learning environment that enables the student to continuously hone the necessary skills required to use available technology as a means of expression and communication. The second objective of our strategy is to familiarize the students with the coded language and subversive and overt objectives of media producers and help them learn to use this knowledge as a basis for making informed decisions regarding their specific media choices. On a regular basis we employ multiple strategies based upon the foreign language classroom for teaching the media's coded language including vocabulary lists, implementation of user specific vocabulary terms, and insist that students use technology driven and image making verbal descriptions when communicating with one another in the media arts and studies classroom. We provide ample opportunities for students to make and develop emotional connections by promoting the integration of topics, tools, and processes within their individualized project outcomes. Our primary goal is to train the student to simultaneously see, conceive, create, emotionally connect with, and interpret his/her surroundings and experiences will use the technology to communicate their feelings and ideas about these connections.

3rd grade

At the beginning of the fall semester, third graders were given an overview of the intended media arts and studies classroom project that would coincide with a scheduled homeroom sponsored, daylong field trip to Henry Ford's "Greenfield Village," a 90-acre outdoor museum featuring more than 300 years of history.

Figure 2: Student portraits taken by 3rd grade students for their Henry Ford–Greenfield Village Microsoft Word Publication.

Figure 3: Example of 3rd grade student digital photography for the Greenfield Village publication.

There are multiple learning opportunities created for the "My Trip to Greenfield Village" book project and include student created sepia toned author's portraits and accompanying biographies, snapshots and descriptive narratives designed to be composited in an eight page Microsoft Word book publishing template. Prior to the daylong field trip students were instructed in digital camera handling and operation, basic camera framing and image capturing techniques, and camera and image making specific vocabulary words. The students were given digital cameras and required to practice capturing images and encouraged to think about the various ways they could control image composition, size, and point-of-view. Students were exposed to turn-of-the century photographic principals including longer exposures, plates versus film and digital capture, and sitter's demeanour. In addition, applicable terms for manipulating images to suggest the turn-of-the-century authenticity were introduced such as sepia, toning, contrast, brightness, oval masks, and cropping.

During the actual fieldtrip students created sepia toned portraits of one another (figure 2) and captured digital images of their tour experiences (figure 3). These images were then uploaded using ArcSoft Photostudio software, manipulated, and saved to their student folders stored on the shared server and later inserted into the Word template.

4th grade

Fourth graders were given an overview of the intended media arts and studies classroom documentary-style production that would emphasize and coincide with Cranbrook Art Museum's "100 Treasures" exhibit. There are multiple interdisciplinary student learning experiences that were designed for this project including the introduction to selected Cranbrook affiliated artists and their artwork, and the overriding conceptual principals behind documentary creation.

Prior to actually gathering images and interviews for the documentary, students were instructed in digital camera handling and operation, basic camera framing and image capturing techniques, and camera, image making, and documentary specific vocabulary terms. The students were given digital still cameras and required to practice capturing images of various aesthetic compositions, upload, log, and evaluate their images. To help prepare for the gathering of the actual documentary materials, the students were asked to sketch storyboards and describe the accompanying voice/over, music, and sound effect that would be heard on the soundtrack (figure 5).

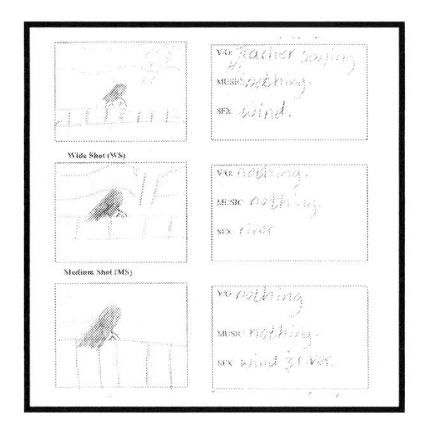

Figure 4: 4th grade student practice storyboard.

The finished documentary-style project will include student captured digital still images and digital video of the artists during interview situations. The artist interviews occurred in the Brookside library (figure 6), at the museum exhibit opening, and via the Internet. Students visited the museum, wrote interview questions and took turns asking the artist about his/her schooling, family life, art styles, and influences. While some students were interviewing the artists and/or education curator, others were documenting the events using Sony Mavica digital still cameras, Sony mini-DV handycams, and sketchpads (figure 7).

Figure 5: 4th grade students interview Cranbrook artist, Ruth Adler-Schnee. Note some students are drawing the interview, some are taking still images, and some are capturing the interview in video.

Figure 6: Digital still images captured by 4th grade students. (a) Samples of the artist's work. (b) Student drawing the interview with the artist.

5th grade

Fifth graders were given an overview of the intended media arts and studies production of a digital yearbook designed to further promote the emotional connecting by capturing their memories at Brookside on an interactive CD-Rom. There are several interdisciplinary student learning opportunities occurring within this project including pre-conceptualization using standard storyboarding techniques, digital image capturing and manipulation, sound design and voice-over recording, and hands-on experience using VR Worx 2.0, HyperStudio 4.0, ArcSoft Photostudio, Super Duper Music Looper, and Microsoft Word software. Students were also instructed in image composition, aesthetic principals, and digital specific vocabulary.

Each student's contribution to the CD-Rom consists of a series of portraits taken by their classmates (figures 7 and 8) supplemented by the student's voice-over describing their reasons for choosing this particular 'favourite' location and accompanied by an original soundtrack. Another element created by each student is a panoramic visual time-line of seven images documenting their 'favourite' grade-level experiences. The finished production will be screened at the 5th grade graduation dinner and a copy of the CD-Rom will be given to each family.

Figure 7: Fifth grade student digital portraits for "Brookside Memories CD Rom".

Figure 8: Fifth grade student digital portraits for "Brookside Memories CD Rom".

5 Conclusion

In conclusion, elementary school educators should strive to become more cognizant of the media surrounding and influencing our children. Acknowledging the existence of the wizard behind the curtain is a beginning, and teaching our children to become more like the wizard is our goal.

References

[1] Hartley, John. Communication, Cultural and Media Studies: The Key Concepts (3rd ed). NY: Routledge, 2002.
[2] Hyerle, David. Visual Tools for Constructing Knowledge. Alexandria, VA: Assoc. for Supervision and Curriculum Development, 1996.
[3] National Institute on Media and the Family. http://www.mediafamily.org/facts
[4] Norton, Priscilla, and Karin M. Wiburg. Teaching With Technology: Designing Opportunities to Learn (2nd ed). Belmont, CA: Thomson Wadsworth, 2003.
[5] Restak, Richard, M.D. The New Brain Modern Age is Rewiring Your: How the Mind. Rodale Press, 2003.
[6] Restak, Richard, M.D. Mozart's Brain and the Fighter Pilot: Unleashing Your Brain's Potential. NY: Harmony Books, 2001.
[7] Sturken, Marita and Lisa Cartwright. Practices of Looking: An Introduction to Visual Culture. Oxford: Oxford UP, 2001.
[8] Sylwester, Robert. A Celebration of Neurons: An Educator's Guide to the Human Brain. Alexandria, VA: Association for Supervision and Curriculum Development, 1995.
[9] Walsh, David. Media and the Mind: A Frank Discussion About the Media's Influence on Your Child's Development. National Institute on Media and the Family, 1997.

Section 2
Strategic issues for the design of new learning systems

Curriculum design and management: a systems view

S. Mecca
Department of Engineering-Physics-Systems, Providence College, Providence, RI 02908-0001 USA

Abstract

Systems thinking has been likened to a science of organizing complexity. Few problems in education have the elements of complexity as that of curriculum. Indeed, within the educational system, the subsystem, curriculum, presents us with a design- or problem solving- challenge that requires tools and approaches that have yet to be fully explored. This paper discusses the basic systems elements of curriculum design and management and highlights the problem underlying the development of curricula that are based on networks of learning standards and benchmarks. Project 2061 Benchmarks for Science Literacy [1] is used as an example of such interconnected learning benchmarks. The first of a suite of tools, TraxLiteracy [2], which tracks benchmarks, curriculum activity blocks and student achievement is used to illustrate the dimensions of the problem and the elements of managing benchmark-based curricula. The implications for education at every level from elementary to university is discussed.

1 Background - a systems definition of curriculum

The educational literature abounds with definitions of 'curriculum'. The assortment of contemporary definitions ranges form those of a parent, Mrs. Stephens,

> "Curriculum is an eclectic framework of learning opportunities, resources, and instructional strategies that empower students to aspire to and to attain national and state standards, learner outcomes, specific teacher-based objectives, while addressing individual abilities.".... Mrs. Stephens.

to that of a Board of Education [3],

> "A series of planned instruction that is coordinated and articulated in a manner designed to result in the achievement by students of specific knowledge and skills and the application of this knowledge",

to that of George J. Posner and Alan N. Rudnitsky [4],

> "Curriculum is not a process. . . . A more precise view of curriculum--and the common understanding of curriculum among lay people--is that it is what is taught in school or what is intended to be learned. It does not refer to what is to be done in school or what is to happen in the learning process. Curriculum represents a set of intentions, a set of intended learning outcomes."

The first definition sees curriculum as a set of resources and strategies aimed at empowering students to achieve various standards; the second emphasizes coordination and planning and the third puts the emphasis on the outcomes themselves. It is important that we establish a working definition at the outset. Let's try viewing curriculum as a subsystem of the education system. There are various definitions of the term system. This paper will consider the definition of Robertshaw, Rerick and Mecca[5],

> " A system is a time-varying configuration of people, hardware and procedures organized to accomplish a certain function(s)."

Viewing curriculum as a system or (subsystem of education), we can begin with a simple definition,

> Curriculum is a time-varying configuration of teaching-learning activities organized to accomplish a set of *benchmarks* for student accomplishment.

In this paper we will use the term benchmarks, learning objectives and standards somewhat interchangeably referring to them generally as *benchmarks* or BMs. Likewise, we will refer to teaching-learning activities as *curriculum activity blocks* or CABs. CABs involve students, teachers, parents, and other participants in a planned learning activity such as a learning unit, an extended lesson, a group or individual project, etc. The specification of a CAB will be discussed later. For purposes of introduction, as long as we keep the aforementioned agreements in mind, we can use as our definition of curriculum,

> Curriculum is a time-varying configuration of learning activity blocks (CABs) organized to accomplish a set of benchmarks BMs.

2 Background - systems design and complex problem solving

Systems design, which is related to engineering design, is the common thread among the engineering and interdisciplinary problem solving disciplines and is applicable to a broad range of complex problems especially those which are non-algorithmic. The methodologies have been well described in many sources. We will briefly illustrate the systems approach as described by Robertshaw, Mecca and Rerick [5] and shown in Figure 1.

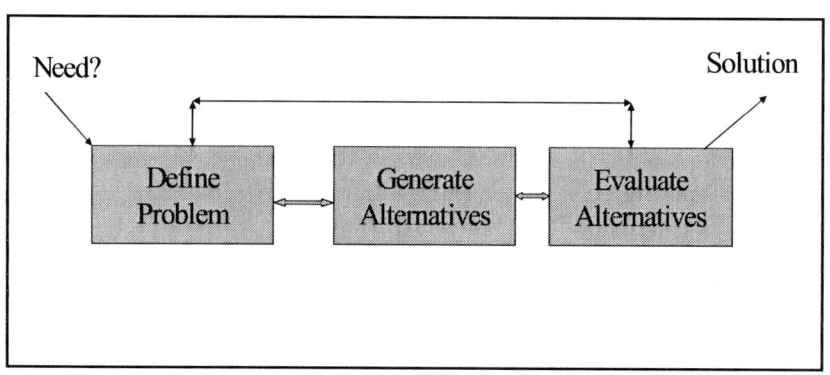

Figure 1: Iterative steps in complex problem solving.

When applied to a real problem, the steps are not necessarily sequential. Yet we will treat each in order and apply this thinking to the design of benchmark-based curricula. Problem definition involves identifying the objectives, deriving the constraints of the problem and establishing the value system of the customer. In the problem of curriculum design, the objectives relate to student accomplishment of learning goals, or in our jargon, benchmarks. Benchmarks may arise from different sources including state or federal mandates, institutional agreements, and partnership or affiliation requirements. Constraints include conditions arising from the time available, e.g. the length of a school day and year, the need for other activities, e.g. lunch and other non-curriculum requirements, and contractual matters, e.g. maximum teacher-student contact hours and teacher preparation time. Generating Alternatives in curriculum design involves the creation of curriculum activity blocks that address benchmarks and the assembly of these in a way that fits the constraints and meets the objectives. Evaluation of alternatives includes consideration of the order in which CABs and hence, benchmarks, are met. As we shall see, the iterative process of generating and evaluating curriculum options introduces a level of complexity that often goes unrecognized in traditional curriculum design. This complexity arises as a result of the inter-relatedness of benchmarks. There are other levels of complexity as well. Coming into a curriculum segment, every student may not have accomplished the same benchmarks or every student may have a different level of accomplishment of prerequisite benchmarks. This introduces a requirement that we closely monitor the progress of every student before and during the learning process. Clearly tools are needed if we are to meet the challenges of curriculum design under the aforementioned conditions.

3 Benchmarks

School districts serving K-12 are increasingly faced with standards and benchmarks from a variety of sources and in a variety of areas (types); this is shown in Figure 2.

Often the benchmarks areas (types) are driven by particular sources. Examples of some of these connections are shown for the Times2 Academy, a Charter School in Providence, Rhode Island USA, is in the arrows of Figure 2. Of particular interest to this paper are the American Association for the Advancement of Science (AAAS) Project 2061 Benchmarks for Science Literacy [1]. Project 2061 grew out of a need to raise the scientific literacy of U.S. students which had fallen sharply in the decades following the late 60s. The effort drew on the talents and thinking of educators, faculty, teachers, researchers, administrators and Nobel laureates from a variety of scientific disciplines and resulted in a collection of some 800 benchmarks representing things students should know or be able to do as a result of their K-12 school experience.

The basis for each benchmark is documented in Science for All Americans, published by AAAS in 1990 [6], Benchmarks are organized into 12 chapters. So many of the topics historically included under the aegis of science literacy are not included in the Project 2061 Benchmarks for Science Literacy. Yet what is included is found on close inspection to be a set of ideas and skills that are significant and fundamental to the scientific enterprise. The great strength and the source of complexity in Project 2061 is that the benchmarks are inter-related on different levels with hierarchies that cross its chapter categories. Some of these connections are documented in the Atlas for Scientific Literacy published by AAAS in 2001 [7]. It is not the intention of this paper to discuss the specific content of *Benchmarks* but rather to emphasize the complexity that arises out of the connections between benchmarks in the development of a curriculum that is based on these standards. Table 1 gives a small segment with maps of interconnected Project 2061 benchmarks to be accomplished by students by grade 2. The numbers represent assigned codes for the benchmarks. Highlighted for example is benchmark number 070A02002 (chapter 07 section 0A grade 02 item 002). Moving from left to right, notice the sequence of benchmarks that arise in each map that must be accomplished before benchmark 070A02002. Of course, the complexity increases many-fold as one traces a grade 12 benchmark through its pre-requisite benchmarks.

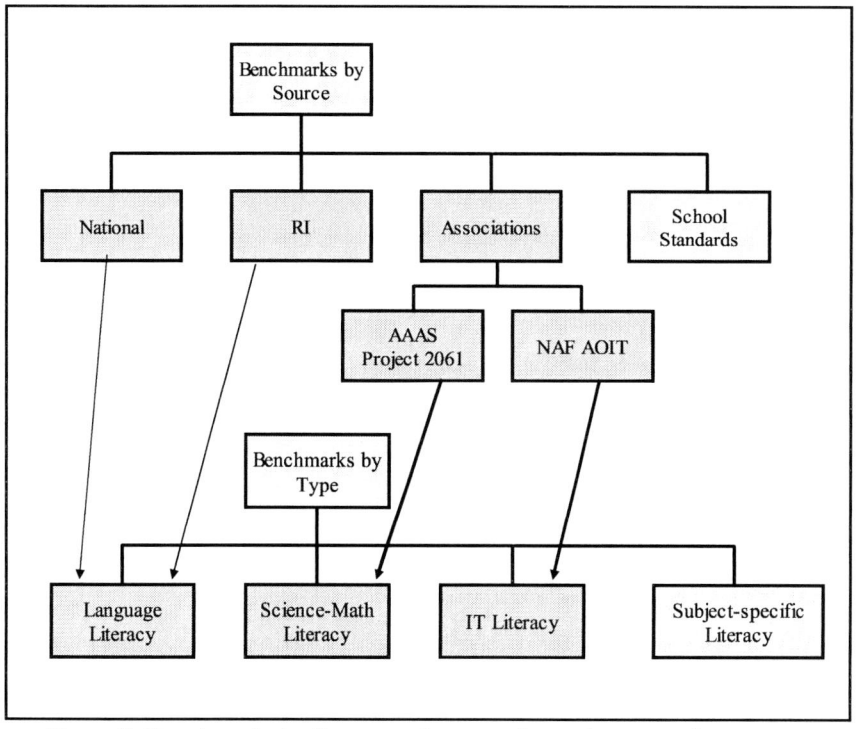

The Internet Society: Advances in Learning, Commerce and Security 53

Figure 2: Benchmarks by Source and type and sample connections source to type for Times² Academy.

Table 1: A small segment of Project 2061 benchmarks. See text.

070A02001	060D02003		
	060F02001		
	060F02002	060F02003	
	070A02002	070B02002	
	070A02003	060D02003	
		070A02002	070B02002
		070B02002	
070B02001	060A02003	*070A02002*	070B02002
		070B02002	

The Internet Society: Advances in Learning, Commerce and Security, K. Morgan & M. J. Spector (Editors)
© 2004 WIT Press, www.witpress.com, ISBN 1-85312-712-4

4 Curriculum activity blocks

Standards based curriculum design must consider Benchmarks in developing the building blocks of a curriculum or, what we have termed, Curriculum Activity Blocks or CABs. A CAB may range from a traditional classroom activity or unit to an individual or team project or problem, which is tied to one or more Benchmarks in one or more areas. CABs may be designed for the full range of learning development and a CAB may even be designed as a terminal Benchmark assessment tool.

New standards should bring a complete re-thinking of the CABs comprising an existing curriculum though all too often CABs get recycled with, at most, an inventory of the related benchmarks tagging each CAB. CABs are assembled to fit the constraints of the school day and school year. The process is depicted in Figures 3, 4 and 5 and more fully described in the AAAS publication, *Designs for Science Literacy* [8], which also documents decades of thinking on the matter. The process, which is termed, Design by Assembly, is likened to a two-dimensional CAD assembly of blocks that fit a given space. But, curricula based on Benchmarks such as those documented in Project 2061 will require much more than a mere assembly of CABs. The process is made complex by a series of factors:

1. The benchmarks are interrelated as discussed earlier.
2. The status of students with respect to benchmark accomplishment varies by student and changes with time.
3. There are often other constraints arising from teacher agreements and state and federal rules related to or affecting scheduling.
4. There is a tendency, in many school settings and in response to shortfalls in teacher preparation time, for teaching staff to re-cycle CABs, a kind of "bend to fit" approach rather than a creative re-thinking of CABs that meet intended benchmarks.
5. There is often an isolation with respect to communications between teachers of different grades.

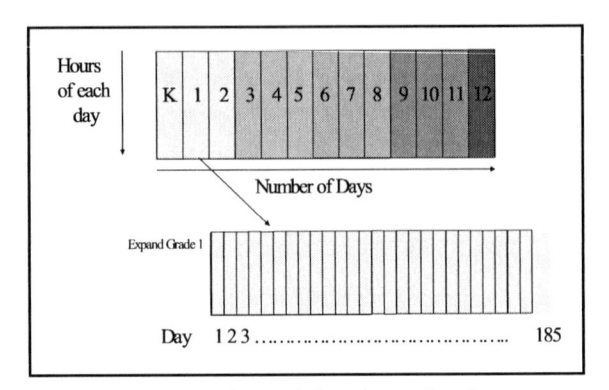

Figure 3: Grades and days in a school year.

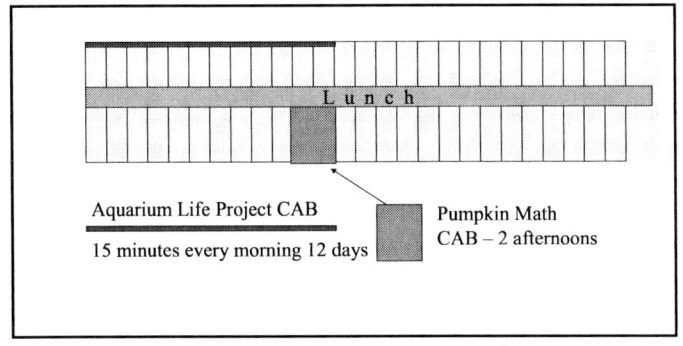

Figure 4: Placing CAB into a school year.

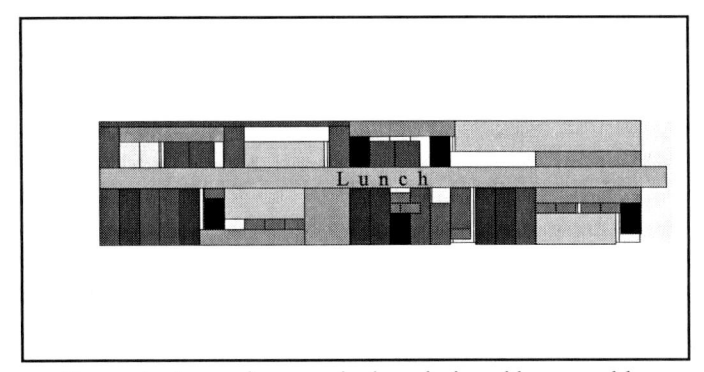

Figure 5: A year-long curriculum designed by assembly.

This is clearly a formidable task with the full range of complexities of the most sophisticated of problems. From a systems perspective a key component of curriculum design is understanding the problem, not just the dimensions noted in this paper but also the issues stemming from the culture of the school. Relating to an understanding of the problem are questions such as: Where are our students? What do we expect them to accomplish (the benchmarks)? How are the benchmarks related? What are the priorities? Are we focusing on broad literacy areas or specialized areas of learning? What are the time frames? What are the constraints? Are all of these imposed or can some of them be negotiated?

5 Tools

As the process moves to considering CABs that address the needs and to evaluating individual CABs and the curriculum as a whole, it is clear that tools are needed. Yet, while many visual organizers and software applications have emerged, much more will be required to fit this problem. In 2001, the author set out to create a wish list of functions that might be served by a tool or a suite of tools. Ultimately, the desired product would assemble a set of CABs, each addressing one or more benchmarks, into a curriculum optimized to meet the benchmarks for every student under the constraints of the situation. [The problem can be formulated as a systems optimization problem with perhaps an evolutionary algorithmic approach, the subject of which will await another paper.] For purposes of this discussion, suffice it to say that some intermediate tools are required to meet the practical application of the aforementioned ideas. One of the suite of tools that has been developed and tested is TraxLiteracy[2]. TraxLiteracy supports benchmarks as these have been defined in this paper from state, national, association (such as AAAS Project 2061 and National Academy Foundation) and school sources.. Benchmarks are expected to be accomplished at certain points in time and accomplishment of these is tracked for each student in the TraxLiteracy system. Figure 6 shows a partial menu frame for this system. Interested readers are encouraged to visit www.traxliteracy.com or contact the author.

From 2002 to present, thorough testing of the system has taken place at the Times2 Academy. A small set of the Academy's Division 1 CABs supporting Project 2061 *Benchmarks* are shown in the following table.

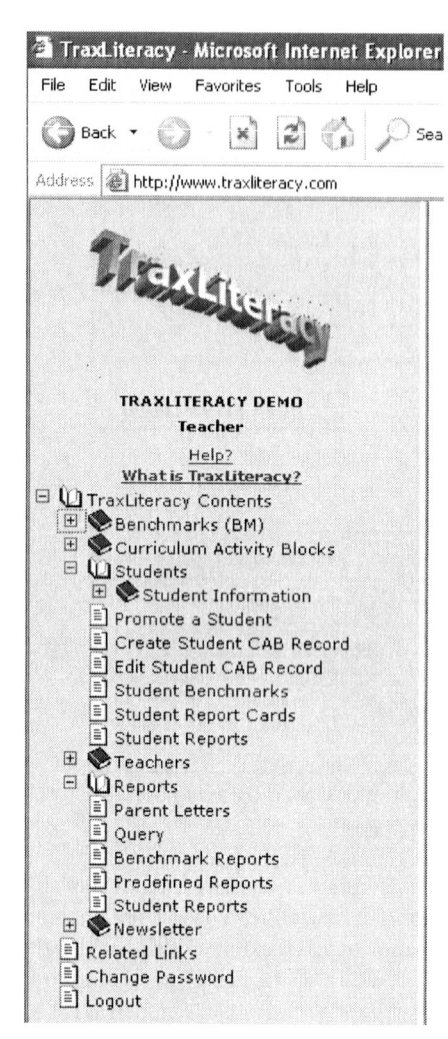

Figure 6: Partial menu frame from TraxLiteracy.com

Grade	0K	0K	0K	0K	01	02	0K	0K	02	0K	02	0K	01
Topic Area	PS	SC	PS	SC	MH	SC	LS	SC	SC	MA	SC	MA	MA
CAB Number	00 00 2	00 00 4	00 00 1	00 00 7	00 00 1	00 00 3	00 00 1	00 00 6	00 00 4	00 00 4	00 00 2	00 00 1	00 00 1

Benchmarks

010A02001	x	x											
010A02002													
010B02001			x	x									
010B02002				x	x	x	x	x					
010B02003						x	x	x	x	x			
010B02004													
010C02001		x				x		x					
010C02002						x	x		x				
010C02003				x		x	x			x	x	x	
020A02001												x	x

Notice that several CABs address several *Benchmarks*, yet there are *Benchmarks* which are not addressed by any CABs in this small subset. Work is in process to display the time-sequence of CABs in the curriculum and to overlay the implied order in which *Benchmarks* are undertaken and the prescribed order in which they are intended to be undertaken. This would facilitate the iteration of CAB development and sequencing that must be done to arrive at a workable curriculum that satisfies the constraints of time and order that must be met. The process is depicted in Figure 7 for a hypothetical and simple system of *Benchmarks* and CABs. Figure 7A shows CABs, X, Y and Z and the Benchmarks that each activity addresses. Figure 7B shows the hierarchy of the Benchmarks, BMs from left to right, 1 and 6 being the most fundamental ones; 5 and 3 require that 1 be completed and 4 and 3 require that 6 be completed; 2 requires 4 and 4 requires 3. This hierarchy suggests two BM sequence options and these are shown in Figure 7C. Finally, each CAB sequence results in a BM sequence shown in Figure 7D.

Each of the CAB-related BMs in the sequence is scored for purposes of illustration with a +1 for being in the right sequence and a -1 otherwise. It is clear from this simple analysis that CAB sequence XZY is the best choice for this hypothetical curriculum. It is also possible in a real situation involving an existing set of CABs addressing 50 or more BMs that no sequence will meet the requirement that all BMs be met in sequence. The practical consequence of this situation is that emphasis in curriculum design should be on CAB design around specific BMs versus a reliance on one's inventory of existing learning activities to assemble a curriculum. Such an approach was suggested and formulated by Wiggins and McTighe [9], who used a design methodology approach that emphasized the framing of learning experiences, what we have termed CABs, as the final stage of the curriculum design process.

CABs	**BMs addressed**
X	1-6-3
Y	5-2
Z	6-4

Figure 7A

BM Hierarchy

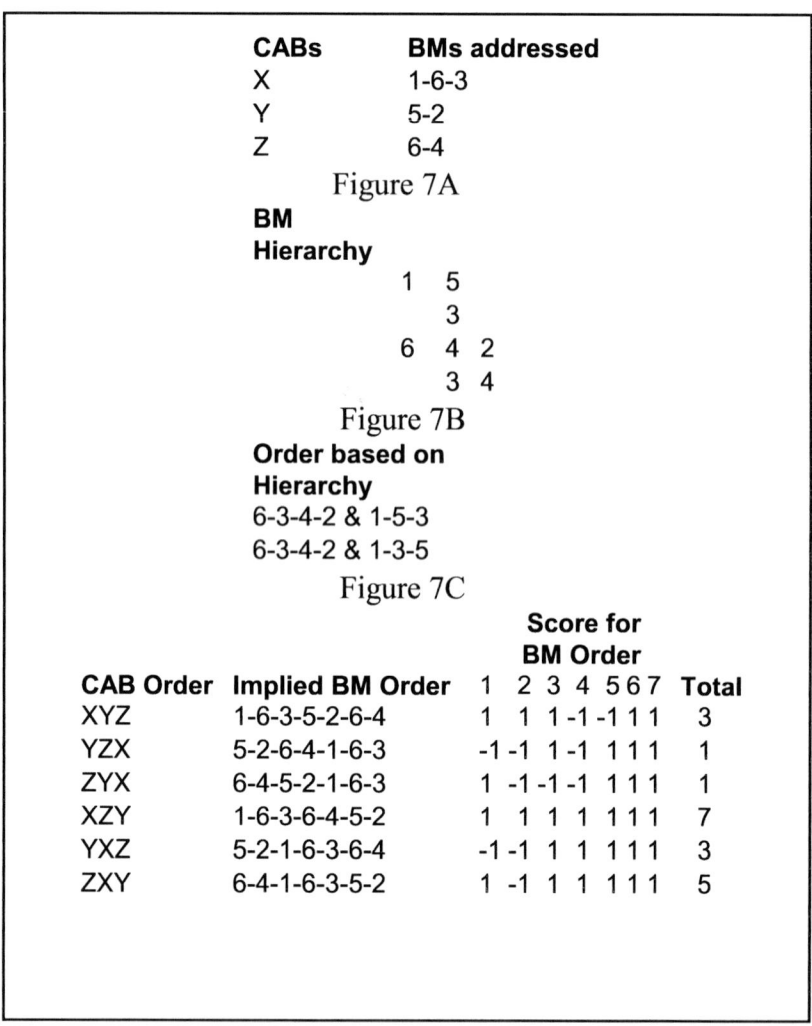

```
      1   5
          3
      6   4   2
          3   4
```

Figure 7B

Order based on Hierarchy
6-3-4-2 & 1-5-3
6-3-4-2 & 1-3-5

Figure 7C

CAB Order	Implied BM Order	Score for BM Order 1 2 3 4 5 6 7	Total
XYZ	1-6-3-5-2-6-4	1 1 1 -1 -1 1 1	3
YZX	5-2-6-4-1-6-3	-1 -1 1 -1 1 1 1	1
ZYX	6-4-5-2-1-6-3	1 -1 -1 -1 1 1 1	1
XZY	1-6-3-6-4-5-2	1 1 1 1 1 1 1	7
YXZ	5-2-1-6-3-6-4	-1 -1 1 1 1 1 1	3
ZXY	6-4-1-6-3-5-2	1 -1 1 1 1 1 1	5

Figure 7: A. CABs X,Y, and Z and the BMs each addresses; B. The hierarchy of BMs is from left to right (see text); C. BM sequencing options based on the BM hierarchy; D. Scoring for each CAB based on its BM sequence (see text).

6 Conclusions

This paper has outlined a systems view of curriculum design and management wherein curriculum is viewed as a time-varying configuration of learners and learning activities, or curriculum activity blocks (CABs), organized to accomplish a set of benchmarks, BMs. Benchmarks are learning outcomes, standards or goals to be achieved at certain times in the continuum of school years and are hierarchically ordered on a number of levels. TraxLiteracy, a web-centric tool for managing CABs and related BMs along with student progress and achievement, has been developed and tested at the TIMES^2 Academy, a charter school in Rhode Island, USA, that has adopted Project 2061 Benchmarks for its K-12 Science Literacy curriculum. The intrinsic complexity of designing curriculum around ordered benchmarks has been discussed and the need for developing tools and practices to aid teachers, administrators, school improvement teams, literacy coordinators has been emphasized. Finally, while this paper used illustrations based on K-12 Benchmarks, similar consideration needs to be given to post-secondary curricula as well. Certain literacy standards are normally assumed to have been met for students entering a college or university program but new course work is often built upon a set of interdependent learning objectives which must be recognized in developing the lessons and learning activities of university-level courses. This will become increasingly important as colleges and universities are held accountable for their teaching-learning practices and outcomes.

Acknowledgments

The author gratefully acknowledges the ongoing efforts of Times^2 Academy administrators and staff, of teachers, Kristen Farrah, Kathy Field, Kimberly Cordeiro Maratto, Alicia Castle, Brooke Harris, and Deborah Wagner for their efforts in testing TraxLiteracy as the product was implemented in year one trials, of their second year colleagues, Kristine Gannon, Seaana Marcks and Natasha Re who make use of the product and provide input for further improvements and of Drs. Stanley Thompson, Dean, Academy and Dr. Geraldine Thomson for their able direction of the Times^2 academic enterprise as it seeks to build a curriculum with the underlying complexities touched upon in this paper. Special thanks to Gail Thomas of Genlex, Inc. for her careful coding of TraxLiteracy and ongoing support of its implementation in K-12 programs.

References

[1] *Benchmarks for Science Literacy*, American Association for the Advancement of Science (AAAS), Washington, DC 1993.
[2] TraxLiteracy is a product of Genlex, Inc., Jamestown, Rhode Island.
[3] Pennsylvania State Board of Education Code Ch. 4, Pennsylvania, USA.
[4] George J. Posner and Alan N. Rudnitsky, *Course Design*, page 8, Addison Wesley Longman, 1997.

[5]   J. Robertshaw, S. Mecca & M. Rerick, *Problem Solving: A Systems Approach*, Petrocelli Books, Inc. 1978.
[6]   *Science for All Americans*, AAAS, Washington, DC, Oxford University Press, 1990.
[7]   *Atlas of Science Literacy*, AAAS and the National Science Teachers Association, Washington, DC, Oxford University Press 2001.
[8]   *Designs for Science Literacy*, AAAS, Washington, DC, Oxford University Press 2000.
[9]   Grant Wiggins and Jay McTighe, *Understanding by Design*, Association for Supervision and Curriculum Development 1998.

Learning objects in use

J. Bennedsen
It University West, Denmark

Abstract

One of the really hot topics in the learning community at the moment is learning objects. Right now a lot of effort is put into developing and describing standards for learning objects – standards like SCORM, Ariadne or Dublin Core. These initiatives will definitely benefit the persons seeking information, but will be an extra burden on the persons supplying the information – the lecturers – since they have to add all the metadata.

In e-learning courses a lot of materials get developed – materials like discussions, essays, taped video sessions etc. – and all these materials are potential learning objects - something that others can reuse. It is therefore important, that it is easy for the lecturer to add metadata to the learning objects, so the objects can be easily found either by other lecturers or by the students attending the course.

In this article we will focus on balancing the need for metadata with the limited time the lecturers have. This is done in several steps: First we define what we think is a minimum amount of metadata and discuss this metadata description to see if it fits requirements of the lecturer, the students and the requirements for describing all the different types of materials. Secondly we propose and develop an open-source tool that can be used to store and retrieve the materials using metadata descriptions and be integrated in a lot of different e-learning systems. Thirdly we will describe how this approach can be expanded to give access to electronic materials like article databases. Finally we give some conclusions and remarks on how to make the creation of learning objects happen.

1 Introduction

In the past decade or so a lot of effort has been put into creating different descriptors for all kind of electronic learning materials. A lot of standards for describing learning materials have emerged like SCORM (SCORM [9]),

ARIADNE [1] and Dublin Core [6] hand in hand with the development and spreading of e-learning systems. One example is the birth of the Dublin Core metadata standard [6]: *"Yuri Rubinsky of SoftQuad (who chaired panels regarding the future of HTML and Web authoring tools) along with Stuart Weibel and Eric Miller of OCLC (who were presenting papers about scholarly publishing on the Web and leading discussions on the delivery of Web-based library services) had a hallway conversation with Terry Noreault, then Director of the OCLC Office of Research, and Joseph Hardin, then Director of the National Center for Supercomputing Applications (NCSA). This discussion on semantics and the Web revolved around the difficulty of finding resources (difficult even then, with only about 500,000 addressable objects on the Web)"*

Describing materials have a much longer tradition in the libraries, where description and cataloguing have been done for a long time (in Hermann [8] an instruction for the library from 1797 is quoted) but the descriptors for learning materials - or learning objects – take into account the teaching and learning aspects.

All of these descriptors use metadata. Metadata (Day [5]) are traditionally defined as data about data, information about information, and are used to describe document contents and structure, relations to other data items, the properties of the corresponding data domains, legal rights etc. Metadata are also useful to provide textual descriptions for non-textual objects, for example, to enable the representation of multimedia document properties in a structured way, simplifying document management, search and retrieval (Yoon and Kim [12]). Today, most collections of articles and other learning objects worldwide have already adopted metadata as the basic tool for resource description. Following this trend, metadata recommendations for educational systems are one of the most productive activities in the standardization of computer-based learning systems (Anido et al [1]).

One of the advantages of e-learning is that all communication and materials are digital. This implies that it can be stored and retrieved at a later stage for the students to look at again; a property that adds a lot of flexibility to a course. In an e-learning course a lot of material gets created. In one example – an introductory programming course – over 100 video mediated materials, 50 program examples, 10 PowerPoint shows and a lot of relevant text based materials were created. For a more detailed description see (Bennedsen and Caspersen [3]). A lot of these materials have a broader usage than the limited usage in the concrete time of the course where they were created; it can be used to give alternative presentations for the topics in the course, as answers to questions etc. This naturally gives rise to the question: "How do the students find the relevant material"? If the e-learning system just uses text-based messages it is possible to do a text search using the search facility that is part of most e-learning systems (given that the search sentence is part of the text based material. If it is needed to add other information (e.g. keywords) metadata is needed for text based materials as well.) But what about the other types of material like videos, applications, images, program examples, etc? These are not searchable, so there is a need for metadata describing the content of these resources.

If we look at the different metadata standards for learning objects, their goal is to add metadata making the materials reusable. One way of saying this is (SCORM [9], p. 21): *"It is intended to provide the technical means for content objects to be easily shared across multiple learning delivery environments"*. SCORM as an example have four major goals: Accessibility, interoperability, durability and reusability – all goals related to the idea of creating learning objects that can be (re)used in many settings. One of the consequences for this reusability is a lot of fields in the description related to property rights; SCORM has nine categories: General, lifecycle, meta-metadata, technical, educational, rights, and relation to other objects, annotation and classification (SCORM [10]).

2 Minimum metadata definition

The approach here is to give the students a possibility of retrieving the different learning resources that is created during a course. Examples of these are streamed video lectures, slide shows with audio speech, solution to exercises etc. This use of the metadata implies that it is not so much reuse of the materials in other course setting that is the goal rather it is descriptions within one course. Therefore the different metadata fields related to lifecycle, meta-metadata, rights and relation to other objects are not needed. As a consequence we have developed a scaled down version of the SCORM metadata model. This metadata description has as its primary goal that the students can find the learning objects again.

The big challenge in developing such a model is to include only the absolutely necessary fields. The main argument for this is that it normally will be the lecturer (or someone with knowledge of the field appointed to the job) who will have the obligation to create the metadata for the learning objects – an extra burden on top of the responsibility of preparing, holding, evaluating the course etc. It is therefore vital for the success to keep the metadata down to a minimum and create a simple and user friendly interface to enter the metadata.

On the other hand Forsyth (Forsyth [7]) asks the question *"Why do you want to deliver your course using the Internet?"* He argues that many institutions do it wrong because they just places translated paper-based materials on the Internet. His point is *"Where the Internet gains credibility in an educational context is the capability to be interactive and resource rich"*. This implies that the metadata descriptions must be able to handle descriptions of many different kinds of material such as images, videos, audios, applications etc. This seems to imply that the metadata description must be very large; a problem when it is the lecturer that has to create the metadata.

The interesting question is therefore: "What are the necessary metadata elements that make it possible for the students to find the relevant learning resources?" The metadata elements should make it possible to describe the content of the resource. We have done this by having the following metadata elements:

- Title: A short sentence describing the resource as a hole.
- Author: The creator of the resource.

- Description: A description of the content.
- Keyword(s): relevant keyword(s) within the course.
- Date: When is the resource created
- URL: The address of the resource

We have found these five metadata elements sufficient for the students. The only element that is not directly related to the possibility of searching the materials is the author. We have included this metadata element in order to give the students a possibility to judge the quality of the resource (i.e. is it created by the lecturer, other lecturers or another students in the course).

3 The system

We have created an open source system based on the XML standard (XML [11]). The metadata are stored as XML files. This way of storing the information gives great flexibility when we want to display the data since we can parse the XML files (for example show the title as a link to the material). By using folders to store the different metadata descriptions (i.e. XML files) the different materials can be categorized. The definition of the category is a special XML file placed in the folder.

The database stores only the metadata descriptions not the content of the material. The content is stored somewhere on the web and is referenced by a URL. This gives a great flexibility since it is possible to add materials that are not created in the course or materials that are accessible on other web-servers. If it is required that the material must be password protected, this is implemented on the web server storing the material.

This way of storing the metadata gives the possibility to use an open source XML database in order to make the metadata searchable. We therefore have the possibility to create a web interface for the material that shows the material in the chosen categories regardless of the actual placement of the material (this is shown in a web-browser):

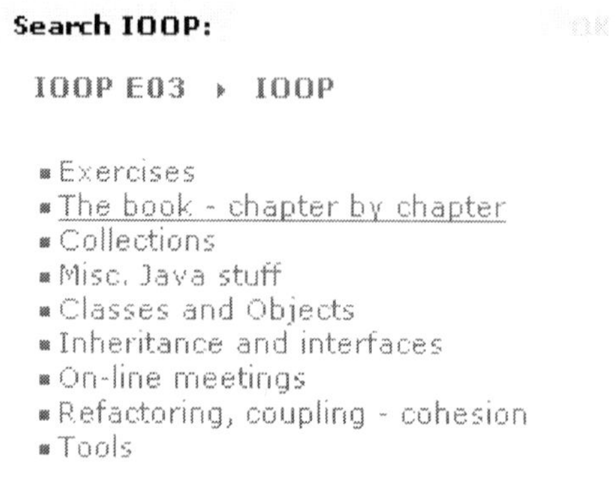

Search IOOP:

IOOP E03 ▸ IOOP

- Exercises
- The book - chapter by chapter
- Collections
- Misc. Java stuff
- Classes and Objects
- Inheritance and interfaces
- On-line meetings
- Refactoring, coupling - cohesion
- Tools

Figure 1: Categories of materials in an introductory programming course.

The categories are defined by the lecturer. A resource can be in more than one category, but replication of the metadata is then needed.

When the user clicks on one of the categories, the metadata for the resources in that category is shown (notice that the resources in the example below are videos):

IOOP E03 ▸ IOOP ▸ Tools

2 links. Showing 1-2.

▸ Connect to videostream
http://www.daimi.au.dk/~ioop/video/WMP.wmv
Description: This shows how you connect to the videostream using Windows Media Player
Author: Jens Bennedsen
Date:
Keywords: Windows Media Player
Type: Windows Media File

▸ Submit vejledning
http://www.daimi.au.dk/~ioop/video/submit-vejledni...
Description: Jens viser hvordan Blue J sættes op til at kunne aflevere

Figure 2: Some learning objects in the tools category.

The really big advantage is the possibility for searching. This implies that the students can find the relevant materials created in the course.

By using XML we have the possibility to create different metadata description by using different XML schemas. This implies that the lecturer (or other creators of metadata) can create their own metadata definition with metadata elements of their choosing.

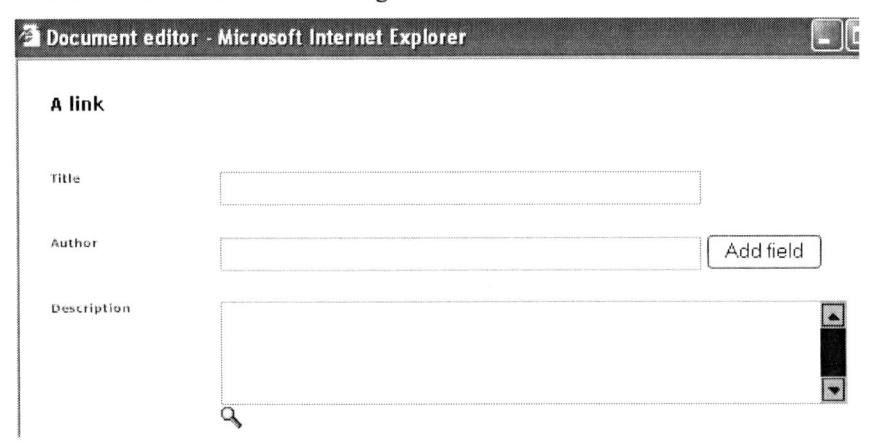

Figure 3: Form for describing metadata.

We have created a web-based interface for the metadata suppliers. We have created two types of interfaces for metadata suppliers: one where it is possible to create categories and one where you just select the category and then add the metadata. The metadata entry interface passes the XML schema and creates input fields for the relevant metadata elements.

4 Evaluation

The system has been in use in one course and is currently being used in two other courses. The one course where it was used was the introductory programming course mentioned above. There were 32 students participating in the course. We have evaluated the usefulness of the system by qualitative interviews with a representative selection of the students from the course (nine students all in all). Furthermore we have interviewed the lecturer and the teaching assistant involved in the course.

4.1 The main results of the evaluation

- Only 50% of the students have used the resource database. The rest of the students did not know that they could search the materials. If they had known, they indicated that they think it would have been very useful.
- The students had hardly any use the system during the course but used it during their preparation for the exam. They explained that the course design (one topic pr. week) implied that they had very little need for extra materials. But at the exam period they needed to understand all the topics and could not only focus on materials for one topic.
- The students found the interface simple to use and the descriptions for the materials useful.
- The lecturer and teaching assistant found the interface for creating metadata a little difficult to use. They would have preferred integration with a web browser.
- The teaching assistant supplied the videos with indexes (the time a given topic starts in the video). This serves both as a description of the video and as a guide for the student showing him what part of the video is relevant.

We will evaluate the use of the system for the two courses in this semester. The use of the system in one of the courses is a little different: The course is based on materials available on the Internet. The system is here used for describing the already available materials (i.e. adding metadata like description, reading depth, mandatory text etc) and making these metadata searchable.

5 Integration of library resources

Particularly in distance education settings we have observed that the students do not use academic articles or other academic materials. Neither do they use the databases available at the library for searching relevant information. At the most they use Google or other search engines, but this approach has many drawbacks. One is the quality of the materials they find. Another is that they probably do not hit any academic articles since they are not freely accessible on the Internet.

The Danish Electronic Research Library was founded in 1996 with the aim of providing electronic access to many articles etc. They have negotiated rights for all students and staff of the Danish Universities to search and read many of the article databases and full text articles. These articles are accessible within the network on the campus or by different solutions (like proxy-servers and passwords) to the students outside the campus.

The solution created here uses the Z39.50 standard for accessing library databases. It is possible to include a database in the search (and which fields in the metadata description) if this database is Z39.50 compliant. This part is work in progress but we believe that this integration of library materials in the e-learning platform will have the effect that the students will use the library materials much more.

The XML database used is also compliant with the Z39.50 standard. It is therefore possible to make all the materials created in a particular course accessible for other than the students participating in the course.

6 Related work

In [4] Collis they noticed five outcomes from practice. *"Of the hundreds of thousands of objects in the TeleTOP database for the University of Twente, the large majority are submissions by learners, many of which are re-used by other learners as study resources. The system has not replaced the book but extended it, so that resources from many different origins, often located by the participants, form a dynamic and growing resource collection".* In their setting this is done as part of a commercial system, not as an open-source component the course designer can add to an existing course web site. As described above we are also working on integrating library resources as part of the system

7 Conclusion

We have described an approach to learning objects where the main purpose for the learning object not so much is reuse by others but reuse within a course. This is relevant in e-learning settings where all the materials are digital. When e-learning uses richer types of materials than merely text based materials, metadata is needed. We have proposed a minimal metadata description and developed an open source system based on the Z39.50 standard in order to make the metadata descriptions available and searchable for the students. Furthermore we have evaluated the use of the system by students and lecturers.

Acknowledgements

We will like to thank DEF – The Danish Electronic Research Library – for their financial support. Without their support this project would not have been possible. We would also like to thank the library at Aarhus School of Business for their support and eager to create electronic access to articles etc. Last but not least we would like to thank the students participating in CS1 and other courses for their help in evaluating the system.

References

[1] Anido, L.E. et al, Educational metadata and brokerage for learning resources, *Computers and Education*, **38(4)**, pp. 351 – 374, 2002
[2] Ariadne, www.ariadne-eu.org/en/publications/metadata/ams_v32.html, last visited December 4, 2003
[3] Bennedsen, J and Caspersen, M., The Rationale for Designing a Programming Course for Adults, Proc. of International Conference on Open & Online Learning, 2003
[4] Collis, B. The TeleTOP initiative: new learning, new technology, *Industrial and Commercial Training*, **34(6)**, p 216 – 222, 2002
[5] Day, M., Metadata in a nutshell. *Information Europe*, **6(2)**. 2001
[6] Dublin Core Metadata Initiative, www.dublincore.org/, last visited 27 November 2003Forsyth, I. *Teaching and Learning Materials and the Internet*, Kogan Page, 2001
[7] Forsyth, I., *Teaching and Learning Materials and the Internet*, Kogan Page, 2001
[8] Hermann, Else, Mod fælles standarder (towards common standards) (in Danish), Biblioteksstyrelsen, 1999
[9] The SCORM overview, version 1.2, available at www.adlnet.org, last visited December 4, 2003
[10] The SCORM content aggregation model, version 1.2, available at www.adlnet.org, last visited December 4, 2003 [SCORM2]
[11] XML reference, www.w3.org/TR/REC-xml, last visited December 4. 2003
[12] Yoon, J. P., & Kim, S., Schema extraction for multimedia xml document retrieval. *Procs. of the 1st International Conference on Web Information Systems Engineering (WISE'00)*. IEEE Press. 2000

Modularization of learning outcomes: a "design-down" competency driven instructional design approach

T. M. Stavredes & S. Clawson
Capella University, USA

Abstract

Traditionally, educational institutions issue degrees based on the participation of the student within their institution, however, a shift is taking place where qualifications are issued on the basis of attainment of specified competency units influenced by industry standards. Designed in terms of the knowledge, skills, and attitudes expected from graduates, competency-based curricula aim to equip learners for enhanced performance in the workplace. Capella University conducted a study utilizing a design-down competency driven instructional design approach linking program outcomes down to the course, the assessments, the resources, and finally to the alignment of each unit within the course. The design was based on the development of content chunks with clearly defined competencies. The learning objects are fine-grained detailed learning outcomes. Aggregated into larger objects, they can be delivered as a unit of instruction or a complete course.

This paper addresses the influence of competency standards on the development of curriculum and related development tools. In addition, the discussion will present the results of a case study on the development process and implications of this competency driven approach to modularized learning outcomes. The results indicate that competency-based course design is a worthwhile approach and leads to the development of courses with superior associations to competencies and comprehensive curriculum.

Keywords: competency-based curriculum, instructional design, modularization, design-down approach, learning outcome.

1 Introduction

A wide variety of stakeholders champion competency-based curriculum. Over the past few years, accreditation agencies such as North Central Association have focused on the assessment of student achievement as linked to learning outcomes [1]. The organization understands that focusing on learning outcomes is the best way to achieve a curriculum that is relevant, rigorous, and current.

Further, "educational stakeholders—students, parents, and government funding agencies—are demanding that education be [held] accountable. Concern over the "value" of education has prompted a rethinking about how colleges and universities function [2]. Learners seeking higher education demand evidence of the value they seek in their institutions. They want opportunities to build on the skills, knowledge, and attitudes they acquire through their education and that are closely related to their professional field.

Through a re-examination of the curricula and courses, institutions can better align their learning outcomes with competencies that are grounded in both general and specialized knowledge and influenced by evolution of specific fields, thereby, maintaining the essence of higher education while changing the way knowledge is transmitted to students so that they can survive in the workplace [2]. Because a competency-based approach to education is outcome directed and assessment oriented, it creates a closer fit between higher education and the needs of society [2].

In response to this focus shift to learning outcomes, Capella University proposed the goal to become a completely competency-based university by the end of 2004 and has developed learning outcomes and associated competencies for all programs of study. The School of Education began the process of identifying program outcomes and competencies for every specialization in September 2002. Beginning in 2003, the School of Education began the process of revising every course in the curriculum to incorporate the stated outcomes and associated competencies within the respective specializations. This project was based on four assumptions: Alignment was the fundamental test. From the University's mission, we had to map the School mission, down to specialization missions and outcomes, down to the course competencies; all outcomes and competencies had to be based on recognized national standards; the definitions of terms would be taken from recognized and respected academic sources, and outcomes and competencies would distinguish doctoral from masters learners.

While multiple, credible models and definitions of competencies are available; we determined that we needed to move forward from the clarification of whose outcomes and competencies we would use [3]. We decided to adopt North Central's language and the Accounting Education Change Commission (AECC) guidelines for outcomes and competencies. Generally, "an outcome is 'what' you expect your student to achieve, whereas a competency demonstrates 'how' your students can achieve that outcome. Think of an outcome as an *end* and a competency as a *means* to that end." [4].

Outcomes were expected to be learner and learning focused, skills and abilities central to a discipline, based on professional standards, and general enough to capture important learning but specific enough to be measurable.

Competencies were expected to: describe the performance of a major skill, be written at the level of application, be measurable and observable, and describe the intended result and not the learning process [3].

To ensure alignment of program outcomes and competencies within the School of Education specializations a "design-down" competency driven instructional design approach was developed. This approach links program outcomes and competencies down to the course outcomes, competencies, assessments, resources, and finally to the alignment of each unit within the course being developed or revised. This approach assures that our learners are able to demonstrate program outcomes and competencies, and it permits a seamless transition from curriculum content to course production--a critical issue for an online university. The content objects that are developed using this approach are fine-grained detailed learning objects. Aggregated into larger objects, they can be delivered as a unit of instruction or a complete course. In order to understand the applicability of this design-down competency driven instructional design approach, we conducted a study to evaluate this approach from the perspective of faculty course developers.

2 Method

The purpose of the study was to evaluate the applicability of a design-down competency driven instructional design approach using a Competency Matrix tool. Because the purpose of this study was not to confirm but rather to gain insight and a better understanding of the process from the perspective of faculty course developers, a case study was employed. The interest was in the process rather than the end product. Insights from this study would help us better understand the effectiveness and applicability of the approach and tool that will inform us in future iterations of the process. The study followed the faculty course developers through the design process using weekly meetings and an end of course development survey.

2.1 Participants

A total of 20 faculty in the School of Education participated in the original course development team using the new design-down, competency-driven instructional design approach and tool. All faculty had experience in developing courses, but no one had prior experience developing competency-based courses.

2.2 Process

The course development team consisted of experienced members of the Capella community and School of Education, who collaborated to design and develop a new or revised course. The team included:

- A faculty course developer: to serve as subject matter expert from School of Education (adjunct or full time faculty designated by School leadership)
- An instructional designer: to lead the project team and the design of online courses, instructional content, and assessment
- A member of School leadership: to review and approve the course content and design

Faculty course developers worked one-on-one with an instructional designer as they developed the course. In addition, the course developer received feedback from the program leadership who reviewed their work throughout the process.

To build a space for dialogue and reflective practice through the course development process, the course development team met on a weekly basis via a telephone conferencing system to discuss the course development process and exchange ideas about best strategies for achieving course outcomes.

At the end of the course development process faculty were sent a survey that asked them their perceptions of the strengths, weaknesses, and difficulties of the course development process.

2.3 The competency matrix tool

In order to ensure that courses within the School of Education specializations reflect the outcome and competency of their respective specializations, a Competency Matrix tool was developed for the first phase of the development process (Figure 1). A course developer is required to move sequentially through a series of design steps, each step building on the decisions of the previous ones as follows:

Curriculum alignment: External standards were used as a basis for creating outcomes that reflect the School and Specialization missions.

Course alignment: Alignment of School and Specialization outcomes and the respective competencies to the individual course are recorded by indicating the course ID in the "Course Alignment" column of the matrix next to the specific competencies it will address.

Assessment alignment: Once the competencies for the course had been determined, appropriate assessments must be chosen to demonstrate that the learner has acquired the stated competencies. All competencies must be assessed in order to be included in the course. The type of assessment is then recorded in the "Assessment Alignment" column.

Resource alignment: It is only after the competencies and assessments have been determined, that appropriate resources addressing the stated competencies and assessments are chosen. Mapping of resources to individual competencies assures that learners are provided with relevant content to gain the knowledge, skills, and attitudes associated with the stated competencies. The name of the resource, as well as the part (i.e. chapter, sections, unit) of the resource addressing the specific competency, is recorded in the Competency Matrix under "Resource Alignment".

Unit alignment: The final step in the alignment process is to determine the order of presentation of the course. The competencies are ordered by "unit" and the associated unit recorded in the column "Unit Alignment".

Although the process appears to be linear, it is actually an iterative process. Course developers continued to revisit the Competency Matrix as they developed the course and make adjustments. The importance of using the Competency Matrix is to ensure that the course development process is driven by the competencies.

The purpose of the Competency Matrix was to ensure that courses aligned with program outcomes and competencies; however, the Competency Matrix organizes content "chunks" with clearly defined outcomes and competencies allowing the modularization of content that can be used to create individual learning objects for storage in a content repository and assembled for use in a variety of individualized learning events.

Capella UNIVERSITY Education. Reborn.

Course Name: ED825 – Curriculum Development			Course Competency Matrix		
Program Outcomes	**Competencies**	**Course Alignment**	**Assessment Alignment**	**Resource Alignment**	**Unit Alignment**
PSE 1: Demonstrate an understanding of effective learning communities and the teacher's role in forming collaborative relationships with learners, colleagues, and the community.	PSE 1c. Analyzing and evaluating existing learning communities in the professional education setting.	ED825	(CourseRoom discussions and postings.)	Gabbert and Gabbert (2003). *The growth of technology*. New York Technology Press. Chapters 1 through 4.	10
PSE 2: Create multiple pathways to knowledge.	PSE 2b. Demonstrating effective communication strategies and techniques related to knowledge acquisition and interactive communication		(Oral, aural, written, and non-verbal, journal, portfolio, CourseRoom discussion based on assigned readings.)	Minkus (2003). *Mastering web searches in the sciences*. Chicago. Ion Press. Chapter 4.	3, 4, 6, 8
PSE 3: Demonstrate an understanding of the social and cultural context of education and the implications of practice.	PSE 3b. Exhibiting appreciation of diversity and multicultural differences.		(Journal, describing experiences in CourseRoom discussions, developing culturally sensitive courses and lessons.)	???	
	PSE 3c. Demonstrating an understanding of the need to accommodate differences in cognition and achievement in instruction and assessment.		(Paper based on text/assigned reading and library research, portfolio.)	North Dakota science resources for K-12 teachers http//www.ndsr.edu/tech lab/articles/	5,6

Figure 1: Capella's competency matrix tool.

2.4 Course development

Once the Competency Matrix had been completed the end product is a set of modularized learning outcomes that can be used as a framework for developing individual learning events such as a unit of instruction or aggregated as a course. During course development the modularized outcomes are aggregated into units of instruction. Each unit of instruction includes an introduction, outcomes statement, presentation of unit, information, action, & discussion assignments, and assessments (Figure 2).

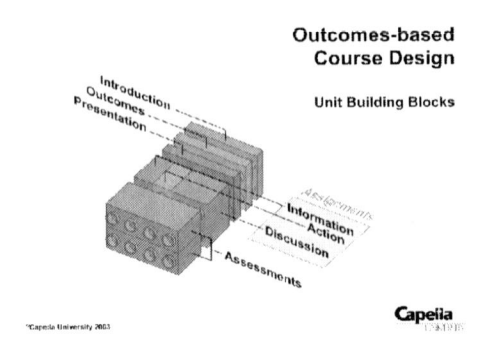

Figure 2. Unit building blocks.

3 Results

The "design-down" competency driven instructional design approach was developed to assure that our learners are able to demonstrate program outcomes and competencies and also to permit a seamless transition from curriculum content to course production, a critical issue for an online university.

At the end of the course development process a survey was sent out to all faculty developers asking them to comment on the strengths and weaknesses of the process as well as degree of difficulty using the Competency Matrix tool. They were also asked to comment on specific ways the process could be improved. A total of 16 of the 20 distributed surveys were completed and returned.

3.1 The competency matrix tool

The survey asked faculty to order the steps in the Competency Matrix tool in order from least to most difficult based on a scale of 1-least difficult to 5-most difficult (Table 1).

Faculty developers indicated that the first step of the process, aligning the course to the competencies, was the least difficult. The most difficult step was developing the course through written presentations and activities after using the Competency Matrix tool to align the various components of the course. During the weekly meetings throughout the course development process, this theme was common in the discussion.

Faculty provided additional comments on the survey relating to the difficulty of using the Competency Matrix tool. The comments explicated the common difficulties in extending the Competency Matrix to develop a competency-based course.

Table 1: Difficulty using competency matrix tool.

Level of Difficulty N=16	Course Alignment	Assessment Alignment	Resource Alignment	Unit Alignment	Course Development
1	9	3	5	1	1
2	4	4	4	5	1
3	0	4	3	4	3
4	1	4	3	3	4
5	2	1	1	3	7

Level of Difficulty: From least difficult (1) to most difficult (5)

3.2 Alignment and comprehensiveness of curriculum

Faculty were asked to indicate their level of agreement (from strongly agree to strongly disagree) to the following statements:
1. The course(s) I developed using the competency-based instructional design approach were more tightly aligned to the competencies/outcomes of the specialization.
2. The Competency Matrix allows the mapping of courses to competencies that lead to a more comprehensive curriculum aligned with the intended outcomes of the specialization.

Of the 16 faculty that returned the survey 88% agreed (n=2) or strongly agreed (n=12) that the course they developed was more tightly aligned to the competencies; 81% agreed (n=2) or strongly agreed (n=11) that the curriculum was more comprehensive as a result of the alignment

3.3 Strengths and weaknesses of the approach

At the end of the survey questionnaire three open-ended questions were asked to help determine the strengths and weaknesses of the competency-based instructional design approach and recommendations for process improvements:

3.3.1 Strengths
The first question was "What are the strengths of using the competency-based instructional design approach?" Faculty comments indicated that as a result of using this process, they had more structure for the course development process. Moreover, the comments illustrate that as a result of this direction faculty produced courses of higher quality:

"I like the strong foundation, direction, and continuity among courses that the competency-based approach provides.

"Leads to more rigor and better quality."

"A defined design process clarifies expectations for course developers, and allows energy to be focused on content, assessment, and resources."

"It forces me to reconsider the promises that we make to our learners. It also ends up with a tighter design, the assessments match the readings, and the project matches the learning objectives."

3.3.2 Weaknesses

The second question was "What are the weaknesses of using the competency-based instructional design approach?" Overall comments indicated a lack of flexibility, increased time, and that courses are only as good as the beginning list of program outcomes and competencies.

"There is less flexibility on occasion."

"Sometimes it seems the course gets too tight when every event, every discussion must match a competency and an assessment."

"Honestly, not enough time. I think the process would be easier if two people worked together on a course."

"The resulting courses are only as good as the competency list you start with. Your courses are limited in that they include only the competencies on the list. There may be other, worthwhile competencies that are ignored."

3.4 Process improvement

The final question on the survey asked, "How this process could be improved?" Comments indicated that more faculty development regarding the use of the Competency Matrix tool and the development of competency-based curriculum could improve the process. They also indicated a need to work more closely with an instructional designer to assist them in the development of instructional strategies and other best practices that support the competencies and assessment alignment.

"Practice and collections of best practices will improve our ability to design competency-based courses."

"In fact, create a model that would detail not only the process itself, but details about the staffing and management requirement to make it happen."

"If possible, a closer collaboration with instructional designers."

"I would like to see faculty development for course design that is also competency-based."

4 Discussion

The main purpose of this study was to evaluate the applicability of a "design-down" competency driven instructional design approach using a Competency Matrix tool. The data collected in this study confirms the applicability of this approach using the Competency Matrix tool to ensure the alignment of the course to program outcomes and competencies.

Faculty course developers had a positive response to the process and tools that were developed to ensure alignment of courses to the respective specialization program outcomes and competencies. The results indicated that the most difficult part of the process is going from the alignment of the course components to the actual development of the course. The additional comments provided by faculty indicated that addition resources are needed to assist them in the course development phase. There was also an indication that faculty development and training prior to the course development work may help alleviate some of the difficulties in using this new approach.

Overall, the results show that aligning the courses to the competencies was least difficult; however, there were individuals who perceived this part as the most difficult in the process. For those who had difficulty aligning outcomes and competencies to the individual course they were developing, additional comments on their surveys indicated a lack of comprehensiveness of the original program outcomes and competencies. This comment indicates the continuous need to revisit the Competency Matrix once all courses have been revised within a specialization to determine the gaps in the program outcomes and competencies to make appropriate adjustments. This process improvement will help to ensure the curriculum and the initial program outcomes and competencies are comprehensive.

It was the perception of faculty course developers that the courses they developed were more tightly aligned to the outcomes and competencies of the specialization and that the courses resulted in a more comprehensive competency-based curriculum. To better understand the reality, additional data must be correlated to the end of course evaluations from learners. In addition, the Competency Matrix needs to be evaluated after all courses within a specialization have been revised as competency-based to verify the comprehensiveness of the curriculum as well as program outcomes and competencies. Through this process, gaps and overlap within the competency design and assessment alignment need to be evaluated. Overlap in the competencies addressed throughout the course should be evaluated to determine if the overlap leads to more complex knowledge, skills, and understanding. If gaps appear in the matrix where competencies have not been addressed, an evaluation of those gaps are needed to determine whether they should be addressed or if the competencies associated with the gaps are actually of value for the specialization.

5 Future implications

Although the "design-down" competency driven instructional design approach currently does not have a learning object repository linked to it, this design was based on the use of learning objects and the development of modularized chunks of content with clearly defined learning outcomes. In the next phase of development, a learning object repository will be developed. The real value of the repository will be in its ability to shorten course development time and costs. This will enhance our ability to produce quality competency-based curriculum and get "just-in-time" products to the market.

One of the challenges in using learning objects to develop learning content is how to handle cross-references and contextual anchors, such as "in the next unit" or specific reference to previous content within a course that we currently have. There is a direct conflict between contextualized content for learning, which provides context for the learner and guides them through the learning process, and the notion of "context independence" which is needed for widespread reuse of learning objects. The solution is to separate the content from the presentation and wrap content for presentation to meet specific outcomes and competencies. This will require re-thinking the roles of instructional designers and faculty course developers that may lead to course developers who bring an expertise in content presentation rather than content knowledge to the design process. Instructional designers may also find their role becoming more focused on ensuring the alignment of learning objects, presentation, and operation within a course management system.

An additional challenge for this future phase is that current courses are delivered irrespective of the current level of competency a learner has already acquired or what learning content should be delivered to the learner for the learner to meet specific course competencies defined in the course. The same set of learning content is delivered to all learners regardless of background or needs. Competency-based curriculum provides the opportunity to develop specific modules of content for delivery based on the learner's known skills and competencies and the competencies covered by each learning object. This will require additional mapping of assessments and resources according to the level of competencies addressed, based on a taxonomy such as Bloom *et al.*'s [5], and assessment rubrics that can indicate levels of prior competence as well as the level of competency when a learner completes the program of study.

However great these challenges are for instructional designers pursuing this design approach, the drive towards competency-based curriculum is one that will benefit our educational institutions and learners and is worth further investigation.

References

[1] North Central Association Briefing, Vol. 11, No. 2, Oct 1993
[2] Evers, T., Rush, J.C., Berdrow, I. (1998). The Bases of Competence: Skills for Lifelong Learning and Employability, San Francisco, Jossey-Bass,
[3] McLenighan, H. (2002). School of Education Outcomes and Competencies Project, Capella University, Unpublished.
[4] Accounting Education Change Commission. "Position and Issue Statements of the Accounting Education Change Commission." Accounting Education Series. Sarasota, Florida: American Accounting Association: 1996.
[5] Bloom B. S., Engelheart, M. D., Furst, E. J., Hill, W. H., Krathwohl, D. R. (1956). Taxonomy of Educational Objectives: The Classification of Educational Goals Handbook I: Cognitive Domain. New York: David McKay.

Work-centred design and decision support in an Adaptive Decision-Enabling and Proficiency Toolkit (ADEPT)

A. Hafich[1], H. B. Sorensen[2] & J. Owens[1]
[1]*CHI Systems Inc., USA*
[2]*United States Air Force Research Laboratory, USA*

Abstract

This paper describes the work-centered design of a system to be used by satellite systems operators and the decision support provided. The United States Air Force (USAF) satellite domain is dynamic, stressful, and cognitively demanding. In this paper, we focus on the specific ways in which ADEPT provides decision and performance support to satellite operators, as well as the benefits of providing such support – improved accuracy, faster task performance times, and greater opportunity for on-the-job learning.
Keywords: decision support, performance support, satellite systems, work-centered design, information comprehension, task performance.

1 Introduction

The Adaptive Decision Enabling and Proficiency Toolkit (ADEPT) was designed using a work-centered design approach with the intention of enhancing a pre-existing satellite ground system. The initial motivation for developing ADEPT came from the significant changes operators are expected to encounter in the coming months. The space community is undergoing significant transition as the U.S. Air Force looks to space technology to help it achieve many of its envisioned Global Engagement capabilities, which led to the creation of the next generation of satellite technology: the Space-Based Infrared System (SBIRS) and the Space Tracking and Surveillance System (STSS). The major components of SBIRS are being introduced incrementally. Once complete, SBIRS will include satellites in geostationary earth orbit (GEO) and highly elliptical orbit (HEO), and will be complemented by the STSS – a constellation of more than 20 satellites in low earth orbit (LEO). Currently, the SBIRS ground segment is operational and is being used to manage GEO satellites. Over the next few years, the GEO and HEO SBIRS satellites, and the STSS constellation will be launched, accompanied by many changes in satellite capabilities and in the way satellite operations are conducted.

With the help of SBIRS and STSS technology, space personnel will be able to contribute to military operations in ways never before possible. However, the introduction of these satellites also presents a number of challenges for space personnel. For example, satellite operators will be required to manage larger numbers of satellites and process larger amounts of information under increased time pressure. In addition, the efficiency and accuracy of satellite operator performance, which was once considered critical due primarily to the cost of satellite systems, will become much more critical due to the dependency of the operational military community on the rapidly evolving satellite capabilities. For example, satellites are increasingly used by the military to support tactical communications, warfighter situation awareness, intelligence gathering, event detection, and sensor-to-shooter information delivery.

SBIRS and STSS personnel will be facing challenges such as those mentioned above without the advantage of any notable advances in the systems they use to manage and interact with satellites. That is, although satellite technologies will be significantly advanced within the SBIRS and STSS programs, the associated ground systems are based on legacy ground system technologies and designs (Lockheed Martin Space Systems Company [1]). Many legacy ground systems were designed without a full appreciation for the ways in which users perform their work, the challenging aspects of that work, or human cognitive capabilities and limitations. Critically, they were not developed with knowledge of the specific work SBIRS and STSS personnel would be performing.

Many of these aforementioned changes were introduced when the SBIRS ground segment became operational. However, operators will likely face additional changes that may include substantial workload increases when the SBIRS HEO and STSS satellites are launched. Despite the possibility of further change, ADEPT was purposefully designed to support operators primarily in their current work environment, although with an eye to the future. This design decision was based on the logic that problematic characteristics of the current operator workstations will become increasingly likely to impair performance as workload and work complexity increase, and that improving upon them will help operators cope with future work conditions.

2 Performance and decision support

2.1 Design process and findings

It is frequently the case that systems and user interfaces are defined with a focus on individual system functions, and not on how the functions would work together to support a user's workflow, i.e., to support users as they work. As noted by Zachary and Bell [2], "Since the system is there to facilitate human work…it should be organized around the work that the person is trying to accomplish (p.1):" it should be work-centered. When users perform demanding and dynamic tasks on systems that are not designed in a work-centered way, the cognitive resources available for task performance are reduced by the demanding information processing and integration tasks. Users may be inefficient in using the system to achieve various task performance goals if the system was not designed to facilitate the conduct of those task performance procedures, and users may have to perform time-consuming information searches that are not supported by the system.

The ADEPT user interface design centers on the ways tasks are performed, and organizes information and resources in functional ways that are adapted to the specific task and situation. Additionally, ADEPT supports work by providing users with a high-level view of the systems they manage, consistent with the tenets of Ecological Interface Design (EID) (Vicente [3]; Vicente and Rasmussen [4]). This high-level view provides users with a real time representation of the satellite systems they manage.

To support the design phase of the project, a domain analysis was conducted that involved several visits to Buckley Air Force Base (BAFB) and Vandenberg Air Force Base (VAFB) to collect data. In addition, one subject matter expert (SME) was interviewed extensively using unstructured interviews to collect data as well as to obtain feedback. As the ADEPT design evolved, iterative storyboards were developed and used to obtain user feedback regarding system design and functionality from our primary SME as well as potential users at VAFB.

During data collection, as well as during the design process, one critical task and multiple common tasks were identified as candidates for performance and decision support. The critical task identified involving responding to satellite and ground system alerts – the SBIRS and STSS satellite systems crews investigate alerts, warnings, and events (AWEs) that appear on their displays to determine if they possibly represent a real problem. If a crewmember determines that an AWE is indicative of a real problem, the crewmember must, based on standard operating procedures, either 'safe' the satellite or inform satellite systems engineers of the current status of the satellite. Then the satellite systems engineers troubleshoot the problem and develop a course of action. In response to ground system alerts, operators can perform quick fixes, or otherwise switch to a back-up system until the primary system is fixed. Common tasks identified include:

o   Perform routine satellite commanding, e.g. to recondition batteries during eclipse season or to safe a satellite component
o   Monitor ground systems for problems; ensure quality and continuous flow of satellite and communications data
o   Detect and respond to (bypass or fix) ground equipment failures
o   Monitor satellites' states of health by regularly checking a set of critical system parameters, or *measurands*, which represent the current value of a satellite component or system (see Table 1 for examples)

- Investigate and monitor satellite and ground system warnings and events, and bring to the attention of engineers as appropriate
- Maintain logs of events and activities

ADEPT was designed to support satellite operators in all the identified – both critical and common. Following a domain analysis and unstructured interviews with a SME, inefficiencies were identified in the following areas:

- Crew communication – not supported technologically. Crews often shout to communicate
- Dependency on paper-based resources – logging, procedure documents, command plans, etc. all still paper-based
- Means by which satellite systems data is represented – data is in measurand form, which consists of a string of alphanumerics
- Organization of satellite systems and other operational data – e.g., information is accessed by drilling down through a hierarchical menu structure, and information necessary for anomaly resolution is located in notebooks at the back of the operations center, etc.

ADEPT consists of five primary support tools, accessed via tabs on the user interface, in addition to a number of support features that are present within all of the primary support tools. The five support tools, or tabs, of ADEPT were designed so that the above inefficiencies may be addressed, and so that the tasks and decisions of the satellite operators may be easier to perform and less cognitively demanding. The *AWE Tab* presents Alerts, Warnings, and Events and all relevant information as well as information pertinent to the particular measurand about which the AWE is occurring. The *Messaging Tab* facilitates crew communication with a prioritized instant-messenger type tool as well as "canned" or commonly-used messages. The *Satellite View Tab* is a pictorial view of the universe and gives the satellites' positions relative to bodies such as the sun, the moon, the earth, and other satellites. The *Logging Tab* allows the satellite systems operators to not only electronically log the daily activities and the status of the different vehicles, but also to share these electronic logs real-time so that the necessary information reaches the necessary crew members. Finally, the *EDocs Tab* is an online resource library that databases crew Temporary Procedures (TPs), Command Plans, and operational manuals, among other things.

To demonstrate the ways in which ADEPT supports the work of satellite operators, an example situation will be described. Specifically in the example, satellite operators are working in a stressful, dynamic, and extremely complex domain. They must make decisions regarding an anomaly's criticality based on knowledge and information resources, often within very strict time constraints. One example of such an anomaly is an alert for a satellite's sun shutter being out-of-limits. The user must first decide if the sun shutter is stuck open or closed—a very important decision. If the sun shutter is stuck closed, the anomaly is still critical, but not as critical as if the sun shutter were stuck open. The sun shutter protects a sensitive satellite component from being exposed to the sun's potentially lethal rays when that particular component is spatially positioned so that it is exposed to the sun. A sun shutter stuck closed is not desirable, obviously, as it could block the satellite component from completing its mission, but a sun shutter stuck open could potentially cripple the satellite. If a sun shutter is stuck open, then there is a very small window of time during which the operator may 'safe' the satellite before any damage is caused. This window of opportunity may also obviously be affected by which direction the satellite is facing and, more specifically, where it is spatially. The operator must decide, based on information resources, as well as the satellite's current alert and position, what the best course of action would be. As previously mentioned, support tools have been added to aid the operator throughout the decision process: measurand labels to help identify the anomaly; checklists, command plans, and procedures resources to help determine possible courses of action; a Satellite Viewer to help the operators determine the spatial position and criticality of the anomaly; a messaging function to notify the proper crewmembers quickly and effectively of the situation.

2.2 Types of support provided

Based on the identified inefficiencies, the goal was to design ADEPT so that a high level of support could be given to the satellite systems operators. For example, tools were needed to facilitate crewmember communication, assist electronic logging of activities, and provide an electronic document library, for example. Two of the performance support tools, the previously introduced Satellite Viewer as well as an alphanumeric explanation function, are described below. Also described is the context for learning and decision support which ADEPT includes.

Table 1: Example measurands.

Measurand	Component Represented
CALFQM	Mainframe Frequency
CCS1SOH	CCS1 Subsystem Health
ADPCAV	EDE-A Power Converter Voltage
ADPCBV	EDE-B Power Converter Voltage
TCHTRA	Thermal Control Heater A

2.2.1 Explanation

Persistent use of alphanumerics in this domain becomes a hindrance to the user as it is not typically immediately clear as to what they represent to the satellite system. Alphanumerics are generally an inadequate means of representing complex information, such as that in the satellite domain. In this domain, one subset of alphanumerics is the measurands, while a second set of alphanumerics used in this domain are command mnemonics. Though many of the satellite measurands have recurring symbology that can aid the satellite operator in discerning its meaning (e.g., an A or B would be present to represent side A or B of a satellite – see Table 1 for examples), many measurands have very little resemblance to the names of the systems and components they are representing.

This presents the operator with the difficult information processing task of discerning which satellite system or component the given measurand represents. One of the functions included in ADEPT helps to alleviate the cognitive demands caused by frequent alphanumerics. Specifically, measurands can be "moused over" to give the satellite operator the full name of the represented component.

2.2.2 Visualization

Often, as in the given examples, tasks that satellite systems operators must perform are contingent upon the particular position of a satellite in relation to other heavenly bodies, knowledge of orbital mechanics, and other spatially-oriented concepts. Research has shown that spatial information is best understood when represented graphically or pictorially (e.g., Bell and Johnson [5]; Kosslyn et al. [6]). The EID approach to display design also advocates high level representations of a domain as a means of providing operators with an externalized mental model (e.g., Vicente [3]). As operators described difficulty visualizing a satellite's orbital position, it became apparent that a visualization tool would be beneficial in this context. A tendency for less experienced operators to be unaware of the onset of various orbital events was another consideration, particularly because an incoming AWE's level of criticality sometimes depends on the spatial positioning of the satellite (e.g., the fault could occur but be non-critical because of the satellite's spatial positioning, or the level of criticality could escalate drastically due to the satellite's proximity to the sun, etc.). Therefore, the Satellite Viewer in ADEPT provides the user with a 'God's-eye view' of the universe, including satellites, the sun, the moon, the earth, and other heavenly bodies. The satellite operator may also overlay on the view relational geometry, such as the Solar Aspect Angle (SAA) or the Sun Azimuth Angle--pieces of information used to make a number of important decisions (For example, the criticality of certain anomalies is based on a satellite's SAA, and the course of action may be contingent upon the satellite's SAA).

Another benefit of the ADEPT Satellite Viewer is operator interest in the functionality. SME response to the Satellite Viewer has been positive and enthusiastic, especially because it provides the operator with the opportunity to explore the 'universe' as well as the various relationships between satellites and heavenly bodies. One feature of the Satellite Viewer that is of particular interest is the time 'fast-forward' and 'rewind' buttons that will advance the position of the different elements so that they are in accurate position for whatever time the satellite operator chooses, be it two months in the future to locate the next satellite eclipse (a commonly occurring event), or ten years in the past.

2.2.3 Building expertise

Decisions, when made repeatedly and supported with knowledge-rich tools that offer guidance and explanation, allow satellite operators to build expertise in their domain. As Zachary and Ryder [7] note, "decision making is a skill that is learned, and ... experts are therefore made not born (p. X)." A relationship is therefore implied between making decisions and learning decisions, and thus a relationship "between decision support and decision training" (Zachary and

Ryder [7]). Based on this theory, designing a tool that provides situated decision and task performance support provides the operator with a good basis for on-the-job training therefore facilitating the transition from neophyte to expert.

Decision-making skill is decomposed into three knowledge/skill components by Zachary and Ryder [7]:
- conceptual knowledge/skill – domain facts and concepts
- procedural knowledge/skill – guidelines and protocols for how to perform the task as well as the ability to perform the task
- relational knowledge/skill – domain-specific decision making skill based on integrated conceptual and procedural knowledge

ADEPT is designed to support operators in each of these three components of knowledge/skill. For example, resources made available by the EDocs tool, such as the operational procedures, checklists, command plans, and temporary procedures support both conceptual knowledge/skill and procedural knowledge/skill, the measurand identifier is an example of conceptual knowledge/skill support, and the Satellite Viewer along with EDocs, for example, is supportive of relational knowledge/skill.

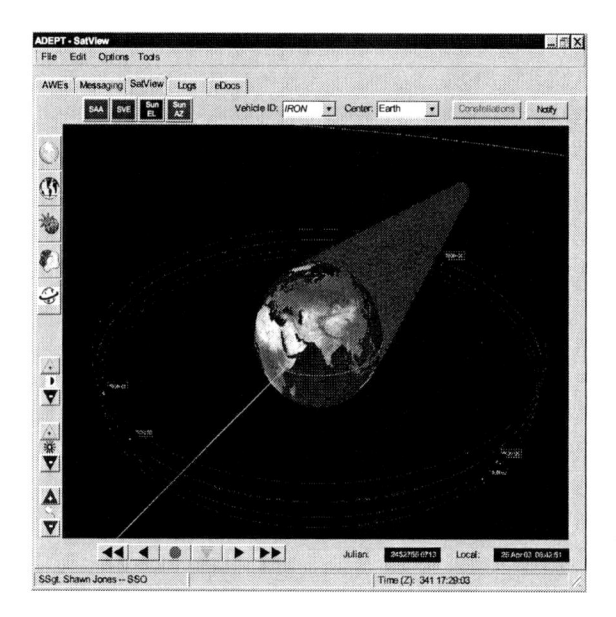

Figure 1: Satellite Viewer.

3 Conclusions

The design phase of ADEPT is closing, as is the research that influenced the design, and the next step will be implementation. Though ADEPT is specifically designed for the USAF satellite domain, it can be transitioned to any domain that involves the maintenance and health of mechanical systems. It could be useful in nuclear power systems, oil rigs, and especially remote systems, such as commercial satellites, undersea equipment, and other types of space craft. ADEPT was designed so that each of the five main tabs (AWEs, Messaging, Satellite Viewer, Logging, and EDocs) may be pulled apart and used independently, but when grouped with other tabs, becomes a powerful decision support tool.

References

[1] Lockheed Martin Space Systems Company (Nov 2002). Highlights [online: http://lmms.external.lmco.com/highlights/pdf/nov2002.pdf]. Lockheed Martin Space Systems Company Communications.

[2] Zachary, W. & Bell, B., Work-centered infomediary layer (WIL): An architecture for adaptive interfaces. *Proceedings of the Fifteenth Annual Conference on Innovated Applications of Artificial Intelligence* (IAAI-2003), Melo Park, CA: AAAI Press.

[3] Vicente, K.J., Ecological interface design: Progress and challenges. *Human factors*, **44**, pp. 62-78, 2002.

[4] Vicente, K.J. & Rasmussen, J., Ecological interface design: Theoretical foundations. *IEEE Transactions on Systems, Man, & Cybernetics*, **22**, pp. 589-606, 1992.

[5] Bell, D., & Johnson, P. Support for the authors of multimedia tutorials. *Multimedia: Systems, Interaction, and Applications*, ed. L. Kjelldahl, Springer-Berlag: New York, pp. 307-323, 1992.

[6] Kosslyn, S.M., Ball, T.M. & Reiser, B.J., Visual images preserve metric spatial information: Evidence from studies of image scanning. *Journal of Experimental Psychology: Human Perception and Performance*, **4**, pp. 47-60, 1978.

[7] Zachary, W. & Ryder, J., Decision Support Systems: Integrating Decision Aiding and Decision Training (Chapter 52). *Handbook of Human-Computer Interaction: Second, completely revised edition*, eds. MM. Helander, T.K. Landauer, P. Prabhu: Elsevier Science B.V., pp.1235-1258, 1997.

Section 3
The evaluation of new learning systems

Privacy and security in digital environments: the psychological issues

K. Morgan
InterMedia, University of Bergen, Norway

Abstract

Over the past 40 years technological advances in the fields of information and communications technology have allowed for the creation of new digital media as a vehicle for human expression, communication and behaviour. These new media are neither better nor worse than the more traditional methods of communication but they do have several differences which raise fundamental questions about how they impact the lives of all who use them whether it be for commercial, entertainment or creative purposes. This paper discusses how the topics of security and privacy underpin all aspects of these new digital media and how psychology can provide a deeper understanding of these problems with the goal of trying to understand ourselves and the challenges the new digital medium provides.
Keywords: digital security, digital privacy, society, education, e-commerce, psychology

1 Introduction: the digital mirror

The subjects of digital Security and Privacy are often viewed as being simple technical matters that are primarily of interest to mathematically orientated computational scientists and entrepreneurs keen on maximizing profit from a potential new market place. However this is a very simplistic view of the profound issues which are addressed within these themes. In fact privacy and security are fundamental to physical and mental well being whether they are in a digital medium or the more traditional physical world. Although many philosophers and science fiction authors have long argued that the new digital advances can be an opportunity for humanity to avoid the inequalities and problems of the more traditional material world the truth is that the fundamental traits and characteristics of human nature are reflected in the behaviours which we see and experience in the new digital medium [1]. In this paper the terms new digital medium or new digital environment are used to cover the cluster of technologies that includes all aspects of Information Communications Technology (ICT), networked computers, hypertext and hypermedia, the World Wide Web, and other adjuncts.

1.1 Hierarchies of authority

The new digital environment can be considered with regard to many different applications but as this conference is specifically addressing the issues of commerce and education within the digital lifestyle this paper will focus on this aspect. Traditionally the introduction of new communication mediums has had the effect of levelling existing hierarchies of authority within the group or society concerned [2]. This has been true whether the society is a business organization, a country or an academic community.

1.2 Digital empowerment or digital enslavement?

As established hierarchies of power are removed by digital mediums certain aspects of control are also surrendered. We have each become our own secretaries and by means of digital tools we have changed the basic skill sets required for almost every career and created career paths that are less defined. This fundamentally changes the goals of education and traditional occupational training. Instead of teaching basic facts and career related skills the rate of change within the digital medium has introduced the concepts of flexible and transferable skills. In effect education has had to acknowledge that the best preparation it can provide for the life of an individual is the ability to learn new skills rapidly. This results in new generations of learners who increasingly rely on the infrastructure of the new medium for their performance in a job and less on basic intrinsic skills that would have taken previous generations of learners a large proportion of their professional lives to acquire. In education students using digital systems can conceptualize higher order ideas without having to spend years working through basic principles that are now often literally embedded in the digital systems and tools that they use in their classes. This does not mean that the quality of education has changed. What it does mean is that the methods and goals of education have to adapt to the new digital medium and that this brings with it dramatic challenges to both education and society. In exactly the same way the introduction of the printed word in the 15th century provided greater access to books and changed the focus of education from complex systems of memory training to a profound reliance and respect for reference books and journals. It is this traditional intellectual respect for printed and fixed references that is challenged by the digital environment.

2 Change in the digital world

Other important differences between the traditional physical environment and the new digital environment are the increases in the speed of communication and sheer volume of information presented to actors (human or software) in the digital world. More fundamentally the very structures that give frames of reference and meaning to support this new digital environment, for example the web sites themselves, often are of short lived duration. The transient nature of the structures in the new digital environment creates a constant state of flux and uncertainty that is quite new to human experience. In previous generations the basic structures within an environment changed relatively slowly. Buildings and physical structures, whether they are medieval cathedrals or the fixed landmarks of nomadic tribes, provide a source of fixed reference for an individual's life. These basic environmental structures often add substantially to an individual's ability to understand not only the world around them but also to understand themselves and their role in existence. When we change the nature of structure in the environment we fundamentally alter the way in which an organism understands itself and its purpose. It is important to realise that the manner in which knowledge is represented and disseminated also plays an equally important role in human well being and self understanding. It is often overlooked that stability in relation to our mental wellbeing is essential for the healthy functioning of the human mind. For example, rapid and unstable changes to the underlying frameworks used to define relationships between individuals, ideas and possessions are also often reflected in unstable behaviour in society as a whole. For better or worse the new medium is driven by an engineering paradigm of constant improvement and rapid obsolescence. This means not only is there rapid change but that change is constantly accelerating. The basic components of the digital world are derived from algorithmic and logical software structures, communications technology, computer hardware, intellectual objects and abstract, often arbitrary links or relationships between them all. The World Wide Web is by definition a rapidly evolving decentralized set of relationships or links between these basic components and a search for a set word or item on two different occasions is likely to produce different results. Even a return visit to the same logical location in the digital space can result in a different result. As a consequence the web is filled with broken links, out of date pages and a huge variation in the quality and content of its presentations.

2.1 Stress

The digital medium has produced a society that is attempting to respond to more and more stimuli in less and less time while the existing framework of reference - the very item that gives stability to understanding and mental health - is becoming transformed into an unstable rapidly changing form and as more systems and groups become involved in the digital medium the rate of change multiplies. Although the Greek philosopher Heraclites was not thinking specifically of the digital world his proposition "There is nothing permanent except change" could not be more apt. Users and indeed software systems themselves are faced with questions about what can they trust, what is reliable, what is constant? Any change in an established environment produces stress in the organism but this constant state of change in our lives can be shown to be harmful. Occupational psychologists have performed the most focused research into these issues. They have found that stress introduced by new working practice and methods influences mood, physical well being and work performance [3]. Other research has shown that many workers feel that computerisation makes work more difficult, increases stress levels and introduces the mental cycles of low self-image and failure [4]. If this environment of change is so harmful for us we should enquire why people would opt for such a dynamic situation. In truth many are not given the freedom of choice. Research that has tried to identify the motivational categories for using new technology has reported finding four motivational clusters that produced behavioural reactions to new technology. These were security consciousness, maximizers, instant gratifiers and hassle avoiders [5]. These findings were consistent over both sexes. This suggests that people adopt these new technologies into their environment in the hope of some improvement in their life-style.

3 Intellectual identity in the digital world

Many authors have noted how the new digital mediums have revolutionized knowledge representation and dissemination [2]. However there is a less well recognized secondary effect to these rapid advances. Previously well defined reference points that had been established for aspects of the intellectual world are now changing not just in terms of how ideas relate to each other but also in how ownership of these ideas is established and maintained. Whilst information travels rapidly and widely there is no established mechanism within the digital medium to protect intellectual ownership and equally there is no established mechanism to establish the worth or authority for any idea or fact.

3.1 Equality for all means identity for none

The problem faced by human and software actors within the digital medium is that of establishing the identity and authority (financial or intellectual) of other individual actors or organizations. The digital medium permits anyone to own a web page or a domain and within limits allows any actor (human or software) to appear to be any other actor. The problem is complex and relates directly to the security and privacy of the actors within a digital medium that by its very nature dis-empowers those in traditional authority and empowers those traditionally without power. These problems affect the whole of the digital environment since ownership is a fundamental aspect of our established society structures. It is one of the most powerful anchors in our mental understanding of self and our relation to the world around us. Without it we risk loss of identity and purpose, since for many it is the things that we own or have created which define our identity. It is no surprise then that one of the most popular crimes within the digital world is that of identity theft. Whether simply as a stolen credit card number or an intellectual idea both are crimes that proliferate in the digital world. The problems associated with this crime are not just financial. They can affect our mental development and also the development of our society and its norms. Any causal observer of the music industry will be aware not just of the problem associated with music piracy but more profoundly the increasing use of samples from other artists work to produce a new work which is a synergy of other and self into a new form. It is true that such synergies have always occurred but the difference is that now the very tools that are used in the creative process have the contributions from others built into them. Often the process of creation no longer even consciously involves a decision about whether or not to use the contribution of another. It simply happens as a natural part of the use of the digital tool. Clip art, search engines and sound libraries have all made the automation of plagiarism go beyond the famous "cut and paste" of the 1990s.

4 Digital creation: a synergy of sources

Increasingly whenever humans use the digital medium for actions of creativity or learning, for example students accessing the Internet for educational materials or designers looking for inspiration, we see problems emerge with regard to recognising and defining intellectual ownership. This problem is made more complex by the amount of incorrect, obsolete or wrong information that exists in the digital medium. Not only do actors in the digital medium have access to enormous numbers of potential sources for their inspiration or entertainment there is no accepted method to tell the valuable from the disposable, the true from the false. Of course there has always been a problem knowing what is true or real. Indeed the most fundamental philosophical questions relate to these issues. But when the medium and tools of creation within the digital world implicitly use the creations of others and there is no way to know the truth, value or ownership of any item this raises some interesting questions about the future of the digital society.

4.1 What happens when identity becomes a variable and not a statement?

We have already said that one of the issues raised by the creation of the new digital medium is that actors (human and software) can assume the identity of anyone they wish. This leads to some interesting insights into human behaviour and also some problems for businesses trying to keep their workforce productive and legally occupied. One of the great paradoxes of the Internet is that it could have been dedicated to the purest of intellectual goals, the pursuit of truth and the dissemination of knowledge for the benefit of all humanity. Some parts of the system do aspire to such goals but a surprisingly high proportion of the total resources of the internet are devoted to activities and interests which are, if not illegal, then highly personal in nature. The very freedom and open access of the medium makes it subject to misuse. Recent surveys of how human actors use the facilities of the internet reveal that nearly 40% of workplace Internet use is not related to the core business of the company supplying the Internet facilities [5]. Again nearly 37% of office workers say they surf the Internet constantly while they are at work [6]. An indication of what content themes occupy this 40% of employees' time can be determined by the fact that nearly 70% of Internet pornography occurs between the normal office working hours of 9am to 5pm local time [7]. It is not a surprise therefore to learn that 77% of major US companies routinely monitor their employees' email, Internet usage and computer files [8]. When we look at home use of the Internet we see sexual content and sexual themes again predominating. Nearly 60% of home users admit to using the Internet to flirt with individuals other than their spouse or long term partner [9] and half of those people admitted telephoning the individual with whom they had flirted online. Nearly 40% admit to engaging with sexually explicit online conversations online and 31% of individuals admitted to having had intimate physical relations with the individuals they had chatted and phoned [9].

4.2 Digital predators and digital prey

The use of the new digital medium for sex is hardly a surprise since reproduction is one of the primary motivating factors within human existence. What is alarming is the realisation that recent surveys estimate that over 24 million children regularly use the Internet [10]. Given the ease with which any actor can assume any identity in the digital medium it is inevitable that many Internet users should view minors as easy prey for their sexual appetites. One child in five using the Internet has been solicited for sex within any 12 month period. One on four have been sent sexually explicit pictures and in the year 2000 in the US alone an estimated 725,000 child Internet users had been aggressively pressured by an adult online to meet physically for sex [10].

4.3 Extremist recruitment

Children are not the only prey for digital predators. Increasingly extremist groups are using the Internet as an effective method for recruiting new members who are then used either as a free workforce to achieve the organisations goals or in extreme cases the new recruits are encouraged to sacrifice their possessions and even their lives. Conversion and indoctrination are present in most human societies so it is natural that we should find them in the new digital society using the digital medium to achieve their ends. Cialdini's six principles that direct human behaviour [11], consistency (justification of earlier behaviour), reciprocity (repayment in kind), social proof, authority, liking and scarcity (not wishing to miss opportunity) can easily be adapted to be used on the Internet. The very characteristics of the digital medium that make it share information quickly and cheaply also make it a near perfect mechanism for mass recruitment. Many Internet users are lonely and searching for answers. The lack of any mechanism to provide checks on the authority or validity of any identity means it is too easy for the innocent and inexperienced to become digital prey. Ironically the very lack of certainty that is inherent increases uncertainty and vulnerability. Indeed the new digital medium begins to assume an air of authority and divinity to many users who report finding the Internet infinite and ethereal, almost a deity in itself [12]. For this very reason the Internet has become the new location of choice for recruiters of both new religions and extremist terrorist groups. The Internet is very economical for cults, e-mail is cheap, and it keeps cult members hooked, wherever they are, with messages of support and propaganda. The groups do not have to rent land or buildings as the Internet itself becomes their virtual commune.

4.4 Who is at risk?

Although anyone can become prey in the digital world those most at risk are people who work intensively around computers, are lonely and who identify with what is happening on screen more than in their physical reality. The lack of a permanent structure to give a framework of understanding combined with the speed and lack of validity checks combine to form a very problematic situation. These factors produce a dis-associative effect, where intensive Internet users lose touch with immediate physical reality, or the social, larger culture outside. With these cues missing social norms disappear and individuals lose their self in a form of identity theft that goes beyond stealing credit card numbers or impersonation.

5 Privacy

Now that we have begun to understand the importance of privacy and security in the digital medium we can also begin to look at the methods which have been developed to try and protect users and society at large from the threat of digital predators. At the level of the state and society as a whole the events of September 11th 2001 changed the world's perspective on global terrorism. In a reaction to Al Qaeda's use of digital communications technology, governments proposed restrictions on the availability of strong encryption technology. On September 13th 2001 US Congress began discussing granting law enforcement agencies access to private encryption keys or secret backdoors to all digital security systems. This has sparked a huge debate with arguments against the proposals from civil liberty groups and also from e-commerce groups who believe such laws would damage consumer confidence in e commerce. In early 2002, as a reaction to the use of the digital medium by terrorist groups, the Bush Administration formed the National Strategy to Secure Cyberspace. This document describes actions that companies, individuals, and schools can take to improve cyber security. The NCSD also created the Cyber Interagency Incident Management Group (Cyber IIMG), an organization dedicated to finding ways to pre-empt cyber attacks and to help the government prepare for future attacks. In 2004 the Bush Government also established a critical infrastructure information network - a private version of the Internet that is not accessible through the public Internet. It is thought that this network is intended to function as a resource in case the Internet and other forms of computer-based communications become inoperable. However its isolation from the public Internet also makes it less vulnerable to threats of privacy and security. At the commercial and organisational level VeriSign, one of the Internet's major controllers of .com and .net registries, indicated in their February 2004 report [13] that site hacks, online fraud and identity theft were rising dramatically. At the same time as Verisign stated that online commerce grew 59% in comparison between the 2002 ($4bn) and 2003 ($6.4bn) holiday season it also reported that attempted hacks rose by 176% in the same period. As a clear indication of global disparity Verisign also reported that those countries which ranked highest in percentage of fraud per transaction were predominantly third world nations. It is believed that this disparity is more a reflection of poorly maintained software and systems and this raises some important questions about hopes that many have expressed of using digital technology as a panacea for the inequalities in wealth in the physical world.

6 Understanding and predicting deception

The Psychology of Deception is a relatively well-established area within psychology. These principles provide a high level conceptual framework from which digital deception and crime can be examined and understood. While many of the detailed techniques involved in data security evolve rapidly, the underlying principles of deception remain the same so when conceptualising digital threats this framework can be extremely useful.

6.1 Principles of deception

To give a complete coverage of the principles of deception would be beyond this paper and is better covered elsewhere [14] however as a summary if you wish to deceive there are only three principle opportunities.

6.2 Preparatory phase

A pre scene strategy involves the alteration of some basic characteristic of either the environment in the location of the planned deception or an object that will be introduced in the deception. This is done so that during the actual deception what appears to be a known and trusted environment or object is in fact aiding the deception. The majority of deception involves some aspect of a pre scene strategy. Within the digital environment viruses, worms and URL redirection are all commonly known deceptions that rely on extensive preparatory phase effort.

6.3 Activity phase

This is the most difficult type of deception if no preparation work has been completed. Activity phase attacks usually involve misdirection, impersonation, substitution or interference. Impersonation in the digital world means assuming the identity of another trusted entity either through gaining their password. With software entities either the appearance (Trojans) or their site certification are false. Misdirection is where the victim (human or software) is made to focus on one area of the environment while the deception is acted out in another area of the environment. Changes in speed, distraction or impersonation are the key techniques used within misdirection. If an object or information is involved in the deception then substitution must usually also occur. Substitution is where a trusted object or item of information is replaced with a pre-prepared object or item. Interference is often included within misdirection and is where a process that is known and trusted is in fact acting in a manner that is not normal.

6.4 Post activity phase

A post activity strategy involves changing or substituting the genuine result of an action, event or item of information with another action, event or item of information. If this is done in the presence of the victim or observers then misdirection, interference or substitution must usually be used. However in most cases post activity deceptions are done after all formal observation is complete and there is no need for misdirection, substitution or interference.

6.5 Protecting against deception in the digital medium

The basic requirements for understanding and controlling digital security against digital deception are based on these principles. In order to ensure against deception the observer must have control over or understanding of the fundamental structures that form the basis of observed reality. Whether that reality is physical or digital the same principle applies. The nature of the digital environment is that it is constantly changing and evolving without any fixed structure. Since a fixed structure is needed to control an environment against deception it is easy to see why data security and privacy are so difficult to maintain. The actions involved in using the digital medium necessitate relying on numerous uncontrolled environments and objects that have no known or trusted pre activity state. To further complicate matters the actors using the digital medium have no way of knowing or observing all aspects of the environment during their activities and finally have little control over the fate of items or environments after the scene is over and they have moved to another part of the digital environment.

7 Conclusions: challenge of a new mobile digital environment

The situations we have described and problems we have discussed in this paper are merely snap shots of the current status within a rapidly evolving environment that mirrors almost all the characteristics of other naturally evolving systems. The latest trends in mobile digital systems and media means that instability with servers, software, connections, and actors are likely to increase with a wireless digital network that will impact our entire lifestyle. The risk is clearly that the lack of a solid framework could mean that we miss the stability necessary for the security, privacy and understanding of our digital lives. We have created an evolutionary system that is forever seeking the next stable optimum solution but never reaches it, an evolutionary system that forces each component to constantly evolve or risk becoming vulnerable either to obsolescence or digital predators. We should not forget however that evolution leads to improvement and such improvements will impact digital media throughout every aspect of society. The challenge facing us in all these arenas is to create conceptual frameworks which can underpin and support the digital lifestyle giving it meaning and permitting security, privacy and understanding.

References

[1]   Morgan, K. & Morgan, M., The Role of Classical Jungian Personality Factors in CSCL Environments, Norwegian Research Council Publications Series 2000 pp183-191 ISBN 1500-7707
[2]   United Nations. The role of information technology in the context of a knowledge-based global economy. Report of the UN Secretary-General, New York, 5 July-1 August 2000
[3]   Stewart, W., & Barling, J., Daily work stress, mood and interpersonal job performance. Work and Stress. 1996, Oct-Dec Vol 10 (4) 336-351
[4]   Seppaelae, P., Experience on computerization in different occupational groups." International Journal of Human Computer Interaction. 1995 Oct-Dec Vol 7 (4) 315-327
[5]   IDC Consulting, Reports on key issues facing organisations relating Internet filtering and security. 2000 IDC Consulting
[6]   Emarketer, Bosses disapprove employees still surf. http://www.emarketer.com/estats/dailyestats/demographics/20001030_work.html: 2000, Emarketer
[7]   SexTracker. Survey of Internet use in the workplace, http://www.vault.com/vstore/SurveyResults/InternetUse/index.cfm: 2004, SexTracker
[8]   American Management Association, Survey of Business Monitoring of Employee Internet Use, June 2001, AMA
[9]   Greenfield, D., Virtual Addiction: Help for Netheads, Cyberfreaks, and Those Who Love Them, 1999, New Harbinger, ISBN: 1572241721
[10] US Congress, Children's Internet Protection Act: Study on threats to minors from the Internet, submitted June 8, 2000, US Congress
[11] Cialdini, R., The Psychology of Persuasion, Quill; Revised edition (October 7, 1998) ISBN: 0688128165
[12] Davis. E., Experience Design (And the Design of Experience), keynote Subtle Technologies, University of Toronto, Canada, 10th May 2002
[13] VeriSign Internet Security Intelligence Briefing Reporting Year-End Trends in Internet Usage, Security, and Fraud, February 9, 2004
[14] Seager, P. B. & Wiseman, R., Fooling All of the People Half of the Time? 1999 Science Spectra, 15, 32-37

Evaluation of learning material in PORTAL project: the case of quality management and benchmarking in public transport

C. Taxiltaris[1], P. Papaioannou[2] & S. Basbas[1]
[1]Dept. of Transportation and Hydraulics Engineering,
Faculty of Rural and Surveying Engineering, School of Technology,
Aristotle University of Thessaloniki, Greece
[2]Dept. of Transport, Infrastructure, Management and Regional Planning,
Faculty of Civil Engineering, School of Technology,
Aristotle University of Thessaloniki, Greece

Abstract

PORTAL (Promotion Of Results in Transport Research And Learning) has been a three year project co-financed by the European Commission within the 5th RTD Framework Programme which aims at accelerating the take up of EU research results in the field of local and regional transport through the development of new education and training courses and teaching materials. The scope of this paper is to present the work done within the Faculties of Civil Engineering and Rural & Surveying Engineering of the Aristotle University of Thessaloniki in incorporating teaching material about the topic "Public Transport – Quality Management & Benchmarking" in the curricula of the graduate and postgraduate relevant courses. The results of an evaluation process involving both students and teachers which was undertaken in order to provide feed back and eventually cater for the improvement of the teaching material is also presented in the framework of this paper.

1 Introduction

PORTAL (Promotion Of Results in Transport Research And Learning) has been a three-year project co-financed by the European Commission within the 5th RTD (Research and Technological Development and Demonstration)

Framework Programme. The PORTAL consortium consisted of 52 partners from the following 24 European countries: Austria, Belgium, Czech Republic, Denmark, Estonia, Finland, France, Germany, Greece, Hungary, Ireland, Italy, Latvia, Lithuania, Norway, Poland, Portugal, Slovakia, Slovenia, Spain, Sweden, Switzerland, The Netherlands, United Kingdom. In each participating country the consortium had a partner as National Focus Point (NFP). In addition a number up to 4 Educational Test Sites (ETSI) from each country were involved for evaluating the project teaching material.

The consortium covered all levels of higher education. Its core was made up of leading educational institutions at university level as well as large national and international commercial training institutes and some experienced research institutions and consultants. An advisory board was set up with the participation of representatives from different sectors such as industry, municipal and local authorities, public transport authorities and road management & transport associations to guarantee that the interests of the most influential policy-makers are safeguarded and that the services and products of PORTAL are brought into line with these target groups. The PORTAL project had duration of 36 months and started in June 2000.

The aim of PORTAL was to accelerate the take up of EU research results in the field of local and regional transport through the development of new education and training courses and teaching materials. The beneficiaries of the project are education and training organisations providing courses and organisations and individuals interested in enhancing their knowledge and skills base in these topics.

Two main target groups are addressed in the project namely educational institutions and end-users. In each group two market segments are focused. The first target group of PORTAL were educational institutions and more specifically:

- Universities and colleges (land use, transport management, transport planning)
- Commercial training institutions in the field of transport

The second target group of the project has been end-users and in particular:
- students (undergraduate/post-graduate).
- decision-makers and multipliers (transport officials, transport manager, transport researchers)
- transport professionals: transport planners, engineers, operators, educators, psychologists.

It must be mentioned at this point that training can be defined in different ways; according to one of them "training is the systematic development of the knowledge, skills and attitudes required by an individual to allow him/her to perform their task or job more effectively". This definition tries to convey that education and training are part of a systematic approach with well defined stages known as the training cycle and is presented in a schematic form in Figure 1.

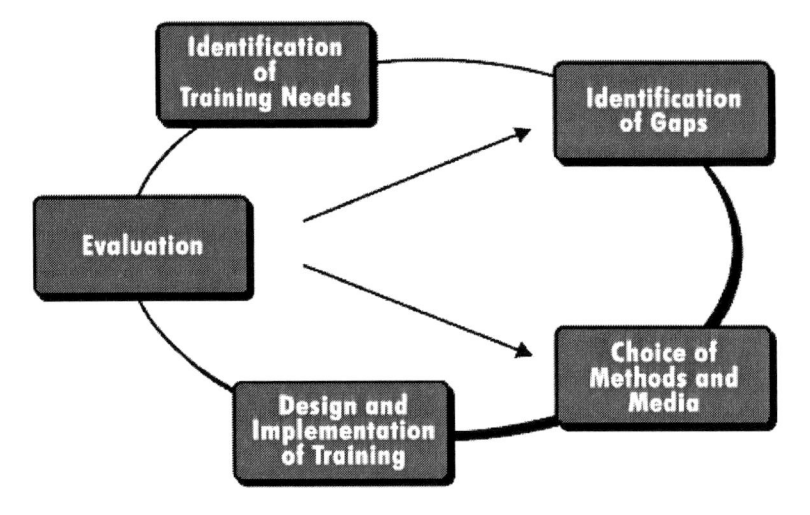

Figure 1: The training cycle.

2 Learning material

The learning materials developed within PORTAL include traditional teaching materials as well as new forms of learning. The main forms of materials on a descending order of preference, as resulted from surveys, include:

- Printable materials and transparencies
- Multi-media materials (including electronic presentations, audio CD)
- Study books for self-learning
- CD ROM
- Video

Special versions of the above learning materials for use in short training courses with duration of 2-5 days were also developed. A need for intensive, "bite sized" modules of free standing courses was widely recognised. It was agreed that these courses must be very practical, focusing on proven techniques, concrete applications and case studies, as well as on examples of best practice and should be offered by educational and training organisations or other providers, in parallel with the long-term courses offered at the Universities.

The above findings about the necessary learning materials were the result of four distinct surveys conducted in the following types of organisations:
- Organisations employing transport professionals and (future) individual professionals
- Providers of educational activities within the transport domain including teachers in leading educational institutions.

Dissemination tools for the PORTAL material included internet web site, newsletters, link management, brochures & postcards, advertisements and conferences presentations [1].

3 Learning material for benchmarking and quality management in public transport

Benchmarking and Quality Management in Public Transport has been one of the 12 topics in transport where new learning material was developed. The other topics are [2]:

- Regulatory frameworks and legislation in public transport
- Integrated transport chains
- Urban traffic management and restraint
- Safety and accident reduction
- Modelling and data analysis
- Environment, energy and transport
- Pricing
- Mobility management and travel awareness
- Urban freight transport and city logistics
- Transport and land use
- Policy formulation & implementation

The learning material was based on research findings from a number of EU research projects. In total 92 EU Transport projects from the 4th Framework Programme and 4 projects from the COST Programme were used for compiling the new teaching and learning material [3]. For each topic a special report was prepared by one or more experts. The material on "Benchmarking and Quality Management" includes the following:

1. Printed material in the form o a coloured text book
2. Power Point presentation material
3. Audio CD

The material for 1 and 2 was prepared in 8 languages, namely English, French, Dutch, German, Italian, Spanish, Portuguese and Greek. The contents covered in this topic include the following [4]:

The quality management tools
- The quality loop: customer-orientated not production-orientated
- Self assessment methods
- Benchmarking
- Standardisation and certification
- Quality partnerships
- Guarantee of service
- The CEN quality framework for public transport
- Links between quality tools

Fundamentals of quality management in urban public transport
- Quality and planning in urban passenger transport
- Urban public transport quality is a shared responsibility
- If you can't measure, you can't manage
- Public transport and quality of the environment
- Quality in public transport results from quality in people management
- Quality is virtuous

Quality contracts and tenders
- The legal framework
- The tender procedure
- The contract itself

Responsibilities of the actors
- General recommendations to improve quality in public transport
- Requirements for public authorities
- Requirements for operators
- Requirements for public transport equipment manufacturers

National Differences/Local Adaptations

Examples and Study Sites
- The service certification of three RATP bus lines
- Oslo Public Transport (OPT)'s customer charter
- financial compensations at London Underground
- Benchmarking clubs: a case study of the CoMET group
- The implementation of ISO 9004/2 by STIB/MIVB in Brussels
- The management strategy of Semitag (Grenoble)
- The ISO 9000 certification of STIB-MIVB (Brussels)
- The hybrid benchmarking framework (HM Customs and Excise)

Exercises

4 Teaching and evaluation process of new learning material

4.1 General

The suitability of the material developed per key topic was evaluated by a number of Academic Institutions all over Europe, the so called ETSI. Academic Institutions from 24 European Countries used the new learning material for evaluation purposes and eventually for permanent teaching purposes. Teaching took place in both undergraduate and postgraduate courses. A number of teaching techniques ware employed such as traditional teaching, seminar type teaching, interactive teaching, teaching with use of audio/video equipment, etc.

Self learning was also one of the selected methods for the evaluation of the new learning material. CD audio and video media involving project partner experts or other well known personalities were used for this teaching technique.

4.2 Teaching and evaluation process at the University of Thessaloniki, Greece

University of Thessaloniki (AUTH) was involved in PORTAL as ETSI with two Faculties; the Faculty of Civil Engineering and the Faculty of Rural and Surveying Engineering. The courses in which the new material on Benchmarking and Quality Management in Public Transport was offered as well as the other details are given in Table 1. It must be noted that the necessary advertisement within the University was made to inform students and other interested about the teaching of this new material.

Table 1: Details about the courses where the new learning material was offered.

Faculty	Civil Engineering	Rural and Surveying Engineering
Faculty Sector	Transport and Construction Management	Transportation and Hydraulic works
Level	Undergraduate	Undergraduate
Course	Public Transport	Urban Mass Transportation Systems
Semester	Ninth	Eighth
Course Information	Compulsory for students selecting transport direction, optional for the others	Optional for students selecting transport direction
Number of students attending	~ Thirty including postgraduate ones	~Thirty
Teaching technique	Traditional lecture / Seminar type 3h duration/lecture	Traditional lecture / Seminar type 3h duration/lecture
Exercises	Yes	Yes
Number of lectures reserved for new material	Two (2)	Two (2)
Other information	Course given since 80's	New course since 2003

The new material was offered by means of video projector presentations using the PPT presentation prepared by the topic experts and translated by the National PORTAL partner. A number of exercises accompanied the teaching of the basic material, other based on the project material and other prepared by the two teachers in the respective courses. All students received a coloured handout with all the material prepared by PORTAL experts and the exercises in the Greek language. The students' participation was on purpose more intense as compared to the regular lectures, in order to enable a credible evaluation of this material.

At the end of the two lectures, all present students were given a standardised evaluation form and instructions in Greek for completing the form. The students returned the completed forms in the following lecture. The evaluation forms contained a number of questions where students had to respond if the agree or disagree by selecting a grade on 5 point ordinal Liekert scale. It should be mentioned that the two teachers in the two Faculties also completed evaluation forms. The evaluation material was forwarded to the responsible PORTAL partner for assembling all the evaluation exercises.

5 Evaluation results

The evaluation results distinguish between the students' and the teachers' results. The former can provide some kind of quantitative type results along with the qualitative ones, while the latter can only provide qualitative results. Figures 2 to 4 present the overall students' evaluation results for both Faculty courses.

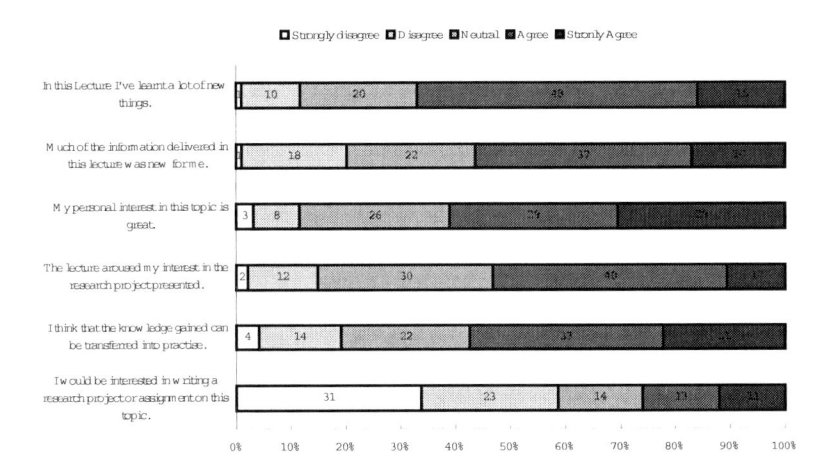

Figure 2: Distribution of students according to their responses to specific questions (questions about the topic)

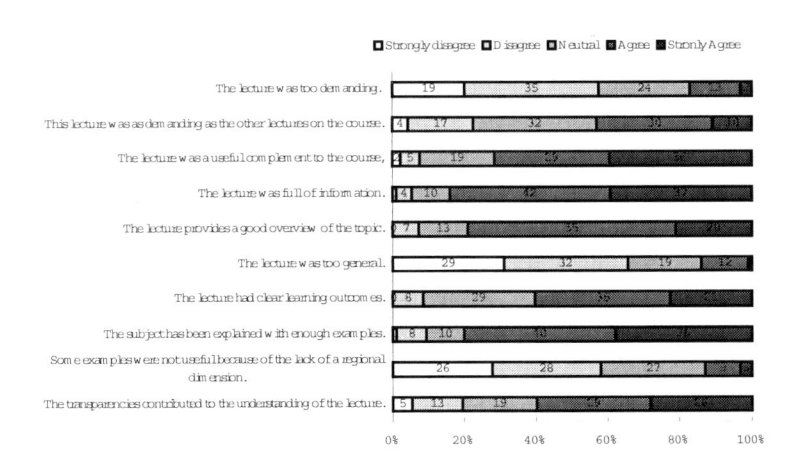

Figure 3: Distribution of students according to their responses to specific questions (questions about the content)

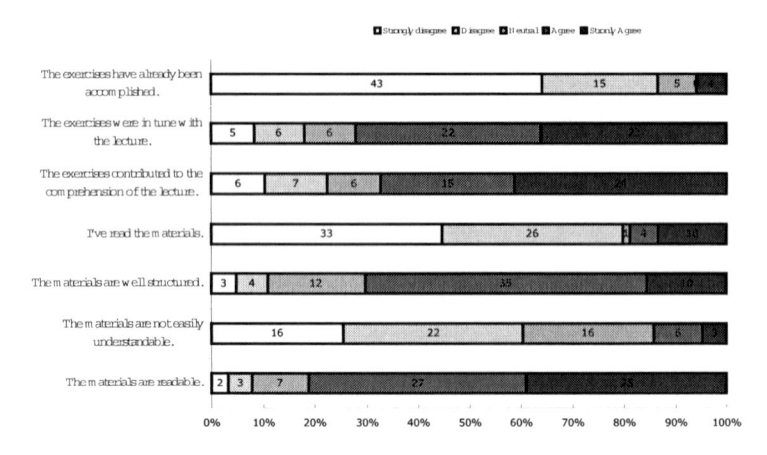

Figure 4: Distribution of students according to their responses to specific questions (questions about exercises & notes)

An evaluation of the audio CD book "Benchmarking and Quality Management in Public Transport", prepared in the framework of PORTAL, also took place as part of the lectures in the undergraduate course "Urban Mass Transportation Systems" in the Faculty of Rural & Surveying Engineering. All the students were familiar with the PORTAL project since they have participated in the questionnaire survey. The students first listen to the audio CD book "Benchmarking and Quality Management in Public Transport" and afterwards there was a discussion with the participation of the students and the lecturer. The lecture and evaluation took place in May 2003.

The main points of this discussion and evaluation include the following:

The majority of the students stated that they want to see images too (while listening to the audio CD). Some of them prefer to have a DVD (multimedia) instead of an audio CD book. They also say that there is no need to listen to the voice of the person who gave the interview (they only want to listen to the narrator). Probably the problem has to do with the different language (e.g., German etc) of the interviewee while the rest in the audio CD is in English. It must be mentioned at this point that other students propose that the audio CD would be more interesting if the interviewee is only speaking (and therefore not to have a narrator). They also prefer to have the lecturer with them, while listening in the classroom, so to comment on the various topics covered in the audio CD. The music (background music at the beginning of each topic) is considered to be rather problematic, in the sense that the students cannot clearly listen to the voice of the narrator. Some students propose to listen to the audio CD in an audio visual centre (each one having its own headset) and not in the classroom because of the problems with noise.

Concerning the topics covered in the audio CD they say that emphasis must be put on implementation and more practical issues and not in theoretical issues (for example they want to listen to the opinion of an expert for a current problem, something which cannot be included in a book). Some students propose to have the audio CD available in a website (on the Internet) so to download it when they need it. They also propose to have updated versions of the audio CD in each topic (so to have series of CDs in each theme/topic). They also want to listen the experiences from all over Europe in each theme/topic. All students say that they do not want to be examined on the material included in the audio CD. Some students stated that there must be a consideration about the students who cannot easily memorize from listening (but other think that its easier to listen than to read). They propose to have a pilot period for the evaluation of the audio CD so to have more time for the evaluation. They also think that no general conclusion can be made on the usefulness and applicability of the audio CD because of the different practices so far in the various European countries concerning the ways of learning. As a result they all agree that if they have to make a final decision, the answer would be "yes but under conditions"

6 Conclusions and suggestions

New learning material was developed in the PORTAL EU project about Benchmarking and Quality Management in Public Transport in the form of textbook, PPT presentation and also CD audio-video material. The testing and evaluation of this new material that was presented in two separate University courses in two Faculties at the University of Thessaloniki reveals the following:

- The contents of the material are of great interest to the majority of students, though some of these are rather difficult to understand and are more fitted to postgraduate level of studies.
- The way the material is presented is quite good and comprehensive for the majority of the participated students.
- The contents of the material provide new knowledge to the students, which are a useful complement to what they learn in the regular lectures.
- The examples provided and the exercises made are quite helpful.
- Use of Power Point Transparencies is also quite helpful in assimilating the contents of this new lecture.
- The new material is well structured and understandable.

From the teachers' point of view the new material is quite useful and helpful, but it covers a wide spectrum of knowledge. Students need additional basic knowledge in order to absorb all this new material. Especially in the case of the two Faculties at the University of Thessaloniki, the students have an engineering background that is not always enough for the assimilation of all this new material.

The use of real life examples from other countries and cities it is quite helpful in understanding some new concepts and the way these are applied in practice, as it is for example the concept of the "contracts" between Public Transport

Operators and the passengers. Employing suitable exercises during teaching is also very helpful and facilitates the comprehension of the new material.

In general the introduction of new material in the curriculum of a course seems to attract students' interest and to create a "potential", especially when it refers to real life examples.

Some useful suggestions can be also made from the experience gained through this testing and evaluation exercise such as:

- Advertising of a new material and/or teaching technique to the students, increases interest, brings more students into class and makes them feel that something special is happening.
- Student participation helps both the learning process and the student acceptability of new material. It is therefore recommended in any case.
- Proper presentation of material, either by coloured textbooks and transparencies or by audio-video CD's helps teachers to accomplish better their tasks and students to understand the contents of the material taught.
- Always use examples from real life and make students active members in the teaching process.

References

[1] PORTAL, Title: Dissemination Plan, VERSION: DP_01_Final2, Author: Dr. H.Kougias/TRADEMCO, Quality Control: C.McNulty, G.Lightfoot /CITI, Approval: R.Pressl / AMOR

[2] PORTAL, Deliverable 3 (Results of WP2), Summary: Overview Report on Key Topics, Author: DTV Consultants, Project Coordinator: AMOR, Quality Assurance: CITI

[3] PORTAL, Deliverable 2 (Analysis on Demand & Supply), Work Package Leader: PTRC, Project Coordinator: AMOR, Quality Assurance: CITI

[4] PORTAL, Summary of projects and results from topic Benchmarking and Quality Management in Public Transport, Author: P.Vincent (CERTU)

Biological science misconceptions amongst teachers and primary students in Jordan: diagnosis and treatment

I. Abu-Hola
Dept. of Curriculum and Instruction, Faculty of Educational Sciences, University of Jordan, Jordan

Abstract

This study was conducted to identify and treat misconceptions in biological science content amongst teachers and primary stage students in Jordan during the scholastic year 2002/2003. The qualitative approach was used in collecting and analysing data. This study emerged from classroom observations during a pre-service science method course in the teacher education program offered at the University of Jordan in 2001/2002. Close observations indicated that teachers and primary students have many biological misconceptions that should be identified and treated properly. Results showed that students and teachers were accommodating many biological misconceptions in all topics covered by this study. Many conclusions were derived from these study findings, and based on these findings, it was recommended that pre-service teacher education programs should be reconstructed so that they account for diagnosing and treating biological misconceptions.

Keywords: biology, misconceptions, alternative concepts, preconceptions, naïve concepts, diagnosis, treatment, students, teachers.

1 Introduction

Misconceptions in biology among teachers and students vary in nature, consequence and tenacity. They cause failure in understanding biological phenomena and may be difficult to discover and address Newton [1]. Reasons for failure to understand biological concepts and phenomena are different. Difficulty in constructing an adequate, coherent mental representation of the phenomena, lack of relevant prior experience or failure in noticing the relationships between different concepts could be a possible factor for not understanding. This failure may exist in wide spectra of thought. Some students believe that acquired characteristics, such as rough hands, strong muscles and playing football skills can be inherited over several generations (Clough and Wood-Robinson [2]). Some kids avoid drinking water after eating fish because of the fear that bits rejoined in their stomachs (Ustinov [3]). But, are there any reasons for the origin of such misconceptions? Misconceptions may appear according to a variety of factors. Misinformation, selective attention, misinterpretation and other factors may stand behind the origin of misconceptions.

Students' understandings of the natural world are not always consistent with accepted scientific beliefs (Wandersee, Mintzes and Novak [4]). For teachers, it is important to know that the most important factor influencing learning is what students already know (Mintzes and Wandersee [5]). Biology and general science teachers should use different strategies to investigate students' concepts. Concept maps, discussion, small group works, specific activities, journal writing and pencil and paper tests have all been suggested to be suitable (Mintzes, Wandersee and Novak [6]; White and Gunstone [7]). Morrison and Lederman [8] analyzed science teachers' planning for evidence of any mention of the assessment of students, ideas. This analysis showed that teachers wrote down abbreviated plans for their lessons, but did not mention any interest in diagnosing students' preconceptions about science topics despite its vital influence in future learning.

The knowledge a student acquires is a result of their interaction with their environment and through special activities with parents, schoolmates, and others. These preconceptions do not always match or are not consistent with real scientific concepts. These discrepancies may confuse students and get in the way of the way they explain or interpret different scientific phenomena. This situation is known as misconceptions, alternative framework, naïve concepts, and primary concepts, or in other terminology used in the science education field. One can describe this misconception as two types, phenomenological and vocabulary (Esler and Esler [9]). Phenomenological concepts are associated with misinterpreting of phenomena; such as respiration is having oxygen through inhaling. Reasons behind this misconception may be as a result of limited experience or passed to students by other persons. The second type, which is the vocabulary one, results through limited experience. For instance students consider the word plant to refer to apple, orange, tomato and other food sources only, although plants are taught in different stages as all living thing that are not animals, fungi, protistans and monerans.

2 Previous studies about biological misconceptions

Many studies dealing with biological preconceptions and misconceptions have been implemented and this study refers to them in order to build the needed theoretical background. Arnaudin and Mintzes [10] implemented concept maps and structured/ clinical interviews to determine knowledge of human circulatory system among different age levels. Confrontation strategies showed an effect of changing preconceptions. Also, Arnaudin and Mintzes [11] observed many alternative conceptions about the human circulatory system among fifth and eighth grade students. Confrontation strategies were also efficient in diagnosing these alternative conceptions. Trowbridge and Mintzes [12] reported that some teachers think that the situation and distribution of alternative conceptions improves with student growth. Although, this was not the case in animal classification concepts, where students still showing alternative concepts throughout all school years, and constructivist view of learning should be implemented.

Gallegos and others [13] chose food chains as a field of studying student preconception. Preconceptions held by students on the construction of food chains were determined. Results showed that classification of herbivores and carnivores was based on children's preconceptions of size and ferocity. Gibson [14] noticed that not only teaching activities are sources of misconceptions, but also textbooks are sources of these misconceptions. An example of these misconceptions is what related to succession concept, which needs textbook revision and improvement. Evolution concept was found by Jensen and Finley [15] to be one of the important biological concept, which should take more consideration in teaching. As an application to treat these misconceptions, many instructional strategies were applied; paired problem- solving in conjunction with the historically rich biological curricula was found to be the best. Ferrari and Chi [16] found that mistaken categorization could cause misconceptions about natural selection, and pushed students to fail in understanding the ontological features of equilibrium processes. During the last year of the twentieth century, Mak, Yip and Chung [17] observed that junior high-level secondary science teachers showed many alternative concepts in biology related topics. Results showed that science teachers are not prepared to teach integrated science curriculum.

Internal body maps were investigated by Cuthbert [18]. The majority of 8-9 year old children thought that their body has no organs. While the majority of 7-11 year old children thought there are small and freely suspended organs. Kinchin [19] studied presetting materials related to photosynthesis through modified concept mapping activities to help students' awareness of their alternative preconceptions. Cartoons were used as a stimulus and encouraging factors for learning and the study found that this technique was efficient. Lewis and Wood-Robinson [20] found that students in United Kingdom seemed to have a poor understanding of the processes by which genetic information is transferred and a lack of basic knowledge about other related concepts such as chromosomes, cell division and inheritance. Also, Bianchi [21] stated that children's conceptual understanding of plants was a problem and it could be enhanced positively by hands-on activities. Alternative concepts about photosynthesis were diagnosed by Griffard and Wandersee [22] and they used the traditional paper-and-pencil tests. In using the second tier in asking students about reasons of their answers, the situation was different and some misconceptions were detected. In looking to inheritance, Marbach-Ad [23] identified many alternative concepts in the relationships between genetic concepts. These results gave recommended improving instructional strategies in teaching genetic concepts for different grades. Nazario, Burrowes and Rodriguez [24] made more investigations. They found that university students taking biology courses showed misconceptions during the pre- and post-tests in different biological topics. Ozay and Oztas [25] implemented a questionnaire to test students' concepts. Diagnosis reported conflicting ideas about photosynthesis, respiration and energy flow in plants among 9 grade (14-15 years old) Turkish students. Results showed that it was difficult to change students' prior concepts about these topics.

All those previous studies revised showed that there is a real problem in teachers and students' understanding of different biological concepts, which made the rationale base of doing this study.

3 How to deal with students' misconceptions

Dealing with students' misconceptions has many steps. Firstly, recognizing that misconceptions exist, and it is well known that concepts grow in students' cognitive structure by gaining more experience and knowledge. Secondly, the real conflicts arise between students' misconceptions and the right scientific concepts should be spotted. Thirdly, these concepts should be grouped into phenomenological and vocabulary ones to make dealing with them more doable and workable. Fourthly, treating these misconceptions by structuring teaching activities that will produce the needed conceptual change. Esler and Esler [9] reported that hands – on – experience is the best in treating phenomenological misconceptions, while defining words in the context of their use is an accepted and desirable mechanism for correcting vocabulary – based misconceptions.

It is well known that some misconceptions are easy to change, while other well - founded concepts in experience or which based on innate knowledge are difficult to change. There are many theories in dealing with misconceptions such as:

- The replacement theory, which treats the process as one of replacing existing mental structures with others. Enrichment and revision are recruited in this theory (Vosniadou [26]).
- Disconnected / Mini theories in which knowledge of the world supposed to be fragmented and composed of small knowledge structures. In this way difficulties in understanding the holistic view of the world arise (DiSessa [27]).
- Multiple representations theory, which mainly described by Caravito and Hallden [28]. This theory sees that we have a range of theories about the different phenomena in the world. Not all of these theories developed, but one or two. These different theories cause the conflict in students' understandings.

Beside these theories, there is more than one strategy adopted in treating different misconceptions. As there are several kinks of misconceptions, it is a mistake to think that one can treat all kinds in the same way. So, teachers should use a range of strategies to treat students' misconceptions. Many strategies were examined in this study such as, diagnosis, integration, differentiation and exchange strategy. Also activating students' prior learning, classroom demonstration, question – answer – explanation worksheets, and peer group discussion was used.

4 Method

This study was conducted to investigate diagnosing and treating of misconceptions in Biological Science content amongst teachers and primary students in Jordan during the scholastic year 2002/2003. This study followed the qualitative approach in collecting and analyzing data. Root of this current study emerged from classroom observations during a pre-service science method course in the teacher education program held in the University of Jordan in 2001/2002. Direct observations indicate that teachers and primary students have many Biological misconceptions, which need an urgent diagnosis and treatment. Aims of this study were dealing with answering the following questions:
- What strategy teachers used to diagnose Biological Science misconceptions?
- What are the misconceptions teachers and students have in primary Biological Science?
- How teachers and students deal and react with these misconceptions?
- What strategy teachers used to treat these misconceptions?
- To what extent teachers success in treating and modifying students misconceptions?

This study was designed depending on the qualitative approach and followed the following procedure in collecting and analyzing data. This process was carried as follows:

- Teachers who implement the Biological content (12 male and female) were asked to collect all data related to student dealing and manipulating of different Biological concepts in order to analyze this data and treat all misconceptions students have. Primary analysis of this data showed that students have many biological misconceptions (Chromosomes, genes and DNA are the same; Mother is the one who is responsible of deciding the sex of the baby; respiration and photosynthesis are the same; mixing between male and female flowers and difficulties in differentiating between vein and artery).

- An open discussion between researcher and teachers was made about what was done inside classrooms exactly in order to be sure that research procedure was carried in the right way.
- The later stage was implementing a program for modifying teachers' misconceptions.
- The last stage was observing and monitoring the effects of the remedial program of teachers' understandings of different Biological concepts, which related to the content covered in this study.

5 Results

After collecting data a thorough analysis was carried out. Many important findings were found. First of all, misconceptions were emerged in Biological Science and not only Physical and Chemical Science as the thought was. Secondly, Biological misconceptions are spread amongst all Biological concepts and not only in the difficult contents like genes, photosynthesis and respiration. Thirdly, teachers and students, both have misconceptions. Fourthly, teaching and learning strategies affect students understanding of Biological concepts and they may cause building these misconceptions.

Units in which misconceptions appeared after analysis were:
Endocrine system, Circulatory system, Digestive system, Respiratory system, Execration system, Inheritance (Human Inherited diseases and Inheritance and Environment), Plants (Parts, Growth, Photosynthesis, Respiration and Nutrition) and Hearing Mechanism

Not all misconceptions appeared among students and teachers were reported in this study. <u>In the different units mentioned above, types of misconceptions, diagnosis strategies, percentage of misconceptions among students and teachers and the treatment strategies were stated respectively and in one complete sentence to make it easy for the reader.</u> In each time of misconception' treatment a disequilibrium situation was achieved by different techniques and strategies such as open discussion in order to help students move to the accepted scientific believes. The full results are as follows:

5.1 Endocrine and circulatory systems

Definition of the somatic gland: open discussion showed that 50% of students and 30% of teachers carry this misconception. To treat this misconception, discussion and knowledge replacement were applied. More gland secretion is a healthy symptom: Paper and pencil test, 100&40%, demonstrations of some human diseases caused by hormones' secretion irregularity.

Ventricles and auricles are the same: Drawings, 90&20%, demonstrations of drawings and film about differences between ventricles and auricles. Ventricles and auricles contract at the same time: Open discussion, 85&70%, demonstration of video film showing the human heart at work. Mixing between arteries and veins: Drawings and direct questions, 100&60%, using circulatory system charts and demonstration of lamb heart with arteries and veins.

5.2 Digestive and respiratory systems

Digestion happened inside living cells: Pencil and paper quiz, 90&50%, deep discussion about stages of digestion and stating differences between digestion in or outside cells. Also, concentrating on differences between digestion and cellular respiration. Water acts as a digestive factor or enzyme: Classroom discussion, 80&40%, applying hands-on-inquiry activities to prove that putting a piece of bread inside the water for long time doesn't change its chemical characteristics. Sugar detecting test was also used. Stomach is the only organ where digestion takes place: Direct questions, 90&35%, group discussion and knowledge replacement to show that the small intestine has a vital role in food digestion.

Inhaling, exhaling and internal gas exchange are used to indicate respiration: Open discussion about respiration mechanism, 75&25%, defining the respiration concept as the reaction of oxygen and food to produce energy. Exhaling gas has no oxygen: Open discussion about respiration, 100&65%, demonstration of one of the first aid activities (artificial breathing) and raising a question of the benefit of this aid. Respiration has nothing to be an activity of oxygen – food reaction to produce energy: Two-tier test about energy producing mechanism, 65&30%, classroom discussion and film demonstration about food journey inside human body.

5.3 Excretion system and inheritance

Sweating protects body from dryness: open discussion, 50&20%, concentration on the role of water in homeostasis and maintaining the body temperature. The relation between liver and kidney in producing urea is absent: group worksheets about producing urea in the body, 100&60%, discussing the stages of producing urea starting from having protein during feeding mechanism.

Concepts of chromosomes, genes, DNA, sex of the baby, sex-influenced characteristics, genotypes and phenotypes, sex-related genes, inherited diseases, and environment and inheritance relationship are all reflecting a real problem among students and teachers of a percentages about 90% or more among both students and teachers. It was easy to determine these misconceptions by classroom discussion. It took a comprehensive class activities and discussion to give the accepted scientific believes about the above concepts with both students and teachers.

5.4 Plants

Mixing between photosynthesis and respiration in plants as both students and teachers mentioned that both activities produce energy: diagnosis test was applied to explore the previous experience about these two concepts, 100% of students and 60% of teachers showing this misconception, using charts for both concepts and discussing each of them in depth, then the relation between the two was highlighted. Respiration happens in nighttimes only, while photosynthesis happens only during daytime: this mixing appeared accidentally during the classroom discussion, 80&60%, the problem appeared as a vocabulary one as the concepts were used in the wrong context. Teachers always said: photosynthesis happens in the light, while respiration happens at night. Mixing between pollination and fertilization: all students and teachers used both concepts as a word and it's meaning without differentiation. Discussing the mechanism of producing seeds was applied by using real flowers and charts with concentration in using each concept in the right place all the time.

5.5 Hearing mechanism

Nerves have nothing to do with hearing mechanism and the human ears do all the job: Simple questions were enough to discover this misconception, 90&40%, deep discussion about the hearing mechanism and the role of the brain was highlighted.

Finally, the remedial program showed a moderate effect on students and teachers' understandings, which means that they still have problems in their explanations and dealings with concepts and more research effort is still needed. This means, more concentration and efforts should be given in teacher education programs to solidify and correct teachers' understandings of Biological Concepts before their real teaching practice.

6 Discussion and conclusions

Results of this study are strongly consistent with results of previous studies (Arnaudin and Mintzes [11], Bianchi [21], Marbach-Ad [23], Ozay and Oztas [25]), which indicate that the problem of having biological misconceptions among teachers and students is an international one. This should encourage researchers around the world to put this issue among their research priorities. This is because any future learning will be influenced positively or negatively of students' prior knowledge. Many conclusions were derived from these study findings. Diagnosis of misconceptions should take place for teachers and students side-by-side and only for students. All Science contents should be studied as a package (Biology, Physics, Geology and Chemistry) and not dealing with these contents lonely. This is because scientific concept is a result of these integrated contents and you cannot deal with blood concept without understanding other component of this concept rooted in Physics and chemistry as an example. Cross-sectional and longitudinal studies should be conducted for all school and college grades in order to indicate these misconceptions and deal with them in the right way and time. It is harmful to ignore any misconception; easily it will be resistant to change later on. Finally, teachers should receive dense teacher education program to be sure they got a good understanding of scientific concepts before the start teaching.

7 Recommendations and implications

The study findings will be helpful for teachers, students and all educators, especially curriculum designers, textbooks authors, trainers, parents, science teacher educators, administrators, teachers, student teachers and students. Finally, science teacher should give big effort for diagnosis and treating misconception as early as possible, otherwise the problem will be more difficult to be solved.

This study recommended applying different approaches in diagnosing and treating misconceptions among students and teachers. Pre-service teacher education programs should have a considerable interest, as it is the key for the future teacher to start his/her job.

References

[1] Newton, D.P., Teaching for Understanding: What it is and how to do it?, Routledge: London, pp.110-124, 2000.
[2] Clough, E.E. & Wood-Robinson, E., Children's understanding of inheritance. Journal of Biological Education, 19, pp. 304-310, 1985.
[3] Ustinov, P., Dear Me, Heinemann: London, 1977.
[4] Wandersee, J.H., Mintzes, J.J. & Novak, J.D., Research on alternative conceptions in science. In Gabel, D.L., (eds). Handbook of Research in Science Teaching and Learning, Macmillan: New York, pp. 177-210, 1994.
[5] Mintzes, J.J. & Wandersee, J.H., (eds). Teaching Science for Understanding: A Human Constructivist View, Academic Press: San Diego, CA, 1998.
[6] Mintzes, J.J., Wandersee, J.H., & Novak, J.D., (eds). Assessing Science Understanding: A Human Constructivist View, Academic Press: San Diego, CA, 2000.
[7] White, R. & Gunstone, R., Probing Understanding, Falmer: New York, 1992.
[8] Morrison, J.A. & Lederman, N.G., Science teachers' diagnosis and understanding of students' preconceptions. Science Education, 87, pp. 489-467, 2003.
[9] Esler, W.K. & Esler, M.K., Teaching Elementary Science: A Full Spectrum Science Instruction Approach, Wadsworth/Thomson Learning Inc. Belmont: USA, pp. 1-45, 2001.
[10] Arnaudin, M.W. & Mintzes, J.J., Students' alternative conceptions of human Circulatory system: A cross- age study. Science Education, 69(5), pp. 721-733, 1985.
[11] Arnaudin, M.W. & Mintzes, J.J., What research says: The cardiovascular system: Children's conceptions and misconceptions. Science and Children, 23(5), pp. 48- 51, 1986.
[12] Trowbridge, J.E. & Mintzes, J.J., Alternative conceptions in animal Classification: A cross –age study. Journal of Research in Science Teaching, 25(7), pp. 547-571, 1988.
[13] Gallegos, L. & Others., Preconceptions and relations used by children in the construction of food chain. Journal of Research In Science Teaching, 31(3), pp. 259-272, 1994.
[14] Gibson, D.J., Textbook misconceptions: The climax concept of succession. American Biology Teacher, 58(3), pp. 135-140, 1996.
[15] Jensen, M.S. & Finley, F,N., Changes in students' understanding of evolution resulting from different curricular and instructional strategies. Journal of Research in Science Teaching,33(8), pp. 879-900, 1996.

[16]   Ferrari, M. & Chi, M.T.H., The nature of naïve explanations of natural selection. International Journal of Science Education, 20(10), pp. 1231-1256, 1998.

[17]   Mak, S.Y., Yip, D.Y. & Chung, C.M., Alternative conceptions in biology-related topics of integrated science teachers and implications for teacher education. Journal of Science Education and Technology, 8(2), pp. 161-170, 1999.

[18]   Cuthbert, A.J., Do children have a holistic view of their internal body maps?. School Science Review, 82(299), pp.25-32, 2000.

[19]   Kinchin, I.M., Concept – mapping activities to help students understand Photosynthesis – and teachers understand students. School Science Review, 82(299), pp. 11-14, 2000.

[20]   Lewis, J. & Wood-Robinson, C., Genes, chromosomes, cell division and Inheritance – do students see any relationship? International Journal of Science Education, 22(2), pp. 177-195, 2000.

[21]   Bianchi, L., So what do you think a plant is? Primary Science Review, 61, pp. 15-17, 2000.

[22]   Griffard, P.B. & Wandersee, J.H., The two-tier instrument on photosynthesis What does it diagnose? International Journal of Science Education, 23(10), pp. 1039-1052, 2001.

[23]   Marbach-Ad, G., Attempting to break the code in student comprehension of genetic concepts. Journal of Biological Education, 35(4), pp. 183-189, 2001.

[24]   Nazario, G.M., Burrowes, P.A. & Rodriguez,J., Persisting misconceptions. Using pre- and post- tests to identify biological misconceptions. Journal of College Science Teaching, 31(5), pp. 292-296, 2002.

[25]   Ozay, E. & Oztas, H., Secondary students' interpretations of photosynthesis and Plant nutrition. Journal of Biological Education,37(2), pp. 68-70, 2003.

[26]   Vosniadou, S., Capturing and modeling the process of conceptual change. Learning and Instruction, 4, pp. 45-69, 1994.

[27]   DiSessa, A., Towards an epistemology of physics. Cognition and Instruction, 10, pp. 105-125, 1993.

[28]   Caravito, S. & Hallden,O., Re-framing the problem of conceptual change. Learning and Instruction, 4, pp. 89-111, 1994.

Expanding online learning exam options with computer-based assessment

E. M. Weeden
*Department of Information Technology,
Rochester Institute of Technology, USA*

Abstract

This paper will discuss how computer-based assessment can help solve the problems of examination administration in an online learning environment. An instructor who is new to the online learning arena may attempt to take traditional classroom examinations and port them over to the online learning format using one of several methods. These methods will be discussed pointing out the issues that arise when they are used.

The advancement of computer-based assessment can help solve the problem of assessing the knowledge of online learning students through examinations that can not be given in a centralized location such as a classroom. The advantages of computer-based assessment over traditional paper-based assessment will be explored as they relate to students, faculty, and administration.

There are numerous computer-based assessment tools available as stand alone software or as part of courseware packages. An exploration of the testing features of one of those tools will illustrate and put into perspective several advantages of computer-based assessment.

Keywords: assessment, computer-based assessment, online learning strategies.

1 Introduction

With the rise of the Internet, there are now diverse ways in which people can learn. Training companies and educational institutions have harnessed the advantages of the Internet to disseminate materials significantly reducing any impact location can play in learning. In a traditional learning environment, the learner has to travel to a certain learning location, like a training center or educational institution. The ability to access learning materials over the Internet has allowed people to learn from home or any other location that has a computer and Internet access.

In an educational setting, when an online learning course is offered there still must be a way to assess a student's knowledge in order to issue a grade. In a traditional educational setting, this may be done via written examinations. Trying to convert traditional examinations to an online learning format raises some challenges based on the method of examination administration selected. Computer-based assessment can significantly reduce these issues to provide an assessment environment that is conducive to the online learning environment.

2 Traditional exam administration

Early on in the history of online education programs, it was not uncommon to have instructors attempt to convert traditional paper-based examinations to the online learning arena. The methods that are discussed below are all examples of asynchronous exam administration [11].

2.1 Administration via postal mail

The conversion method closest to a traditional classroom exam is to use postal mail to send and receive an examination. The instructor would compose a traditional paper-based exam, make photocopies of it and mail a copy to each student. Once received, the student would complete the exam and mail it back. The instructor would then correct the exam and convey the result to the student possibly again through postal mail.

There are several issues with this type of examination delivery. One issue is cost. Mailing potentially bulky exams could prove costly for the educational institution, especially if it pays the return postage for the students as well.

Consistency in delivery is also a concern. Due to postal mail operations, students will not receive the examination at the same time. Therefore, the instructor would need to provide enough of a window for all students to receive and complete the examination. This means that students wouldn't have equal time to complete the exam.

Another issue is the amount of time the entire cycle (send, complete, return, grade, return) could take. It is entirely possible for the process to take over a week, maybe two or more. This causes a large gap from the time a student takes an exam, until they receive the results and are able to view their mistakes. This is not an ideal situation for students in online programs.

This method of exam administration also has aspects where student honor and integrity are needed. One aspect involves being honest about when the exam was received. Unless the educational institution sends the examination as certified mail requiring a signature upon receipt, the instructor has to take the word of the student as to if the exam was received and when. Therefore, unethical students could lie to their instructor about when they received the mailing to provide themselves extra time to complete the examination.

The procedure by which the student completes the examination can also be compromised. If an instructor wants to enforce a closed-book exam, then a proctor may be required to administer the exam to the student. However, trust is given that the proctor will actually enforce the rules specified.

If a trustworthy proctor is not used then there is a possibility that students could collaborate or cheat on an exam. This places additional responsibility on the instructor to look for similar answers, whereas in a traditional testing environment the instructor can monitor the room for suspicious behaviour. Also if an instructor finds multiple examinations with similar answers, proving that collusion or cheating occurred could be very hard.

2.2 Electronic distribution with date range

Given the severe disadvantages of exam distribution via postal mail, a better alternative is to have an electronic distribution with a date range within which students can submit their exams for grading. Although the grading turnaround time is quicker, this method shares some of the same disadvantages as a postal distribution such as potential cheating or collusion.

Having a range of dates provides students with time management flexibility. They can take the exam at a time that is convenient for them as long as it is within the acceptable dates.

An instructor can choose to limit the amount of time students have to complete the exam by noting the difference between the download time of the document and the time it was submitted by the student. However, this difference is not a foolproof indication of true time spent completing the exam. For example, after having downloaded the exam, the student's computer could have locked up causing the student to spend examination time getting the computer operational.

If there is no time limit to enforce completing the examination in one sitting, then the student can have the flexibility to complete the exam in one sitting or across multiple sittings. Completing the exam in multiple sittings could maximize time flexibility for online students trying to complete coursework while balancing work and family. It also allows the student to stop working on the examination if the environment he or she is working in becomes distracting (crying baby, loud music, etc.).

2.3 Electronic distribution with specific date and time

In this third method, a process similar to the previous one occurs, however the date and time is the same for all students. This simulates a traditional examination environment where students arrive on a set date and time to take the exam. This process greatly reduces the time gaps that occur in the first two methods.

Given the time limitation, students may not have time to collaborate with classmates on answers. Cheating by taking another's exam is still possible.

One major problem with this method is that the time flexibility that online learning offers is eliminated. All students must attend the online testing session regardless of time zone differences. Also if the exam is to be proctored, then there is the potential for additional scheduling conflicts.

2.4 Overall issues

Given the above methods of examination distribution, there are overarching issues that are common to the methods discussed. First, in each scenario the exam is given directly to the students, allowing them to retain a copy of its contents. This essentially makes that exam public knowledge and its integrity is compromised for later use.

Another overall issue is that the methods discussed apply primarily to paper-based examinations or converted electronic counterparts. For some knowledge it is necessary to test whether or not a student can apply what he or she has learned to perform an action as part of a practical examination. The extent to which this could be done with the previously discussed methods is to have the students describe what actions were performed or the results received. In a study performed by Hunt et al., 75 percent of students sampled found written exams to be more demanding than a computer-based exam because they found it more difficult to explain actions rather than perform them [4].

An additional drawback is that students are not able to practice taking exams unless the instructor provides samples that he or she has composed or has gathered from other sources. In order for the students to assess performance on practice exams, instructors have to distribute a key. This key could be abused by students who have not attempted to practice for the exam, but are rather just trying to find out answers to questions that might appear on the actual exam.

All of these methods require the instructor or a grader to manually grade the examinations. The instructor must then manually track the grades of the students. Students would have to do the same to track their progress in the class.

3 Computer-based assessment

The power of computer-based exams can be seen when applied to assess knowledge from different perspectives, via various assessments, to gather information that can be used to tailor online learning to the needs of the student. This power is based on the different types of assessments that can be performed as well as the types of questions that can be included in assessments.

3.1 Types of questions

The types of questions asked via a traditional paper-based exam can also be asked via a computer-based exam. However computer-based assessment questions can incorporate multimedia elements such as images, video and sound to make the testing experience more robust than a paper counterpart. The types of questions available are summarized below.

3.1.1 Selecting [10]

Selection questions allow users to select from a list of choices. The most basic selection question involves two choices: true or false, yes or no, etc. The next step up is where there are more than two choices and the user selects one choice as the correct answer. A variation is to allow the user to select more than one answer as correct.

Selecting questions can also be based on non-textual choices such as images, video, or sound. The overarching idea is that the user selects something as an answer. Shepard identifies scenarios where this can be harnessed, "users may be asked to select from a number of images, to click on a part of an image; to drag selected items into a target area;…to stop an audio or video sequence at a point where they recognize a particular event or situation is occurring." [10]

Selecting questions are designed to test whether the correct answer(s) can be recognized by the student.

3.1.2 Supplying [10]

Supplying questions are answered by users typing in their response. This is synonymous with short answer, essay, or questions where students are to provide a list.

Supplying questions test whether or not the student can remember facts or apply knowledge [3].

3.1.3 Ordering/ranking [10]

This question type involves organizing a list of items in a correct sequence.

3.1.4 Matching [10]

Matching questions entails identifying linkages between two lists of items. As with prior question types, the choices may be textual or of a multimedia format.

3.1.5 Locating [10]

This question type involves identifying something from a larger form. For example, given a picture of a house, click on the roof.

3.2 Instructional practices

Computer-based exams can be combined with a learning management system to provide education tailored to the student. This tailoring can be accomplished through the use of different types of assessment as described below.

3.2.1 Pre-tests [3]

Computer-based pre-tests can be utilized to assess the amount of knowledge a student already has on a given topic. The results from the test can be analyzed to determine what learning objectives are met and what objectives the student needs to learn. This can allow a learning management system to tailor learning to focus on what the student truly doesn't know.

3.2.2 Remediation [3]
This type of assessment allows identification of knowledge that the student is not possessing for the purpose of suggesting or providing remedial activities that the student can perform to gain the knowledge.

3.2.3 Post-tests [3]
Post-tests can be used at the end of a course to assess the amount of mastery a student has over the material. From the results of the post-test both the student and the instructor see if the material was mastered. The instructor can also analyze the overall results from the post-test to identify weak areas to determine course effectiveness.

3.2.4 Adaptation [3]
Adaptation questions attempt to assess student strengths and weaknesses. From an analysis of the results, learning can be adjusted accordingly, such as increasing or decreasing the pace of the course, providing more or less practice opportunities, etc.

3.2.5 Personalization [3]
This type of assessment is geared toward acquiring background information about the student. This information, such as name, educational background, job position, etc., can be used to build a profile of the student. The profile along with data obtained through the other types of assessments can then be use to personalize the student's learning experience.

4 Advantages of computer-based assessment

Computer-based assessment can help solve some of the problems of examination assessment in an online learning course. Computer-based assessment can go beyond distributing a traditional examination electronically, as discussed earlier, and harness database, multimedia and Internet technologies to create a synchronous assessment environment that is beneficial to students, instructors, and administration.

4.2 Student benefits

4.2.1 Immediate feedback
Depending on how computer-based assessment is implemented, the system may be able to grade an examination immediately after a student completes it, allowing the student to receive immediate feedback [4]. If short answer or essay questions are included in the examination, then the instructor must grade them. However for multiple-choice or true/false questions, the system would be able to automatically grade them.

4.2.2 Opportunity for practice
Using a computer-based assessment tool that composes an exam from a pool of questions stored in a database allows students the opportunity to take several

different practice examinations. These exams could provide not only grading results but also feedback on questions missed. Hence, the students have the potential of using the system also as a learning tool.

4.2.3 Task-based questions feasible
In a traditional examination it is very difficult to have task-based questions included. The student can perform a task and then explain what he or she did and explain the results, but this is often more difficult for the student than just performing the task [3]. With computer-based assessment, students can interact with a software application and the application can track their actions and grade them [4].

4.2.4 Comfortable testing environment [11]
With computer-based assessment, students can have the flexibility as to where they take their exams. This flexibility allows students to take an exam in a comfortable location that may relax them and reduce their anxiety.

4.3 Faculty benefits

4.3.1 Reduction in grading
If multiple-choice or true/false questions are utilized, a computer-based assessment tool can potentially grade the exams and enter the grades into a database. If short answer or essay questions are also included, the tool can grade the questions it is able to and leave the other questions for the instructor to grade.

4.3.2 More efficient use of time
Once the initial time is spent by the instructor setting up the assessment tool and populating it with questions, it can be re-used for several subsequent terms. Storing questions in a database allows them to be added, edited, or deleted at any point in time. Also since exam grading can be automated, much of the work that goes along with traditional examination administration is removed.

4.3.3 Grading is more consistent [11]
The grading performed by an assessment tool will be consistent. Instructors or graders are human, and when grading exams by hand a mistake is possible.

4.3.4 Grading is done faster [11]
Again due to the assessment tool being able to potentially do some, if not all of the grading of the exam, the students get feedback on their progress sooner.

4.3.5 No interpretation of handwriting [11]
Because responses to the exam will either be selected by using the mouse or the keyboard, the instructor does not have to struggle with hard to read handwriting.

4.3.6 Ability to re-test students [5]
Since pools of questions can be stored in a database, an instructor can compose a new exam by selecting different questions for a makeup exam, or by having the

questions be randomized so that each student receives a randomized exam. In a traditional environment, the instructor might have to compose a new exam or find an old exam to re-use.

4.3.7 Test analysis can be automated
To ensure the reliability and validity of a paper-based examination, the instructor would have to perform a manual analysis. Since the majority of computer-based assessment tools utilize a database, exam data can be collected and analyzed automatically [3].

4.4 Administration benefits

4.4.1 Printing and copying costs are reduced
In earlier methods of exam distribution the institution incurred costs associated with copying or postage. With computer-based assessment, these costs are eliminated because students complete and review exams using a computer.

4.4.2 Faculty time can be more effectively used
Utilization of a computer-based assessment tool by faculty members allows them to use their time more effectively and therefore accomplish more.

5 Overall assessments

There have been several studies done on computer-based assessment. In a study done by Peat and Franklin, they describe a variety of computer-based assessment tools that they have utilized at the University of Sydney along with feedback that they have obtained from students using the tools [7]. Overall, 75 percent of the sampled students preferred computer-based quizzes to paper-based quizzes. In addition, 67 percent of the sampled students preferred questions that included diagrams, photographs, or graphs. When asked what was the best aspect of quizzes delivered via the computer 17 percent stated instant feedback, 15 percent like the multiple-choice format, and 13 percent liked that the quizzes were quick to complete.

A study by Hunt, Hughes, and Rowe involved the development and student evaluation of the Formative Automated Computer Testing (FACT) system [4]. This system automated the assessment of information technology skills obtained by students. When asked, 97 percent of the students in the study preferred a computer-based exam to a written exam citing reasons such as no handwriting and the exam took less time.

Multiple studies have commented on the impact of a person's comfort level using computer on performance [6]. For someone who is scared of a computer, using one to complete an examination could increase anxiety and reduce confidence. However as computers and the Internet become universal in society the issue of comfort level should significantly decrease.

6 Example

There are several learning management systems on the market today. In December 2002, Dean [2] listed 31 learning management systems. Out of those 31, 19, or 61 percent, included computer-based testing functionality. These products will continue to evolve to stay competitive in the marketplace. To illustrate some of the computer-based testing functionality that can be included Prometheus, a courseware package produced by Blackboard Incorporated will be explored [8].

The Rochester Institute of Technology uses Prometheus for both on-campus and online learning courses [9]. The main features of Prometheus that will be discussed are related to testing. Within Prometheus, testing, an optional feature, can be enabled or disabled by the instructor(s) of a particular section of a course.

Once testing has been enabled, the option for testing appears in the system menu on the right side of the screen. If selected, the instructor is taken to a page that allows him or her to create, edit, or grade an exam as well as view summary information about the test such as the total number of points in the test.

When the option to create a test is chosen, the instructor is taken to a page that allows specifications for the exam to be entered. These specifications include test title, whether it will be a survey or test, grading specifics such as whether students can view their grades, comments for students after completing the test, and if the grade is automatically inserted into the grade book portion of the system. For added security the instructor can specify a password for the exam, when the test will be made available to students, whether questions within a test section are to be randomized, and whether a certain number of questions will be pulled randomly from a pool of questions. After the instructor has made his or her selections a test will be created.

Once a test is created, the instructor is able to add sections to the test. Once a section is added the instructor can insert questions into the section. A section can have many different types of questions within it, such as multiple-choice, true/false, short answer, and long answer. Initially, the instructor specifies how many of each type of question he or she would like to add to the pool of questions for that section. Then for each type of question, the instructor can specify the default points. Also if the instructor is having questions pulled from a pool he or she can specify how many questions of that type are to appear in the section. For multiple-choice questions, there is an additional parameter for how many options (the key plus distractors) the instructor intends to have for each question. The key to a multiple-choice question is the correct alternative or answer [1]. A distractor is a non-correct alternative [1]. Also the instructor is able to see how many questions of that type have been entered already.

Once the instructor has specified those parameters, he or she can then begin composing questions. For any question, the instructor can select to "always include this question." For all question types, with the exception of short answer and long answer, there are text boxes available for the instructor to provide feedback for correct and incorrect answers for students to see when they review their results.

After composing an exam, an instructor has several options available, such as adding, editing, or deleting content. The instructor can view the exams that he or she has created, but only students can take exams. For new instructors to the system, it makes it really difficult for them to see the student perspective of the exam and to test out how grading is done.

When students select an exam to take, the test appears in one scrollable window. Once finished with the exam the system will grade multiple-choice and true/false questions and store the students' exam answers and results in a database for the instructor to refer to later.

Grading of student exams can be done either in student order or in question order. When done by question the individual responses are shown without the student's name appearing by the response. The instructor is shown the total number of points that question is worth and is allowed to enter a value equal to or less than that number. A space for the instructor to type in feedback to the student for that question is also provided. An instructor can also chose to go back and re-grade a question, even a question that was graded by the system.

When grading exams in student order, the instructor is shown the names of the students who have taken the exam from which he or she can select a student to grade. In addition to showing the first and last name of the students a timestamp of when they started the exam, along with the amount of time taken to complete the exam. If for some reason a student needs to retake an exam, a button appears by each student's name allowing the retest to occur.

After all exams have been graded, the instructor can then view the results. The instructor can view a listing of students that took the exam with the points each student received and the percentage scored. The instructor can also view the distribution of answers for each question. After doing so, if an instructor feels that a question should be eliminated from the exam results he or she can chose to do so and the system will recalculate the grades. An instructor can also view summary graphs and statistics on the exam by both points and percentages.

After the instructor has finished grading a student's exam, he or she is now able to view the results. Each question will show the total number of points and the number of points received. For true/false and multiple-choice questions the correct answer is displayed along with a general response that the instructor may have entered for the right or wrong answer. For short and long answer questions, the student's answer appears along with any customized feedback the instructor entered when grading.

7 Future research

Cheating in any type of examination is always a concern. For online assessment, where exam location can be anywhere, it is very hard to know for certain who is taking the examination. Applying biometric technologies such as retinal scanning, face or voice recognition, and fingerprinting, is not a silver bullet; there could be another person with the student who still provides assistance [10]. Research should be done to provide testing equipment that would allow the test taker to have video including sound taken during the examination.

Another area for continued research is computer adaptive testing. By evolving this area computer-based assessment can be taken to another level, where the test is truly tailored to each individual student.

One final area that can be utilized to take computer-based assessment to another level is simulation. Companies such as Cisco, Microsoft, and Novell are either planning or already using simulations in their certification exams [12]. By exploiting this technology for assessment, testing can be focused on problem-based scenarios [12]. Vallejo adds that, "when you integrate the power of simulations into testing environments, the result is not just an alternative way of doing things; it is a fundamentally new and better way to be evaluated." [12] Eric Wenck addresses the security issue when he explains, "simulations provide a higher level of test security because the exam is not simply constructed with multiple-choice questions that may be memorized and exposed." [13]

8 Conclusion

Online learning is becoming a popular venue for people pursuing education. Just as assessment is a topic of research for the traditional educational environment, it is becoming a topic for online learning. Some online learning instructors have discovered that it is inefficient to try and make traditional paper-based examinations work in an online learning setting. With the available technology and advancing research, tools are continually being developed and refined that allow assessment to occur in online learning format through computer-based assessment. This format harnesses database, multimedia, and Internet capabilities to create assessment tools that are suited to online learning environments.

References

[1] Cucciarelli, A., Panti, M., & Valenti, S. (2000). Web-based assessment in student learning. In M. Khosrowpour (Ed.), *Web-based learning and teaching technologies: opportunities and challenges* (pp.175-197). Hershey, PA: Idea Group Publishing.

[2] Dean, C. (2002, December). *Technology based training & on-line learning.* Retrieved August 25, 2003, from http://www.peak.co.uk/AuthoringSystem.pdf

[3] Driscoll, M. (2001, June). Building better e-assessments. *Learning Circuits.* Retrieved September 10, 2003, from http://www.learningcircuits.com/2001/jun2001/driscoll.html.

[4] Hunt, N., Hughes, J., & Rowe, G. (2002). Formative Automated Computer Testing (FACT). *British Journal of Educational Technology, 33,* 525-535. Retrieved August 3, 2003 from Wilson Web.

[5] Jacobs, L. C., & Chase, C. I. (1992).*Developing and using tests effectively: a guide for faculty.* San Francisco: Jossey-Bass Publishers.

[6] Latu, E., and Chapman, E. (2002). Computerised adaptive testing. *British Journal of Educational Technology, 33,* 619-622. Retrieved August 3, 2003 from Wilson Web.

[7] Peat, M, & Franklin, S. (2002). Supporting student learning: the use of computer-based formative assessment modules. *British Journal of Educational Technology, 33,* 515-523. Retrieved August 3, 2003 from Wilson Web.

[8] Prometheus (Version 5.1) [Computer software]. (2002). Washington, DC: Blackboard Incorporated.

[9] Rochester Institute of Technology. (1999). [myCourses page, which uses Prometheus]. Retrieved August 25, 2003 from mycourses.rit.edu

[10] Shepard, C. (2001). *Checking out.* Retrieved September 10, 2003 from http://www.fastrak-consulting.co.uk/tectix/features/checkingout.htm.

[11] Thomas, P., Price, B., Paine, C., & Richards, M. (2002). Remote electronic examinations: student experiences. *British Journal of Educational Technology, 33,* 537-549. Retrieved August 3, 2003 from Wilson Web.

[12] Vallejo, N. (2002, July). Simulations: virtual reality for certification. *Certification Magazine.* Retrieved September 10, 2003 from http://www.certmag.com/issues/jul02/feature_vallejo.cfm.

[13] Wenck, E. (2002, July). Simulations: The next generation of testing. *Certification Magazine.* Retrieved September 10, 2003 from http://www.certmag.com/issues/jul02/feature_vallejo.cfm.

Preliminary results exploring the use of alternate instructional methods in mathematics

D. Bond-Hu
*Instructional Design, Development and Evaluation Department,
Syracuse University*

Abstract

Many classrooms across the world contain students with disabilities. This study examined four instructional methods that have been suggested to be appropriate for educators to utilize in classroom environments to improve student mathematical understanding. The study was conducted in a multi-level, inclusive classroom in the United States with a mixture of learning disabled and non-learning disabled students. This study examined four different mathematics-instructional methods designed specifically for students with dyslexia. Over a 20-day period, 17 students were taught mathematical concepts using one of the four instructional methods. Students provided ratings for each lesson based on a specific set of criteria. The instructor also kept a reflective journal to assist in the comparison of the students' perceptions to her own perception of how the students reacted to each lesson. The study found that lessons involving manipulation, guided problem solving and interaction with others were perceived as the better instructional methods. The study also discovered that the instructor's perception correlated with the students' perceptions of the methods.
Keywords: dyslexia, learning disabilities, mathematics education, instructional teaching methods, middle school education.

1 Introduction

Learning disabilities are not isolated to one geographic area of the world, one race, or one culture. Dyslexia occurs at a rate of 3% to 9% in the world's population (Shaywitz et.al. [1]). Thus, a mathematics instructor in primary or secondary school is likely to have students with dyslexia in their classrooms at one point in their career. Dyslexia does not have a cure and cannot be prevented, but through careful consideration of lesson creation an instructor can be proactive by making careful selections in their lesson design strategies. James Carrier states that 'learning disability researchers misconstrued their object of study, unexplained underachievement, interpreting it neurologically and ignoring classroom practices and events and the social forces shaping them as possible causes. As a result the theory masks societal forces as they affect academic performance (Carrier [2]). This research study examined how dyslexic and non-dyslexic students in a mainstream middle school classroom responded to dyslexic teaching methods.

2 Literature review

Dyslexia has its earliest recording in 1817, Professor Lardart of Montpellier wrote of his inability to read and write. Since Professor Montpellier's record, dyslexia still mystifies researchers as to its cause. Though, with mysteries come misconceptions. Having dyslexia has often been associated with mental retardation and brain damage, which there are no true correlations. In fact, dyslexia has it roots in two other disorders: alexia (loss of reading ability) and aphasia (loss of speech) (Huston [3]). One of the first documented cases of dyslexia was reported by Pringle Morgan in the *British Medical Journal* in 1896. Morgan wrote about a boy, Percy F., who had difficulty with both reading and writing language even though he was 'bright and of average intelligence' (Huston [3]).

In the 1940's the context of dyslexia broadened to include topics such as numeracy skills, interpretation of musical notations and mapping skills (Critchley [4]; Chinn and Ashcroft [5]). An experiment conducted by Joffe concluded that 60% of dyslexic subjects have some degree of difficulty with mathematical skills (Miles and Miles [6]). With the introduction of mathematical difficulties into the realm of dyslexia there were questions that arose about ways to teach dyslexics mathematics. To date there is no one prescribed method seen as superior for teaching dyslexics mathematics. That is counter to the areas of reading and writing in which the Orton-Gillingham approach has prevailed. Furthermore, there has been little research on the utility of dyslexic teaching methods to assist dyslexics and non-dyslexics with learning mathematics in mainstream classrooms.

This study explores four specific instructional methods that have been documented and recommended as helpful tools to teach dyslexics mathematical skills. These four methods were: 1 – ELPS, 2 – Six-Step, 3 – Learn by Example and 4 – Cooperative Learning. Each of these methods will be described in higher detail in the paragraphs that follow. The exploration of these different dyslexic teaching methods one hopes to discover ways to identify best practices for teachers.

The first method used in this study was the ELPS method. This name for this method is shortened for the steps a student using while working through mathematical problems. The E = Example, in this stage the teacher would present the student with concrete examples to create meaningful relationships between the mathematical concept and real world activities. The L = Language, in this stage the instructor would work on introducing the concept using the common mathematical terms. The P = Pictures, this stage focuses on introducing the mathematical concepts using pictures to make meaning. Finally the S = Symbols, in this stage the student begins to relate mathematical symbols to the concepts taught during the previous stages. Overall, this method intertwines students' experiences, language, mathematical symbols and meanings (Liebeck [7]).

The second method used in this study was the Six-Step Mastery method. The stages in this method are 1 – introduce the students to numerical words and numerical symbols they will use during the process of learning the mathematical concept, 2- the students will create a relationship between the mathematical symbols and words, 3- the students will focus on discussing the steps to work through a problem, 4 – the students will discuss working backward on a problem, that is given an answer the students can work back to the symbols. 5 – students use graphical representations to help them recall the procedure for working forward and backward to solve problems and 6 – the students will link both the symbols and their numerical value to each other. Overall, this method's focus is on student mastery of mathematical concepts through modelling, pictorial representations of the concept, application and communication (Chinn and Ashcroft [5], Newman *et al.* [8]).

The third method used in this study was known as the, 'Learn by Example method'. This method revolves around supporting materials given to students to teach an attribute of a particular problem, or group of problems (Miller *et al.* [9]). This method consists of two major components, supplying students with prescriptions of solving problems dealing with a particular mathematical concept, and counter-examples dealing with that same concept.

Final method used was known as the Cooperative Learning method. This method used student's physical interaction with mathematical manipulative to explore mathematical concepts. Students were placed in heterogeneous groups to work through problems together and share the ways in which they arrived at particular solutions to the problem. This method focused on using active learning, teaching, and student discourse in groups.

These lessons were implemented into a middle school classroom as part of the daily curriculum and used student perceptions and teacher's reflective journals to examine correlations between teacher perceptions of the lessons and students perception of the lessons.

There were two hypotheses tested in this study. The first hypothesis: the teacher's and the students' perception of the lesson would correlate. Thus, if a teacher perceived the lesson as being effective, the students should have also perceived the lesson as being useful and informative. The second hypothesis: there would be no differences in the perceptions of students in terms of the instructional methods used. This stems from the fact that each instructional method was a dyslexic teaching method, and has been documented as an effective way to teaching students with dyslexia in mathematics.

3 Method

3.1 Subjects

This study was conducted at a small private school on the West Coast of the United States. 20 mini-lessons were used over a six-week period. These lessons, no more than 15 minutes in length, used one of four instructional methods described in the literature review. In total there were 8 ELPS lessons, 6 Six-Step lessons, 3 Learn by Example lessons and 3 co-operative learning lessons.

The students' racial composition included 1 African American, 2 Asians and 14 Euro-American students. There were 7 girls and 10 boys in the classroom with 40% of the students having documented learning disabilities. In terms of academic level, there were 11 students in the 7th grade and 6 students enrolled in the 8th grade. Many students had been enrolled at this private school for at least 2 years, come from households with two working parents and have high socio-economic status.

3.2 Procedure

Each day during the six-week period, the students followed their traditional classroom activities. Students would walk into the classroom, sit at their seats, give the homework to the instructor and then have their notebooks open for a mini-lesson to introduce the mathematical concept for that nights' homework assignment. The instructor also followed the same patterns she had prior to the study, she would great the students, remind them to turn in their homework, take attendance, and then begin the mini-lesson. The research was conducted in March, and students had been in this routine since late August. The only items modified were the teaching methods used to teach the class.

At the conclusion of each lesson the instructor would walk to the main office to return the attendance sheet and write a reflective journal entry on how she felt the lesson was perceived by her students and any other information she felt was relevant to that day's lesson. Upon returning from the office, the instructor would walk around the room and record students' ratings for that day's mini-lesson.

Each mini-lesson was prepared two days prior to teaching the students. This was done for two reasons. First, sometimes the students in the classroom needed an extra lesson for reinforcement of a concept. Second, to ensure the students were not being subjected to a method that was hindering their mathematical abilities or perceptions of themselves.

At the start of the study, it was expected to have 5 lessons for each teaching method. Yet, difficulties with the Learn by Example method and instructor planning for the Cooperative Learning method that only 3 of each of those methods would be conducted. The researcher did not want to cause undue frustration to the students in the classroom or a feeling a failure amongst the students. Furthermore, the planning and implementation of the Cooperative learning method went beyond the time the instructor had available.

When the study was completed, a rubric was created to assign a value to the instructor's journals. This rubric was based upon the same criteria as the student's ratings recorded by the instructor. This ensured that the value assigned to the instructor's perception followed the same measures as the value the students assigned to each lesson. There were four persons that rate the instructor's journal; the researcher and three independent persons not associated with the study.

It was difficult to control for students missing classes, students arriving to class during the lesson, or even student's reactions to particular lessons. For example, only 7 of the 17 students were present during all 20 lessons. Though, the focus of this research study was to explore different types of instructional methods for learning disabled students and how students in a mainstream middle school classroom reacted to those methods. Furthermore, the study used the data collected above to observe if students enjoyed a particular method the teacher would enjoy it also, and which of the four types of lessons implemented into middle school classrooms were the most enjoyable for students to participate in.

4 Results

The results for this study are preliminary in nature. This stems for the fact that there was a small population being tested, and that only 40% of the students in the class had learning disabilities. Though the preliminary results that follow are important to begin understanding what types of alternative methods work well in mathematics classrooms.

The ratings for the teacher and the students were compared with a Spearman's rho (ρ) calculation. The hypothesis that the teacher's perceptions of the lessons (M = 2.43, SD = .6) would correlate with the students' perceptions (M = 2.20, SD = .41) was accepted at both p=.05 and p=.01 levels. Thus, the strength of the relationship between the teacher's perception and the student perception, this analysis yielded a significant relationship with ρ = .75.

Though, after further exploration of the data set, there was one lesson that appeared to be an anomaly: the first Learn by Example lesson. This lesson was unlike all the other lessons that transitioned between instructional methods. This particular lesson was a review lesson of the material learned in the prior five ELPS lessons. The instructor's journal revealed a classroom that was confused and bored, though the lesson scored a 2.31 student average and a 1.8 instructor average. Below is an excerpt from that journal entry that helps to justify the deletion of that lesson from the correlation calculations.

"The students appeared to be slightly confused by this lesson...They seemed to be distant from me. They didn't ask any questions today, and seemed very frustrated by the notes, they didn't understand why I wasn't giving them theory. I just couldn't believe the student's unwillingness to be involved with the lesson"

The perception rating by the students is in no way inappropriate using the rubric provided to the class (a rating of 2 represented the students had learned something and could see when to apply it in the future). Furthermore, the students' were using much more prior knowledge because of the ELPS lessons. Therefore, a second Spearman's rho was calculated without using the first Learn by Example lesson. There was a significant relationship at $p = .01$ with a Spearman's rho of .81. Thus, both analyses above show that the first hypothesis that the teacher's perceptions of the lessons were equal to that of the students was accepted.

There were several issues which arose during the analysis to test the second hypothesis: there would be no differences in the perceptions of students in terms of the instructional methods used. The first issue is the variation of content presented in the lessons. Topics being taught to the students ranged from introduction to geometry to calculating simple compound interest. Thus, the use of the instructor's journals became essential in making conclusions about the students' perceptions of the different types of lessons.

As stated earlier, there were issues as to the order in which the lessons were presented to the students. Though to assist in the exploration of the second hypothesis a one-way ANOVA was run on the students' ratings. The results revealed a significance of .041. A Duncan post-hoc was conduced using Harmonic Mean Sample of 4.174. This post-hoc revealed (significance = .75) that there were differences in the rating of the Learn by Example method and the other three teaching methods used in the study.

To further the exploration of the findings in the above ANOVA calculations, it was of interest to examine the instructor's ratings for each of the lessons to see if there were differences between her perceptions and the different teaching methods. When this one-way ANOVA was conducted it revealed a significance of .001 and the Duncan post-hoc revealing (significance = .39) the same results as the students; that is, the Learn by Example method was statistically different from the other three teaching methods.

One must be aware of the limitations to this study. It is difficult to use solely pure numerical tests to indicate the statistical significance of the relationships between the methods. Yet, with an examination of the instructor's journal a pattern was established. The Learn by Example method was given the lowest ratings by both the students and the instructor. Typical statements used in the instructor's journal when implementing these lessons were, *"the students were confused", "the students were frustrated", "they [the students] had blank expressions on their face", and "the students were bored out of their minds".* Though, ELPS, Six-step and the Cooperative Learning methods seemed to rate the highest with both the students and the instructor. The instructor does mention that those (ELPS, Six-Step and Cooperative) types of lessons are typical to her teaching styles. The instructor's reflections in her journal about these lessons were drastically different from the journals from the Learn by Example method. Entries included statements such as, *"the class was begging to come to the [chalk] board", "these questions allowed me to keep the students engaged",* and *"the students liked being able to talk their way through the problems".*

Overall, after examining both the quantitative and qualitative data the second hypothesis was rejected with a likelihood of having a type I level error. This is due to the limitations in the design and implementation of the study. Thus, it is likely that the students did not perceive the lessons as being equal.

5 Discussions and conclusions

This study was unique in the sense that it brought about an understanding of how teachers and students perceive mathematical teaching methods. It was also unique in the sense that the methods utilized were those designed to assist dyslexic students in learning mathematics. The population was a heterogeneous group of seventh and eighth grade students with and without learning disabilities, the classroom also consisted of students with varying levels of mathematical skills and doing homework from different textbooks. This mix of subjects makes it difficult to make concrete statistical conclusions as to what methods used above work best, but with the integration of the teacher's journals one can examine the extent to which methods seemed to work well for this particular group of students.

It came as no surprise that the ELPS method and the Six-Step method had the high ratings by both the instructor and the students. The instructor related her typical teaching techniques to this method. Furthermore, the reflective journals continually made reference to how the student enjoyed the lessons if the material was shown to be applicable to the students' lives and past experiences. At one point the instructor commented on the greediness of her students when conducting an ELPS lesson that used focused on calculating interest. Furthermore, the Cooperative method was also rated high by both the instructor and the students. This can be attributed to the instructor believing in social learning theory as a way to teach. At one point, the instructor's journal mentioned that one of the cooperative lessons the students were *"learning in a Vygotskian type of way"*.

Again, it is essential to state that the conditions in this study were not controlled to the extent that would be needed for the numerical data analyses to stand on their own in concluding the differences in teaching methods. Though, by showing that there were not statistical differences between the students' ratings and the teachers ratings, and with a high correlation between student and teacher ratings one can argue that the Learn by Example method could be a method that would not be the premier method to teach students mathematics.

There should be further studies done using the instructional methods described above but using an experimental design or a quasi-experimental design. This could lead a definite conclusion on the methods that work best for classrooms with both learning disabled and non-learning disabled students. Though, it is essential to continue research in this area to discover the best practices middle school teachers should use in there classroom, and to pin point a teaching method in mathematics which shows to be the most promising in teaching students with dyslexia.

References

[1] Shaywitz, Bennett A.; Shaywitz, Sally; S., Mark M. Growth Hormone and Prolactin Response to Methylphenidate in Children with Attention Deficit Disorder. Life Sciences, 46(9), 625. 1990.

[2] Carrier, J. Masking the Social in Educational Knowledge: The case of Learning Disability Theory. The American Journal of Sociology, 88(5), 948-947. 1993.

[3] Huston, A. Understanding Dyslexia: A practical Approach for Parents and Teachers. London: Madison Books. 1992

[4] Critchley, M. The Dyslexic Child. London: William Heinemann Medical Books Limited. 1970.

[5] Chinn, S., & Ashcroft, R. Mathematics for Dyslexics: A teaching Handbook. London: Whurr Publishers Ltd. 1993.

[6] Miles, T.R., & Miles, E. Dyslexia and Mathematics. London: Routledge. 1992.

[7] Liebeck, P. How Children Learn Mathematics: A Guide for Parents and Teachers. London: Penguin Books. 1994.

[8] Newmann, F., Brandt, R., Wiggins, G. An Exchange of Views on "Semantics, Psychometrics, and Assessment Reform: A Close Look at 'Authentic" Assessments. Educational Research: a publication of the American Educational Research Association. 27 (6), 19 – 22. 1998.

[9] Miller, S.; Mercer, C.; Dillon, A. CSA: Acquiring and Retaining Math Skills. A Systematic, Practical Approach to Teaching Basic Math Skills at the Concrete, Semiconcrete, and Abstract Levels. Intervention in School and Clinic, 20(2), 105. 1990.

[10] Pollock, J., & Waller, E. Day to Day Dyslexia in the Classroom. London: Routledge. 1997.

Tools for teaching molecular spectroscopy

M. Dalibart
LPCM, UMR 5803, Université BORDEAUX I, France

Abstract

From our experience in teaching molecular spectroscopy it appeared that specific teaching tools could be useful. We describe here self-training packages, instrument simulators and tools for classroom demonstration developed for this purpose and report on their usefulness for teaching various target groups: university students, chemical school engineers, and technicians during part time courses.

Keywords: self-training, self-assessment, e-learning, FTIR, UV, Raman, luminescence, optical spectroscopy, spectrometer simulator, classroom demonstration.

1 Introduction

Teaching spectroscopy means teaching several disciplines at the same time: chemistry, optics, classical mechanics, quantum mechanic, electronics and data processing. Many students have gathered some basic knowledge in these fields during their studies; it is nevertheless always difficult and time consuming to refresh memories. From our experience in teaching molecular spectroscopy to audiences such as university students at various levels, technicians, and engineers, it appeared that specific teaching tools might be useful for this purpose. They would be particularly useful for the in-house crash or part time courses nowadays often in demand. For this purpose, we have been working on self-training programs, spectrometer simulators and classroom demonstration software. Descriptions of these tools and reports on their introduction through teaching practices are presented in this paper.

140 The Internet Society: Advances in Learning, Commerce and Security

2 Description

2.1 Self-training software

The first self-training software was already written in the eighties, at the very beginning of FTIR spectroscopy. This was partly motivated by the fact that at that time FTIR spectrometers were too expensive for our teaching laboratory. However, we had received a donation of small personal computers (4 K memory, two 80 K floppies), the French "Goupil 3". Using BASIC and machine language, chaining programs and using one floppy as common memory, we were able to illustrate the concepts on which FTIR is based, i.e. Fourier transformation, resolution, sampling, aliasing, etc. This software was subsequently distributed by Bomem and Mattson, two FTIR manufacturers. A few years later, a special issue was made available under the European Program "COMETT II" Dalibart [1].

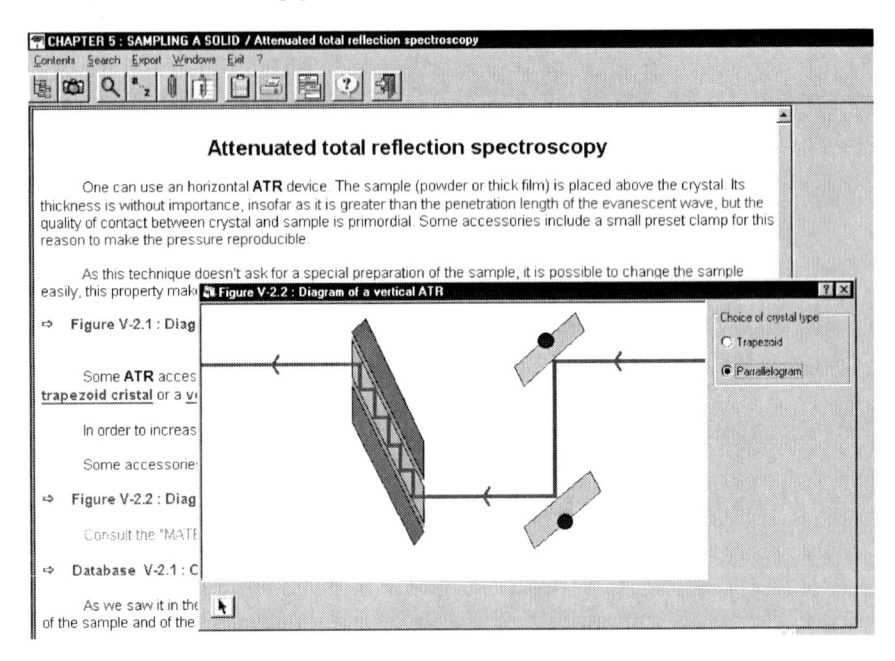

Figure 1:   A screen capture from ISIR.

Today, we make available more elaborate software Dalibart [2] which allows self-teaching in Fourier transform infrared spectroscopy (ISIR), photoluminescence spectroscopies (ISPL) and Raman scattering (ISR). Modules covering ultraviolet absorption are presently under development. In the near future, all molecular spectroscopy techniques will thus be covered. Besides molecular spectroscopy, a special package (IC) devoted to colour and colorimetry was also written. The packages are distributed by WinLab [3]. A demonstration package can be downloaded [4].

Each package includes modules for theory, instrumentation, and practice. Theory obviously includes some amount of revisited classical and quantum theory. The instrumentation part introduces interference, gratings, monochromators, the Michelson interferometer and also spectral sources, detectors and optical fibers. A large section is devoted to data treatment, introducing sampling, subtraction and specific spectral corrections. Numerous sampling methods for liquids, solids and gases are described. For example, in ISIR, we start from a simple KBr pellet, moving to more advanced methods like attenuated total reflectance, specular reflectance and diffuse reflectance. Reflectance theory, accessories and specific data treatments are included (see figure 1), chromatography and microscopy coupling are not forgotten.

More practical aspects such as spectral interpretation, spectral searching, and modern quantitative analysis are also covered extensively. Various databases dealing e.g. with instrument manufacturers, accessories dealers, optical properties of materials, and solvents are also supplied. Numerous web links are available through a mouse click.

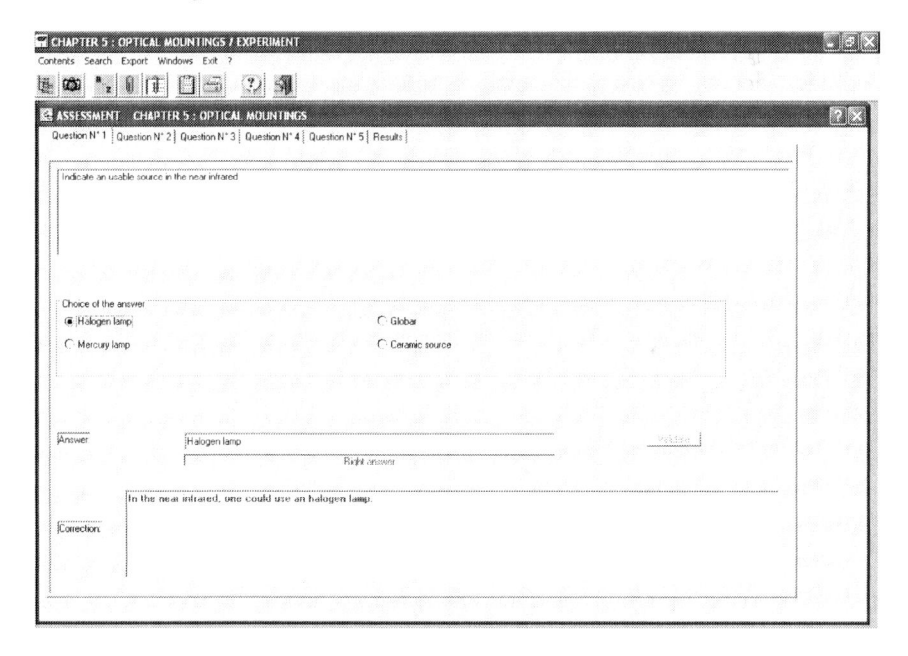

Figure 2: Self-assessment in action.

Each chapter contains lessons and a tutorial for experiments. A self-assessment is proposed to check the advancement of learning and the correct answers can be consulted (see figure 2). Being an e-book, the software makes use of navigation tools such as search functions, glossary and bookmarks. Thus, using these interfaces the user can access the desired topic instantly. Help is available through an email interface. In order to allow an easier understanding of this encyclopaedic content, numerous figures, applets and movies are used showing e.g. black body curves, vibrational modes of molecules and instruments in action. Two levels (a basic level and an advanced one) are available and the user can readily choose his own curriculum.

The ISIR and ISPL software was first used as a didactic support in classroom teaching. These packages have proven to be very efficient tools for teaching students. Tedious concepts such as Fourier transform or convolution product are easily illustrated. Movies showing vibrational modes of molecules such as acetone, nitromethane or benzene are more efficient that a descriptive text! Furthermore, this allows students to practice open lectures and to focus easily on specific problems.

Students at the Engineering School of Chemistry and Physics of Bordeaux (ENSCPB) are evaluated in spectroscopy on the basis a short oral presentation. Typical topics are e.g. ATR, diffuse reflectance, FFT, IR sampling methods, 3D fluorescence spectra, synchronous scanning etc. They can be easily researched by the student with the help of the software. It is true that on several topics a web search could yield similar results, but for a beginner it is quite time consuming to find the perfect query giving related links and only relevant links, not to mention language problems. ISIR and ISPL were also available in the spectroscopy teaching laboratory and some instructive projects have been elaborated using this software.

During in-house courses, technicians have been successfully instructed on molecular vibrations and Fourier transform. However, such people are often afraid to of the self-learning approach due to the encyclopaedic contents and want more guidance. Thus, we have undertaken to develop a new line of basic packages dedicated to applied spectroscopy for in-house use. A first version dealing with near-infrared and chemometry applied to quality control is under development. After a brief introduction to mid-infrared and near-infrared spectroscopies the specific instrumentation is presented. A third step is devoted to PLS data processing through chemometry: clustering and prediction.

The future of new learning leads to e-learning. Of course, updating and helping will be easier on-line, but at the present time, limited range web colours and access time required for such large movies are limiting this approach.

2.2 Spectrometer simulator

Nowadays a relatively cheap computer can be turned into another powerful tool: a spectrometer simulator. A tedious and time-consuming training is always necessary to acquire experimental skill. This is particularly true in the case of luminescence and Raman scattering since numerous artifacts are possible and the number of parameters to be optimized is very large. In this view, a spectrofluorimeter simulator Dalibart and Belin [5] appears to be a valuable tool to render this training easier and faster. After choosing a set of experimental parameters, the computer displays immediately the corresponding spectrum. The influence of all experimental parameters is simulated: monochromator slit width, excitation or emission wavelengths, xenon source type, photomultiplier tube high-voltage, etc. The nature of solvents with first and second orders Rayleigh and Raman scattering is taken into account. Sample geometries and concentrations with corresponding inner filter are also simulated. Obviously, there is no risk of damaging the virtual photomultiplier tube! Figure 3 exhibits a screen capture from this simulator.

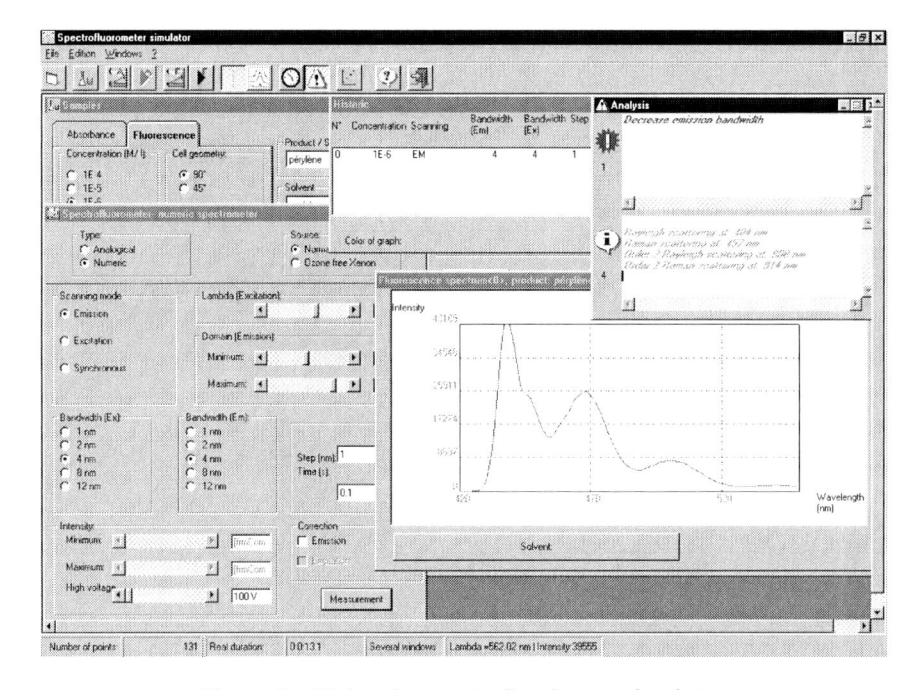

Figure 3: Using the spectrofluorimeter simulator.

2.3 Classroom demonstration

Computers are essential for modern spectroscopy. Unfortunately, experimental skills disappear concomitantly and the instrument appears as a black box. In order to demystify the instrumental layout, our last development is a software dedicated to low cost "Ocean Optics optical fiber spectrometers", allowing classroom demonstrations. Using a notebook, an usb spectrometer, a diode-laser, a linear variable filter, a halogen-deuterium source, some optical fibers, and a cell holder it is easy to build "real life" typical instruments and then to demonstrate how they work. Besides the spectrum window, the video frames coming from an usb webcam are displayed on the screen.

Figure 4 shows an ultraviolet-visible absorption spectrometer in action. Introducing a band filter and moving the collecting fiber to the 90° port leads to a spectrofluorimeter as shown in figure 5.

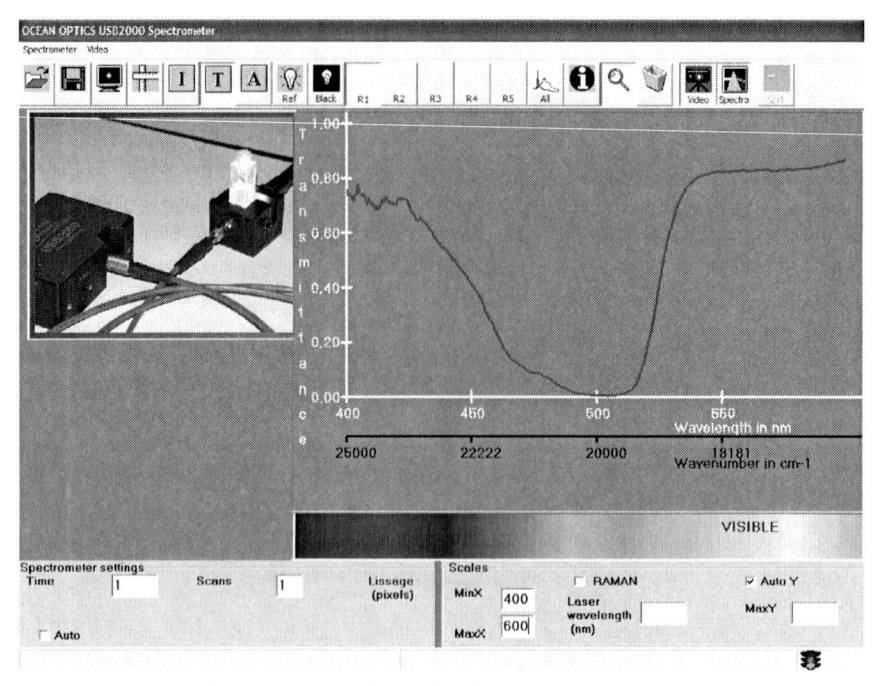

Figure 4: Manufacturing the UV spectrometer.

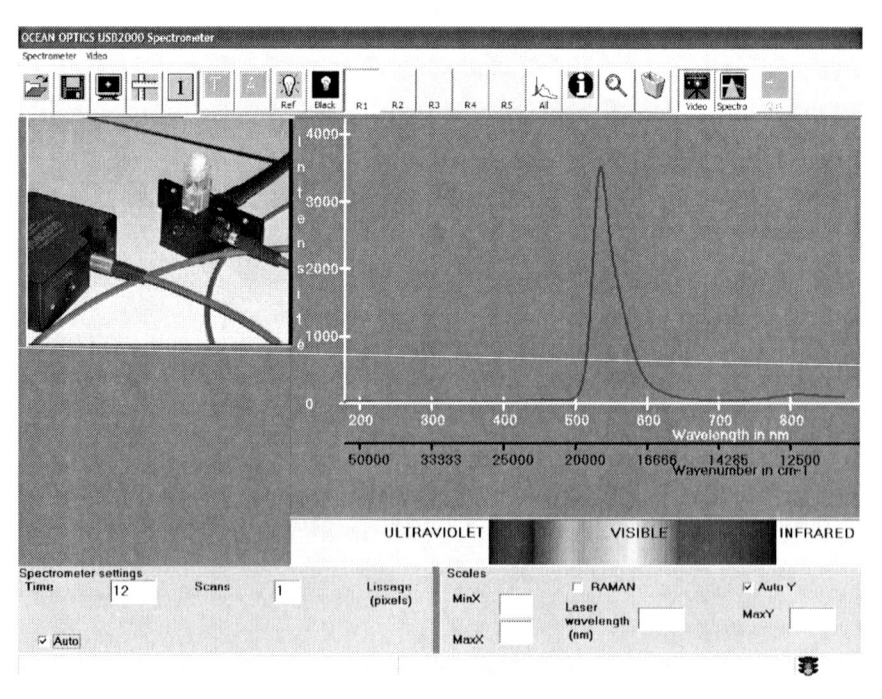

Figure 5: Demonstrating fluorescence.

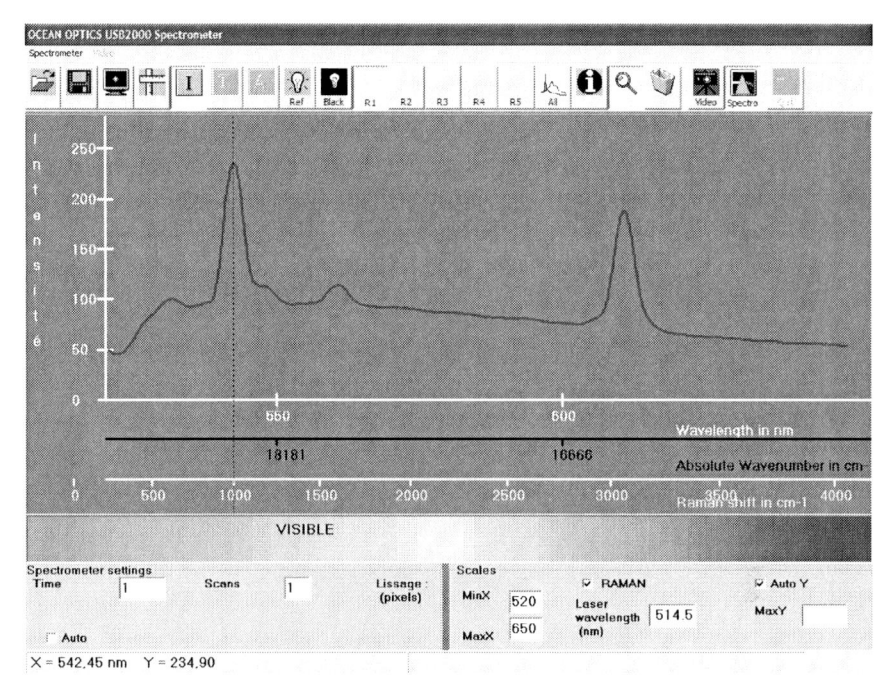

Figure 6: Demonstrating Raman scattering.

Finally, a Raman spectrometer can be manufactured if a (rather expensive) green (532 nm) solid laser or an ionised argon laser (514 nm) is available (see figure 6).

3 Conclusion

At the University of Bordeaux and at the Engineering School of Chemistry and Physics of Bordeaux (ENSCPB) we have introduced some didactic tools for spectroscopy in our teaching practices. These packages have proven to be efficient tools for teaching students in traditional classroom teaching and open lectures. Specific tools are currently developed for in-house course. Spectrometer simulators are efficient for acquiring experimental skill and may save money.

References

[1] Dalibart M., *Spectra 2000*, **185**, p17, 1995
[2] Dalibart M., A new package for teaching molecular spectroscopy, *J. Mol. Struct.*, **651-653**, pp787–789, 2003
[3] WinLab Instruments, 33 Avenue Gambetta, F-93170 Bagnolet, France,
[4] http://mrc.chem.tue.nl/countries/france/examples-F.htm
[5] Dalibart M. and Belin C., New tools for learning fluorescence: a spectrofluorometer simulator, *Journal of Fluorescence*, **10**, p 217, 2000

[6] Lerner J.M and Thevenon A., The Optics of Spectroscopy, *Jobin Yvon-Spex*, pp. 21, 25, 1988
[7] Marshall A.G. and Verdun F.R, Fourier Transforms in NMR, optical, and mass spectroscopy: A user's handbook, *Elsevier*, Amsterdam, pp. 38-56, 1990
[8] Perkanpus H-H., UV-VIS spectroscopy and its applications, *Springer-Verlag*, Berlin, pp. 220-22, 1992

Evaluation of CBT for increasing threat detection performance in X-ray screening

A. Schwaninger & F. Hofer
Department of Psychology, University of Zurich, Switzerland

Abstract

The relevance of aviation security has increased dramatically in recent years. Airport security technology has evolved remarkably over the last decade, which is especially evident for state-of-the-art X-ray screening systems. However, such systems will only be as effective as the people who operate them. Recognizing all kinds of prohibited items in X-ray images of passenger bags is a challenging object recognition task. In this article we present a method to measure screener detection performance based on signal detection theory. This method is applied to measure training effects resulting from individually adaptive computer based training (CBT). We have found large increases of detection performance and substantial reductions in response time suggesting that CBT is a very effective tool for increasing effectiveness and efficiency in aviation security screening.

Keywords: X-ray screening, computer based training, aviation security, object recognition, signal detection theory, training effectiveness.

1 Introduction

Working at an aviation security checkpoint is an important and demanding task. This is especially evident for the X-ray screener who has only a few seconds of inspection time to decide whether an X-ray image of a passenger bag is OK or needs to be manually searched (NOT OK). The X-ray screening task can be described as a signal detection situation in which prohibited items represent the signal and the remaining visual information in the X-ray image of the bag represents noise. Screener detection performance can be calculated using sensitivity measures from signal detection theory such as d', Δm or Az (Green and Swets [1], MacMillan and Creelman [2]). These measures are based on hit rates and false alarm rates and are relatively independent of response biases. This is of special importance for measuring detection performance in X-ray screening tests. If the false alarm rate is not considered, it is not possible to distinguish between good detection performance and a "liberal" response bias (Schwaninger [3]). This can be illustrated by a simple example (Schwaninger [4]). Let us assume that two screeners A and B take a test in which 200 X-ray images of passenger bags are shown and half of them contain prohibited items. Both screeners detect threat items in 90% of the cases (hit rate). When the bag contains no prohibited items, screener A judges bags as being NOT OK in only 11% of the cases (false alarm rate). In contrast, screener B has a false alarm rate of 78%. Whereas screener A has a high detection *performance*, screener B achieves a high hit rate *at the expense* of efficiency, which would result in substantially longer waiting lines at the checkpoint. This difference becomes apparent when detection performance is measured by $d' = z(H) - z(FA)$, whereas H denotes the proportion of hits and FA the proportion of false alarms. In the formula z denotes the z-transformation, i.e. H and FA are converted into z-scores (standard-deviation units). In the example mentioned above screener A would have a detection performance of $d' = z(0.90) - z(0.11) = 2.51$ whereas screener B has a $d' = z(0.90) - z(0.78) = 0.51$. In other words, detection performance of screener A is almost 5 times higher!

If a CBT system is effective, it should be expected that detection performance d' increases as a result of training. Moreover, if threat items are seen repeatedly during training it could also be expected that they become better represented in visual memory, which could result in faster response times.

However, several methodological considerations need to be taken into account in order to achieve reliable measurements of CBT effectiveness in terms of d' increases and response time decreases. Schwaninger [5] identified three image-based factors that influence X-ray detection performance. Threat items can be more or less superimposed by other objects (effect of superposition).

Second, the number and type of other objects in a bag challenge visual search and recognition processes such that threat items in more "complex" bags usually result in a lower detection probability (effect of bag complexity). Third, when objects are rotated away from the canonical view (Palmer et al. [6]) they usually become more difficult to recognize (effect of viewpoint). Since these effects have been shown to affect detection performance (Schwaninger [5]), image-based difficulty of X-ray images needs to be carefully controlled in a longitudinal study designed for evaluating CBT effectiveness. Moreover, display duration could be an important variable as well and should therefore be varied.

Finally, only X-ray images of bags and threat items that have not been seen during training should be used in order to measure CBT effectiveness reliably.

These considerations were taken into account using a pilot study, a pre-selection test, and a Latin Square counterbalanced design with four tests of equal difficulty and four groups of screeners with comparable average threat detection ability.

2 Method

The CBT used in this study was X-Ray Tutor, an individually adaptive training system based on object recognition and visual cognition (for recent reviews on these topics see Graf et al. [7]; Schwaninger [3]).

The main aim of the system is training object recognition by increasing the number and strength of view-based representations in visual memory. X-Ray Tutor is driven by software algorithms that monitor student performance and adjust images presented to provide threat types and bag difficulty needed for the student to learn and progress based on performance deficiencies. For further information see Schwaninger [8] and [9].

2.1 Pilot study

Threat images were created by combining X-ray images of improvised explosive devices (IEDs) with X-ray images of passenger bags using a customized TRX algorithm. In the pilot study, 4000 X-ray images were used, i.e. 2000 harmless bag images and 2000 threat images (125 IEDs * 16 bags per IED). Image difficulty was rated by eight expert screeners of Zurich Airport using a slider control (rating scale 0-100). Inter-rater reliability was estimated by calculating Cronbach's Alpha among raters. Alpha for IEDs (averaged across the 16 X-ray images) was .96. Alpha for X-ray images (without averaging) was .82. Images were ordered by average rated difficulty so that 16 difficulty levels were obtained per IED.

2.2 Training library

In the training system 64 of the 125 IEDs were used. Thus, the training library consisted of 1024 X-ray images containing a bag with an IED (64 IEDs * 16 bag difficulty levels) and 1024 harmless X-ray images showing the same bags without IED.

2.3 Participants

Seventy-two screeners (fifty female) at the age of 23.9 – 63.3 years ($M = 48.3$ years, $SD = 9.0$ years) took part in this study. None of them had received a special IED or computer based training before. These screeners were divided into four groups (group A: $N = 17$, group B: $N = 18$, group C: $N = 18$, group D: $N = 19$) as described in the next paragraph.

2.3.1 Grouping of participants
Prior to training, a pre-selection test was used to distribute the screeners among four groups of equivalent detection performance. To this end, 16 IEDs rated in the pilot study were used, which were not contained in the training library. Each IED X-ray image was combined with a bag image of medium and high difficulty (difficulty level 9 and 15 estimated in the pilot study as described in section 2.1). The entire pre-selection test consisted of 64 trials: 16 IEDs * 2 difficulty levels *

2 trial types (threat images vs. harmless bags). The order of image presentation was counterbalanced across screeners. The task of the screeners was to decide whether the presented luggage contained an IED or not. After each answer, they rated the difficulty of each image on a slider from 0 (very easy) to 100 (very difficult). Statistical analyses showed that the standardized ROC curve is best described by a linear trend, $R^2 = .93$, $p < .001$. Thus, the parametric detection performance measures Δm and d' (Green and Swets [1], MacMillan and Creelman [2]) could be calculated for each screener and four groups of comparable mean detection performance were created (Table 1). Three of the 72 screeners did not participate in this pre-selection test because they were not available during the period of testing which lasted 32 days (compare the number of screeners in Table 1 and section 2.3).

Table 1: Mean Δm, d' and their correlation, listed separately for each group of screeners. Values in parentheses represent standard deviations. All correlations (r) are significant with $p < .01$.

Groups of screeners	Δm	d'	r
Group A ($N = 16$)	1.58 (0.76)	1.75 (0.70)	.90
Group B ($N = 17$)	1.98 (2.14)	1.87 (1.02)	.89
Group C ($N = 18$)	1.63 (0.82)	2.07 (0.91)	.88
Group D ($N = 18$)	1.58 (0.73)	1.90 (0.88)	.84

A one factor ANOVA with group as between-subjects factor confirmed that the created groups were comparable in terms of their detection performance. There were no significant differences, neither for the Δm-values, $F(3, 65) = 0.40$, $p = .75$, nor for the d'-values, $F(3, 65) = 0.38$, $p = .77$. For both measures, no post hoc pairwise comparison between groups reached a statistic significant value (all p-values $> .25$).

2.4 Training blocks

The 64 IEDs used for training were distributed among four blocks of 16 IEDs so that all blocks were of comparable mean difficulty according to the difficulty ratings of the pilot study. One training block consisted of 512 images, i.e. 16 IEDs * 16 bags (difficulty levels) * 2 trial types (threat images vs. harmless bag images).

Standardized measures of difficulty ratings were subjected to one-way repeated measures ANOVA with training block as within-subjects factor. This analysis confirmed that the four training blocks were of equal difficulty. There was no effect of training block, $F(1.72, 12.04) = 0.47$; $MSE = 0.004$; $p = .94$ and pairwise comparisons between the training blocks showed no significant differences for any of the comparisons (all p-values $> .25$).

During training each IED was first presented in its easiest difficulty level. The order of IEDs was randomized across participants. The difficulty level was increased successively for each screener based on achievements in training (for more information on X-Ray Tutor see Schwaninger [8], [9]). Each training session was automatically terminated after 20 minutes.

The order of training blocks was counterbalanced across the four groups of trainees using a Latin Square design (see Figure 1). Between each training block the detection performance was measured in testing blocks.

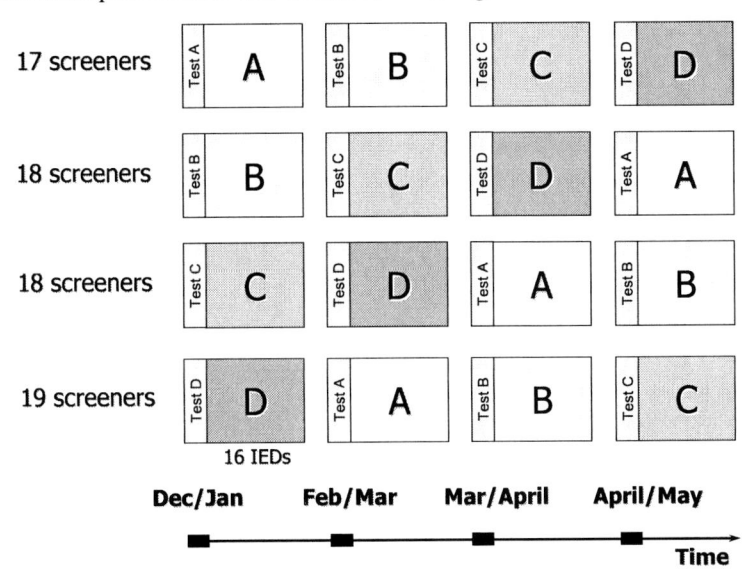

Figure 1: Latin Square design. A-D: Training blocks. Each training block consisted of 16 IEDs in 16 difficulty levels (bag images). Before each training block, a detection test containing the IEDs of the following training block was used to measure the training effects (see text for details). The study was carried out during six months starting December 2002 (see x-axis).

During training, each X-ray image was presented for a maximum of 8 seconds. Trainees had to decide whether the bag contains an IED or not by a clicking on one of two buttons. Subsequently, they judged the difficulty of the X-ray image from 0 (very easy) to 100 (very difficult) using a slider control. Screeners received immediate feedback to their answers. For X-ray images containing an IED the feedback messages were either "Threat detected" (hit) or "Threat missed" (miss). For innocent X-ray images the feedback messages were "False alarm" or "Bag OK" (correct identification of a harmless bag). In addition, an information window could be displayed which showed a labelled X-ray image and photograph of the IED.

2.5 Testing blocks

The participants were always tested using IEDs they had never seen before. This was achieved using testing blocks which contained the IEDs from the next training block (see Figure 1). At test, each IED was presented for 4 and 8 seconds in bags of the two highest image difficulty levels (15 and 16). As in training, each bag was also presented without the IED in order to obtain a better signal detection measure.

As in training, participants judged whether the presented luggage is NOT OK (contained an IED) or OK (contained no IED) and subsequently rated the difficulty of each X-ray image using a slider control.

All four tests consisted of 128 trials: 16 IEDs * 2 display durations * 2 difficulty levels * 2 trial types (threat images vs. harmless bags). The order of presentation was randomized. In contrast to the training blocks, no feedback and no additional information about the IEDs was available during tests.

3 Results

3.1 Descriptive statistics

There was a large increase in detection performance measured by signal detection d' (Figure 2a). In order to assess training effectiveness we calculated % increase values as compared to baseline measurement (first test results), averaging the two display durations. Relative detection performance d' was increased by 70.76% (Figure 2b). This is a remarkable effect if it is taken into account that on average screeners took only 28 training sessions during the six months period ($SD = 10$ TS). Moreover, for a subgroup of 52 screeners, who on average took 31 training sessions ($SD = 8$ TS), the training effect was even more pronounced; relative detection performance was increased by 84.46%!

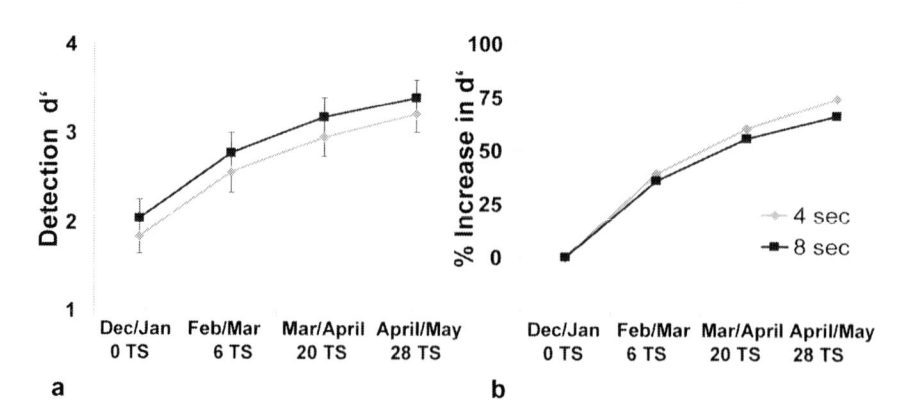

Figure 2: Absolute detection performance (a) and relative increase of detection performance (b) averaged across all 72 screeners. Display durations were 4 and 8 seconds. Error bars represent standard errors. TS = Number of training sessions.

3.2 Inferential statistics

Only significant effects are reported using the conventional cut-off of $p < .05$. Effect sizes η^2 are reported and can be judged based on Cohen [10].

3.2.1 Statistical analyses of detection performance d'

Mean detection performance d' at the four test dates of each group are shown separately for the two display durations in Figure 3.

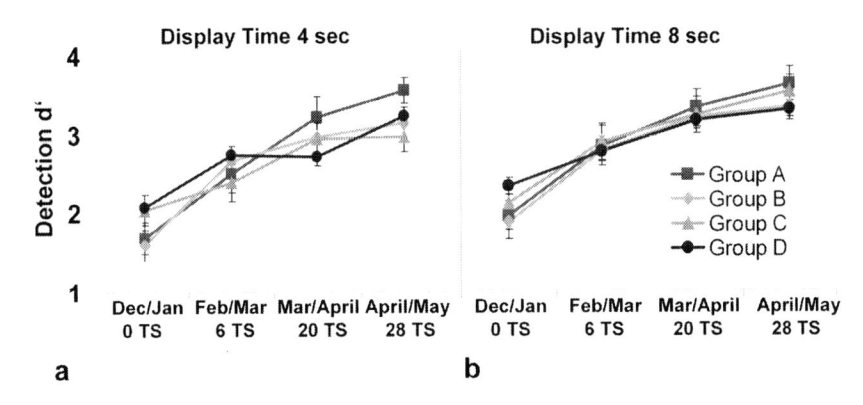

Figure 3: Detection performance d' of the four test dates for the four groups and the two display durations. Error bars represent standard errors. TS = Number of training sessions.

Again, the general training effect can be seen clearly. Detection performance d' of each group increased after each training block. A three-way analysis of variance (ANOVA) with the two within-subjects factors test date and display duration and the between-subjects factor group showed significant effects of test date, $F(2.81, 190.54) = 124.15$, $MSE = 0.44$, $p < .001$, and display duration, $F(1, 68) = 44.15$, $MSE = 0.14$, $p < .001$. With effect sizes of $\eta^2 = .65$ for test date and $\eta^2 = .39$ for display duration. The two-way interaction between test date and group was significant with an effect size of $\eta^2 = .10$, $F(9, 204) = 2.42$, $p < .05$. There was also a significant three-way interaction between test date, display duration and group, with an effect size of $\eta^2 = .09$, $F(9, 204) = 2.18$, $p < .05$.

In short, whereas the groups did not differ in their mean detection performance, there were slight differences in terms of how fast their detection performance increased across training when tested with 4 and 8 seconds of image presentation.

All Bonferroni-corrected pairwise comparisons between different test dates were significant confirming training effectiveness for the whole period of six months (all p-values $< .001$, with the exception of the comparison between test dates 3 (Mar/April) and 4 (April/May) with the p-value $< .01$).

3.2.2 Statistical analyses of reaction times

Figure 4 (top) shows reaction times for bags containing an IED separately for the four screener groups and the two display durations of 4 and 8 sec. Similarly, Figure 4 (bottom) depicts reaction times for harmless bags.

Only reaction times of correct responses were analysed. For threat images (bags with IED), a three-way ANOVA with test date and display duration as within-subjects factors and group as between-subjects variable showed a significant effect of test date, $F(1.71, 116.44) = 52.54$, $MSE = 1961145.60$, $p < .001$. The effect size was $\eta^2 = .44$. There was also a main effect of display duration ($\eta^2 = .57$), $F(1, 68) = 91.26$, $MSE = 476870.94$, $p < .001$. The two-way interaction between test date and display duration was also significant with $\eta^2 = .10$, $F(1.82, 123.72) = 7.30$, $MSE = 636920.93$, $p < .01$.

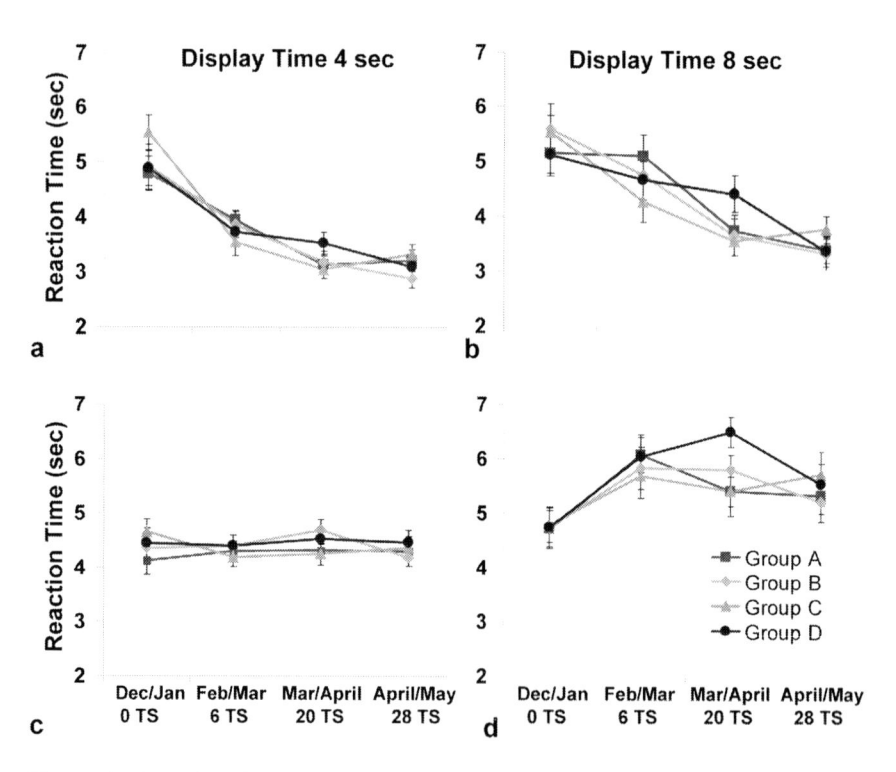

Figure 4: Reaction times of the four test dates for the four groups and the two display durations of 4 and 8 seconds. Top: Reaction times for bags containing an IED for 4 seconds (a) and 8 seconds (b). A clear decrease of reaction time was observed. Bottom: Reaction times for harmless bags for 4 seconds (c) and 8 seconds (d). Error bars represent standard errors. TS = Number of training sessions.

Bonferroni-corrected pairwise comparisons revealed significant differences for all comparisons between the reaction times of test dates (all p-values < .001, except for the comparison between test date 3 (Mar/April) and 4 (April/May) with $p < .05$). In short, response times for threat images decreased across training for all participant groups to a similar extend.

The same three-way ANOVA was used to analyze reaction times for harmless bags. Again, there was a main effect of test date, $F(1.99, 5.96) = 5.17$, $MSE = 2752802.22$, $p < .01$, with an effect size of $\eta^2 = .07$, which is much smaller than observed for threat images (see above). There was also a main effect of display duration ($\eta^2 = .74$), $F(1, 68) = 190.02$, $MSE = 901246.42$, $p < .001$, and a significant two-way interaction between test date and display duration ($\eta^2 = .28$), $F(2.49, 169.01) = 26.58$, $MSE = 463610.22., p < .001$.

Except for the comparisons between test date 1 (Dec/Jan) and 2 (Feb/Mar) and 1 (Dec/Jan) and 3 (p-values < .05) no Bonferroni-corrected pairwise comparison revealed significant differences between the reaction times of different test dates. Thus, in contrast to response times for threat images, there was no substantial reduction of response times for X-ray images of harmless bags.

4 Discussion

The aim of this study was to develop a method in order to evaluate effectiveness of CBT for increasing threat detection performance in X-ray screening. Signal detection measures take the hit rate and the false alarm rate into account and provide more valid and reliable measures of detection performance than the hit rate alone (Schwaninger [3], [4]). ROC linearity analyses revealed that parametric measures d' and Δm can be computed (Green and Swets [1], MacMillan and Creelman [2]). The two measures were strongly correlated as revealed in a pre-selection test that was used to create four groups of screeners with equivalent detection performance. Four tests of equal X-ray image difficulty were created based on difficulty ratings by eight expert screeners. Inter-rater reliability was sufficient suggesting that difficulty ratings could serve as estimates of objective detection performance.

A Latin Square counterbalanced design was used to measure CBT effectiveness in a longitudinal study of six months during which each screener took about 2 training sessions of 20 minutes per week. None of them had received a special IED or computer based training before. Only new X-ray images were used in the four tests in order to measure training effectiveness in terms of generalisation to new threat items. Remarkable increases in detection performance d' were observed. Relative increase in detection performance d' as compared to the first test was 71% after an average of 28 training sessions during the six months period. For a subgroup of 52 screeners, who on average took 31 training sessions, relative increase in detection performance d' was even higher, i.e. 84%.

Image display duration at test had a small but reliable effect. When images were displayed for 4 seconds, performance was a bit worse than for 8 second display durations. This effect remained relatively stable across the four tests conducted during the six months period.

More interesting was the decrease in response time for detecting threat items as a result of training. This finding is consistent with the assumption that individually adaptive CBT increases the number and strength of view-based representations of threat items in visual memory and thus could explain a reduction of detection time. Since no response time reduction was observed for harmless bag images, the learning effect indeed seems to be more related to visual memory representations than to increased general visual processing capacities.

In sum, the results of this study suggest that individually adaptive CBT is a powerful tool for increasing threat detection performance in X-ray screening of passenger bags.

Acknowledgements

We are thankful to Zurich State Police, Airport Division for their help in creating the stimuli and the good collaboration for conducting the study. This research was financially supported by Zurich Airport Unique.

References

[1] Green, D. M. & Swets, J. A., *Signal detection theory and psychophysics*, Wiley: New York, 1966.

[2] MacMillan, N. A. & Creelman, C. D., *Detection theory: A user's guide*, University Press: Cambridge, 1991.

[3] Schwaninger, A., Object recognition and signal detection. *Praxisfelder der Wahrnehmungspsychologie*, eds. B. Kersten & M.T. Groner, Huber: Bern, in press.

[4] Schwaninger, A., Evaluation and selection of airport security screeners. *AIRPORT,* **02**, pp. 14-15, 2003.

[5] Schwaninger, A., Reliable measurements of threat detection. *AIRPORT*, **01**, pp. 22-23, 2003.

[6] Palmer, S.E., Rosch, E. & Chase, P., Canonical perspective and the perception of objects. *Attention and Performance IX*, eds. J. Long & A. Baddeley, Erlbaum: Hillsdale, N.J., pp. 135-151, 1981.

[7] Graf, M., Schwaninger, A., Wallraven, C. & Bülthoff, H.H., Psychophysical results from experiments on recognition & categorisation. *Information Society Technologies (IST) programme, Cognitive Vision Systems – CogVis; IST-2000-29375*, 2002.

[8] Schwaninger, A., Training of airport security screeners. *AIRPORT,* **05**, pp. 11-13, 2003.

[9] Schwaninger, A., Computer based training: a powerful tool to the enhancement of human factors. *Aviation Security International*, in press.

[10] Cohen, J., Statistical power analysis for the behavioral sciences, Erlbaum: Hillsdale, New York, 1988.

The training environment support system: a system designed to enhance dynamic satellite operator training

H. B. Sorensen[1], K. Neville[2], C. Barba[2], R. Kellermann[3] & R. Andrade[3]
[1]U.S. Air Force Research Laboratory, USA
[2]CHI Systems, Fort Washington, USA
[3]Space and Missile Systems Center, Los Angeles, USA

Abstract

The introduction of advanced satellite technologies has necessitated the development of new satellite operations centers and, likewise, new training facilities. This paper describes the design of a training system that is intended to benefit simulation training facilities being developed to support emerging satellite operations capabilities. The objectives of this training system are threefold: (1) to increase training fidelity by emulating applications used in satellite operations but missing from the new training facilities; (2) to provide training support tools that will present trainees with explanation and guidance as well as dynamic support in the form of agent-based performance assessment and feedback; and (3) to provide an instructor operating station from which instructors can monitor and manage training.

Keywords: satellite operations, simulation-based training, agent technology, intelligent agent, training management.

1 Transformation in space operations

The U.S. military's strong foothold in space has given it a great advantage over the rest of the world. During recent operations in Iraq, for example, space-based capabilities enabled joint military communications; the control of uninhabited aerial vehicles (UAVs); precision-guided munitions; enemy launch detection; intelligence, surveillance, and reconnaissance (ISR); and more [1]. Warfighters benefited from and relied upon space capabilities in almost every aspect of their operations.

However, as the U.S. military ambitiously expands its space capabilities, the human component of space-based systems — the personnel who maintain and operate the systems — must advance at the same rate. The development of new space technologies gives rise to greater complexity in space operations, which increases the risk of human error. At the same time, growing reliance on space technology makes the repercussions of such errors much more grave and far-reaching. Further, if space becomes the battlefield of the future [2], space operations personnel may find themselves serving as frontline warfighters, which would increase not only the stress and complexity of space operations work but the consequences of human error, as well.

> *"Today space enables virtually everything we do."*
> *- Colonel Steven Fox, Director, Army Space Program Office, March 12, 2003*

Space operations personnel must receive training commensurate with the complex and critical work they perform. Training programs need to prepare them to think and react like warfighters. Operations personnel must be capable of responding effectively to time-critical events, coping with high workload and stress levels, and reacting to a wide variety of situations that may arise. In other words, training should prepare them to be adaptive and agile, a goal called out by the Air Force Space Command (AFSPC) strategic master plan for FY06 and beyond [3]. Adaptive expertise and agility typically depend on an accumulation of experience, the development of a repertoire of response strategies, and a deep comprehension of complex and dynamic concepts and relationships within a given domain [4,5]. Thus, the development of effective and agile space operations personnel would ideally involve training that provides opportunities to develop the core elements of adaptive expertise.

In reality, to produce mission-ready personnel in a minimal amount of time, satellite operator training tends to focus on the execution of procedures rather than on the knowledge underlying such procedures. For example, trainees who will work with the Space-Based Infrared System (SBIRS) learn the basics of managing satellite state of health (SOH) and then are assisted on-the-job by contract personnel who have had years of experience and are knowledgeable about satellite systems. The same training scenario will likely apply to the future Space Tracking and Surveillance System (STSS). USAF space operations would benefit, however, from more-knowledgeable and -expert operators. Reduced dependence on contract personnel may save money, but perhaps more importantly, having operators with greater levels of knowledge and expertise reduces the likelihood of an error and additionally improves the overall effectiveness of the operations. Basically, all operators in such a critical domain should understand what they are doing and why, and they should understand at as deep a level as possible given time and other resource constraints.

The work of space personnel is thus becoming increasingly critical to military operations. The costs of the space systems they manage are growing, and the cost of losing communications with any given satellite for even a short period of time is growing. Accordingly, while efforts are made to improve the capabilities of satellite technology, parallel efforts must be made to improve the training of space personnel. Ensuring the proficiency of space personnel during this period of rapid transformation is essential.

The SBIRS and STSS are examples of new space technologies that constitute major change. In this paper, we describe an effort to design technology that meets the training needs of operators working with these technologies in the mission control station (MCS). The goals of this effort are threefold: to contribute needed basic training resources; to provide trainees with support tools to enhance learning; and to provide instructors with support tools to enhance training management. In the paragraphs that follow, we elaborate on the basic training needs that this training system hopes to fulfill.

2 Fulfilling basic training needs

Simulation training facilities for satellite operations crews exclude certain system applications that are used by operators in the MCS. Consequently, certain procedures must be skipped or pantomimed by trainees. In the SBIRS integrated training suite (ITS) excluded applications include:

- a space weather reporting application;
- the New Tactical Forecast System (N-TFS) for terrestrial weather warnings;
- the Electronic Scheduling Dissemination (ESD) system to be used to schedule unanticipated commanding sessions; and
- an email application called the Defense Message System (DMS).

In the SBIRS and STSS domains, as in others, operators and training personnel have stated the requirement that simulation-based training facilities mirror the operations center. This parallelism makes it possible for personnel to practice complete procedures from start to finish in the training environment. As a result, they are able to perform those procedures during real world operations without utilizing significant cognitive resources. In other words, those procedures become automatized or proceduralized and more cognitive resources are available for dealing with other aspects of task performance. This allows the operator to devote cognitive resources to the many other tasks they have to perform. Further, interacting with these particular support applications in a training environment will allow operators to develop knowledge and expertise about, for example, space weather, orbital mechanics, scheduling, resource constraints, and the network of organizations with which they interact (e.g., via the DMS).

In addition, inclusion of the support applications listed above in training facilities is needed to support mission ready (MR) qualification training, upgrade and requalification training, and proficiency training. Specifically, a number of SBIRS job performance requirement lists (JPRLs) are associated with use of those support applications and specify tasks and procedures that are not currently supported by SBIRS simulation-based training facilities. In addition to reducing the quality of training, this mismatch between job requirements and training resources can potentially create a serious staffing shortage if it delays the MR certification of needed personnel. Furthermore, personnel do not become as proficient at performing tasks in the absence of associated training resources as they would otherwise. Without these support applications, SBIRS training facilities do not support acquisition of basic job requirements and, by implication, do not prepare trainees to perform their jobs as proficiently as they could.

3 Training system design approach

To address shortcomings of simulation training facilities for satellite operations, we have developed an initial design for a training system that will augment and enhance simulation-based training. This training system will emulate missing applications described in Section 2 as well as trainee and instructor support tools. To design the system, a training requirements analysis was conducted to identify training requirements such as JPRL proficiencies and the need to develop task performance routines that span the use of multiple systems. In addition, survey data were obtained from satellite operations subject matter experts (SMEs). These data suggested that SBIRS simulation-based training would benefit from support tools that help instructors:

- detect trainee errors,
- provide trainees with one-on-one attention and guidance, and
- tailor or select scenarios to better meet the training needs of various groups of trainees

In addition to using the identified training requirements to design this training system, the training environment and the ways in which satellite operations training is conducted were considered. There are two major challenges associated with the training environment that the training system design must address. The first of these is the technology currently used to run and store exercise scenarios. The training system will need to be able to used in a synchronized manner with existing training suite workstations during simulation training exercises. The second challenge has to do with limitations on the way training can be presented during real time simulation exercises. For example, real time expert advice, context-specific explanation, and feedback associated with error detection were all identified as useful training resources, but each must be implemented it in a way that does not interfere with time-pressured task performance.

To meet these challenges and address all identified design considerations adequately, the initial training system design, described below, will be subject to additional design iterations based on feedback from SBIRS training personnel and technical staff. Feedback will be obtained on multiple iterations of this design and subsequently on iterative versions of the functional training system once the implementation stage of development is reached. Our goals in these iterative feedback sessions are primarily to:

- educate SMEs about the approach and technology we are utilizing so they can better evaluate the system and make informed suggestions and
- obtain SME feedback about the training system design and functionality.

4 Training system design

In this section, we describe the initial design of the training system we are developing to augment and enhance simulation-based training for SBIRS and STSS personnel. This system, called the Training Environment Support System, or TESS, has the primary objectives of providing personnel with:

- the opportunity to perform tasks during training in the same way they would perform them during real world operations;
- opportunities to learn how to interact with support systems and use their information in a training environment rather than on the job; and
- experience responding to alerts and warnings generated by those support systems.

TESS is intended to augment simulation-based training by providing clones of support applications that are used during MCS operations– namely, the DMS, N-TFS, ESD. TESS is furthermore designed to enhance simulation-based training by providing trainees and instructors with training support tools and resources. The instructor application will feature instructor support tools including scenario development, trainee performance monitoring, and training management tools.

The TESS training application would be installed on a single PC within each training facility, and this PC is to be networked with the system on which the TESS instructor application resides. This latter system may reside on the instructor system currently used to manage training, or it may be an adjacent system that is networked to the existing instructor system. TESS furthermore would be integrated with other training suite workstations. This would allow TESS to detect and react to changes in the simulation environment, such as the occurrence of a satellite anomaly. In addition, it would allow TESS to track and adapt to the progression of the exercise scenarios. As described in more detail below, a performance support toolkit called the Agent-based Decision Enabling and Proficiency Toolkit (ADEPT) that is being developed by CHI Systems for use by satellite systems crews may be integrated with TESS to facilitate the linkage with the training suite workstations.

4.1 The TESS training application

The TESS training application design specifies two modes of use. Specifically, the application may be used in *basic application mode* to provide trainees with high fidelity versions of the MCS applications and thereby a more complete operational context. Alternatively, a user can toggle to the *training support mode*. In the training support mode, the cloned applications are reduced to one-third of the display so that the training support environment may be expanded.

This training support mode is intended to expedite the development of proficiency with the MCS support applications contained within TESS. It is also designed to help trainees acquire a 'bigger picture' understanding of when and how to use the cloned support applications, including an awareness of the sometimes subtle relationships among the applications (e.g., a space weather alert may necessitate a schedule change request due to the loss of an asset caused by a geomagnetic anomaly). TESS trainee support tools and resources available to trainees when TESS is used in the training support mode will include the following:

- *TESS cognitive agent* – the TESS cognitive agent will track and assess trainee performance.
- *TESS cognitive agent output* – trainees will be given real time feedback on their performance as well as context-sensitive explanations and guidance.
- *Managed Exploratory Learning (MEL)* – TESS will, via the TESS cognitive agent, provide expert mentoring and guidance that is tailored to the current situation within an ongoing training exercise. Guidance will change based on whichever clone application is active.
- *Adaptive Decision Enabling and Performance Tracking (ADEPT) decision support tools* – ADEPT is a decision support toolset CHI Systems, Inc. is developing for satellite operators to use in the MCS as part of a Phase II SBIR effort. Reusing the ADEPT application in training facilities by integrating it with TESS will give trainees access to the ADEPT tools, including the:
  - *AWE tool* – trainees can access this tool to view a prioritized list of alerts, warnings, and events (AWEs). Among other things, AWE codes are defined, time limits on time critical AWEs are given, and course of action recommendations are provided.
  - *Messaging tool* – this tool will allow instructors to give trainees individualized attention and guidance.
  - *Satellite position viewing tool* – this visualization tool provides trainees with a 3-D view of satellite locations relative to the sun, earth, moon, penumbrae, and umbrae, and facilitates understanding orbital mechanics.
- *Self-directed training tool* – when TESS is used in standalone mode, trainees can choose from a categorized list of training events that are specific to the TESS clone applications, and train using TESS in the absence of an instructor or when personnel are not available to support a full training exercise.

4.2 The TESS instructor application

The TESS instructor application will be used to give instructors tools and resources to help them manage training sessions. The TESS instructor application features five primary modes of use – automated, manual, scenario editor, analysis, and help. It is designed to provide varying levels of automated control over the execution of a training session, and additionally offers manual control for situations in which automated control is not desired. The proposed set of instructor support tools to be provided within the TESS application include:

- Scenario management tools, including:
    - *Automated scenario controls* – instructors will be able to select and launch predefined scenarios from a menu. Each scenario will be associated with a script that may be edited and printed.
    - *Scenario development controls* – instructors will use these controls to organize multiple training events into a single training scenario and script. These controls will include a scenario development filter that will allow instructors to view and select from training events that are associated with a particular training objective. Example objectives include various JPRs, skills such as proactivity, crew coordination, and 'comm' discipline, and proficiency using various applications.
    - *Manual event insertion controls* – instructors will be able to insert events into the training environment one at a time instead of using scenario controls to present a predefined series of events.
    - *Event editing controls* – these controls allow instructors to tailor selected events with respect to, for example, severity, satellite system affected, ground system affected, start time, and duration.
- *Training session viewer* – this tool allows instructors to view time-stamped interactions between the trainee and the TESS clone applications during scenario execution, as observed by a TESS cognitive agent. The tool additionally features the detection and report of trainee errors by a cognitive agent.
- *Messaging tool* – this tool, made available via the ADEPT toolkit mentioned above, will allow instructors to give trainees individualized attention and guidance.
- *Performance evaluation capabilities* – instructors will have the ability to specify performance measures to be collected for a given event using the event editing controls. These measures will be collected using the TESS cognitive agents and the results will be entered into a database and subsequently accessed by the TESS instructor application that instructors will use to develop and print training summary reports for training exercise participants.

5 Conclusions

This paper describes the design of a training system developed to augment and enhance the simulation training facilities of satellite operators. Space operations are rapidly advancing and transforming, and these changes pose a constant challenge to training effectiveness. It is especially challenging to adapt training to fundamental changes in the complexity, stress, and degrees of freedom in the operational environment. It is our hope that this training system design and subsequent development effort will provide a vehicle for upgrading training technologies and introducing tools that will facilitate simulation-based training from both the instructors' and the trainees' perspective. Future work will involve working with space operations training personnel to iteratively refine the functionality and user interface design of TESS, and then to iteratively develop the training system.

References

[1] Bosker, A.J., *Space is the ultimate high ground.* Spacedaily Website, http://www.spacedaily.com/news/milspace-03p.html, June 4, 2003.

[2] Zakaria, T. *U.S. General sees space as future battlefield.* Survivability/Vulnerability Information Analysis Center (SURVIAC) website:http://www.bahdayton.com/surviac/e-news/PDF/CGSC_Space_News_03-43-28Oct03.pdf, October 28, 2003.

[3] Air Force Space Command (AFSPC). *Strategic master plan: FY06 and beyond*, Peterson Air Force Base, Colorado, 2003.

[4] Holyoak, K. J., Symbolic connectionism: Toward third-generation theories of expertise (pp. 301-336). *Toward a General Theory of Expertise*, eds. K. A. Ericsson & J. Smith, Cambridge University Press: Cambridge, England, 1991

[5] Kozlowski, S. W.J., Developing adaptive teams (pp. 115-154). *Making Decisions Under Stress: Implications for Individual and Team Training*, eds. J. A. Cannon-Bowers & E. Salas, APA: Washington, DC, 1998

Content management systems for e-learning: an application

A. Cucchiarelli & S. Valenti
DIIGA - Università Politecnica delle Marche, Via Brecce Bianche, 60131 Ancona, Italy

Abstract

This paper discusses our approach to the tailoring of an open source Content Management System to use it as a Learning Content Management System, by providing modules for the management of Learning Objects and for their retrieval and indexing via Metadata. Both the description of what a Content Management System is and the key requirements that a Learning Content Management System must posses will be presented in the paper. Then, a working definition of Learning Object will be provided, and finally we will show how this model can be implemented using MD-PRO.
Keywords: content management systems, learning content management systems, learning objects, MD-Pro.

1 Introduction

In the last few years, one of the main interests of the researchers in e-Learning has been the development of sophisticated frameworks for the storage and the deployment Learning Material. Eventually, this research led to the development of powerful Electronic Learning Environments such as WebCt, Blackboard, Lotus Learning Space and many others more. Currently, it is becoming clear that an e-Learning system comprises three main components: a Learning Management System, a Learning Content Management System (LCMS) and a Virtual Class [7]. According to recent reports from industry analysts as IDC, WR Hambrecht & Co and Gartner Group, LCMSs represent the next big wave in e-Learning [3].

An LCMS is a Content Management System (i.e. a system that supports the creation, management, distribution, publishing, and discovery of information) tailored for e-Learning applications.

This paper is aimed to discuss our approach to the tailoring of an open source Content Management System [8] to use it as a LCMS, by providing modules for the management of Learning Objects and for their retrieval and indexing via Metadata. Thus, we discuss our design approach for the implementation of such modules, in the realm of the existing international standards [2, 4].

2   Content management systems

A Content Management System (CMS) is able to support the creation, management, distribution and publishing of contents [11]. It covers the complete lifecycle of the pages on a Web site, by providing tools ranging from their creation through their publication. It also provides the ability to manage the structure of the site, the appearance of the published pages and the navigation provided to the users.

The key goal of a CMS is the increased integration and automation of the processes that support efficient and effective Web delivery.

The functionality of a content management system can be broken down into four main categories: content creation, content management, publishing and presentation.

Content Creation. At the front of a CMS there is an easy-to-use authoring environment designed to work as a common word processor. This provides a non-technical way of creating new pages or updating content, without having to know the HTML language. A typical CMS also allows the structure management of the site that is where the pages go, and how they are linked together. Many systems even offer simple drag-and-drop restructuring of the site, without breaking any links. Almost all CMSs now provide a web-based authoring environment, able to further simplify implementation that allows content updating to be done remotely. This authoring tool is the key to the success of the CMS: by providing a simple mechanism for maintaining the site, authoring can be devolved out into the content itself.

Content Management. Once a page has been created, it is saved into a central CMS repository. All the content of the site, along with the other supporting details is stored in such repository, which allows a range of useful features to be provided by the CMS:

- keeping track of all version of a page, and who changed what and when;
- ensuring that each user can only change the section of the site they are responsible for;
- integration with existing information sources and IT systems.

Most importantly, the CMS provides a range of workflow capabilities to track the evolution of a document from the creation by the author, to the approval of the manager to its publishing by the central web team. At each step, the CMS manages the status of the page, notifying the people involved and escalating jobs as required. In this way, the workflow capabilities allow more authors to be involved in the management of the site, while maintaining strict control over the quality, accuracy and consistency of the information.

Publishing. Once the final content is in the repository, it can be published out to the web site. CMSs boast powerful publishing engines that allow the appearance and page layout of the site to be applied automatically during publishing. It may also allow the same content to be published to multiple sites. The CMS lets also the graphic designers and web developers specify the appearance that is applied by the system. These publishing capabilities ensure that the pages are consistent across the entire site, and enable a very high standard of appearance. This also allows the authors to concentrate on writing the content, by leaving the look of the site entirely to the CMS.

Presentation. The CMS can also provide a number of features to enhance the quality and effectiveness of the site itself. These features are usually carried out by "modules" that are typically add-ons to the core CMS, sometimes integrated as part of the base system, and can vary greatly from one system to another. The presentation layer also makes it easy to support multiple browsers, or users with accessibility issues. The CMS can be used to make the site dynamic and interactive, thereby enhancing the impact over the users, and even if the content providers are not creative or artistically challenged, there are a plenty of resources around to help them. They come in the form of templates and themes designed by more creative minds, and can be downloaded and added to the site, giving a complete makeover to it. Some of the best CMSs even allow the registered user to pick up and choose the "skin" or theme of the site. Sometimes this is referred to as "personalization", and it adds an element of flexibility for both the user and the site manager. Users will be pleasantly surprised by the ability to customize their "view", and the site manager get credit for setting up an environment where users have more control, without breaking or reprogramming the structure of the site.

So far, we focused on the creation of HTML content for websites. While this is the strongest aspect of most CMSs, many can do much more. Central to the power of many systems is the concept of "single source publishing", where a single topic can be published automatically into different formats. This could include printed formats (PDF, Word, etc.), wireless/PDA formats (WAP, etc.), or XML.

3 From CMSs to LCMSs

One of the emerging application domain of CMS technology is e-Learning. In this field, the new term LCMS has been coined. LCMSs are CMSs used to manage content in the form of learning objects to serve the needs of individuals [5]. Note that in this context, we will consider the instructional designers and the teachers as the target users of the LCMS, while the learners will be the main users of both LMSs and Virtual Classes.

With LCMSs it is possible to create libraries of Learning Objects (LOs) that can be used either independently, or as a part of larger instruction sets. Just like in a CMS there would be workflow processes around a LCMS too:

- Instructional designers would create either new LOs targeting specific performance goals, or new courses by assembling already created LOs;

- Editors would view the submitted LOs and either approve or reject them. If approved, the LOs would be made available to all to use, otherwise they would be sent back for revision;
- Personalization rules would set in, targeting the new LOs to those who fit (or, have subscribed to) its profile;
- LOs that have outlived their usefulness would either be backed up and archived, or just deleted from the repository [9].

For instructional designers, the idea of LOs requires a small but immense change in thinking: learning is no more considered as linear processions with beginning, middle and end, but as clusters of independent, stand alone chunks of knowledge. They are certainly related to each other and they may be viewed together, but they may also be viewed singly. Just as anyone can enter a web site at any page and leave at any point, so too can learners. They can come in at nearly any point in the training, stay as long or as short as they wish and leave either when they are bored or when they have learned what they want. Chunks of knowledge may be used in dozens of different trainings for different people. Designers will now develop instructional goals, piece together knowledge chunks based on those goals and develop clear navigation. A much greater emphasis must be placed on developing clear instructional goals, for it will be these goals which guide what should be offered. In addition, navigation becomes crucial. Trainings must be developed to allow, indeed to help the learner get to exactly the point they wish, and then helping them learn and understand that exact piece of information, knowing that once they get what they want, they will leave.

According to the above goals it is clear that a LCMS moves beyond the simple content authoring, storage and delivery to include [12]:

- *Support for reuse.* Every piece of knowledge within the LCMS must be stored as a reusable learning object - a chunk of distinct knowledge that can be kept as a resource for content designers within the LCMS, or delivered as a stand-alone object. This enables organizations to gain leverage and consistency of knowledge, while reducing redundant and contradictory knowledge across the enterprise.
- *Administrative applications.* The LCMS must be able to function as a stand-alone system that manages enrollment and progress of learners, as well as course content, timing, and tracking.
- *Assessment tools.* In order to link learning to individual performance, the LCMS must assess the learner's prior knowledge and what he/she learns from a particular LO. Robust management and reporting features that analyze the effectiveness of courses and individual learning objects must be available. The system should be able to accommodate multiple assessments of varying levels of difficulty and security.
- *Security.* Due to the proprietary nature of content within an LCMS, the system must contain robust security and encryption mechanisms to protect content and user data. A secure set of user privileges (which determine permission levels that users need to control, manage, and update content) must be provided.

- *Open interface with external systems.* In addition to serving as a stand-alone application, the LCMS must interface effectively with external systems, including the ability to download user and application domain information and upload performance and completion data.
- *Facilities for content migration.* Most organizations maintain a body of proprietary knowledge and learning content in a wide variety of file formats. The ability to rapidly re-purpose content for online use can accelerate deployment times, therefore, the LCMS must offer easy-to-use conversion tools.

All the above characteristics can be satisfied by using a proper CMS, tailored to manage content in the form of learning objects and to act on them by using specific functional elements (modules), able to extend its basic functionalities of content creation and management, publishing and presentation.

4 Learning objects

In this paper we use the term Learning Resource (LR) to address "any digital resource that can be used to support learning". This definition limits our interest to digital resources only, as f.i. figures, tables, pictures, HTML pages, presentations and so on.

A Learning Object is a digital object that complements a LR by including Metadata and an explicit representation of a Learning Design.

Metadata represents the key to resource discovery, to effective use of resources and to interoperability across protocol domains. According to the IEEE Learning Technology Standards Committee [4] metadata is information about an object, be it physical or digital. Thus, metadata contain all the instructional characters of every LO along with the complete information on their physical location The structure of Metadata inside our system has been chosen coincident with the one proposed by IEEE [4]. Other standardization initiatives are converging on the same model as for instance ARIADNE (www.ariadne-eu.org) and PROMETEUS (www.prometeus.org).

The Learning Design is composed by a Metacognitive Framework and by some Navigational Aid that will be used to support the learner in the exploitation of the LO (fig. 1).

The Metacognitive Framework is originated by the current research on metacognition. Metacognition refers to high order thinking which involves active control over the cognitive processes engaged in learning. Teaching metacognitive skills must be one of the goals of instruction, so that the learners have a bundle of strategies that will encourage significant learning, i.e. the process by which a learner puts new information in relation with existing knowledge. In this view, we define a metacognitive framework as a manifest that must be defined for every LR to transform it, along with some additional information, in a LO.

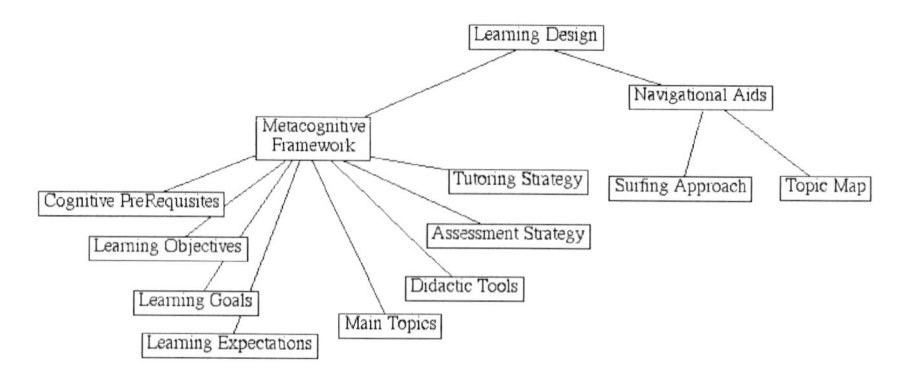

Figure 1: The structure of the learning design.

The Metacognitive Framework is composed by the following items: Cognitive PreRequisites, Learning Objectives, Learning Goals, Learning Expectations, Didactic Tools, Main Topics, Assessment and Tutoring Strategy.

The *Cognitive PreRequisites* describe the knowledge and the skills that the learner must possess in order to gain access to the different entry points of the LR that is encapsulated by the LO. In fact, if the LR is complex, as for instance a composite unit or a course [2] it is possible to predefine different entry points of the same material according both to the background knowledge and to the skills owned by the learner. The background competence may be elicited though a placement assessment that must referenced in the assessment strategy, and included along with the LR to complete the LO.

The *Learning Objectives* describe the purposes for which a given educational path has been designed and the targets that the learner is expected to reach. This item is mandatory since it allows the learner to explicitly associate the attribute of metacognition to an educational path. In fact, the declaration of the learning objectives allows the learner to understand why, to what extent and under which perspective the topics are covered in the LO.

The *Learning Goals* describe the goals that led to the development of the LO in its current form. This item is mandatory to allow the learner to reach a better/deeper understanding of the material and to place it in a wider framework of significant learning without limiting its pure learning objectives.

Learning Objectives and Goals allow to make a distinction between the competence that the learner will be asked to show at the end of an educational path without any concern of what has happened during its progress (Objectives), from the results that the teacher/organization responsible for the learning material wants to obtain from the learning process (Goals).

The *Learning Expectations* describe the results to be attained by the learner at the end of the use of the LO, expressed in terms of cultural goals, cognitive expectations, skills and operational abilities. This item allows the learner to gather a better understanding of what she is supposed to know on completion of the educational path.

The *Main Topics* describe the arguments covered by the LO, and provide details on their organization, structure, timeline, interleaving. The explicit description of the topics covered by the LO allows to provide the learner with continuous cognitive reinforcement and to drive her throughout the educational path.

The *Didactic Tools* describe the tools that will be used inside the LO, as f.i. compilers of programming languages, simulation packages, virtual-reality environments, laboratory instruments, robots and so on. The description of the styles used for the presentation of the topics covered, represent a natural add-on of the didactic tools adopted. This includes descriptive, narrative, persuasive, or expositive approaches along with interactive, dialogic or sequential forms of delivery of the material.

The *Assessment Strategy* describes the policies that will be used to evaluate the attainment of the learning objectives. As a side effect, this item allows the learner to infer which results will be met by the accomplishment of the LO, thus making explicit the competence or skill gain provided by the educational path.

The *Tutoring Strategy* describes the policies that will be used to support the student in the use of the learning material. This may range from the simple provision of Frequently Asked Questions or Searchable Knowledge Bases to the description of the duties and activities that a human tutor will perform during the availability period of the LO.

Finally, the *Navigational Aids* have been included to provide some indication to the learners on how to traverse the LR. The Navigational Aids include a Topic Map that allows the learner to clearly identify the point in which a given topic is discussed and the organization and structure of the topics covered.

The *Surfing Approach* contains a description of the ways in which the LR may be traversed according to the competence of the learner. Thus, learners with different background knowledge may adopt different approaches (as f.i. depth first vs. breadth first) to the use of the learning material.

Therefore, a set of HTML pages dealing with a topic, a bunch of electronic slides, an animated presentation, a questionnaire require some Metadata, an explicit discussion of the Learning Design adopted expressed in terms of Metacognitive Framework and of Navigational Aids to become a LO. Furthermore, the same LR may be used for different type of learning approaches and for different learning goals and perspectives simply by adopting different Learning Design models.

5 MD-Pro for LCMS implementation

We were unable to identify an existing LCMS able to implement in a simple and natural way our model of L.O. Therefore, we decided to build our own LCMS starting from a generic CMS. We tried identify a system able to cope with the needs of a LCMS by selecting a set of key requirements grouped into the same four main categories used to break down the functionality of a CMS, as summarized in table 1. This selection has been adapted to LCMSs starting from the work by Robertson [10]. With these requirements in mind, we looked at many different open source CMS (the choice of open source software being mandatory in the perspective of free dissemination of the project results).

Key requirements for content creation	<ul><li>*Integrated authoring environment*</li><li>*Separation of content and presentation*</li><li>*Multi-user authoring*</li><li>*Metadata creation*</li><li>*Non-technical authoring*</li></ul>
Key requirements for content management	<ul><li>*Workflow*</li><li>*Security*</li><li>*Integration with external systems*</li></ul>
Key requirements for Publishing	<ul><li>*Stylesheet*</li><li>*Extensibility*</li><li>*Support for multiple formats.*</li><li>*Personalization*</li><li>*Usage statistics*</li></ul>
Key requirements for Presentation	<ul><li>*Accessibility*</li><li>*Cross browser support*</li><li>*Limited client-side functionality.*</li><li>*Speed.*</li><li>*Valid HTML*</li><li>*Effective navigation.*</li></ul>

Table 1: Key requirements for content creation, management, publishing and presentation.

As result of our evaluation process, we adopted MD-Pro [8] a CMS maintained by an international community of programmers devoted to the development of high quality open source software. It is a direct evolution of two successful open source CMSs, PostNuke and eNvolution, is coded in PHP, a wide used script languages for Web applications, and stores contents in a MySQL database, the most used open source DBMS.

It is based on a "core system" with modules for all the basic CMS functionalities (creation, management publishing and presentation of content), and has a very powerful "theme engine", AutoTheme, to define the "skin" of the site. The basic functionalities can be extended by adding more modules, chosen from a large collection of third party free components. The development of "ad hoc" modules to satisfy specific requirements is easy, due to the characteristics of the PHP language used for coding, and to the clean interface between the modules and the core system.

MD-Pro appears to satisfy the most part of key requirements allowing a CMS to be used for a LCMS implementation, and in the following section we shows how we accomplish this task.

6 Implementation issues

In this section we will provide some details regarding the approach adopted to transform MD-Pro in a LCMS.

First of all, a layout has been defined so that the content page is divided in three sections: one on the left of the user, listing the LOs organized in topics and sub-topics along with modules for text-searching and for logging-in, a central section containing the material associated with each learning object, and a section on the right that shows contextual menus.

Among the contextual menus, the user of the our LCMS will find a topic map as required by the Navigational Aids of the Learning Design (fig.1) that is dynamically created by MD-Pro according to the current content page and a link to the Metacognitive Framework

One of the first issues that we had to solve was to decide how to implement a LO. We decided to implement each of the elements composing the manifest of a LO (i.e. Metadata, Learning Design and LRs) as a content page. A content page is a page that may contain both data and links to other sub-content pages, thus allowing to re-construct the tree structure of the Learning Object in a easy and simple way.

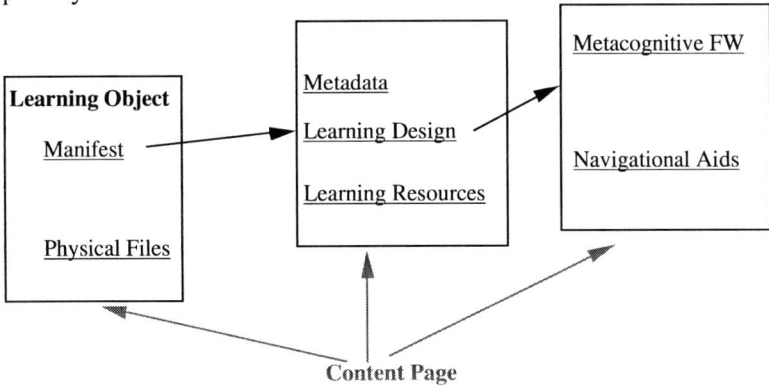

Figure 2: Our approach to LO implementation.

Each content page is created via the Content Express Module of MD-Pro.
A module named LOH (Learning Object Handler) has been implemented, so that any time an author wishes to create a LO, an empty template organized as discussed in section 4, is automatically created.

Another module named PFH (Physical Files Handler) allows the author to assemble all the content pages belonging to a LO in a zipped file that can be downloaded for further use outside the LCMS. This choice ensures the portability of the learning material over other platforms.

The metadata, expressed according the LOM specifications [4], have been implemented for the time being as simple content pages. A background database storing the metadata has not been implemented yet. Thus it is still possible to make a text search among the Metadata of each LO, but it is not possible to create specific queries that allow both to simplify and to optimise the search process. The implementation of the Metadata DB using MySQL, and the creation of PHP procedures for the handling of the database represents one of our next goals for the tailoring of MD-Pro as an LCMS.

Assessment is considered to play a central role in the educational process. Thus, it is mandatory for the LCMS we are developing, to implement the modules that allow an easy management of questions and tests by the instructional designer. Currently, we are developing a Question Management Module based on PHP and MySQL that will provide a friendly interface for the creation of closed-answer question and tests in the realm of current standardization initiatives [5].

References

[1] Browning P., Lowndes M. - Content Management Systems. JISC Techwatch report TSW 01-02.2001. http://www.jisc.ac.uk/index.cfm?name=techwatch_report_0102

[2] CEN/ISSS. CEN/ISSS/WS-LT Project 1 Draft Report .2000.

[3] Chapman, B. LCMS Report: Comparative Analysis of Enterprise Learning Content Management Systems, Brandon-Hall.com, 2003

[4] Final Draft Standard for Learning Object Metadata - IEEE 1484.12.1-2002 http://ltsc.ieee.org/doc/wg12/LOM_1484_12_1_v1_Final_Draft.pdf

[5] IMSWP-1 Version A - IMS Question & Test Interoperability Specification: A Review. A QTI White Paper from IMS. IMS Global Learning Consortium, Inc.2000.

[6] Koolen R. Learning Content Management Systems - The second way of e-Learning. A Knowledge Mechanics White Paper. Knowledge Mechanics, Grand Rapids, Michigan, USA.2001.

[7] Lennox, D. (2001). Managing Knowledge with Learning Objects. WBT Systems White Paper. 2001.http://www.wbtsytem.com

[8] MD-PRO. 2003. http://www.max-dev.com.

[9] Nichani, M.LCMS = LMS + CMS [RLOs]. ElearningPost. May, 2001. http://www.elearningpost.com/features/archives/001022.asp

[10] Robertson J.– How to evaluate a content management system? Step Two Designs Pty Ltd. 2002. http://www.steptwo.com.au/papers/kmc_how/index.html

[11] Robertson J. - So, what is a content management system? Step Two Designs Pty Ltd. 2003. http://www.steptwo.com.au/papers/kmc_what/index.html

[12] Shepherd, C. Making the case for content.2002. http://www.fastrak-consulting.co.uk/tactix/Features/lcms.htm

Section 4
Identification and verification

Identification of parts in identity-based encryption

G. Stephanides[1] & N. Constantinescu[2]
[1]*Department of Applied Informatics, University of Macedonia, Greece*
[2]*Department of Informatics, University of Craiova, Romania*

Abstract

After Shamir proposed his scheme, other authors proposed many Identity-Based Encryptions. The models were assumed in the random oracle model with a variant of the computational Diffie-Hellman problem. In our paper we propose a new variant of Identity-Based Encryption (IBE), using elliptic curves schemes and prove his security completeness. Also, we are doing a complete description of the necessary system used in the present scheme in order to secure a communication. The performance of our system is comparable to the performance of ElGamal encryption in F_p^* and the security of the system is based on the elliptic curve calculus intractability.
Keywords: identity-based encryption, Diffie-Hellman problem, elliptic curves cryptography, Escrow ElGamal.

1 Introduction

In the last twenty years many authors have developed security algorithms of information based on making the Public Key System that has an equivalent in an identity system, Shamir [1]. Initially, this system was created in order to assure the confidentiality of the communication between a member of a group who knows some identity information of another member and is going to communicate with him. This is, for example, the email address, the surname, the first name, a code on the identity card, etc. Informally, this kind of scheme consists of the following algorithms:
    (a)   Setup: generates the control parameters in order to identify the users and creates the master key.

(b) Extract: it uses the master key in order to generate the private key corresponding to public key that was generated in function of the Identity String (IS).
(c) Encrypt: the description of the encryption algorithm that will be applied on the plain text. It uses the public key.
(d) Decrypt: the decryption algorithm of the ciphered message. It uses the corresponding private key.

Many of other proposed schemes, [2, 3, 4, 5], use a considerable quantity of processor-time in order to calculate the private key, or they consider a dedicated hardware as being pre-existent.

To describe in this paper our model, we'll first illustrate a general model of the scheme. This model is based on the creation of the public key, which is not necessary to be taken from a server. By convention, it considers that the public key is made by the concatenation of the complete name of the receiver and the current week. So, we obtain the IS (Identity String). It will create an algorithm that transforms some kind of string in a key and this key will become the encryption public key used to encrypt the plain text and it will be sent through the communication channel.

The receiver will request the private key from the Private Key Generator (PKG). This private key is corresponding to the public key that is characteristic to this user (receiver). The decryption will be produced with this key, so Private Key Generator holds the control of all the decryption keys and the public keys associated with every user. To communicate with Private Key Generator, any participant has a secret code that is also known by the PKG. It is used to assure the Challenge-Response algorithm in order to make the secure communication between PKG and any participant.

2 Our secure IBE scheme

In this part of the article we describe the modality of secure information that will be transferred to another participant through the communication channel. This scheme has four parts:

Setup
Every participant of the group has a control key, a personal parameter noted ID, known by himself and by a trusted authority, the Private Key Generator. It is used to assure the secure communication between him and PKG.

Extract
Using the personal parameter ID and a message key communicates the private key for the participant. The private key will be generated by the PKG at the request of a participant authenticated by an ID.

Encryption
Another participant, using the transformation algorithm of an identity string (IS) in a public key $pk \in \{0,1\}^*$, will encrypt the plain text with this key and the cipher text obtained in such a way will be transferred through the communication channel.

Decryption

Using the private key, obtained from the Private Key Generator, one participant will decrypt a message that is destined to him.

As we already have mentioned, the algorithm used to obtain the private key from the Private Key Generator is of a Challenge-Response type. Therefore, for its construction we'll use, in the same way as in Boneh and Franklin [6, 7], the following phases:

Definition

The expression $x^3 + 1$ is a permutation of F_p, where E is an elliptic curve given by the equation $y^2 = x^3 + 1$, defined over F_p, and p is a prime number that satisfies $p = 6q - 1$, where q is a prime number, $q > 3$.

Let $P \in E/F_p$ be a generator in a group of points of order $q = (p+1)/6$.

Choice

For an integer coordinate $y_0 \in F_p$, there is a unique integer coordinate x_0, so that $(x_0, y_0) \in E/F_p$.

Transformation

Let $(1 + \zeta) \in F_{p^2}$ be a solution of the equation $x^3 - 1 \equiv 0 \pmod{p}$. A transformation equation $\phi(x, y) = (\zeta x, y)$ is a group automorphism on the elliptic curve E. If $P = (x, y) \in E/F_p$, then $\phi(P) \in E/F_{p^2}$, but $\phi(P) \notin E/F_p$.

Determination

The points $P, \phi(P)$ generate an isomorphic group $Z_q \times Z_q$. We note this group of points by $E[q]$. These points can be calculated as in Boneh and Franklin [6, 7].

Transformation IS-PK

The public key, which will encrypt the plain text, is made from a string obtained through the concatenation of the complete name of the receiver and the current weak. Once we have a string, it is necessary to transform it in a key, PK. For this reason, at the beginning, we code the string (in accordance with *ASCII*) to obtain $IS^{(1)} \in \{0,1\}^*$. Using a cryptographic hash function, $H: \{0,1\}^* \to F_p$, we construct the point $Q(x_0, y_0)$: y_0 will be equal to $H(IS^{(1)})$ and $x_0 = (y_0^2 - 1)^{1/3} \equiv (y_0^2 - 1)^{(2p-1)/3} \pmod{p}$. Thus, $Q(x_0, y_0) \in E/F_p$, and we compute $Q_{IS^{(1)}} = 6Q$ in order to obtain the necessary order of Q (this is denoted in [6, 7], as being a random oracle model).

2.1 Lifetime of key and key transmission

As we pointed out before, IS is made by the concatenation of the complete name of a participant and the current weak. This means that the key will be changed in every weak. Therefore, the validity of a pair of the key (public key and private key) is maintained only for one weak.

2.2 The functional scheme

In this part of the article we will describe the four steps of the algorithm that assures the confidentiality of the communication.

Setup

As we described before, we chose an elliptic curve E generated through a prime number p, $p = 6q-1$, and a prime number q, $q>3$. We chose $P \in E/F_p$ according to the transformation IS-PK. Also, we select $s \in Z_q^*$ and $P_{pub} = sP$. The master key is $s \in Z_q^*$.

Extract

Once we have $IS^{(1)} \in \{0,1\}^*$, the Private Key Generator will construct a private key, therefore: $H(IS^{(1)}) = IS^{(2)} \in \{0,1\}^*$. From this point it results that $Q_{IS^{(2)}} \in E/F_p$ of order q. The private key will be $d_{IS^{(2)}} = sQ_{IS^{(2)}}$, where s is the master key.

Encrypt

Let be T the plain text to be encrypted by a sender. The ciphered text C will be obtained as being $(rP, T \oplus H(Q^r))$, where $Q = (Q_{IS^{(2)}}, P_{pub}) \in F_{p^2}$ and r is chosen with random oracle, $r \in Z_q$.

Decrypt

We have $C = (U, V)$ a ciphered text with the public key $Q_{IS^{(2)}}$. We'll obtain again the plain text from the ciphered text as follows: $T = V + H(R)$, where $R = (d_{IS^{(2)}}, U) \in F_{p^2}$.

2.3 Security

The security of the system is given by the security of public keys system based on elliptic curves. These notions are described in detail and proved in Blake et al [8] and Verheul [9]. The mode of creation of the public key and private key doesn't offer advantages in the determinations of plain text to any attacker.

3 Conclusions and future work

In this paper, the authors proposed a new encryption scheme of *IBE* type based on elliptic curves. This scheme represents a powerful method to assure the confidentiality of communication in a group that has a *PKG*. The advantages are given by the facility of the generation of the private and public keys and by the fact that a user *A* that wants to send a message to another participant *B*, doesn't allow to establish a link with *PKG* in order to obtain the public key of *B*. It is enough to know the name of *B*. Also, only *PKG* knows about the key system of every user and the code allocated to everyone.

As a first application, we want to implement this scheme in a network with 163 systems. The next step consists of the creation of an hierarchy system in the network, in order to have access to the information, so that any user is able to read all the messages that circulate in the tree, between the users who are hierarchies situated in their descendant nodes of the tree.

References

[1] Shamir, A., Identity-based cryptosystems and signature schemes. *Advances in Cryptology - CRYPTO '84, Lecture Notes in Computer Science, vol. 196*, Berlin: Springer Verlag, pp. 47--53, 1985.

[2] Desmedt, Y. & Quisquater, J., Public-key systems based on the difficulty of tampering (Is there a difference between DES and RSA?). *Advances in Cryptology - CRYPTO '86, Lecture Notes in Computer Science, vol. 263*, Springer Verlag: Heidelberg, pp. 111-117, 1986.

[3] Tanaka, H., A realization scheme for the identity-based cryptosystem. *Advances in Cryptology - CRYPTO '87, Lecture Notes in Computer Science, vol. 293*, Springer Verlag: Heidelberg, pp. 341-349, 1987.

[4] Tsuji, S. & Itoh, T., An ID-based cryptosystem based on the discrete logarithm problem. *IEEE Journal on Selected Areas in Communication*, vol. 7, no. 4, pp. 467-473, 1989.

[5] Maurer, U. & Yacobi, Y., Non-interactive public-key cryptography. *Advances in Cryptology - EUROCRYPT '91, Lecture Notes in Computer Science*, vol. 547, Springer Verlag: Heidelberg, pp. 498-507, 1991.

[6] Boneh, D. & Franklin, M., Identity-Based Encryption from the Weil Pairing. *Advances in Cryptology - CRYPTO '01, Lecture Notes in Computer Science*, vol. 2139, Springer-Verlag: Heidelberg, pp. 213-229, 2001.

[7] Boneh, D. & Franklin, M., Identity based encryption. Full version available at http://crypto.stanford.edu/ibe.

[8] Blake, I.F., Seroussi, G. & Smart, N.P., *Elliptic Curves in Cryptography*, Cambridge University Press, 2000.

[9] Verheul, E., Evidence that XTR is more secure than supersingular elliptic curve cryptosystems. *Advances in Cryptology - EUROCRYPT '01, Lecture Notes in Computer Science*, vol. 2045, Springer Verlag: Heidelberg, pp. 195-210, 2001.

Authenticating mobile device users through image selection

W. Jansen
The National Institute of Standards and Technology

Abstract

Adequate user authentication is a persistent problem, particularly with mobile devices such as Personal Digital Assistants (PDAs), which tend to be highly personal and at the fringes of an organization's influence. Yet these devices are being used increasingly in military and government agencies, hospitals, and other business settings, where they pose a risk to security and privacy, not only from sensitive information they may contain, but also from the means they typically offer to access such information over wireless networks. User authentication is the first line of defence for a mobile device that falls into the hands of an unauthorized individual. However, motivating users to enable simple PIN or password mechanisms and periodically update their authentication information is difficult at best. This paper describes a general-purpose mechanism for authenticating users through image selection. The underlying rationale is that image recall is an easy and natural way for users to authenticate, removing a serious barrier to users' compliance with corporate policy. The approach described distinguishes itself from other attempts in this area in several ways, including style dependent image selection, password reuse, and embedded salting, which collectively overcome a number of problems in employing knowledge-based authentication on mobile devices.
Keywords: user authentication, mobile devices, computer security.

1 Introduction

The current trend toward a highly mobile workforce has spurred the acquisition of handheld devices such as Personal Digital Assistants (PDAs). Handheld devices are characterized by small physical size, limited computing resources and battery life, and the means for exchanging data with a more capable notebook or desktop computer. They also support interfaces are oriented toward mobility, for example, a touch screen and a microphone in place of a keyboard. One or more wireless interfaces, such as infrared (e.g., IrDA) or radio (e.g., Bluetooth, WiFi, GSM/GPRS), are usually built-in for both local and wide area wireless communications. Most handheld devices can be configured to send and receive electronic mail and browse the Internet. While such devices have their limitations, they offer productivity tools in a compact form and at relatively low cost, and are quickly becoming ubiquitous in today's business environment.

Security-related issues loom over the use of such devices, however, including the following items:

- Handheld devices gradually accrue sensitive information and over time gain access to wireless services and organizational intranets.
- Because of their small size, handheld devices may be temporarily misplaced, lost, or stolen, and exposed to an unauthorized individual.
- If user authentication is not enabled, a common default, the device's contents and network services fall under the control of whoever possesses it.
- Even if user authentication is enabled, the authentication mechanism may be weak (e.g., a four number PIN) or easily circumvented [1].
- Once authentication is enabled, renewing the authentication information periodically is seldom done on the initiative of the user.

Enabling user authentication and accurately verifying an individual's claimed identity is the first line of defence against unauthorized use of a handheld device. Three basic techniques commonly used to verify identity involve either some information known by an individual (i.e., knowledge-based authentication), something possessed by an individual (i.e., token-based authentication), or some measurement taken of an individual's physiological or behavioural traits (i.e., biometric-based authentication). Implementing authentication solutions on handheld devices can be problematic. For example, hardware tokens drain power and biometric scanners can be cumbersome to interface and use.

Knowledge-based mechanisms involving passwords are the oldest and most common form of authentication technique in use today. Password systems are straightforward to implement on most devices. While password systems can be effective, users tend undermine them by using easily remembered character strings as their password (e.g., "password"), which an intruder may easily guess or systematically match against dictionaries of such commonly used strings [2, 3]. To combat weak or easily broken passwords, organizations apply measures that compel users to include special, upper case, and numerical characters in their password string, to change passwords regularly (e.g., every 90 days) with completely different strings, and to avoid common or easily guessed strings [4]. Unfortunately, the measures put in place to ensure strong passwords usually result in complex and meaningless passwords that users often record and keep near the computer system to recall quickly.

The method described in this paper authenticates a user to a device using a visual login technique called Picture Password. Its aim is to provide users with a simple and intuitive means of authentication through image selection that avoids the pitfalls of alphanumeric passwords, yet is as effective a mechanism.

2 Background

The strength of password systems lies in the large set of character strings possible, from which an intruder would have to identify the one needed to impersonate a specific user. For example, for an eight-character string populated from the set of 95 printable ASCII keyboard characters, the number of distinct strings is 95^8. Password controls that eliminate weak passwords reduce the size of the password space somewhat, and computer systems that support multiple users offer an even broader target base to an intruder. Nevertheless, passwords remain a cost effective solution that serves as the benchmark for other authentication techniques. Researchers continually look at ways to improve password systems. Experimental results, suggesting human memory is well suited to visual and cognitive tasks involving the recall and selection of images, have stimulated the development of visual login techniques. Image selection inherently avoids traditional dictionary attacks and is especially relevant to PDAs and other devices that interact via a touch screen and stylus.

The earliest general description of a system and method for applying graphical passwords to a handheld device appears in United States Patent 5,559,961 [5]. The authentication mechanism displays a set of image areas or cells that comprise a single graphical image. To enter a password, the user selects and repositions some of the cells in a sequence with an area of the display. The mechanism then uses the selected sequence of cells as a password, though no details are given of how the mechanism uses this information. One drawback for small size screens is that the cells, which in effect form the alphabet for composing a password, may provide a smaller size alphabet compared with alphanumeric passwords. That is, while more cells result in a larger alphabet, their size is diminished, which at some point makes it difficult to select one from another using a pointing device, resulting in entry errors.

Visual Key [6] is a commercial product that also uses cells of a single graphical image as the password elements. A user selects a specific sequence of image areas (e.g., objects in the image) from the display to authenticate. A selection matrix, kept hidden from the user, logically divides a single image into individual cells. During selection, the grid is dynamically adjusted so that a cell centre aligns with an enrolled touch point. The strength of the password depends on the effective size of the password alphabet, which directly corresponds to the number of cells that make up the image. Approximately 85 distinct cells with a size of 30x30 pixels can fit on a standard size 240x320 pixel display of a PDA, which results in a smaller size alphabet than available with alphanumeric passwords. Another limitation is that, because the cell boundaries are invisible, no visual cues exist to help determine areas of the image to select where objects in the image encompass more than one cell. Moreover, cells comprised of 30x30 pixels or less are a bit small, which can contribute to selection errors.

PointSec for Pocket PC [7] is a commercial product that includes several authentication-related components that can be managed centrally. PicturePIN is a graphical counterpart to a numeric PIN system, which uses pictograms rather than numbers for entering a code via a keypad-like layout of 10 keys. The symbols are intended to form a mnemonic phrase, such as the four-symbol sequence of ♟ - men / ♥ - love / 𝄞 - to listen / ♪ - to music. The sequence of symbols can be 4-13 symbols long. To increase security against a bystander observing hand motion and inferring the PIN, the symbols are scrambled at each login. PicturePIN, with a limited alphabet size of 10 items, is equivalent in strength to a numeric PIN. Even if more symbol keys populated the screen, the same tradeoffs between cell size, selection errors, and password strength would arise as with visual Key and result in the same upper limit on alphabet size. SafeGuard PDA [8] is another commercial product whose Symbol PIN authentication technique works nearly identically and with the same limitations.

3 Picture password

The visual login techniques described above face two main problems. First, due to screen size limitations, the size of the alphabet is smaller compared with traditional alphanumeric passwords, resulting in a weaker mechanism. Second, the user must select and remember a new set of images or image areas periodically whenever a password expires, which raises the level of difficulty for a user, especially if done within the context of the previous image set. Picture Password was devised to overcome both of these problems.

As with textual password authentication mechanisms, Picture Password uses elements of an alphabet to form a password entry of a given length. However, instead of the user having to remember a string of random-like alphanumeric characters, the sequence of images that form a passcode must be recalled and selected. Moreover, an image sequence that has some meaning or is of interest to the individual user (e.g., images of sport team logos in order of preference) can be used. If forgotten, the sequence may be reconstructed from the inherent visual cues.

3.1 User interface

The presentation of visual images to the user for selection is based on tiling an area of the graphical interface window with thumbnail images. Various ways exist to tile an area, the simplest being squares of identical size grouped into a two-dimensional matrix. The surface of each tile displays a bit-mapped representation of some thumbnail image supplied in a predefined digital format. The goal is to strike a balance between providing clear recognizable and easily selectable images within the display area and having a sufficient number to enable the formation of strong passwords. Picture Password uses a template of 30 identically sized squares for its thumbnail images, grouped into a 5x6 matrix, as shown in the screen shots in Figure 1.

A message area at the top of the display guides the user actions. The buttons at the bottom allow the user to clear out incorrect input or submit an entered image sequence for verification. When an image sequence is initially enrolled, users can choose from among several available predefined themes. An option exists to shuffle images between authentication attempts, where appropriate for the theme, to make input monitoring by a bystander difficult. While each thumbnail image is distinct and individually recognizable, several of them may be used collectively to form a composite mosaic image. Users may define new themes using a theme builder tool and their own images.

Figure 1: Example PDA Screens (Copyright of Hemera Technologies Inc. All rights reserved).

Image selection and other interactions are done with an available pointing device – a stylus in the case of most PDAs. Two styles of thumbnail image selection are provided: individual selection and paired selection. Individual selection requires choosing a single thumbnail, which represents one element of the alphabet. Paired selection requires choosing and linking a pair of consecutively selected thumbnail images, which when coupled together this way also represent one single element of the alphabet. The idea is similar to using a shift key to select uppercase or special characters on a traditional keyboard. In this setting, however, each thumbnail image can serve as a shift key for every other image.

Individual selection is done with a quick single pick of the stylus on a thumbnail image. Paired selection requires a touch and hold of the stylus for the first image, such that the stylus rests on a thumbnail image until it is highlighted, followed by a quick single pick of the second image. Using similar but distinct styles of selection offers significant benefits. First, it greatly expands the effective alphabet. Second, the subtle differences in selection style make eavesdropping difficult, especially since the narrow viewing angle of most handheld device screens already limit the viewing ability of a bystander.

The number of alphabet elements that a user can select when enrolling an image sequence is determined by the number of singly selectable thumbnail images, n, plus the number of possible paired thumbnail images selectable, n*(n-1), if a thumbnail image is not paired with itself, or n*n, if self pairing is allowed. For the 5x6 image matrix used, the total number of selectable elements with self-pairing allowed is 30+(30*30) or 930 in total. The result compares favourably with the conventional 95 printable ASCII character alphabet and significantly overshadows virtual keyboard emulation used on many PDAs, where a touch screen and stylus often prove cumbersome for entering characters.

With an effective alphabet size of 930, the resulting password space becomes extremely large. For example, 7-entry long passcodes have 930^7 possible values or a password space of approximately 6.017e+20, which is an order of magnitude greater than that for 10-character long passwords formed from the 95 printable ASCII character set whose password space is 95^{10} or approximately 5.987e+19. The general relationship between the password spaces of passwords formed these two ways can be represented using the following formula:

$$Lp = \lceil \tfrac{2}{3} \times Lt \rceil,$$

where Lt is the required character length for textual password input, Lp is the corresponding passcode length required for Picture Password, and $\lceil y \rceil$ denotes the ceiling function (i.e., the least integer greater than or equal to y). In simple terms this means that the length of a passcode formed using a 5x6 image matrix is approximately one-third less than that of a traditional alphanumeric password, yet results in a comparable password space. Table 1 gives a comparison of input lengths between the two methods over a range of sizes. Note that the values in the table presume that just as additional keystrokes are needed to select special and capital characters on a keyboard, a comparable number of additional strokes are used when forming a passcode involving paired image selections.

Table 1: Input length comparison.

Textual Password Length	6	7	8	9	10	11	12
Visual Passcode Length	4	5	6	6	7	7	8

3.2 Password derivation

It is relatively straightforward to use the indices of the image matrix to form the elements of an alphabet, which in turn are used to compute an associated password value based on the images selected, in much the same way as is done for textual passwords. A one-way cryptographic hash applied iteratively to the clear text password value formed by concatenating individual alphabet values produces the cipher text value of the password. While a visual login technique inherently avoids dictionary attacks associated with textual passwords, it may be possible for an intruder to compile commonly used set of image selections (e.g., the four corners of the image matrix) and use them in an attack. To ward off specialized dictionary attacks, the clear text password value can be prepended with a random value, referred to as a salt, before the applying the hash. Adding a salt significantly increases the work factor for the intruder, in proportion to the size of the salt and whether both a public and a secret salt are applied [9, 10].

Many organizational policies require users' passwords be replaced after some period of use. Password expiration stymies an intruder, who somehow obtains the cipher text value of the password, from cracking it and determining the input string, over an indefinite lifetime of use. Though the safeguard is effective, it is also a nuisance for the user, who must follow this practice on numerous systems. Ideally, the user would prefer to continue using the same image sequence indefinitely. The solution is to allow the same image sequence to be used during a password change over, but generate a completely new password value.

Allowing password reuse required the addition of a value matrix with the same dimensions as the image matrix. The value matrix holds the values to be applied when the corresponding image is selected. Each entry in the value matrix is randomly assigned a value drawn from the set of values previously associated with singly selected images. Thus, instead of using the indices of an image sequence to derive the clear text password, the corresponding elements of the value matrix are used. As before, the values are concatenated together, in the sequence the images were selected, to form the clear text password. The mapping of elements of the value matrix to the assigned values is retained by the authentication mechanism, and remains constant from one authentication attempt to another. Only during password changeovers are the elements of the value matrix automatically updated and randomly reassigned values. Thus, the value matrix allows users to retain the same theme and image sequence over multiple password changeovers, yet produce completely different password values.

One additional use for the value matrix is to hold individual salt values for each element of the alphabet, rather than prepending the clear text value of the password with a single salt value. This can be particularly advantageous when the memory allocated for each value matrix element is larger than that needed to hold the values of the alphabet. In such situations, the unneeded bits can be populated with random values each time a new password is enrolled. This, in effect, creates a new way of salting the password through the embedding of salt values within the alphabet value entries of the value matrix.

3.3 Organization

Picture Password has two main functions: enrolment and verification. Figure 2 gives an overview of these processes. For mobile devices, normally only a single user exists that needs to be authenticated. During start up, the system prompts the user to login or, if an image sequence is not yet enrolled, to enrol one as the passcode. Unlike desktop systems, powering off a handheld device suspends all processes, rather than stopping them and shutting down the system. Powering on the device simply resumes any suspended processes without having to initiate a time-consuming system boot up. To be effective, the authentication mechanism must assert itself at device power on as well as at system boot up, effectively turning the power button into a secure attention key for establishing a trusted path to the authentication mechanism.

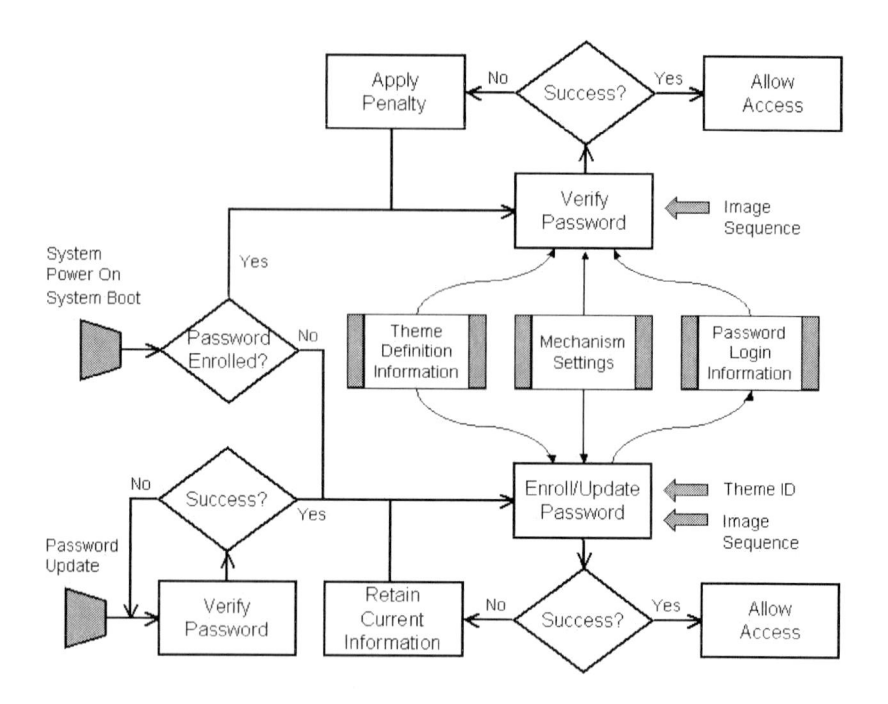

Figure 2:   Functional flow diagram.

Enrolling the password requires the user to select a theme and image sequence, and repeat the sequence a second time to ensure accuracy. If a discrepancy arises, the user can continue the process until successful. Enrolment uses several files. The theme definition information file identifies each theme, the images to display, and other related information. Similarly, the mechanism settings file contains information related to computing the password, such as the number of login attempts to allow, restrictions on passcode length, and the number of hash iterations to apply. When a successful enrolment occurs, the theme identifier and image sequence entered by the user are saved away within the password login information file, along with the value matrix and salt information generated, and the user gains access to the device.

Once enrolled, subsequently powering on or booting up the device prompts the user to enter a correct image sequence for verification. The verification process uses information from the password login information file to display the correct theme and from the mechanism settings file to compute the clear text password for the image sequence. It then applies the hash algorithm as prescribed in the mechanism settings file. A correct match against the enrolled value in the password login information file results in successful authentication, and access granted to the device. If too many authentication failures occur, the user account is locked temporarily to prevent unrestricted password guessing.

Any time after gaining access, a user can update the password by using an available icon to launch the process and entering the correct image sequence for verification, which then follows the same steps described earlier for verification at power on or boot up. In Figure 2, the "Verify Password" box associated with password update does not show the information flows discussed earlier, which are present implicitly. Successful verification allows the user to select a theme and enrol a new image sequence. Choosing the same theme and image sequence produces a completely different password value. A successful enrolment updates the password login information file and the user regains access to the device.

As with any authentication mechanism, Picture Password relies on the security of the operating environment to protect critical pieces of authentication information, including the salt value, the value matrix, and the enrolled password value. Strict file access control settings ensure the confidentiality and integrity of this information. The binaries of the authentication mechanism must also be protected against unauthorized replacement or deletion. Additional system policy controls can be added to enforce these restrictions and lockdown the device until authentication successfully completes [11].

4 Related work

Draw-a-Secret (DAS) is a scheme for graphical password input, targeted for PDA devices [12]. Rather than selecting images, a user draws them on a display grid for use in generating a password. The size of each cell of the grid must be sufficiently large to allow the user enough tolerance when making a stroke to avoid cell boundary ambiguities. Each continuous stroke is represented as the sequence of cell grids encountered. Strokes can start within any cell and go in any direction, but must occur in the same sequence as the one enrolled for the user. Each continuous stroke maps to a sequence of coordinate pairs by listing the cells in the order in which it traverses cell boundaries. The grid sequences for each stroke that compose a drawing are concatenated together in the order they were drawn to form a password. The size of the password space for graphical passwords formed using this scheme on a 5x5 grid is argued to be better than that of textual passwords.

5 Summary

Picture Password is a visual login technique that matches the capabilities and limitations of most handheld devices and provides a simple and intuitive way for users to authenticate. Besides user authentication, Picture Password may also be used in other security applications where conventional passwords have been used traditionally. While the solution is particularly well suited for handheld devices, Picture Password can also be used in a wide range of computing platforms.

References

[1]   Kingpin and Mudge, Security Analysis of the Palm Operating System and its Weaknesses Against Malicious Code Threats, Proceedings of the 10th USENIX Security Symposium, August 2001.

[2] Robert Morris, Ken Thompson, Password Security: A Case History, *Communications of the ACM*, 22(11), pp. 594-597, November 1979.

[3] Daniel Klein, Foiling the Cracker: A Survey of, and Improvements to, Password Security, Proceedings of the 2nd USENIX Unix Security Workshop, pp. 5-14, August 1990.

[4] Eugene Spafford, OPUS: Preventing Weak Password Choices, *Computers & Security*, 11(3), pp. 273-278, May 1992.

[5] Greg E. Blonder; Graphical Password, US Patent 5,559,961, Lucent Technologies Inc., Murray Hill, NJ, August 30, 1995.

[6] Visual Key – Technology, sfr GmbH, 2000, http://www.viskey.com/technik.html.

[7] PointSec for Pocket PC, PointSec Mobile Technologies, November 2002, http://www.pointsec.com/news/download/Pointsec_PPC_POP_Nov_02.pdf.

[8] SafeGuard PDA, Utimaco Safeware AG, March 2003, http://www.utimaco.com/eng/content_pdf/sg_pda_eng.pdf.

[9] Udi Manber, A Simple Scheme to Make Passwords Based on One-Way Functions Much Harder to Crack, *Computers & Security*, 15(2), pp. 171-176, 1996.

[10] Martın Abadi, T. Mark A. Lomas, Roger Needham, Strengthening Passwords, SRC Technical Note 1997-033, Digital Systems Research Center, December 1997.

[11] Wayne Jansen, Tom Karygiannis, Michaela Iorga, Serban Gravila, Vlad Korolev, Security Policy Management for Handheld Devices, International Conference on Security and Management (SAM'03), June 2003

[12] Ian Jermyn, Alain May, Fabian Monrose, Michael Riter, Avi Rubin, The Design and Analysis of Graphical Passwords, Proceedings of the 8th USENIX Security Symposium, August 1999.

Section 5
Interface design issues

Cognitive style and interface design: findings from the HomeNetToo project

L. A. Jackson, F. Biocca, A. von Eye, Y. Zhao & H. Fitzgerald
Michigan State University

Abstract

In the HomeNetToo project we designed alternative user interfaces and examined whether interface design and user's cognitive style independently and/or interactively influenced learning and attitudes about health information (www.HomeNetToo.org, NSF-ITR #085348). Participants were 161 low-income African Americans who resided in urban communities in the midwestern United States. Findings indicated that: (1) interface design influenced attitudes about the source of health information; (2) Cognitive style influenced intentions to use the health information presented in the interface and evaluations of the interface; (3) Gender was related to cognitive style; (4) Participants significantly increased their basic and behavioral knowledge about high blood pressure by viewing the interface presentation, regardless of interface type, cognitive style or gender. Implications for the design of technology to enhance learning are discussed.
Keywords: cognitive style, interface design, learning.

1 Introduction

Cognitive style is defined as an individual's culturally attuned ways of perceiving, organizing, remembering and evaluating information [1]. It is the individual's preferred mode for perceiving and processing information about the social and physical world [2]. Although some researchers argue for a distinction between cognitive style and learning style, most agree that the two constructs share the following core assumptions: (1) Individuals differ in how they seek, model, and learn information from the environment; (2) Individual differences are systematic and reflect stable differences in perceptual and processing preferences; (3) Individuals tend to selectively absorb, use, and manipulate information presented in a manner that matches their cognitive style, and avoid or ignore information presented in a manner that does not match their cognitive style; (4) Individuals perform better at cognitive tasks when information presentations match their cognitive style than when they do not [3-14].

A growing body of evidence suggests that adapting the information technology (IT) interface to user characteristics and preferences (e.g., personality, affective preferences) affects a variety of important outcomes in computer-mediated environments (e.g., performance, affect; [15-28]). In particular, adapting the interface has been shown to influence user satisfaction and motivation for computer-mediated activities, computer usage, access to information databases, attention to information, and the learning of computer programs and spatial cognitive skills [29-35]. However, studies vary considerable with respect to the quality of research design and hence in the confidence we can place in their conclusions.

In the HomeNetToo project we designed user interfaces adapted to two dimensions of cognitive style: visual preferences and interpersonal preferences. Kolb's Learning Styles Inventory [36] was used to measure the perceptual and processing preference dimensions of cognitive style. An experiment examined whether cognitive style and interface design, independently and interactively, would influence learning and attitudes about health information presented in the interface.

2 Methods

Three levels of interface design were created: a 3-D spatial interface, an interpersonal interface and a "magazine-style" (control) interface. Two levels of perceptual style and two levels of processing style were created by median splits on Kolb's Learning Style Inventory. Three by two multivariate and univariate analyses of variance (ANOVAs) were used to examine main and interactive effects of perceptual/processing style preferences and interface design on the following dependent measures: changes in basic and behavioral knowledge about high blood pressure (i.e., pre-post difference scores); attitudes about the information source (i.e., American Heart Institute), intentions to use information presented in the interface, evaluations of the interface

2.1 Participants

Participants were 161 African Americans (73% females) recruited from low-income neighborhoods in Detroit, Michigan (n=91) and Lansing, Michigan (n=70). Recruiting and participation took place in local community centers (e.g., Black Child and Family Institute, Lansing, MI, n=55) and churches (e.g., Generation Ministries, Detroit, MI, n=90). In addition, 15 participants were recruited from phase one of the HomeNetToo project, all from Lansing, MI. Community centers and churches were financially compensated for provided facilities and assisting with recruiting. Participants received a $25 gift certificate for their one-hour participation.

2.2 Procedures

Research sessions began with an overview of the experiment. The participant then completed the first part of the survey (see Measures, below). Next, the participant was escorted to an adjacent room and seated on an elevated platform about 4 feet from a large rear-projection screen (3m X 2m) and at eye-level with the randomly assigned interface. The participant's facial expression was videotaped throughout the 30 minute-interaction with the interface. The participant also wore noise-cancellation headphones to filter out extraneous noise. After viewing the interface participants completed the second part of the survey (see Measures, below).

Table 1: Experimental interfaces.

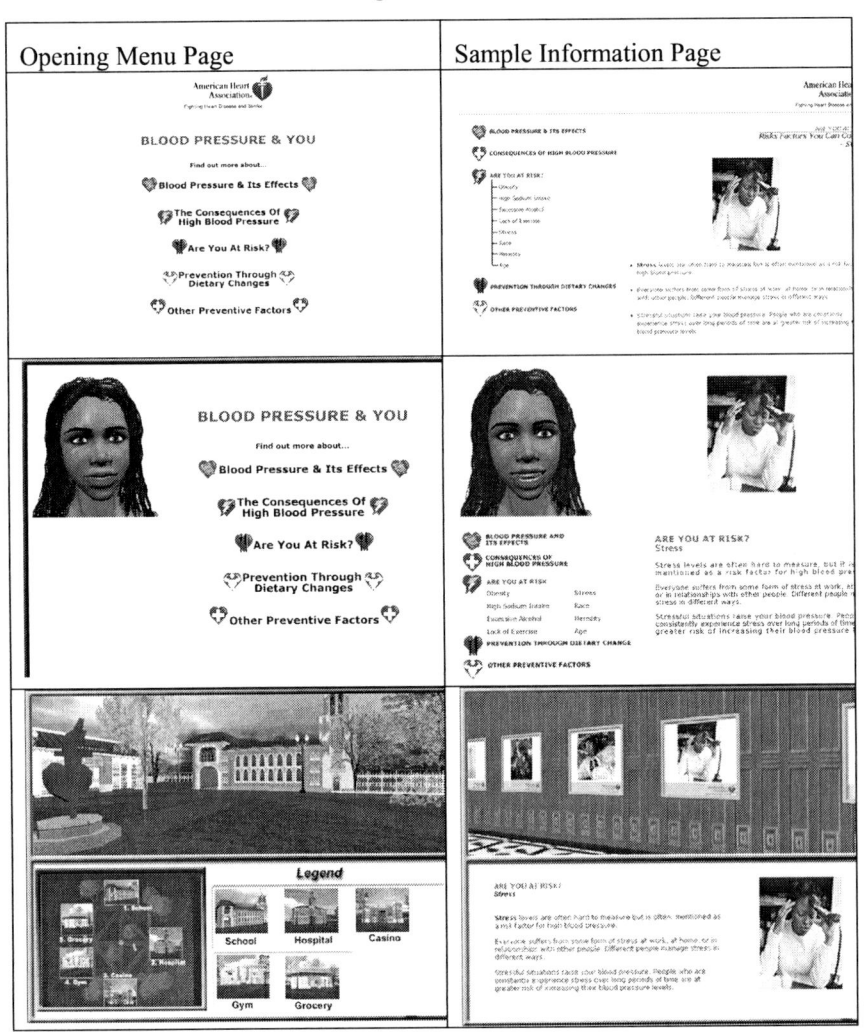

2.3 Interface design

Three interfaces were designed to present identical textual and graphic information about high blood pressure, but using different organizational metaphors, navigation methods and adaptations to cognitive style. Snapshots of the three interfaces are presented in Table 1.

Information about high blood pressure was obtained from the American Heart Association Web page (2002) and divided into five sections: (1) effects; (2) consequences; (3) risks; (4) prevention through behavior change; and (5) prevention through dietary change. For all three interfaces, icons were used to represent each of these sections, respectively: (1) a book; (2) a red cross; (3) a lightning bolt; (4) a man exercising; and (5) a fork and knife. According to previous research, icons assist users in comprehension of and memory for medical and medicinal information (McDougall, de Brujin, & Curry, 2000).

2.3.1 Magazine-style (control) interface

Information in the control interface was presented in standard magazine-style format. All information was presented as text or images. Participants navigated through the three layers of information by clicking on hyperlinks. Each main heading, which consisted of one or two sentences, was followed by bullet points of supplementary information. A two-dimensional picture related to each main heading was displayed adjacent to it (Table 1).

2.3.2 Three-dimensional spatial interface

Information in the 3-D spatial interface was organized into thematic buildings similar to the top level of the hierarchical menu in the control interface. Participants navigated through a three-dimensional courtyard to select a building, which placed them within a large room. Each of the five buildings in the urban setting contained posters with links equivalent to those provided at the second level of the magazine-style interface menu. Users selected a page by clicking on a poster. The page appeared in a new window, and contained the same text and images as in the other interface conditions (Table 1).

2.3.3 Interpersonal interface

The interpersonal interface contained an anthropomorphic, African-American character - an intelligent agent, "Cardie," who guided the participant through the information. The information was presented on web pages identical to those used in the control interface. At the start of the session the agent introduced herself (orally) and asked the participant to select a topic from a list of the same topics included in the other interface conditions. The participant made her/his selection with an oral request to the agent. The page containing information about that topic was then displayed, with the agent introducing the main points (but not the bulleted points) on the page (Table 1).

2.4 Measures

Part I of the survey, administered before viewing the interface, contained the following measures: (1) basic knowledge about blood pressure (10 items, e.g., A normal blood pressure reading is: a) 20 over 10, b) 70 over 30, c) 140 over 90, d) 200 over 100); (2) behavioral knowledge about blood pressure (10 items, e.g., Which of the following will not help to reduce high blood pressure? a) reducing sodium intake, b) eating more fruits and vegetables, c) increasing alcohol intake, d) prescribed medication from a doctor.); (3) Kolb's Learning Styles Inventory [36].

The Kolb inventory consists of ten items, each having four choices about preferred ways to learn. Scoring is based on Cartesian coordinates of Active Experimentation (doing) versus Reflective Observation (watching) on the x-axis, and Concrete Experience (experiencing) versus Abstract Conceptualization (thinking) on the y-axis. The coordinates yield two scores, one for the perceptual style preference dimension (y-axis, Abstract Conceptualization plus Concrete Experience) and one for the processing style preference dimension (x-axis, Active Experimentation plus Reflective Observation). High scores on the perceptual style dimension indicate a preference for perceiving by abstract conceptualization and low scores indicate a preference for perceiving by concrete experience. High scores on the processing style dimension indicate a preference for processing by reflective observation and low scores indicate a preference for processing by active experimentation.

Part II of the survey, administered after viewing the interface, reassessed basic and behavioral knowledge about high blood pressure (1 and 2, above), plus: (3) attitudes toward the information source (American Heart Association, 3 items, e.g., I trust the American Heart Association, 1=strongly disagree, 7=strongly agree); (4) intentions to use the information about high blood pressure (19 items, e.g., I will eat a healthy diet. 1=strongly disagree, 7=strongly agree); and (5) evaluations of the interface (7 items, e.g., The site I just visited is enjoyable, 1=strongly disagree, 7=strongly agree. Demographic information was also obtained (e.g., gender).

3 Results

For each participant the following measures were computed: (1) number of correct answers to basic knowledge questions about high blood pressure and number of correct answers to behavioral knowledge questions about high blood pressure, both pre- and post-interface presentation; (2) pre-post difference scores for basic and behavioral knowledge about high blood pressure; (3) composite measure (average) of attitudes toward the information source; (4) composite measure (average) of intentions to use the information; and (5) composite measure (average) of evaluations of the interface. All composite measures were reliable (.80<alpha<.93). Also computed were composite scores (sums) for the perceptual and processing style dimensions, followed by median splits to categorize participants into high and low perceptual preference groups and high and low processing preference groups.

ANOVAs revealed a main effect of interface design on attitudes toward the information source (American Heart Institute), $F(2,155)=6.11$, $p<.01$. Participants in the 3-D spatial (N=60) and interpersonal (N=41) interface conditions had more favourable attitudes (Ms=6.01, 6.35, respectively, SEs (standard errors)=.145, .176, respectively) than did participants in the magazine-style (N=60) interface condition (M=5.54, SE=.146). There was no difference between the spatial and interpersonal interfaces on this measure. There were no differences related to interface design on measures of basic knowledge or behavioral knowledge about high blood pressure. Scores on both measures increased from pre-interface presentation (Ms=5.30, 5.42, out of 10 maximum points) to post-interface presentation (Ms=6.39, 6.21, respectively), indicating significant learning by viewing the interface, regardless of its design. Note that the three interface design groups were equivalent on both knowledge measures prior to the interface presentations (i.e., there were no pre-existing differences in knowledge about high blood pressure among the three interface design groups).

There was a marginally significant main effect of perceptual style preference on intentions to use the information about high blood pressure presented in the interface, $F(1,155)=3.08$, $p<.08$, and a significant main effect on evaluations of the site, $F(1, 155)=3.97$, $p<.05$. Participants who preferred concrete learning experiences were less likely to intend to use the information (N=75, M=6.05, SE=.103)) and had less favourable evaluations of the site (M=5.85, SE=.123) than did those who preferred abstract learning experiences (N=86, Ms=6.30, 6.19, respectively, SEs=.096, .114, respectively). There was no interaction between interface design and perceptual style preference.

There was a marginally significant main effect of processing style preference on intentions to use the information presented at the site, $F(1, 155)=2.95$, $p<.09$, and a significant main effect on evaluations of the site, $F(1, 155)=5.30$, $p<.05$. Participants who preferred reflective observation were less likely to intend to use the information found at the site (N=66, M=6.03, SE=.108), and evaluated the site less favourably (M=5.79, SE=.129) than did those who preferred active experimentation (N=95, Ms=6.23, 6.18, SEs=.092, .109, respectively). There were no interactions between interface design and processing style preference.

Gender differences were obtained for both perceptual and processing styles preferences. Males preferred abstract conceptualization (N=42, M=6.10, SE=.318) whereas females preferred concrete experience (N=112, M=5.30, SE=.198; $F(1, 152)=4.39$, $p<.05$). Females preferred reflective observation (M=4.34, SE=.195) whereas males preferred active experimentation (M=3.67, SE=.295; $F(1, 152)=3.39$, $p<.068$). However, there were no gender differences in learning (basic or behavioral information), attitudes toward the source of information (i.e., American Heart Association), intentions to use the information about high blood pressure, or evaluations of the site.

4 Discussion

Findings indicated that: (1) interface design influenced attitudes about the source of health information. Participants who experienced the 3-D spatial interface or the interpersonal interface had more favourably attitudes than those who experienced the standard magazine-style interface; (2) Cognitive style influenced intentions to use the health information presented in the interface as well as evaluations of the interface. Participants who preferred concrete learning experience and reflective observation were less likely to intend to use the information, and evaluated the interfaces less favourably than did participants who preferred abstract conceptualization and active experimentation (respectively). (3) Gender was related to cognitive style. Females preferred concrete experience and reflective observation whereas males preferred to abstract conceptualization and active experimentation (respectively). (4) Participants significantly increased their basic and behavioral knowledge about high blood pressure by viewing the interface presentations, regardless of interface design, cognitive style or gender.

Our findings have implications for the design of technology to enhance learning in members of underserved groups. They suggest that 3-D spatial interfaces and interfaces that contain anthropomorphic "helping" agents produce more favourable attitudes about the information presented than do standard "magazine-style" interfaces. Although these adapted interfaces did not result in better learning, it is important to note that our participants were never explicitly instructed to learn the information presented in the interface. Had they been so instructed, then the 3-D spatial and interpersonal interfaces may have resulted in better learning as well. Our findings that cognitive style may interact with interface design to influence intentions to use the information presented in the interface suggest that more attention should be given to cognitive style and possible cultural influences on cognitive style in the design of technology for learning.

References

[1] Shade, B. J., Kelly, C., & Oberg, M. (1997). *Creating culturally responsive classrooms.* Washington, DC: American Psychological Association.

[2] Witkin, H. A., & Goodenough, D. R. (1981). *Cognitive styles: Essence and origins.* New York: International University.

[3] Kolb A., & Kolb, D. A. (2003). *Learning styles and learning spaces: Enhancing experiential learning in higher education.* Academy of Management: Learning and Education.

[4] Epstein, S., Pacini, R., Denes-Raj, V., & Heier, H. (1996). Individual differences in intuitive-experiential and analytic-rational thinking styles. *Journal of Personality and Social Psychology, 71*, 390-405.

[5] Gardner, H. (1983). *Frames of mind: The theory of multiple intelligences.* New York: Basic Books.

[6] Golding, J., & Cavangh, M. P. (1997). *Learning styles: How and what we learn*. Learning Resources Center.
[7] Reid, J. (1995). (Ed.). *Learning styles in the ESL/EFL classroom*. Boston: Heinle & Heinle.
[8] Riding, R. J. & Douglas, G. (1993). The effect of cognitive style and mode of presentation on learning performance. *British Journal of Educational Psychology, 63,* 297-307.
[9] Riding, R. J., & Watts, M. (1997). The effect of cognitive style on the preferred format of instructional material. *Educational Psychology, 17,* 179-183.
[10] Sadler-Smith, E. (2001). The relationship between learning style and cognitive style. *Personality and Individual Differences, 30,* 609-616.
[11] Sloman, S. A. (1996). The empirical case for two systems of reasoning. *Psychological Bulletin, 119,* 3-22.
[12] Witkin, H. A., & Goodenough, D. R. (1977). Field dependence and interpersonal behavior. *Psychological Bulletin, 84,* 661-189.
[13] Grigorenko, E. L., & Sternberg, R. J. (1995). Thinking styles. In D. H. S. M. Zeidner (Ed.), *International Handbook of Personality and Intelligence* (pp. 205-229). New York: Plenum.
[14] Knight, K. H., Elfenbein, M. H., & Messina, J. A. (1995). A preliminary scale to measure connected and separate knowing: The Knowing Styles Inventory. *Sex Roles, 33,* 499-513.
[15] Bostrom, R., Olfman, L., & Sein, M.. (1988). The importance of individual differences in end-user training: The case for learning style. *Applied Social Psychology, 10,* 371-391.
[16] Bransford, J., Brown, A., & Cocking, R. (1999). *How people learn: Brain, mind, experience, and school.* Washington, DC: National Academy Press.
[17] Butler, K. (1997). *The strategy chart for learning styles, levels of thinking, and performance*. Columbia, CT: The Learner's Dimension.
[18] Gorayska, B., & Mey, J. L. (1996). *Cognitive technology: In search of a humane interface.* Amsterdam, Oxford: Elsevier.
[19] Dunn, R. S., Dunn, K. J., & Perrin, J. (1994). *Teaching young children through their individual learning styles: Practical approaches for grades K-12.* Boston: Allyn and Bacon.
[20] Nielsen, J. (1990). *Designing user interfaces for international use.* New York: Elsevier Science.
[21] Nielsen, J. (2000). *Designing Web usability.* Indianapolis, IN: New Riders.
[22] Nielsen, J., & Del Galdo, E. M. (1996). *International user interfaces.* New York: Wiley Computer
[23] Barret, G. V. (1968). Relationship between perceptual style and simulator sickness. *Journal of Applied Psychology, 52,* 304-308.
[24] Chamillard, A. T., & Karolick, D. (1999). Using learning style data in an introductory computer course. Paper presented at the SIGCSE'99, New Orleans.

[25] Gagnon, D. M. (1986). *Interactive versus observational media: The influence of user control and cognitive styles on spatial learning.* Cambridge, MA: Harvard University Press.

[26] Ossner, J. (1990). Transnational symbols: The rule of pictograms and models in the learning process. In J. Nielsen (Ed.), *Designing user interfaces for international use.* New York: Elsevier.

[27] Oviatt, S., & Cohen, P. (2000). Multimodal interfaces that process what comes naturally. *Communications of the Association for Computing Machinery 43,* 45-53.

[28] Van-der-Veer, G. C., Tauber, M. J., Waern, Y., & Van-Muylwijk, B. (1985). On the interaction between system and user characteristics. *Behavior and Information Technology, 4,* 289-308.

[29] Dugdale, S. (1994). Using students' mathematical inventiveness as a foundation for software design: Toward a tempered constructivism. *Educational Technology Research and Development, 42,* 57-73.

[30] Greco, A., & McClung, C. (1979). Interaction between attention direction and cognitive style. *Educational Communication and Technology, 27,* 97-102.

[31] Jih, H. J., & Reeves, T. C. (1992). Mental models: A research focus for interactive learning systems. *Educational Technology Research and Development, 40,* 39-53.

[32] McClurg, P. A., & Chaille, C. (1987). Computer games: Environments for developing spatial cognition? *Educational Computer Research, 3,* 95-111.

[33] Nass, C., Moon, Y., Fogg, B.J., Reeves, B., and Dryer, D.C. (1995). Can computers be human personalities? *International Journal of Human Computer Studies, 43,* 223-239.

[34] Reeves, B., & Nass, C. (1996). *The media equation: How people treat computers, television, and new media like real people and places.* Cambridge, MA: Cambridge University Press.

[35] Tan, B. W., & Lo, T. W. (1991). The impact of interface customization on the effect of cognitive style on information system success. *Behavior and Information Technology, 10,* 297-310.

[36] Kolb, D. A. (1984). *Experiential learning: Experience as the source of learning and development.* Englewood Cliffs, NJ: Prentice-Hall.

A learning tool for the visualization of general directed or undirected rooted trees

K. Paparrizos, N. Samaras & A. Sifaleras
Department of Applied Informatics, University of Macedonia, Greece

Abstract

This paper presents a new learning tool developed for the visualization of general directed and undirected rooted trees. This visualization tool for teaching graph and network algorithms provides an interactive view of the subject being taught to the students. The tool is designed for three different groups of users: developers, instructors and students. It could be used for the visualization of any algorithm that generates a sequence of trees. This new tool minimizes the instructor's effort and gives him the possibility of drawing trees easily with many different properties. It can be used efficiently in courses like Graph Theory or Network Programming or in an introductory course like Algorithms and Data Structures. We believe that this tool will be an effective supplement to traditional classroom education. It is a commonly accepted fact that teaching can be vastly amplified when it is done visually and interactively instead of in the traditional way. Therefore, a summary of other educational tools concerning tree drawing is presented. Benefits and drawbacks are thoroughly described in order to support the efficiency of modern learning technology.
Keywords: interactive learning environment, intelligent tutoring systems, tree visualization, Matlab.

1 Introduction

Data Structures and Algorithms is a fundamental course in Computer Science. However, many students find it difficult because it requires abstract thinking. It would be very helpful for students, if there was a visualization tool of some basic data structures such as trees and graphs. Students are able to learn interactively by receiving feedback provided either by the instructor or by a computer program. The tool would allow students to see how a tree is traversed in different traversals (pre-order, in-order, post-order, and level-order). This tool could be used as an effective supplement to the traditional classroom education and textbook for Data Structures and Algorithms courses. Usually an instructor who teaches Graph Theory topics such as trees had to draw on a whiteboard a tree and explain its pre-order using a pen. That surely is not a flexible way to make many different examples, furthermore it is very much time consuming. This paper describes how the teaching of Graph Theory topics such as trees can be improved in compare to the traditional tutoring system.

The teaching of an algorithm or a data structure can be greatly enhanced with such a visualization tool. It is a commonly accepted fact that teaching can be vastly amplified when it is done visually and interactively instead of purely theoretically, Tal and Dobkin [1] and Naps [2].

The paper is organized as follows. In section 2 we briefly describe any previous work which has been done. In section 3 we give the motivation which led us to develop this visualization tool. In section 4, we present the analysis and design of our tool and give an illustrative example. In section 5 we focus on implementation principles. Finally in section 6 we show that the implemented visualization tool can be extended in order to visualize Simplex type algorithms for Network Programming problems.

2 Previous work

There is a vast amount of research of different visualization tools conducted over the years. The development of technologies and the evolvement of the World Wide Web have influenced education. Instructional Web sites and courses on the Web have grown dramatically. Web-based courses that consist of the syllabus, assignments and lecture notes are now widely used. Two interesting Web sites are the ones developed by Duane [3] and Mukundan [4]. In particular, Mukundan's homepage has a comprehensive applet which demonstrates the three different types of binary tree traversals, i.e., pre-order traversal, in-order traversal, and post-order traversal. The user can see the three types, but not create his own general trees. Our educational function is intended to aid Computer Science students facing for the fist time Data Structures and Algorithms. Therefore, as mentioned by Foley [5], ease of use becomes our main consideration. The design of educational software needs to be learner centred rather than user centred Soloway et al [6].

There are many tools for graph drawing. A very good source containing a large collection of graph drawing tools is a link provided by Tamassia [7] homepage. This paper is based on ideas presented in the books by Battista et al [8] and Goodrich and Tamassia [9]. Both books are very good sources and contain useful information. Also, *GraphEd* is a graph editor, by Himsolt [10], which provides graph layout algorithms and an interface for application modules. It provides a wide variety of graph drawing algorithms including spring embeddings and special algorithms for drawing trees, and planar graphs. Graphlet [11], the successor of *GraphEd*, is a toolkit for graph editors and graph algorithms. Both of them have been developed at the University of Passau, Germany.

Many tools have been based on *VGJ* tool, (Visualizing Graphs with Java, McCreary C.) The VGJ Graph Drawing Tool [12] is a tool for graph drawing and graph layout. Graphs can be input into *VGJ* in two ways: with a textual description (GML) or through a drawing the user creates using the graph editor. The user can then select an algorithm to layout the graph in an organized and aesthetically pleasing way. Also there is the aiSee [13] tool, created in *AbsInt, Angewandte Informatik GmbH Germany*, which reads a textual graph specification and visualizes the graph. Its design has been optimized to handle large graphs generated by applications automatically. Another graphic tool which can handle tree - tuple automata is Taja 2.0, by Lecland and Rety [14]. Furthermore, data structures libraries in Java, *JDSL,* have been developed. Information for tree structures can be found in the following papers: Tamassia *et al* [15] and Goodrich *et al* [16].

Finally, commercial graph drawing systems are available from Tom Sawyer Software [17]. There are systems and libraries for UNIX and MS-Windows, mostly written in C++.

3 Motivation

Recently many scientists and engineers are using Matlab [18] not only as a modeling and analysis tool, but also as a visualization tool. There is a function in Matlab which plots undirected trees, the *treeplot(p)* function, where *p* is the vector of parent pointers, (the node *i* is the root if and only if $p(i) = 0$). There is also the *treelayout(parent,post)* function, where parent is the vector of parent pointers and post is an optional post-order permutation on the tree nodes. Function *treelayout(parent,post)* does not plot trees, it just computes the coordinates of the nodes.

Function *treeplot(p)* does not plot the tree structures correctly. For example, if the tree defined by the vector p = [0 1 1 1 1 2 2 2] is plotted in Matlab by typing *treeplot(p)* in the command window, the tree shown in Figure 1 is drawn.

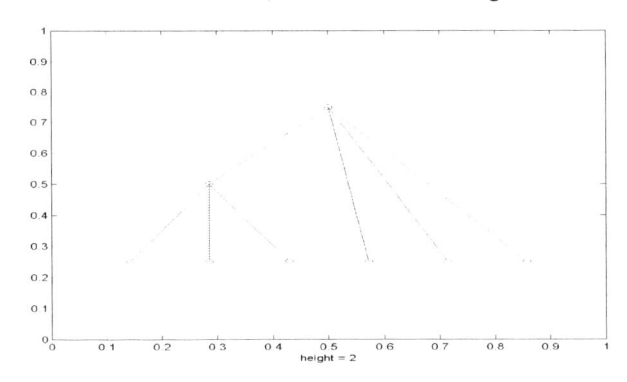

Figure 1: An incorrect tree plot.

We see in Figure 1, that some leaves of the tree are not drawn at the correct level. In fact, all leaves are drawn at the bottom level. Furthermore *treeplot(p)* does not support directed trees and it does not show the label of each node.

4 Design and implementation issues

We developed a new function for the correct visualization of general directed and undirected rooted trees. Our function *Drawtree(p, pre, x)* is an educational purpose function which has the following three inputs:

a. *p* is the vector of parent pointers in which $p(r) = r$ implies that *r* is the root.
b. *pre* is the vector of the pre-order traversal.
c. *x* is a vector which describes the arc's directions.

For any non root node *i*, $x(i) = 1$, ($x(i) = -1$) implies that arc *(p(i), i), (arc (i, p(i)))* is contained in the tree. Also, it is set $x(r) = 0$ for the root node *r*. This vector is an optional choice for the user. In case it is passed as an argument to the function the tree will be directed.

For aesthetic reasons we slightly modified Matlab function *quiver*. In particular the size of the arrow head and the width of the base is 25% instead of the size 33% used in Matlab.

Currently *Drawtree(p, pre, x)* consists of 186 lines of source code. *Drawtree(p, pre, x)* exploits the power of Matlab Programming Language, see for example Marchand and Holland [19], and therefore it is not only flexible and customizable, but also easy to use. The student, who wishes to install the Drawtree.m file, can install it as he would have done with any other Matlab m - file. First he will select File → Select Path → Add with subfolders and then choose the appropriate folder which contains the above file. In addition, the student can choose some parameters with the help of certain pop up lists. He may select the color and the shape of the nodes. The pop up menus are illustrated in Figures 2 and 3.

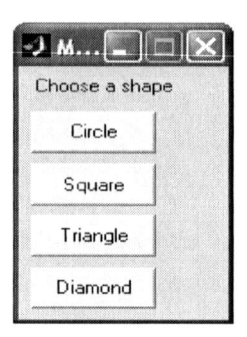

Figure 2:   Selection of the node's shape.

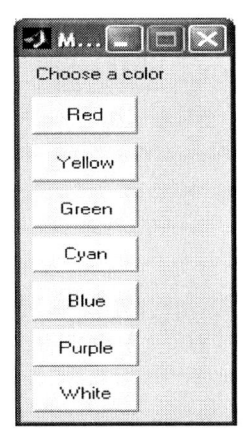

Figure 3: Selection of the node's color.

In order to use our software, the user may type the next commands in the Matlab Command Window:

p = [18 1 1 2 2 2 3 3 18 15 12 9 15 12 9 15 12 18 3];

pre = [18 9 12 14 17 11 15 16 10 13 1 2 4 5 6 3 8 7 19];

If the user wants the tree to be undirected, he may now type the command *Drawtree(p, pre)*. The resulting tree is the one illustrated in Figure 4.

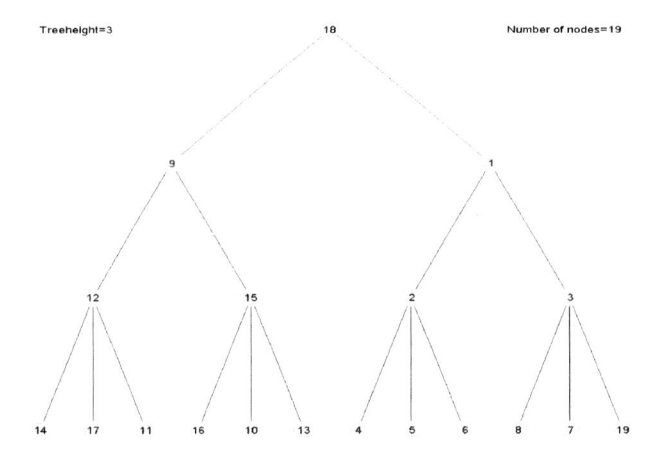

Figure 4: An undirected rooted tree plotted by function Drawtree.

In case the user wants the tree to be directed, he must insert as an input in the function the following *x* vector:

$$x = [1\ 1\ -1\ -1\ -1\ 1\ 1\ 1\ 1\ -1\ -1\ 1\ 1\ 1\ -1\ 1\ 1\ 0\ -1];$$

Now, the command *Drawtree(p, pre, x)* will plot the tree in Figure 5.

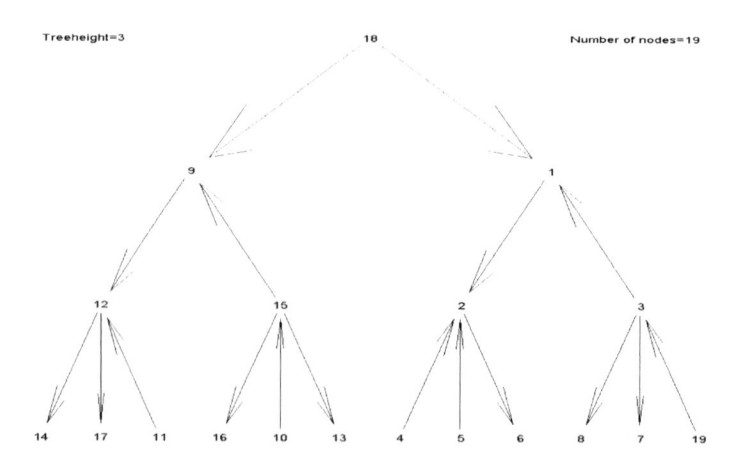

Figure 5: A directed rooted tree plot plotted by function Drawtree.

The difference between the trees shown in Figure 1 and Figures 4 and 5 is now clear. In figures 4 and 5, the trees are drawn correctly. In particular, the nodes are drawn at the right level. Moreover the plot includes the tree height and the total number of nodes.

File *Drawtree.m* contains analytical instructions, so that the user can verify the facts mentioned earlier. It is obvious that instructors can draw any kind of tree easier than they do at the traditional classroom teaching of trees. Besides, they can interactively modify the tree structure and finally the students can adjust easier to this new learning environment.

In order to achieve the results just mentioned, an algorithm drawing trees has been developed. The main part of the algorithm is devoted to the calculation of the nodes coordinates. The tree is drawn in such a way, so that its arcs do not cross with each other.

In order for the tree to be drawn correctly, all the nodes should have appropriate coordinates. The root node is drawn, of course, at the top of the tree. All the nodes being in the same level are at the same distance, in the y axis, with the nodes of the previous and the next level. Therefore, the distance in the y axis, between all the nodes of the first and the second level is the same as for the nodes of the second and third level.

As far as concerns the x axis, the computation of the nodes x axis coordinates begin from the x axis coordinates of the leaves. Specifically, the node being at the bottom level, at the left corner has been assigned with zero for the x axis coordinate. Every next node of the same level has such coordinates for the x axis, so it is at the same distance from its left or right side, node.

At this point the tree is not ready yet to be drawn. In order to avoid the edge's intersection, for all the nodes above the bottom level, their coordinates for the x axis are being edited so that the parent node is drawn in the middle of its children distance (node's movement). Hence, all the nodes at the final tree will be drawn at the correct place.

The details mentioned before, concerning the node's coordinates for the x, y axis, are shown in Figure 6. It is the same as figure 5, except that now the user can see the axis.

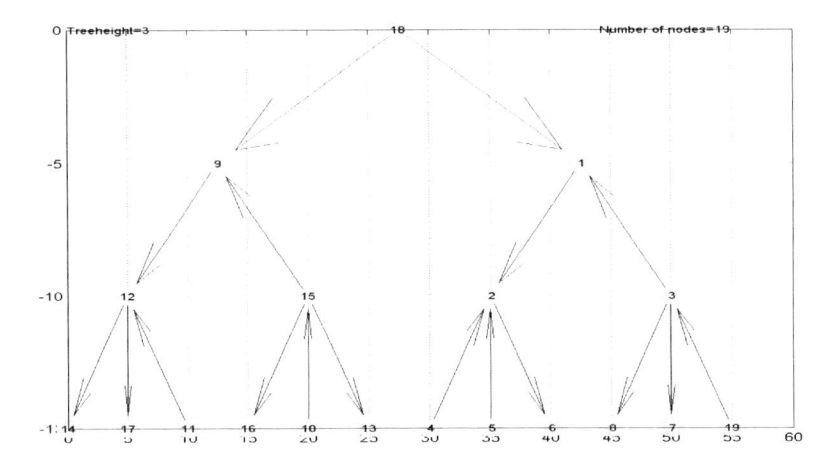

Figure 6: The user can verify the x, y coordinates.

In order to achieve this result, the pre-order traversal is used. In particular, the order of the nodes in each depth level is the same with that in the pre-order traversal. Therefore, a vector including the tree's pre-order, *pre*, is used.

The optional directions of the tree arcs are visualized using the *x* vector. The *Drawtree* function is programmed in such a way that can have two or three inputs, depending on the user's choice. Finally the user can select any time the nodes colour and shape.

5 Conclusions and future work

In this paper, we have presented a visualization tool designed to aid computer science students learn basic Data Structures. This tool not only lets students see the visualization of a general, directed or undirected, rooted tree, but also allows them to customize their own trees and make use of the pre-order traversal.

This new tool minimizes the instructor's effort and gives him the possibility of drawing trees easily with many different properties. It can be used efficiently in courses like *Graph Theory* or *Network Optimization* or in an introductory course like *Algorithms and Data Structures*. We believe this tool will be an effective supplement to traditional instruction.

Should we want to find the educational value of our tool; then certain tests must take place inside the classrooms during the lectures, for the needs of our Department's courses. More significant is to find how students make use of this specific software, rather than just explaining to them what might be the potential benefits, Hundhausen *et al* [20] and Lawrence *et al* [21]. Other researches show how to use algorithm animations in learning situations, as for example Kehoe *et al* [22]. This is the best way for measuring the efficiency of any software dealing with Algorithm Visualization, described by Price *et al* [23], as a subclass of software visualization, concerned with illustrating computer algorithms in terms of their high-level operations, usually for the purpose of enhancing computer science students' understanding of the algorithms' procedural behaviour. We shouldn't forget on the contrary, the fact that there have been conducted researches which support that pedagogical advantages can be only partially attributed to Algorithm Visualization Technology, as for example Byrne *et al* [24].

A possible future enhancement for our educational tool is to add options for post-order and in-order permutation and to visualize the Simplex Algorithm and also some exterior point Network Flow Algorithms as for example, Paparrizos [25], where we meet significant tree modifications. This tool would help the student to better follow the steps of these specific type algorithms.

References

[1] Tal A. & Dobkin D. Visualization of Geometric Algorithms. *IEEE Transactions on Visualization and Computer Graphics*, 1(2), pp. 194-204, 1995.

[2] Naps T. L., Incorporating Algorithm Visualization into Educational Theory: A Challenge for the Future, *The European Online Magazine for the IT Professional*, 2(2), 2001.

[3] Duane J. J., www.seas.gwu.edu/~idsv/idsv.html

[4] Mukundan R., www.cosc.canterbury.ac.nz/people/mukundan/dsal/BTree.html

[5] Foley B. J., Designing Visualization Tools for Learning. *Proc. of the ACM SIGCHI Conference on Human Factors in Computing Systems,* Los Angeles, pp. 309–310, 1998.

[6] Soloway E., Guzdial M. & Hay K. E., Learner - centered design: the challenge for HCI in the 21st century. *Interactions*, 1(2), pp. 36-48, 1994.

[7] Tamassia R., rw4.cs.uni-sb.de/users/sander/html/gstools.html

[8] Battista G., Eades P., Tamassia R. & Tollis I. G., *Graph Drawing: Algorithms for the Visualization of Graphs,* Prentice Hall: Upper Saddle River, N.J., 1999.
[9] Goodrich M. T. & Tamassia, R., *Data Structures and Algorithms in JAVA,* Wiley, 1998.
[10] Himsolt M., GraphEd: A graphical platform for the implementation of graph algorithms. *Proc. of the Graph Drawing, DIMACS International Workshop,* pp. 182-193, 1994.
[11] Graphlet, www.infosun.fmi.uni-passau.de/Graphlet
[12] VGJ, www.eng.auburn.edu/department/cse/research/graph_drawing/vgj.html
[13] aiSee, www.absint.com/aisee
[14] Lecland B. & Rety P., Taja 2.0, 2001, www.univ-orleans.fr/SCIENCES/LIFO/Members/lecland/taja.php
[15] Tamassia R., Goodrich M. T., Vismara L., Handy M., Shubina G., Cohen R., Hudson B., Baker R. S., Gelfand N. & Barandes U., JDSL: The data structures library in java, *Dr. Dobb's Journal,* 26(4), pp. 21–31, 2001.
[16] Goodrich M. T., Handy M., Hudson B. & Tamassia R., Accessing the Internal Organization of Data Structures in the JDSL library, *Lecture Notes in Computer Science,* 1619, pp. 124-139, Springer-Verlag Heidelberg: Baltimore, 1999, selected papers from the *International Workshop Algorithm Engineering and Experimentation ALENEX '99,* 1999.
[17] Tom Sawyer Software, www.tomsawyer.com
[18] The MathWorks, Inc., MATLAB: The Language of Technical Computing, Massachussetts, © 1994-2003.
[19] Marchand P. & Holland O., T., *Graphics and GUIs with MATLAB,* 3rd. Edition, CHAPMAN AND HALL/ CRC, 2002.
[20] Hundhausen, D. C., Douglas, A. S. & Stasko, T. J., A Meta-Study of Algorithm Visualization Effectiveness. *Journal of Visual Languages and Computing,* 13(3), pp. 259-290, 2002.
[21] Lawrence A. W., Badre A. N. & Stasko J. T., Empirically Evaluating the Use of Animations to Teach Algorithms. *Proc. of the IEEE Symposium on Visual Languages,* St. Louis, 1994.
[22] Kehoe C., Stasko J. T. & Taylor A., Rethinking the evaluation of algorithm animations as learning aids: an observational study. *International Journal of Human-Computer Studies,* 54, pp. 265-284, 2001.
[23] Price B. A., Baecker R. M. & Small I. S., A principled taxonomy of software visualization. *Journal of Visual Languages and Computing,* 4, pp. 211–266, 1993.
[24] Byrne M. D., Catrambone R. & Stasko J. T., Evaluating animations as student's aids in learning computer algorithms. *Computers and Education,* 33, pp. 253–278, 1999.
[25] Paparrizos K., An infeasible (exterior point) simplex algorithm for assignment problems. *Mathematical Programming,* 51, pp 45-54, 1991.

Contributions of an electronic performance support system to learning a complex cognitive skill

A. Darabi
The Learning Systems Institute, Florida State University, Florida, USA

Abstract

van Merriënboer [1] defines complex cognitive skills as skills that have a number of constituent skills some of which are cognitive. Based on this definition, conducting a performance systems analysis (PSA) of an organizational performance issue can be considered a complex cognitive skill. PSA contains many whole and sub tasks whose accomplishments require complex cognitive strategies that learner needs to execute in order to successfully "diagnose" the systemic causes of the performance issues and "prescribe" the right performance interventions. The 4C/ID model (van Merriënboer [1]) lists "supportive information" and "just-in-time information" as two major components of its "training blueprint" for complex learning. In this study, an electronic performance support system (EPSS) was employed to provide supportive and just-in-time information to students in a performance technology course. Twelve students divided into three groups used the EPSS while they conducted performance analyses of actual performance problems in three professional organizations. Students' self-efficacy scores, measured before and after using the EPSS to conduct a performance systems analysis, indicated that their self-confidence in conducting PSA on their own improved. Also qualitative and quantitative analysis of students' feedback on the experience demonstrated that EPSS was a valuable tool for learning the skill and supporting their self-regulatory behaviors.

Keywords: EPSS, electronic performance support systems, performance analysis, complex cognitive skills, human performance technology.

1 Introduction

Performance Systems analysis (PSA) is an application of Human Performance Technology (HPT), which the International Society for Performance Improvement (ISPI) defined as "the systematic and systemic identification and removal of barriers to individual and organizational performance" [2]. For successful application of HPT, the performance analyst should rigorously adhere to a data-driven methodology, yet flexibly respond to unanticipated cues that arise during the analysis (Stolovitch and Keeps [3]; Rossett [4]).

According to van Merriënboer's [1] definition, conducting performance systems analysis can qualify as a complex cognitive skill because of its numerous cognitive components. He defines complex cognitive skills as skills with a number of "constituent skills," the majority of which are performed cognitively. He has also developed the empirically based Four Components Instructional Design Model (4C/ID Model) specifically for instruction and training of this type of skills. The four components of this model are "Whole Tasks," "Part-Tasks," "Support Information," and "Just-in-time Information" that are wrapped in a 10-step blue print, prescribed for developing instruction and training for complex learning (van Merriënboer [1]).

In a graduate level course on teaching how to conduct performance analysis, the required skills were analyzed and decomposed according to the strategies recommended by instructional guidelines such as Cognitive Apprenticeship (Brown et al. [5]) and the 4C/ID models. The "whole tasks" and Part-task" were identified, designed, and sequenced to provide students with a mix of instruction in theory, practice at the use of strategies and tools, and real-world experience. An Electronic Performance Support System (EPSS) was employed to provide students with "support information" and "just-in-time information." The learning goals for students were to acquire competence and confidence in using HPT strategies and tools in a gradual, cyclical process of self-regulated learning. The following sections of the paper present a description of the course, its learning activities and the theoretical basis of the study.

2 The performance systems analysis course

The "whole tasks" identified and designed for the PSA course were complex skills such as systems analysis, workforce performance problems identification and analysis, identification and analysis of the problem's causes, and finally, recommending appropriate performance interventions for eliminating those causes. The "part-tasks" were the components of each of these whole tasks and the skills required for accomplishing them. Skills such as conducting an interview, conducting a focus group, using a cause analysis technique, dealing with clients, making a presentation, participating in a meeting with the client, etc... were among the "recurrent" and "non-recurrent" skills emphasized when students were provided with information. The complexity of these tasks and the application of a situated learning approach (Brown et al. [5]), provided the students the opportunity to coordinate and integrate the constituent skills (van Merriënboer [1] of performance analysis.

The students were introduced to three clients who requested assistance with solving performance problems in their organizations. The instructor grouped students with complementary skills to address the designated performance problems. Each team was assigned to a project, considering the individuals' preferences for the organizations and the performance issues.

During the three phases of the project, EPSS provided students with the support information and guidelines required for conducting the tasks in that phase. It also was available to the students on the Web for their instant access to the just-in-time information regarding any of the tasks performed in that phase.

3 EPSS for performance analysis

$ePlan^{TM}$ is a Web-based Electronic Performance Support System designed and developed by the Learning Systems Institute of Florida State University for the United States Navy. $ePlan^{TM}$ assists performance consultants in the analysis of performance problems that have been identified by clients. $ePlan^{TM}$ draws on a synthesis of several HPT models to provide directions and support for the following analysis activities: identify performance problems, analyze workforce performance, select specific organizational results to be examined, select data collection methods, weigh and prioritize performance gaps to be closed, identify potential causes of performance problems, and identify solutions to close performance gaps. Throughout these activities $ePlan^{TM}$ generates nine reports to be used by analysts and clients.

$ePlan^{TM}$ provides numerous tools to aid the novice performance analyst to investigate causes of, and recommend solutions for performance problems. It programmatically structures the analysis activities in three phases: Define, Analyze, and Select. It updates the existing information used in activities and reports throughout the use of $ePlan^{TM}$ as analysts enter new data. $ePlan^{TM}$ also allows users access to reports from multiple projects and facilitates a threaded discussion for users to communicate across projects, thus promoting a community of practice.

The present study examined students' reactions to the use of EPSS and compared their pre- and post-treatment reports of self-efficacy on conducting performance analysis. Students' perceived self-efficacy to perform the constituent skills of performance analysis, and the use of an EPSS for that purpose, was expected to increase during the period of treatment.

4 Methods

The design of this investigation concentrated on how the EPSS, as a component of the PSA course, enhanced students' acquisition of competence. Students started the course with an introductory discussion of the HPT concepts, theoretical basis, and general tasks involved in the process of performance analysis. In the second session of the class, the instructor grouped the students into three teams according to their previous experiences in coursework, research methodology, work experience, and use of computers. The pre-selected performance problems were then randomly assigned to the teams as their projects for the semester.

At the third session, the instructor and his assistants presented an overview of $ePlan^{TM}$, its contents, and its role in the students' implementation of their team projects. Subsequently, teams met with teaching assistants for a total of three out-of-class sessions during the course of the semester. In each session, students reviewed and completed the three phases of $ePlan^{TM}$, the Define phase, the Analyze phase and the Select phase. It was the teams' responsibility to contact the teaching assistants and begin $ePlan^{TM}$ activities.

During the class instruction, teams learned about the tasks involved in each of these phases and started collecting data required for their projects in their initial meetings with their clients at the project locations. Each team was instructed to use the collected data and start the first phase of $ePlan^{TM}$. At the beginning of each phase, teams were presented with an overview of the $ePlan^{TM}$ session. Although the students worked with clients in groups and conducted analyses of workforce environments in teams, they were required to individually log into $ePlan^{TM}$ and enter their team data. This flexibility provided students the opportunity to experience the $ePlan^{TM}$ individually while sharing the experience of collecting, analyzing, and interpreting the data as teams. They were encouraged to discuss the issues of their assignments with one another during the use of $ePlan^{TM}$. At the conclusion of the last $ePlan^{TM}$ session, students were asked to respond to a series of questions presented in data collection instruments and participated in focus group discussions concerning their experiences with $ePlan^{TM}$.

4.1 Measures

Qualitative and quantitative data collection methods were employed at different points of the students' experiences with the $ePlan^{TM}$. The following is a description of these methods and instruments:

4.1.1 Self-efficacy measure

Bandura and Schunk [6] discussed the conceptual framework and application of self-efficacy measure in a study of mathematical efficacy. Based on their application of this measure, a five-item instrument was developed to measure students' self-efficacy and their perceived competence at conducting performance analysis and its component skills (see Table 2). This instrument specifically addressed the complex skills involved in the performance analysis corresponding with the phases and application of $ePlan^{TM}$. Each item presented a scale of 10 to 100 to represent values ranging from "Not sure" to "Very Sure". Items included questions such as, "On scale from 10 to 100, how sure are you that you will be able to successfully conduct a Performance Systems Analysis after completing this course?"

Table 1: Students' feedback on the usefulness of the EPSS by phase of team PSA projects.

PSA Phases	Feedback Questionnaire Items	1 (Not at all)	2	3	4	5	6 (Very much)	M	SD
Organizational Analysis	Helpful in formulating the team approach	8.3	16.7	0.0	25.0	0.0	50.0	4.17	1.03
	Informative in preparing issues to explore	0.0	16.7	16.7	0.0	0.0	66.7	4.17	1.27
	Instructive in providing the appropriate direction	8.3	8.3	0.0	33.3	33.3	16.7	4.25	1.49
Work Environment Analysis	Helpful in formulating the team approach	8.3	8.3	16.7	41.7	25.0	0.0	3.67	1.23
	Guiding how to analyze the issues	8.3	8.3	16.7	25.0	33.3	8.3	3.92	1.44
Gap and Cause Analysis	Helpful in formulating the team approach	8.3	0.0	25.0	16.7	41.7	8.3	4.08	1.38
	Informative in preparing issues to explore	8.3	0.0	25.0	16.7	41.7	8.3	4.08	1.38
	Guiding how to analyze gaps & causes	8.3	0.0	25.0	16.7	33.3	16.7	4.17	1.47
Solution Identification and Selection	Helpful in formulating the team approach	16.7	8.3	16.7	25.0	16.7	16.7	3.67	1.72
	Guiding how to analyze the issues	8.3	16.7	16.7	33.3	0.0	25.0	3.75	1.66

The pretest instrument was administered after the overview of *ePlan*[TM] and before students began their *ePlan*[TM] projects. The posttest instrument was given to students immediately after completion of their *ePlan*[TM] projects.

Table 2: Differences in students' reported self-efficacy before and after using the EPSS.

Self-Efficacy Items Range: 10-100	M	SD	M	SD	Mean Difference	t	df	p
How sure are you that you can successfully use an EPSS in support of a PSA project?	63.64	24.61	90.91	7.0	27.27*	3.96	10	0.003*
How sure are you that you can successfully conduct PSA projects after this course?	82.73	14.90	92.73	10.09	10.00*	2.34	10	0.041*
How sure are you that you can successfully conduct the organizational and environmental analysis for a PSA project?	72.73	22.84	94.55	8.2	21.82*	3.01	10	0.013*
How sure are you that you can successfully conduct the gap and cause analysis for a PSA project?	79.09	23.00	93.64	9.24	14.55	1.84	10	0.096
How sure are you that you can successfully conduct the selection and recommendation of solutions for a PSA project?	75.45	22.07	93.64	8.09	18.18*	2.56	10	0.029*

* $p < 0.05$

4.1.2 Student feedback

A questionnaire was designed to collect information on the usefulness and quality of $ePlan^{TM}$. Two types of questions were used to measure students' reactions to the quality and technical features of $ePlan^{TM}$. Questions specifically focused on whether $ePlan^{TM}$ was helpful in formulating their team approach, informative in their preparation, and instructive in guiding them through the phases of performance analysis projects. One series of questions, constructed on a six-point Likert-type scale, corresponded to the phases of performance analysis. A set of open-ended questions provided students the opportunity to describe their personal experiences with using $ePlan^{TM}$ and offer suggestions for its improvement.

4.1.3 Focus group sessions

At the completion of the students' $ePlan^{TM}$ projects, each team of students participated in a focus group discussion of their experiences with $ePlan^{TM}$. These discussions mainly derived from students' previous reactions to the use of $ePlan^{TM}$ throughout the semester. Discussions included themes of personal experiences, difficulties using the tool, revisions of the tool, its alignment with the course design, and the relevance of the various features of $ePlan^{TM}$ to real world projects. The focus group discussions were tape-recorded and later transcribed for analysis purposes. This transcription provided a set of qualitative data that complemented information collected with other instruments.

5 Data analysis and results

The quantitative data collected by self-efficacy instruments and the feedback questionnaire were analyzed to study the students' use of the EPSS and differences in their self-efficacy before and after the use of the EPSS. A simple descriptive analysis was performed on students' reactions data. A paired samples t-test was used to analyze the pre- and post- self-efficacy scores.

The qualitative data collected through tape recording the focus group discussions were transcribed and segmented into a list of discrete statements. The responses to the open ended questions in the feedback survey were compiled into a second list. Each list was reviewed and analyzed looking for students' references to their experiences with the use of $ePlan^{TM}$. The author then categorized statements according to those references. In the second round of analysis, the two lists were combined and the two sets of categories were merged.

The revisions included compiling the list of references under two major headings, "Use of $ePlan^{TM}$ in the PSA Course" and "Technical Difficulties with $ePlan^{TM}$," (see Tables 3 and 4 respectively). Without exception, all the students' feedback that referred to the technical aspects of $ePlan^{TM}$ was critical and all of their positive feedback referred to the use of the software and the support it provided for the students projects. At the end of this iterative refinement and abstraction process, students' statements were categorized into more general themes which characterized the use of $ePlan^{TM}$ in this PSA course.

5.1 Students' feedback

Table 1 summarizes the students' feedback on how supportive and helpful the $ePlan^{TM}$ was regarding the major components or the "whole tasks" designed for teaching this course.

5.2 Student's self-efficacy

Students reported a significant improvement in their self-efficacy regarding the uses of the EPSS in support of a performance analysis project compared to their statements prior to their use of $ePlan^{TM}$ (see Table 2). At the end of this experience, they found themselves more confident in using an EPSS in support of their future projects (t [10] = 3.96, p = .003).

5.3 Students' discussion of the experience

Table 3 displays the categories of students' references extracted from their comments made during the focus group discussion of their experience and in response to open-ended questions in the Feedback survey.

Table 3: Categorization of students' feedback responses and frequency of references

Use of $ePlan^{TM}$ in PSA Course	Frequency of References
• Channels your thoughts throughout the process	22
• Structures your thoughts by providing a framework and context	21
• Helps the novices by clarifying the performance issues	5
• Provides a sense of realities of practicing PSA as profession	4

Students' negative comments were directed toward the design of $ePlan^{TM}$, its instructional design problems, and its interaction with the course layout. Table 4 displays the number of references students made to these issues

Table 4: Categorization of students' responses on technical aspects of *ePlan*^{TM} by frequency and percentage of references

Technical Difficulties with *ePlan*^{TM}	Freq.	%
EPSS Design Problems:		
• Not intuitive interface	14	16.1
• Awkward Navigation	10	11.5
Instructional Design problems:		
• Not user-friendly Content/functions	14	16.1
• Redundant data entry requirements	7	8.0
• Presentation of PSA phases lacked declarative and predictable	3	3.4
Sequencing of events		
• Too much text	3	3.4
• Unclear instructions on how to modify or what to fill in	2	2.3
Course Related Problems:		
• Lack of sync and alignment with the course schedule	20	22.1
• Not relevant or appropriate for every PSA project.	9	10.3
• Inhibitive to thinking out of the box to include other existing theoretical paradigms	5	5.7
Total number of references	87	100%

6 Discussion and conclusions

The PSA course that provided the context for this experience was designed to accommodate for the current shift in instructional design programs toward the performance technology. Students who enroll in this course are interested in learning how to conduct performance analysis as a complementing skill to their instructional design competencies. Using a performance support system is what performance analysts may recommend to assist clients for improving performance. The use of the EPSS provided the students themselves with a tool to enhance their skills as performance consultants in a course designed for an authentic learning experience.

Conducting a performance analysis is a complex cognitive task that requires learners to engage in a significant amount of concentration and planning, as well as self-regulation. The analysts usually experience several organizational and performance issues at once and perform multiple tasks simultaneously. They observe and analyze performance problems, performance gaps and their causes over a span of multiple visits to client agencies. As the performance technologists recommend job aids and EPSS as support systems for workers, they themselves ma benefit from having the supportive and just-in-time information when they needed. In the present study, students, in response to different questions in multiple instruments, reported that their use of $ePlan^{TM}$ provided the information they needed for performing their tasks.

The qualitative data presented previously illustrate that $ePlan^{TM}$ facilitated students' performance of the tasks required for their course projects. Student's reports on the open-ended questions included statements that $ePlan^{TM}$ provided information for their systemic and systematic analysis of client organizations, performance gap and cause analysis, and selection of performance interventions. Responses such as "it help me to more clearly understand the components and function of the organization," "helped organize and form specific cause & gap," "helped me think more systematic & piece by piece," "made us rank cost-effectiveness," and "ePlan walked me through the solution I.D. process in a clear manner" specifically demonstrated this facilitation.

The EPSS evidently contributed to students' planning and goal-setting behavior promoting their self-regulatory processes. Supporting data reported in Tables 1 and 3 were inducted from specific statements such as that $ePlan^{TM}$ "helped us organize and focus initial analysis," and that it "established process goals." These statements indicated that $ePlan^{TM}$ elicited specific goal-oriented behavior among some students, and that those students found the EPSS to be useful to help them set and monitor goals. Furthermore, the EPSS was found to support the students' self-reflection and self-reaction. These findings, categorically tabulated in Table 3," are drawn from specific statements such as "It forces you to sit down and think about what direction you want to head in," "I think it's useful as a tool and to get the brain starting to work through things before a paper or a proposal is ever done," and "…you're forced to write out all of your opinions and rethink them and restate them for another audience."

Bandura and Locke [7] found self-efficacy to be highly predictive of learners' accomplishments. Accordingly, the reported improvement in students' self-efficacy in the current study may be an indicator of their future success. The aggregate effects of their personal development and their experience in an authentic learning environment provided by this course will assist them in working and succeeding in the real work environment. Students' comments in their discussion of the use and application of the EPSS further confirmed these arguments. Based on their focus group data, the students' use of the EPSS provided them with a positive learning experience and a framework for their activities, and assisted with keeping them on track while executing the components of a complex skill.

Given the significant role that EPSS plays in students' performance and learning, as $ePlan^{TM}$ did in this course, they must be designed and developed based on a sound instructionally design approach. According to students' comments on the features and functions of $ePlan^{TM}$, an EPSS should support the performance, rather than hinder the effort, of the user. Failure to address issues such as the intuitiveness of the interface, smooth navigation, user friendliness, and non-redundant data entry requirements inhibits users' performance and learning.

In summary, the use of the EPSS in this study was found to be a positive experience for the users. They used it successfully to perform the tasks they were assigned, partly because this particular EPSS was specifically designed for the type of use that was the subject of the course and for users like these students. In other words, this EPSS was tailor-made for the profession of performance analysis and, therefore, students found it rewarding to use because it was beneficial for practically supporting their projects. The author argues that this is an important issue for future developers of EPSSs to ensure their products are at least provisionally designed to support novices in a particular profession. He also recommends that there should be an accurate alignment between the features of the software and the context in which the EPSS is presented. In this case, the course activities might have been better synchronized with the phases of $ePlan^{TM}$.

Nevertheless, the students' reports of using the EPSS are viewed as evidence that it expanded their understanding of HPT by providing them the information, direction, guidelines, and support they needed in the application of their acquired competencies. Finally, the EPSS seemed to increase students' self-efficacy on the complex cognitive skill of performance analysis. It reportedly aided them to monitor, record, reflect upon, and evaluate their own performance in the completion of class projects. Based on these findings one can argue that providing an EPSS to support learning a complex cognitive skill can be a valuable asset for the learners to develop knowledge and skills, enhance their self-efficacy, and support their self-regulated learning of performance analysis.

References

[1] Van Merriënboer, J. J. G., Training complex cognitive skills: A four-component instructional design model for technical skills, Englewood Cliffs, NJ: Educational Technology Publications, 1997.

[2] International Society for Performance Improvement Web site, http://www.ispi.org.

[3] Stolovitch, H. D. & Keeps, E. J., Handbook of human performance technology, 2nd ed. San Francisco: Jossey-Bass Pfeiffer, 1999.

[4] Rossett, A., Analysis for human performance technology (Chapter 8). Handbook of Human Performance Technology, ed. H.D. Stolovitch and E.J. Keeps, San Francisco: Jossey-Bass Pfiffer, pp.139-162, 1999.

[5] Brown, J. S., Collins, A., & Duguid, P., Situated cognition and the culture of learning, Educational Researcher, **18(1),** pp. 32-42, 1989.

[6] Bandura, A., & Schunk, D. H., Cultivating competence, self-efficacy, and intrinsic interest through proximal self-motivation, Journal of Personality and Social Psychology, **41(3),** pp. 586-598, 1981.

[7] Bandura, A., & Locke, E. A., Negative self-efficacy and goal effects revisited, Journal of Applied Psychology, **88(1),** pp. 87-89, 2003.

Metacognitive questions to improve surfing and learning activities on the Web

G. Chiazzese, A. Chifari, S. Ottaviano, L. Seta & M. Allegra
Institute for Educational Technologies, Department of Palermo, National Research Council, Italy

Abstract

The purpose of this paper is to present the set of metacognitive questions included in the Did@browser System, a meta-tool for Web surfing, developed at the Institute for Educational Technologies, with the aim of helping pupils to reflect on their own surfing strategies when they study on the Net.
Keywords: metacognition, learning environments, Web surfing.

1 Introduction

Although free navigation is an important part of the process of learning on the Net, we think that it is useful to give some prompts to encourage students who use the Web to be more aware of their surfing process; in this way it is possible to mitigate some negative effects such as disorientation, random browsing of hypertext documents, or surfing guided mainly by interface elements, and so on.
From a psycho-educational point of view the prompts are a cognitive aid or rather provide scaffolding [1] to the learner and are later removed gradually as he becomes able to perform parts of an activity autonomously.
Since the activity of surfing information on the Web may come about in a more or less haphazard way, the introduction of specific prompts is considered to be of use to a novice learner who still needs to acquire familiarity and awareness of his actions.
   Valid prompts may consist in questions which aim to guide the learner in exercising executive control of his behaviour thereby employing strategies which allow him to assess the effectiveness of the procedures used to carry out a task.
The strategy of answering questions is both well known and effective [2] especially regarding reading comprehension, because it simplifies the

organization of topics and the linking of new information with previous knowledge. Recent research shows the effect of using metacognitive questions as a support for activating and engaging learners' awareness thus facilitating their learning and improving the outcomes of a task [3].

Starting from these considerations we hypothesize that connecting metacognitive questions to strategic surfing elements could improve the user's awareness during Web activities. As in a virtuous circle, we hypothesize that improving awareness during surfing could have a positive spin-off in the comprehension of online contents.

2 The Web-surfing meta-tool

The Web-surfing meta-tool has been developed to support the didactic surfing activities of inexperienced students.

As already discussed, in the context of teaching and learning activities based on the Web, specific cognitive tools have been designed for the acquisition and monitoring of metacognitive processes, so that these can be a more productive and enjoyable experience [4]. One of these tools is the meta-tool for Web surfing, developed at the Institute for Educational Technologies. It will be a part of a network learning environment named Did@browser, aimed at eliciting metacognitive and cooperative processes and so becoming itself a guide to promote awareness of Internet surfing [5].

From a technological point of view, the Did@browser system has a client/server architecture; in particular it is composed of two client software components and one server. The two clients are specific for teachers and students and are integrated in the browser. Both components send information to the server.

The teacher client allows the teacher to :
- program a set of metacognitive questions personalized for each student to administer during surfing;
- associate metacognitive questions to any links on a Web page;
- group the questions together according to categories chosen by the teacher;
- review student surfing from the data saved on the server;
- monitor a student during surfing.

The student client allows the student to:
- reflect on and respond to metacognitive questions associated to the links;
- be followed by the teacher during surfing.

The server communicates with the teacher and students components through the Cooperative Activity Control Protocol [6] which has been extended with the functionalities described above. All information sent to the server is organized and saved in a database and includes user profiles, the questions and their associations with the links and surfing trace.

Student surfing can take place with or without the support of metacognitive questions; the teacher decides whether to enable the functionality.

In both cases the following parameters are saved: date, time, name of the link, URL [7]. When the functionality of the metacognitive question is active, the server also saves the question with the student's corresponding answer. The question appears when the student clicks on the hot word.

The particular meta-tool functionality we wish to consider in this work is the possible association of meta-cognitive questions to the strategic elements of Web surfing. Using this tool, the teacher can select specific questions and activate them during the student's surfing, in order to motivate their choices and to increase their awareness when surfing through information on the Web.

3 Metacognitive questions for Web surfing

Our method for defining the questions to integrate into our system followed the steps listed below:
- identify strategic elements of the interaction user/Web (Web pages, hot words, buttons included in the page, buttons of the browser toolbar, indexes, images, etc.);
- associate to these elements the most common behaviours related to them;
- define metacognitive questions connected to each behaviour such as:

- Why have I clicked on this link?
- What information do I expect to find?
- What other surfing tools were there on the page?
- Why have I selected this link rather than the others on the page?
- Have I already explored the other objects on the page (images, links, text)? If not do I expect to do so?
- Do I intend to return to this page? Why?
- Why have you returned to this page?
- Has the image which I've seen helped me to understand better?
- Have I found the information I expected on this page?
- What has interested me most on this page?

As we can see, some questions can be asked at the moment when the student clicks on any surfing object, while other questions are adapt to specific actions.

The purpose of these questions is not to provide explanations about how to surf but to act as a counsellor and to encourage and lead the learner to carry out his study on the Net more effectively.

This set of questions will be integrated in the Did@browser system and will be submitted, during the experimental sessions which we are planning, to an experimental group of students.

Another set of questions was defined to motivate students to evaluate the results of their activities regarding both the process and the quality of information obtained. These questions are:

- What have I learnt surfing on this site?
- What topics are dealt with on this site?
- What sequence of actions have I followed to surf the information on the site?
- Has my strategy of surfing enabled me to reach my aim?
- What do I think will help me to surf better next time?

These latter questions will be submitted both to the experimental group and the control group to assess whether the subjects in the former group have acquired more information and have become more aware of their strategies for surfing than the latter group.

The analysis of stored data during the surfing activities will also allow us to identify the cognitive and metacognitive strategies which the subjects adopt and to establish whether the use of the meta-tool modifies the style of Web surfing.

In particular, it will be clear whether there are any differences between the two groups regarding the main behaviours observed during net-surfing. According to the literature [8, 9], the main behaviours are:

- Backtracking: frequent use of the back button to return to a page already viewed;
- Scrolling: reading of the whole text present on a page and activation of links at the centre and at the end of the page;
- Target: surfing activity aimed at finding a specific site or link;
- Exploratory moves: surfing activity aimed at understanding how the information is organized within the site;
- Looping: returning repeatedly to the same pages.

4 Ongoing project

Testing of the system will involve 30 middle school pupils in Palermo. They will be divided into two groups: 15 of them, the experimental group, will be involved in a Net-surfing activity supported by the metacognitive tool; 15 others, the control group, will be surfing the net to reach the same didactic aims, but without the support of the experimental tool.

The two groups of students will be chosen randomly, so as to include children with heterogeneous Net-surfing skills.

The experimentation activity will consist in surfing a Web site prepared on purpose. The activity will be divided into three phases, for both groups of pupils.

Phase 1. The pupils surf the Web site without a specific aim, for a limited time (about 20 minutes).

Phase 2. The pupils have to identify the main topic of the site.

Phase 3. The pupils surf the site to collect as much information as possible regarding a specific topic. This phase is repeated several times with different topics.

The results obtained from the experimentation will allow us to assess whether the use of metacognitive questions included in the meta-tool promote greater awareness during the surfing activity. Moreover, we will verify whether the use of meta-cognitive tool improves the comprehension of Web topics.

The feedback obtained from the experimentation will be used to optimize the features of the tool and to develop other new functionalities.

Reference

[1] Wood, D., Bruner, J., Ross, G., The role of tutoring in problem solving. *Journal of Child Psychology and Psychiatry*, **17(2)**, pp. 89-100, 1976.

[2] De Beni, R, Zamperlin, C., Benvenuti, M. & Vocetti, C., *Imparare a studiare la geografia*, Erickson, Trento 1995.

[3] Guterman, E., Integrating written metacognitive awareness guidance as a psychological tool to improve student performance. *Learning and Instruction*, **13(6)**, pp. 633-651, 2003.

[4] Lloyd, A., A software tool for supporting the acquisition of metacognitive skills for Web searching. *Proc. of AIED 2001* Online. www.cogs.susx.ac.uk/users/bend/aied2001/lloyd.pdf

[5] Allegra, M, Chiazzese, G., Chifari, A., Ottaviano, S. & Seta, L., A metacognitive tool for Web surfing (CDROM). *Proc. of International Conference IASTED 03*, 2003.

[6] Chiazzese, G., Cortopassi, C. & Laganà, M.R., A Virtual Secondary School Classroom on the Net (Chapter 2). *International Perspectives on Tele-Education and Virtual Learning Environments*, ed. G. Orange & D. Hobbs, Ashgate: Aldershot, pp. 15-31, 2000.

[7] Cockburn, A. & McKenzie, B., What Do Web Users Do? An Empirical Analysis of Web Use. *International Journal Human-Computer Studies*, **54(6)**, pp. 903-922, 2001.

[8] Bilal, D., Children's use of the Yahoolings! Web Search Engine: I. Cognitive, Physical, and Affective Behaviours on Faced-Based Search Task. *Journal of the American Society for Information Science*, **51(7)**, pp. 646-665, 2000.

[9] Slone, D.J., The Influence of Mental Models and Goals on Search Patterns During Web Interaction. *Journal of the American Society for Information Science and Technologies*, **53(13)**, pp. 1152-1169, 2002.

Section 6
Security in e-commerce settings

Cryptography as a formal method and model for security in electronic payments

T. Tsiakis, G. Stephanides & G. Pekos
Department of Applied Informatics, University of Macedonia, Greece

Abstract

The development of electronic commerce makes the issue of paying over open networks very important. Electronic payment is the backbone of e-commerce transactions. The paper defines the role of cryptography and introduces its basis such as the mathematics principles of public key cryptography. Next it identifies the infrastructure for secure payments over the Internet, compares the existing payments mechanisms and methods and gives the general properties. It concludes that electronic payment systems should be developed to satisfy all requirements of (security through encryption models) electronic commerce. That means that the main idea of systems which convert conventional money to electronic equivalent is achieved in such a way.

Keywords: cryptography, computer & network security, electronic payments, data security, PKC, digital signatures, e-commerce.

1 Defining data security

An etymological analysis of the word secure defines its meanings: se - without and cure - to protect. Computer security is usually defined as the: protection of the system and the data stored therein against unauthorized access, modification, destruction or use, and against actions or situations that deny authorized access or use of the system. Security is a frame of mind, not a set of rules [1, 2]. The problem of protecting data (representation of information) and information (subjective interpretation of data) on computers has become even more critical and challenging since the widespread adoption of the Internet and the Web [3].

The definition of security covers three aspects [4].
- Confidentiality: prevention of unauthorized disclosure of information. The terms secrecy (protection of data belonging to an organization) and privacy (protection of personal data) are included.

- Integrity: prevention of unauthorized modification of information.
- Availability: prevention of unauthorized withholding of information resources.

Referring to network we have to include some other security services [5].

- Authentication: is concerned with assuring that communication is authentic. The entities participated in communication are connected and the source data is the claimed one.
- Non-repudiation: prevention of both sender and receiver from denying taking part into all or part of a transaction.

Securing a computer for electronic commerce means that the system must be available for use and the information will be delivered without being corrupted. It guarantees to the seller that no one will be able to acquire the goods without paying the price the seller demands. The corresponding expectation on the part of the buyer is that the goods paid for will be delivered in a timely manner and will be as represented [6]. The concerns of e-commerce security focus on the flow and protection of financial assets. There is a wrong impression that data security comes along with computer security. The need for security in communication arises from every person's need to achieve two basic preconditions: confidentiality (the ability to send data to another person without a third person being able to identify what is being sent) and authenticity (the ability that the message can be verified that was sent from A to B). The use of computer systems in communications places some other dimensions. A computer system has three structurally separate components: software, hardware and data. Each one of them offers distinguishable value that is influenced by the system. In order to analyze security, we can examine the ways in which the system or the information can be lost or damaged. Consequently we have to define security within the environment of computer systems. In general, computer security is defined as the process of securing the system and the files stored in there, against unauthorized access, modification, catastrophe or use.

Security can be broken out in a number of ways. A useful approach is by network security versus computer security. Network protection is different from computer protection. Both depend on operating systems and software. Much more concentration has been given to the infrastructure of developments to establish security and privacy

A definition of security falls into two categories:

- Unconditional Security: any amount of computing power cannot break the system.
- Computational Security: the (polynomial) computing power cannot break the system.

There are three major facets of computer security [7]:

Theory: as with any field, there are some parts of computer security that constitute the basic theory. These are Cryptography and Network Security Protocols.

Process: much of computer security can be viewed at the process of building computer security systems.

Management: once a computer security system has been deployed it needs to be managed to insure that it works correctly.

Cryptography (mathematics), is the theoretic evaluation, Public Key Infrastructure (PKI) is the process, and Virtual Private Networks (VPN) along with legal operation is the management

There are many approaches to privacy and security. Cryptography is the method of transforming data represented as unreadable binary numbers. Modern cryptographic methods are mathematical and are based on mathematical functions (modulo function, prime numbers, factoring large numbers, and permutations).

2 Identification of electronic transactions

Electronic commerce (E-commerce or e-commerce) is the common use of business information, the maintenance of business relationships, and the execution of business processes and market transactions while using information technology [8]. *E-business* is the carrying out of business activities that lead to an exchange of value, where the parties interact electronically, using network or telecommunications technologies [9]. E-business includes 'consumer-oriented storefronts, business-to-business applications as well as behind-the scenes business functions like electronic payment systems and order management'. The process of carrying out and paying electronically is very complicated. One of the major characteristics is that partners do not necessarily have to know each other prior to their business interaction [10].

Concerning the parties involved, Knorr and Röhrig [11] differentiate four categories of e-business: Business-to-Business (B2B), if two companies establish a trade relation, Business-to-Consumer (B2C), if a company and a consumer establish a trade relation, Business-to-Public (B2P), if a company and a public administration do business, and Public-to-Consumer (B2P), if a public administration and a consumer do business.

Electronic Commerce is effective in reducing the cost of business together with the formation of new services. Meanwhile, the side of doing business electronically leaves out a feeling of insecurity due to the fact that there is no central control from a head authority. The entrance of companies to Business-to-Consumer (B2C) model of marketing means that they have to select and establish a safe and friendly in use payment method or system.

We consider that the electronic payments systems are obliged to sustain and vindicate:
- A wide spectrum of communication
- Appliance to Security principles
- Infrastructure for evolving new technologies
- Expanding and adaptation to users (both companies and consumers)

3 Electronic Payment Systems

We can define Electronic Payment Systems (EPS) as a well accepted instrument of settlement, between merchants and customers, for their transactions through Internet (payment completed through electronic means).

Except from the discrimination between e-commerce models we have to notate that in e-commerce there is a payer and a payee who exchange money either for goods or for services. In EPS we use for differentiation the two parts as an issuer (the payer) and an acquirer (the payee). It would be a mistake not to mention the necessity for a central bank as a financial institution, which takes the role of an issuer in payments.

In such way, it arise the first need to distinguish the payments into on-line and off-line. [12, 13, 14] On-line: it means that the systems requires from the payee to contact a third party (the bank), so that can verify the process, and Off-line: without the need of contacting and verifying the transaction of payment. The majority of proposed electronic payments are on-line payment systems. This can be simply explained from the fact that a big mass of payment is conducted through Internet which helps interactivity and on-line access to services.

Payments can be divided in two categories, depending on how they are carried out: payment per transaction and payment through accounts. In proportion to different types of payment methods and transaction environments, Hsiao-Cheng *et al.* [15] divide electronic payment systems into online credit card payments, electronic cash, electronic checks, and small payments. In spite of the similarities what separates the payments systems is the procedure. Dani *et al.* [16] in a uniform comparison divide EPS into five types: electronic cash, electronic fund transfer, credit cards, debit cards and electronic checks. The main differences that perceive between these systems are anonymity of payer and payee, the level of default risk to payee, permission of credit to payer and the level of authorization. Next, Abrazhevich [17] gives out a classification based on the way in which money transfer is organized: electronic currency systems (or electronic cash) and credit-debit systems. Continuing, based on the type of information that is exchanged, it distinguishes the "account-based" and the "token based" systems. Referential to different transaction system, Putland *et al.* [18] consider three types of EPS: card, cheque and cash systems. Cards and cheques are indirect payment mechanisms and cash is a direct mechanism.

3.1 Principles of Electronic Payment Systems

What comes as a conclusion is that the taxonomic evaluation of EPS arises from the way the payments materialize, the security procedure they follow and the affiliation with computer networks. The EPS must follow in general some principles:

Security: A non-stoppable procedure, both in software and hardware, for authentication, in order to succeed: 1) User identification, 2) message integrity, and 3) non-repudiation.

Transferability: The amounts of payments (coins) must be transferred from another computer to another through networks, without the intercession of the issuer.
Off-line capability: The need for the parties to conduct payments without being connected to a system or an on-line process.
Divisibility: The tokens must be capable to be divided into smaller amounts (in token based payments).
User Acceptance and Easiness in use: The need for a well-performing and user-friendly payment system.
Traceability: When there is a need, to trace the sources of money.
Availability: The electronic payment systems must work continuously and be available on and on.
The list may look incomplete but it gives a general overview on what the EPS should follow as a guide to create a safe infrastructure.

4 What does cryptography as a security method-model provide to the participants in a transaction

In order to build secure e-commerce applications, we need to establish the definitions of security requirements. Cryptography is a branch of mathematics that is concerned with the development of algorithms that transforms, an intelligible message into an unintelligible one and vice versus. Cryptography can be seen as a part of a security solution, never as the whole solution. It transforms a security problem into a key management problem. The wide use of computers and communications systems brought up a need in the private sector to find ways to protect digital information.

The communication through the Internet is achieved with the use of Transmission Control Protocol/Internet Protocol where packets (of information) are being sent from one computer to another. The role of Public-key cryptography is the creation of mathematical functions capable to construct public-key themes, to allow the parties involved to the transaction of exchanging information to maintenance the aspects of authentication and non-repudiation. Public-key schemes are scalable: their operation is well-suited to environments with lots of users. The advent of large-scale open networks like the Internet necessitates this property.

4.1 Public-key cryptography

Public-key encryption (named also asymmetric encryption) [19, 20, 21] involves a pair of keys, a public key (known by anybody, can be used both to encrypt messages, and verify signature) and a private key (used to decrypt messages, and sign - create signatures).

The establishment of a public-key cryptosystem is of a network of users where each user in the network has a pair of keys associated with him (resulting too many keys in the system ($n(n-1)/2$ if there are n users)), the public key, which is published under the user's name in a public directory accessible for everyone to read, and the private-key which is known only to the user. The pair of keys is generated by running a key-generation algorithm. In order to send a secret message to a user, everyone in the network uses the same exact method, which involves looking up the public key from the public directory, encrypting the message using the public key, and sending the resulting cipher text to the user. Upon receiving the cipher text, the receiver can decrypt by looking up his private key.

The relation between public and private key is achieved by the use of the mathematical 'one-way' hash function. From the moment the plaintext is encrypted with such a function, it cannot be decrypted with the same key used to encrypt. In practice that means that given x, $f(x)$ can be easily produced, but given $f(x)$, we can't practically calculate x.

The opponent knows how the message was encoded, but he cannot decode it. The message to be encrypted is an integer m, which might represent a letter of the alphabet, or an entry in a codebook or a quantity of cash. The algorithmic process is the one that designates the value of security.

4.2 The RSA public key algorithm

It was first proposed in 1978 and named by the initials of his creators Rivest, Shamir and Adleman. It is based on modular arithmetic. The encryption and decryption are operated by raising numbers to a power modulo, a number which is the product of two large primes. To encode a message using RSA [22], a user needs a pair of keys. To generate the two keys, we consider:
p,q, as the two primes, large enough and of equal length
n, the public key, the product of p and q, $n=nq$
e: the public key, randomly chosen number which is less than n and relatively prime to $(p - 1)(q - 1)$, (e has no factors in common with $(p - 1)$ and $(q - 1)$),
d: the private key, the inverse of (e mod $(p - 1)(q - 1)$) such that $ed \equiv 1$ mod $(p - 1)(q - 1)$.
Compute $\Phi(n) = (p-1)(q-1)$
Choose a random integer, $0 < e < \Phi(n)$ with $\gcd(e, \Phi(n)) = 1$
Compute the inverse $d = e^{-1}$ mod $\Phi(n)$,

We divide the message into blocks so that each block can be represented as a number less than the modulus n. To compute the cipher text C (encryption), we use the following function:
$C = M^e$ mod n
and to compute plaintext M (decryption) we use the function:
$M = C^d$ mod n

4.3 Digital signatures

A product of Public-Key Cryptography is the digital signature (equivalent to a hand written signature) that both authenticates and guarantees that the message is original and is being sent by the person it was originally supposed to be sent from. We make an assumption of the use ness of digital signatures in a bank

account. The bank generates two large (prime) numbers p and q. The product of p and q is the modulus for all of user exponentiation. The two keys system works as:
$$x^{(p-1)(q-1)} \equiv 1 \mod (pq)$$
and the bank chooses values e and d in order to have:
$$ed \equiv 1 \mod (p-1)(q-1)$$
Next the bank relinquish user d, (private key) and register e (public key). That means that the user's bank transaction is encrypted with d and decrypted with e:
$$(x^d)^e \equiv x \mod (pq)$$
We must note that modulus pq is in public and of course the public key e.

5 Conclusion

Electronic payment systems-methods are reliable mechanisms that allow each person to carry out his financial activities. It might be risky viewed from a business perspective and induce loss of funds from fraud, however, they give a competitive edge and a unique business opportunity by reducing cost and time. The on-line capability offers a lot of opportunities but it has to assume and secure that the parties involved in the transaction are the supposed one, as well as, the exchanged information remains confidential and finally that the payment is valued. Further exploitation of the Internet and Web requires extensive research in areas such as cryptography in both algorithmic and implementation.

Cryptography is a very important security measure in the design and operation of electronic payment systems. It allows payment systems to become part of our daily commercial and financial transactions. Vital role in this relationship is laid on banks. Making payments using cryptography means that the coins in the payment by merchant are encrypted using the banks public key before sending to merchant, to prevent from being stolen or being modified during transaction. Updated and highly sophisticated systems are required to maintain security and competitiveness.

References

[1]   Turn, R., Security and privacy requirements in computing, Proceedings of 1986 fall joint computer conference on Fall joint computer conference, November 1999.
[2]   Howerton, W. P., Computer security: a tutorial. Proceedings of the 1985 ACM annual conference on The range of computing: mid-80's perspective: mid-80's perspective, October 1985.
[3]   Yang, T. A., Computer security and impact on computer science education, The Journal of Computing in Small Colleges, Proceedings of the sixth annual CCSC northeastern conference on The journal of computing in small colleges, Volume 16 Issue 4
[4]   Gollmann, D., Computer Security, Wiley: England, pp. 5-9, 2001
[5]   Stalling, W., Network Security Essential: Application and Standards, Prentice Hall: New Jersey, pp.9-13, 2003

[6] Whitfield, D. E-commerce and security Volume 6, Issue 3 Pages: 116–117, September 1998

[7] Fung P., Kwok L. & Longley, D., Electronic Information Security Documentation, Australasian Information Security Workshop (AISW2003), Adelaide, Australia. Conferences in Research and Practice in Information Technology, Vol. 21. C., 2003.

[8] Jones, S., Wilikens, M., Morris, P. & Masera, M., Trust Requirements in E-Business: A conceptual framework for understanding the needs and concerns of different stakeholders, Communications of the ACM, Vol. 43, No. 12, December 2000.

[9] Zwass, V., Electronic Commerce: Structures and Issues. International Journal of Electronic Commerce, 1(1):3 23, 1996.

[10] Nabil,, A. & Yelena, Y.,(Eds.). Electronic commerce: Current Research Issues and Applications. LNCS 1028, Springer, Heidelberg, 1996.

[11] Knorr, K. & Röhrig S., Security Requirements of E-Business Processes, in: Proceedings of the First IFIP Conference on E-Commerce, E-Business, and E-Government (I3E), Zurich, pp. 73-86, Oct. 3-5 2001.

[12] Schoenmakers, B., Security aspects of Ecash Payment System, B. Preneel, V. Rijmen (Eds.): COSIC'97 Course, LNCS 1528, pp. 338Springer-Verlag Berlin Heidelberg 1998

[13] Tsiounis, Y., Efficient electronic cash: new notions and techniques. http://www.ccs.neu.edu/home/yiannis/papers/thesis.ps, November 13, 2000.

[14] Tennant, H., 5 Payment models on the Internet. http://www.htennant.com/hta/askus/5models.htm, November 13, 2000.

[15] Hsiao-Cheng, Y., Kuo-Hua, H., & Pei-Jen, Kuo, Electronic payment systems: an analysis and comparison of types, Technology in Society 24, 331–347, 2002.

[16] Dani, A.R. & Krishna P. Radha, An E-check Framework for Electronic Payment Systems in the Web Based Environment, EC-Web 2001, LNCS 2115, pp. 91-100, 2001

[17] Abrazhevich, D., Classification and Characteristics of Electronic Payment Systems, EC-Web 2001, LNCS 2115, pp. 81-90, 2001

[18] Putland, P, Hill, J. & Tsapakidis D., Electronic payment systems, BT Technol J Vol 15 No 2 April 1997

[19] Halevi, S. & Krawczyk, H., Public-Key Cryptography and Password Protocols, ACM Transactions on Information and System Security, Vol. 2, No. 3, Pages 230–268, August 1999.

[20] Bell, T., Thimbleby, H., Fellows, M., Witten, I., Koblitz, N. & Powell M., Explaining cryptographic systems, Computers & Education 40, pp 199–215, 2003.

[21] Vanables, P., A commercial future of Public Key Cryptography, Information Security Technical Report, Vol. 2, No. 4, pp 32-40, 1998.

[22] RSA Laboratories Cryptography FAQ, http://www.rsasecurity.com

MARAH: an RBAC model and its integration in a Web server

P. Díaz, D. Sanz & I. Aedo
Departamento de Informática, Universidad Carlos III de Madrid

Abstract

Hypermedia systems, whether implemented as web sites or not, should support security policies offering different views of the same information and different manipulation abilities to users with different needs and responsibilities in a particular context. Several experiences have demonstrated that role-based access control policies are a powerful mechanism to simplify management tasks. This paper describes the MARAH model that provides security designers with mechanisms to specify security rules using elements and abstractions of the hypermedia domain (nodes, links or contents). From a functional point of view, the model provides security designers with mechanisms to specify the rules that ensure a proper operation of any hypermedia system. Thus, one of the basic assumptions of this work is the use of abstractions belonging to the hypermedia domain in a broad sense, so that security modeling could be integrated into any hypermedia design method. Moreover, MARAH has been implemented as a module integrated into a well known web server (Apache).

Keywords: hypermedia, RBAC model, web server.

1 Introduction

Hypermedia systems, widely represented by web-based applications, offer more and more services and contents to fulfill the needs of different kinds of users. This fact, together with the growing use of web technology for enterprise computing lead to the need of an efficient access control technology, capable of offering different views of the same information and different manipulation abilities to users with different needs and responsibilities in a particular context [1]. Due that current approaches are normally based on users or groups, the efficiency of security management is compromised in large-scale web systems. Role-Based Access Control

(RBAC) has proven to be an useful approach to simplify management tasks [2], but the interpretation of the model for hypermedia can be faced from rather different levels of abstraction, as shown in Figure 1.

Most RBAC models focus on the highest level, called the *Application Layer* in figure 1, where there are identified a number of roles and operations belonging to the domain of the specific application for which security rules are being specified. Operations encapsulate objects so that security managers are only concerned about operations and are not aware about the objects being accessed by them. Therefore, permissions are expressed as tuples <role, operation>. This is quite convenient from the security manager point of view since the elements they have to deal with are closer to their view of the application. However, from the implementation point of view the encapsulation of objects into operations makes difficult to reuse a security module, which is context dependent, from an application to another.

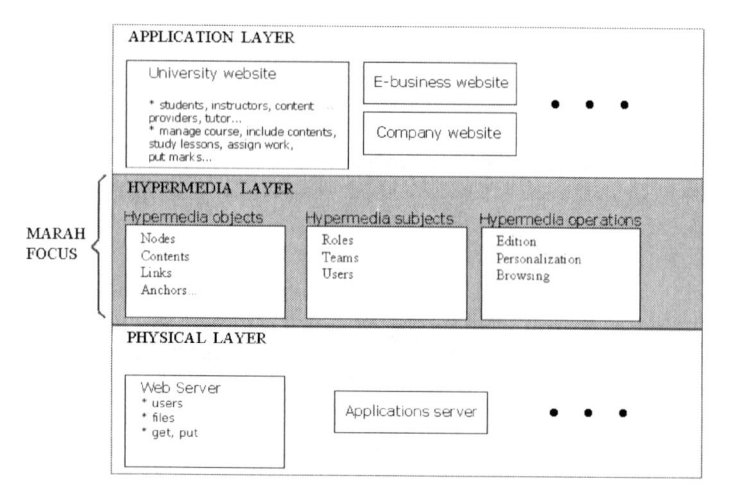

Figure 1: Abstraction layers of security models.

At the lowest level, called *Physical Layer*, some RBAC implementations for the web deal with physical entities [3, 4], such as files or HTML documents, and operations are those supported by the HTTP protocol (put and get, basically). At this point, permissions need to involve not only operations but also objects in order to support some kind of richer RBAC policy, so that they become a tuple <role, object, operation>. This kind of models are completely reusable for different applications since their abstractions are context independent. However, the monolithic view of an object as a file and the very low-level operations difficult security management, losing part of the benefits of applying RBAC models.

Between these two views, there is a big conceptual gap that can be filled by an intermediate level providing a more flexible and reusable mechanism to specify RBAC policies for the web: the *Hypermedia Layer*. The focus of this level is to provide security designers with a model to specify security rules using elements and abstractions of the hypermedia domain (such as nodes, links or contents), considering a web site as a special case of hypermedia. Thus operations would be less basic than those of the Physical Layer, including kinds of processes performed in hypermedia systems (editing, browsing, personalizing...), and more reusable than those of the Application Layer. Objects in the Hypermedia Layer will be more generic than those of the Physical Layer, offering possibilities to define complex structures supporting different relationships (such as spec-gen or part-whole) as well as multilevel security policies. The security model resulting from this layer can be implemented in different platforms (Physical Layer) and used in different environments (Application Layer) for which generic hypermedia abstractions have to be translated into domain components.

The work presented here focuses on this intermediate level, introducing an RBAC model for hypermedia called MARAH (Role-based Access Method for Hypermedia Applications). Moreover, MARAH has been implemented and integrated as a module into an existing web server (Apache) and has been applied in different domains to test its feasibility and efficiency.

The remaining of this paper is organized as follows. Section 2 introduces the MARAH model and section 3 describes its implementation as an Apache module. Section 4 outlines some related works and, finally, section 5 draws some conclusions and future works.

2 MARAH: An RBAC model for hypermedia and web systems

From a functional point of view, the model provides security designers with a series of mechanisms to specify the rules that ensure a proper operation for any hypermedia system. Thus, one of the assumptions of this work is the use abstractions and concepts belonging to the hypermedia domain in a broad sense, so that security modeling could be integrated into any hypermedia design method dealing with other hypermedia features (e.g. navigation structures, multimedia presentations, interaction mechanisms) such as HDM [5], OOHDM [6] or Ariadne [7].

Some classical security principles have been assumed in the model: (1) the system is only accessed through well-formed transactions, that are the operations of the Labyrinth hypermedia model [8]; (2) only authenticated users can perform operations (but the authentication mechanism lies out of the scope of the model); (3) users and processes are assigned the least privilege required to accomplish their objectives; (4) authority is delegated so that not too critical actions are under the author's responsibility; (5) positive and negative authorizations are considered as suggested in [9]; (6) data abstraction is supported so that security rules are specified using abstractions belonging to the hypermedia domain; and separation of duties is also supported.

2.1 MARAH components

From an structural point of view the MARAH model is composed by a number of elements and relations among elements that are summarized in Table 1.

Table 1: MARAH model components.

Model Element	Specification
Subjects	$S = R \cup T \mid R \cap T = \emptyset$
Roles	$R = \{r_i \mid i = 1, \ldots, q_r \ (q_r \in \mathbf{N})\}$
Teams	$T = \{t_i \mid i = 1, \ldots, q_t \ (q_t \in \mathbf{N})\}$
Users	$U = \{u_i \mid i = 1, \ldots, q_u \ (q_u \in \mathbf{N})\}$
Allocation	$A : U \to R^n$
Objects	$O = N \cup C \mid N \cap C = \emptyset$
Nodes	$N = \{n_i \mid i = 1, \ldots, q_n \ (q_n \in \mathbf{N})\}$
Contents	$C = \{c_i \mid i = 1, \ldots, q_c \ (q_c \in \mathbf{N})\}$
Operations	$Op = \{op_i \mid i = 1, \ldots, q_{op} \ (q_{op} \in \mathbf{N})\}$
Security Categories	$Sc = \{sc_i \mid sc_i \subset sc_{i+1}, \forall sc_i \in Sc, (i = 1..3)\}$
Separation of Duty	$SD = \{\langle s_i, s_j \rangle \mid s_i, s_j \in S, s_i \neq s_j\}$
Classification of Operations	$\omega : Op \to Sc$
Classification of Objects	$\delta : O \to Sc$
Confidentiality	$\psi : O \to S^n$
Clearance	$\phi : O \times S \to Sc$
Authorization Rule	$\forall s \in S, \forall o \in O, \prod(s, o) = \begin{cases} \text{denied} & \text{if } s \in \psi(o) \\ \phi(o, s) & \text{if } s \notin \psi(o) \end{cases}$
Transition	$\theta : Op \times O^n \times S \to O^m, \ (n, m \in \mathbf{N})$ $\theta(op, \{o_1, o_2, \ldots, o_N\}, s)$ results in a safe state if $\forall o_i, i = 1, \ldots, N \begin{cases} \omega(Op) \leq \delta(o_i) & \text{and} \\ \prod(s, o_i) \neq \text{denied} & \text{and} \\ \omega(Op) \leq \prod(s, o_i) \end{cases}$

First, there are a number of **subjects** (S) who can access the hypermedia application exercising different permissions. Two kinds of subjects are considered: roles (R) and teams (T), having different meaning and security implications (see sections 2.3 and 2.4). **Users** (U) are assigned one or more roles to be able to use the system trough an **Allocation** function (A). This function reflects the classical role-assignment relationship in RBAC.

The **objects** (O) are the nodes (N) and contents (C) making up the hypermedia application [8]. Nodes are abstract containers of information items, called contents.

For example, a web page is a node containing a number of items such as texts, images, videos and so on. Composition mechanisms are supported, as discussed in section 2.2, to be able to define complex structures.

A number of **operations** (Op) are supported for the different components of the hypermedia application, such as createNode, createContent, placeContentNode, createLink, activateLink and so on. For a comprehensive list of operations see [10].

Security categories (Sc) are the kinds of access categories supported in any hypermedia system. There are three categories making up a partial order: *Browsing*, to retrieve information (nodes and contents) whether selecting links or using other means such as indexes, maps or search engines; *Personalizing*, adds the ability to include personal elements (such as private contents, nodes or links), that is, the possibility of creating and updating personalized or private spaces; and *Editing*, adds the ability to modify elements accessed by all users of the system.

The **classification of operations** (ω) function is used to assign each operation the privileges needed to perform its task. For example, the createNode operation requires an Editing category while activateLink is assigned a Browsing one. This classification is embedded into the specification of the Labyrinth operations [10].

Objects can be assigned also a security category to disable any authorization rule for a while by using the **classification of objects** (δ). This function assigns each object with the most permissive kind of access allowed for it, so that the object will not accept operations whose execution require more privileges.

The **confidentiality** (ψ) function assigns objects with subjects who are not granted any kind of access to them, by means of *negative access control list* (nACL). Positive authorizations are managed by means of the **clearance function** (ϕ) where a subject is granted a security category for an object. Both relationships are gathered together in the **authorization rule** ($\prod$), that determines the manipulation abilities each subject will have in a specific domain. This rule reflects the classical permission-assignment relationship in RBAC.

Finally, the **transition function** (θ) is responsible for guaranteeing that only safe operations are performed. Three conditions are checked: the operation can be executed on that object, the user is not included in the n-ACL of the object and the user can execute the operation on the object.

2.2 Object modeling: nodes, contents and domains

MARAH considers two kind of objects in a hypermedia system: nodes and contents. A node is an abstract information holder that can contain any type and number of information items which are called contents. By separating nodes from contents multilevel policies can be supported so that different subjects can have different views of the same nodes [1].

The other basic component of a hypermedia system, the link, is defined as a set of sources and targets (called anchors) both of which are collections of nodes and/or contents, so that from a security point of view they can inherit the same rules that apply to their components. For instance, to modify a link, a subject should be allowed to modify any of its anchors.

Two composition mechanisms are supported for nodes and contents: generalization (*is-a*), implying inheritance, and aggregation (*whole-part*), used to refer to a group of objects as a whole. Composition is provided not only for security purposes but for gathering the hypermedia system structure. Thus, the object set takes the form of a DAG (Directed Acyclic Graph), whose nodes can be connected by means of two relationship types. On the basis of the composition mechanism, the concept of domain is introduced to refer to the hierarchical structure defined from an object as follows:

$$\text{domain}(o) = o \cup \text{domain}(o') \cup \text{domain}(o''), \forall o', o'' | o \underset{a}{\succ} o', o \underset{g}{\succ} o'',$$

where, $\forall o, o' \in O,$ $\begin{cases} o \underset{a}{\succ} o' \Leftrightarrow o' \in \text{set of objects aggregated by } o \\ o \underset{g}{\succ} o'' \Leftrightarrow o'' \in \text{set of objects generalized by } o \end{cases}$

Domains can be used to refer to a number of objects. The domain of the root node of a hypermedia system includes all the nodes in the system.

2.3 Subject modeling: roles, teams and users

A role is an organizational position or job function that appears in the domain of application, whereas a team is just a group of users established whether to represent collaborative group or to simplify the administration tasks. For example, the web site of a research group at the University is accessed by roles like teacher, student, researcher or anonymous. In turn, the research group is a team made up of different kinds of users sharing a common goal.

Roles and teams support composition mechanisms to be able to deal with complex user structures. To gather the complexity of most organizations, hierarchies of roles can be defined as a DAG where general roles are specialized into more specific ones using a generalization relationship. Teams are aggregations of roles and teams, a composition relationship which makes possible to refer to a number of subjects as a whole while maintaining independence among components.

Each user must have at least one role but she can not directly take part in any team but as acting on behalf of a specific role. Static separation of duties is supported by means of a set of pairs of mutually exclusive roles. An user will not be able to be assigned simultaneously to two roles if these roles are a pair of SD set.

2.4 Authorization propagation

Privileges are propagated in the subjects structure according to the following rules:

R1. Direct propagation. Each role inherits the permissions given by the confidentiality and clearance functions applied to its parent:
$$\forall s_i, s_j \in S, \forall o \in O \mid s_j \underset{g}{\succ} s_i, \Rightarrow \prod(s_i, o) = \prod(s_j, o)$$
R2. Authorization overriding. Authorization propagation is inhibited if the child role is assigned a permission for the same object. Then R1 is rewritten to:

$$\forall s_i, s_j \in S, \forall o \in O \mid s_j \underset{g}{\succ} s_i, (\prod(s_i, o) = x \wedge \prod(s_j, o) = y), x, y \in \{denied\} \cup SC \Rightarrow \prod(s_i, o) = x$$

R3. Propagation in nested relationships. If there is a nested generalization, the child assumes the security rules that apply to the most specialized role, that is, to its immediate predecessor.

$$\forall s_i, s_j, s_k \in S, \forall o \in O \mid (s_i \underset{g}{\succ} s_j \wedge s_j \underset{g}{\succ} s_k), \Rightarrow \prod(s_i, o) = \prod(s_j, o)$$

R4. Propagation in parallel relationships. If a child role is generalized by several parallel roles, it assumes the most permissive authorization. The order considered in Δ is *browsing<personalizing<editing<denied*.

$$\forall s, s_i \in S, (i = 1, \ldots, n), \forall o \in O \mid s \underset{g}{\succ} s_i, \Rightarrow \prod(s, o) = \Delta_1^n(\prod(s_i, o))$$

R5. Direct assignment of authorization. If a role takes part in a team and it has no authorization, neither directly specified nor inherited, it assumes the team authorizations.

$$\forall s_i \in S, \forall o \in O \mid s_i \underset{a}{\succ} s_j, s_j \in S \wedge \not\exists \prod(s_i, o) \Rightarrow \prod(s_i, o) = \prod(s_j, o)$$

3 MARAH implementation

MARAH has been applied in various domains [11, 12], but all of them embedded the Hypermedia Layer into the Application Layer. This is the rationale for splitting both layers, so that the Hypermedia Layer can be implemented regardless of the application domain. An implementation, integrated with the Apache web server, has been developed. In order to achieve maximum integration with the server, an Apache module has been implemented, although the Hypermedia Layer components are reusable. This decision allows to improve the efficiency, as well as get all knowledge about the internal behavior of the server. Like [4, 3], all processing is done in the server, so any web browser can be used. Once the XML configuration file is read, the model is built, and the $\prod$ function is computed using some graph iteration strategies. This leads to an access matrix, built at server startup time.

The system architecture is depicted in figure 2, that describes the Apache request cycle, focusing on the RBAC phase. The modular design of the Apache request loop allows to modify the behavior of the server at any stage of the cycle,

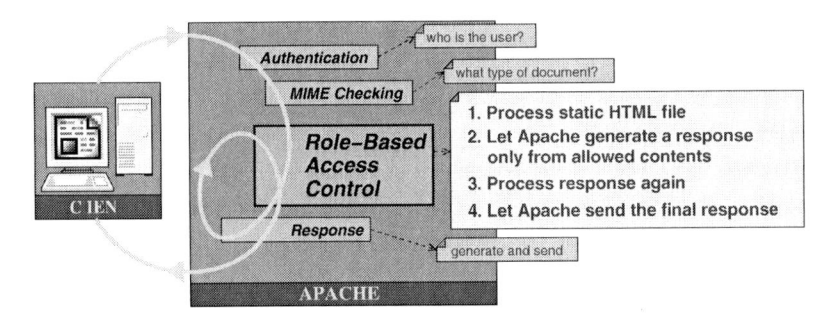

Figure 2: System architecture.

Table 2: Filtering scheme for contents delivered by RBAC module.

Phase	Involves	Action
Pre-handler	Static HTML files	Filter the file.
Handler	Everything that produces HTML result	Execute Apache handler, producing HTML content into a temporary file. If pre-handler was executed, Apache works on its result.
Post-handler	HTML responses	Filter temporary file, skipping the forbidden elements that may have been dynamically generated by some Apache handler.

leaving the rest untouched. The Apache *fix-up* phase has been chosen for placing the RBAC functionality, since it occurs just before the response phase, and just after the rest of Apache cycle. This allows RBAC module to gather all request data (user, object, MIME type, HTTP related information...) previously determined by the server. Note that tasks such as mapping URLs to filenames, checking access based on client's IP, authenticating users (e.g basic authentication scheme) and determining the MIME type of the document are performed by Apache before the phase where RBAC module executes. When RBAC module start its work, Apache has determined all relevant information about the request, so the only responsibility of the RBAC module is preparing a response for the user according to security rules. Again, the task of sending the response to the browser is better done by the Apache handlers.

In order to enforce the security rules, and taking into account the dynamic nature of web, the module must provide generic support for dynamic web generation technologies (e.g. PHP, SSI, index generation). This is achieved using a three phase filtering scheme (described in Table 3), ensuring that (1) server will generate contents only from allowed fragments of the original resource; and (2) once the dynamic content is generated, only allowed fragments will be sent to the client.

Two reasons make this scheme work fine with any MIME type: (1) Apache knows how to generate the content (i.e. parse PHP comments) so the HTML filter (implemented using flex/bison) do not need to filter anything different of HTML, and (2) some phases can be skipped, depending on MIME type (i.e. for images, no phase is executed, while for dynamic indexing the two last phases are executed). For now, only browse and edit operations are implemented. Each operation can register its own functions for filtering the contents, so that the HTML filter triggers the registered function when a given tag is found. The operation register interface is similar to the offered by the expat XML parser. Although the operation is determined by the URL query, sometimes the HTTP method helps to know the phase of execution. When editing, the GET method means the user has requested to edit o, so the edition form is prepared with the fragments of o which can be edited by the user. When the user finishes, the form is submitted, and the server executes again the "edit" operation on o, but now the method is POST, so the edition operation now reads the request body and uses other filter functions in order to assure that the incoming contents are allowed. This avoids, for example, to put a link to an object the user can't edit.

4 Related works

The RBAC model described in [1], together with the proposed NIST Standard [2] are the main references of this work. The integration of RBAC policies into web servers has been already discussed in [3, 4]. Despite of performance considerations, the proposed design maps the operations directly into HTTP methods, takes URLs as the system objects and translates the URL to filenames. Operations are tied to the transmission protocol, so abstract manipulation abilities over the hyperdocument are not considered. The object concept does not take into account relationships among objects, nor consider other hypermedia elements, so that fine grained access to objects is not supported. On the other hand, these works support some dynamic properties of RBAC models (i.e. role activation). Other works propose architectures in order to support RBAC for the web. Some of them (secure cookies, LDAP and certificates) are explained in [13]. The proposed solutions do not consider the application of a RBAC model based on roles for hypermedia, and therefore do not cover the object composition mechanisms and link management. Finer granularity is supported if XML documents are used as in [14], where objects are defined using a hierarchical structure, but the access control is based on credentials instead of roles.

5 Conclusions and future work

The experience gained during the implementation of the module demonstrates that MARAH can be incorporated into the normal behavior of the web server without a considerable degradation of the level of service. The complexity of the model does not affect the response time, assuming that all properties of the different model elements (particularly $\prod$ function) have been computed during the server startup process, so new constraints (i.e cardinalities) and relationships can be added in the future for improving the model. Some aspects of the MARAH model should be improved to deal with more sophisticated features such as dynamic properties (role activation, dynamic SD) or temporal roles. Moreover, it should be studied how to integrate it into a hypermedia design method, so that security can be modeled using the same abstractions employed to define other properties.

Acknowledgements

This work is part of the MARAH project funded by the "Dirección General de Investigación de la Comunidad Autónoma de Madrid y FSE" (07T/0012/2001).

References

[1] Díaz, P., Aedo, I. & Panetsos, F., Modelling security policies in hypermedia and web-based applications. *WebEngineering: Managing diversity and complexity of web application development*, eds. S. Murugesan & Y. Deshpande, Springer Verlag (LNCS 2016), pp. 90–104, 2001.

[2] Ferraiolo, D., Sandhu, R., Gavrila, S., Kuhn, R. & Chandramouli, R., Proposed nist standard for role-based access control. *ACM Transactions on Information and System Security*, **4(3)**, pp. 224–274, 2001.

[3] Barkley, J., Cincotta, A., Ferraiolo, D., Gavrilla, S. & Kuhn, R., Role based access control for the world wide web. *20th National Computer Security Conference*, 1997.

[4] Ferraiolo, D., Barkley, J. & Kuhn, R., A role-based access control model and reference implementation within a corporate intranet. *ACM Transactions on Information Systems Security*, **1(2)**, pp. 34–64, 1999.

[5] Fraternali, P. & Paolini, P., Model-driven development of web applications: The autoweb system. *ACM Transactions on Information Systems*, **19(2)**, pp. 323–382, 2000.

[6] Schwabe, D. & Rossi, G., Developing hypermedia applications using oohdm, 1998.

[7] Díaz, P., Aedo, I. & Montero, S., Ariadne, a development method for hypermedia. *Proceedings of 12th International Conference on Database and Expert Systems Applications (DEXA) Munich, Germany*, pp. 764–774, 2001.

[8] Díaz, P., Aedo, I. & Panetsos, F., Labyrinth, an abstract model for hypermedia applications. description of its static components. *Information Systems*, **22(8)**, pp. 447–464, 1997.

[9] Bertino, E., Jajodia, S. & Samarati, P., A flexible authorization model for relational data management systems. *ACM Transactions of Information Systems*, **17(2)**, pp. 101–140, 1999.

[10] Díaz, P., Aedo, I. & Panetsos, F., Modelling the dynamic behavior of hypermedia applications. *IEEE Transactions on Software Engineering*, **27(6)**, pp. 550–572, 2001.

[11] Aedo, I., Díaz, P., Fernández, C. & Castro, J., Supporting efficient multinational disaster response through a web-based system. *E-Gov Conference Aix-en-Provence (France)*, pp. 215–222, 2002.

[12] Montero, S., Aedo, I. & Díaz, P., Generation of personalized web courses using rbac: Courba, a practical experience. *AH 2002*, pp. 419–423, 2002.

[13] Park, J., Sandhu, R. & Ahn, G., Role-based access control on the web. *ACM Transactions on Information and System Security*, **4(1)**, pp. 31–71, 2001.

[14] Bertino, E., Castano, S. & Ferrari, E., On specifying security policies for web documents with an xml-based language. *Proceeding of SACMAC 01*, pp. 57–65, 2001.

Forced encryption solutions

H. B. Wolfe
University of Otago, P.O. Box 56, Dunedin, New Zealand

Abstract

This paper is intended to introduce the reader to various techniques and tools that can be used to force a solution of encrypted data without the use of cryptanalysis. The relevance of these techniques becomes apparent when attempting to view potential evidence files that have been encrypted and the suspect refuses to cooperate by providing their keys.
Keywords: electronic evidence, surveillance, forensics, chain of evidence, evidentiary copy, evidence acquisition, encryption.

1 Introduction

Investigation and capture of electronic evidence inevitably includes encrypted data. In the first instance, the Court can and usually will direct the accused to provide their keys. If this directive is successful then no further action is necessary and the techniques outlined in this paper will not come into play. However, when keys are not forthcoming the investigator is faced with the difficult problem of trying to find them. The first thought after watching some teenager on TV break encryption codes in a few minutes at his PC is to break the code. TV and movies are fictional and the common portrayal of such activity is also a fiction. If strong encryption is used, breaking it is not an option. The investigator is left with a few options, however, and they will be outlined in this paper.

2 Data encryption

Encryption is the art/science of codes and ciphers. Its main usage is to protect data in transit and at rest. Data in transit refers to communications and data at rest refers to data being stored. In today's world it is an advanced branch of mathematics. People spend their whole life on the pursuit of this complex topic.

Information is protected by transforming useful understandable data (plain text) into a form that is not understandable (cipher text) - thus making it secure from unauthorized use. And, of course, transforming back to its original form. The process of encryption creates cipher text from plain text using a procedure (algorithm) that is controlled by a key phrase. A single plain text file repeatedly encrypted with successively different keys would produce a number of different and unique cipher text files each of which would need to be solved individually (if no key were provided for the respective files). The process of solving or transforming a cipher text file without its key is referred to as cryptanalysis.

3 Cryptanalysis

Cryptanalysis is a very complex field based on the advanced mathematics mentioned above. There are a number of attack strategies developed by cryptographers (those who practice the art/science of creating and/or attacking cryptographic algorithms) over the years. Linear cryptanalysis, differential cryptanalysis, differential fault analysis, plain text attack, and brute force attack are a few. Because this is not a paper about cryptanalysis, it will be left to the reader to pursue these attack strategies further - with one exception. That is the brute force attack.

A brute force attack will cycle through the entire key space until the exact key is found. If the key space is small enough for this to be accomplished in a reasonable time using one or more computers, then the algorithm would be deemed to be weak. Part of the strength of any cryptographic algorithm is based on the size of the key space and that is represented by the number two as raised to the power of some value. For example, the DES [1] has a key space of 256 or seventy-two quadrillion keys. To cycle through all of these keys to find the exact key required to decrypt any given cipher text - even with the fastest computer of the day will take many hours or days. As the key length grows so too does the amount of time required to solve using the brute force technique.

The other aspect of an algorithm that defines its strength is the algorithm itself. Some of the other attack strategies make their attack on the weaknesses inherent in a poorly designed algorithm. The cryptographic community constantly analyses various algorithms for their weaknesses. Those that emerge without being found to be weak may only be attacked successfully by brute force. For example IDEA [2] has a key space of 2128 which equates to more than all of the atoms in the entire universe. Since, after many years of assessment and testing, its process is thought to be secure, a brute force attack would be computationally impractical, Data properly encrypted using the IDEA algorithm and a properly formed key [3] would be impossible to solve in a time that would make the information of any use. For example, if we had a CPU that could test 1 billion keys per second and if we were able to create a parallel machine comprised of 1 billion of these CPU's it would take 10,790,283,070,806 years to cycle through the entire key space that IDEA uses.

4 Detecting cryptographic use

This is harder than it might at first seem. There are forensic tools like IsEncrypted [4] and others that do just that. However, IsEncrypted is designed, as a companion utility to the Password Recovery ToolKit (PRTK), to find files that have been encrypted by specific applications software and can only identify that software that it knows about. IsEncrypted is a very useful forensic tool but it would not find any files that were encrypted by software applications that it was not designed to detect. Many standard applications such as Word or Excel (and there are many others as well) make encryption with strong algorithms optionally possible. While the algorithm implemented may be computationally secure and theoretically unbreakable, the way it has been implemented within other software may be flawed and successful attack may be achieved as a result. AccessData Corporation's Password Recovery ToolKit is specifically designed to resolve the password used from files encrypted by one of fifty or so designated applications. In other words, if your suspect uses the encryption option that Word offers to protect his documents, then the PRTK will be able to derive the keys for all documents protected in that way – even if the suspect refuses to provide their keys.

Another method of finding out whether encryption has been used is to look for known encryption software that is installed on the target system. Some forensic tools will do this based on a known signature pattern - a technique much like searching for a known virus. Encryption that is unknown to the methods described thus far may be more difficult to detect. Moreover, some encrypted files may be hidden within other files where steganography [5] has been used. As you can see, determining whether cryptography has been used is not a simple matter.

5 Social engineering

Once the determination has been made that encryption has been used and that the suspect will not cooperate by providing their keys, there are a number of other techniques that may be used (with varying effectiveness) to obtain particular keys. The first may be referred to as social engineering. This technique makes use of whatever information is available about the suspect. Most people do not construct their keys in a way that make them difficult to guess. Their main concern is being able to remember the key themselves. Therefore, the probability is that the key will be something that they have an interest in. For example, in a particular case, the suspect was a police officer. He had a pretty good knowledge of computing and used strong encryption and it was well implemented. The chances of "breaking to code" were nil. We compiled a dossier containing personal information about this individual (his children's names, his wife and girlfriend's names, his badge number, etc.). The next step was to search the evidentiary hard drive copy for incarnations of some of these names and phrases. As it turned out, the very first search (on his badge number) turned up six candidate keys -- the third one tried was it. While this was a real life successful example the investigator could have spent many hours trying the various bits and come up with a dead end.

6 Physical techniques

There are two places where physical intervention can be used. The first is where the suspect is under investigation (such as the much publicized Nicodemo Scarfo [6] case) and is not likely to cooperate with the investigators by providing their keys. This intervention takes place prior to the actual seizure of hardware. The rationale is that the key may be captured in real time and always without the knowledge of the suspect.

The second place is after the seizure has occurred. An example is where a suspected child pornographer was believed to have illegal images on his computer but would not provide the key to decrypt his system. A warrant was obtained to perform the surveillance and a key logger was installed on his machine. Within three hours of returning his machine, the authorities had the needed keys and were then able to unlock the evidentiary copy of the encrypted hard disk revealing enough pornographic material to result in nineteen counts on the incitement.

The tools used to accomplish the acquisition of subject keys for both scenarios described above are varied. There are physical devices and there are software devices. Physical devices break down into a few types: the first is a radio transmitter, next is the interception of electromagnetic emanations, and finally there are devices with internal memory that record keystrokes. All three must be physically installed on the target computer.

The radio transmitter would be installed somewhere between the keyboard and the CPU depending on its design. It would pick up keystrokes and transmit them over a designated radio frequency (or frequencies if spread spectrum or frequency hopping is used by the specific transmitter). These transmissions would be picked up and recorded at a surveillance receiver elsewhere. The investigator then analyses those keystrokes and finds the various keys that are being used by the suspect. These will be used for later decryption and analysis of the suspect's seized computer. A video camera and transmitter might be used to record the keystrokes. While not actually being connected to the computer, it would still have to be placed where it could record such activity – not a particularly easy task.

All electronic devices radiate electromagnetic emanations. These signals can be received with the appropriate equipment at a distance and translated back into their original form. Keystrokes and the image on the screen can both be recreated and recorded in real time. In the case of keystrokes, these are recorded and analyzed as above for later use.

The third type of device is a small plug like device that is inserted between the keyboard and the CPU or soldered inside the target's keyboard (this takes about 15 minutes). Two examples of this type of device are KeyGhost and KeyKatch. KeyGhost has both external and internal models. You simply install them and retrieve them after the surveillance is completed or periodically as required. They are then installed on a forensic computer, given a password and the contents of the device's memory are then downloaded to a WordPad text file for later processing. These have a distinct advantage over software key loggers in some circumstances. These devices will record ALL keystrokes on a given machine. Software key loggers can only begin recording AFTER the logging software becomes operational. In the event that the target machine uses CMOS based encryption, the keys are not available to such software until after the entire boot-up process is completed and therefore after the keys have actually been entered.

These are a sample of the kinds of hardware approaches that might be taken in an investigation. In the past they have provided good results and if used with the appropriate authorities (warrants) evidence gathered in this way can make or break a case.

7 Software techniques

There are a number of software surveillance tools available that can capture keystroke data albeit with the proviso stated above and are used to capture and record useful evidence before seizure is affected. These are stealth type applications designed to operate without the user's knowledge. Some of them have the capability to report over the back channel of the user's Internet connection. Most of these tools have the capability of recording many things including keystrokes. Normally, the recorded data is encrypted and compressed before being stored so that it will not be recognizable to the user should it be seen accidentally.

Some examples are *STARR*, *D.I.R.T*, *ABCKeylogger*, *Ghost Keylog*ger and the FBI's recently announced *Magic Lantern*. All of them must be installed on the target machine, however, that installation is accomplished in a number of different ways. Some are installed through a Trojan, others are installed by having physical access to the target machine, and still others are installed through the computer virus vector (as admitted in the Magic Lantern's description by the FBI). No matter what the vector, this class of surveillance tool has produced good results.

AccessData's *Forensic ToolKit* has an interesting capability. One option is to create a target profile of the suspect and then use it to perform a dictionary search. As mentioned earlier, knowing the background of your suspect can be fruitful when attempting to gain access to encrypted data. Additionally, this tool has a wide range of other dictionaries that can also be used to attempt to find keys of an uncooperative suspect.

8 Reverse engineering techniques

Reverse engineering also holds some potential. While there may be laws in some jurisdictions that make this avenue illegal, it can produce results if you're not in one of them or if you can get the target encryption software reverse engineered in a jurisdiction where it is not illegal. If an encryption application can be broken, then files that have been encrypted using it may no longer be secure. This is different than "cracking" the encryption code. This technique takes the software apart to see how it works. There are lots of software producers out there but there are not a lot of cryptanalysts out there. For practical purposes, many encryption product creators are not cryptographers and are making use of public or licensed algorithms by incorporating the cryptographic code within their product. Occasionally, this is done in a way that weakens the potential security that might have otherwise been provided. Within law enforcement circles, this information is circulated and used where appropriate.

Some manufacturers of cryptographic applications also build into their products back-door access in case a client has a problem using the vendor's product. These vendors have been helpful when asked by the appropriately identified parties and may also be a source of a solution to a cryptographic problem.

9 Conclusions

Encrypted files can be dealt with in many instances, however, the notion that "breaking the code" is the way to solve the problem may not be the answer that produces results. This paper has attempted to introduce the reader to the potential methods that can be used to circumvent encryption and to pave the way to producing good evidence from what might have previously been considered too hard.

One last comment: on encountering data that is encrypted, it might be natural to assume that the suspect is guilty merely because he/she has chosen to use this powerful privacy tool. That would be a wrong assumption. In 1948 more than 100 nations adopted the *Universal Declaration of Human Rights* [7] which enshrines in *Article 12* the most basic of human rights - the right to privacy. Everyone, good and bad, has the right to opt to maintain their privacy and should, in no way be penalized for choosing to exert that right.

References

[1]   *DES* - The U.S. **D**ata **E**ncryption **S**tandard. This algorithm was adopted as a federal standard on 23 November 1976 and approved for private sector use in 1981. A key space of 72,057,594,037,927,900 keys.

[2]   *IDEA* - **I**nternational **D**ata **E**ncryption **A**lgorithm. This algorithm has been analyzed and attacked (unsuccessfully) since its creation by Xuejia Lai and James Massey in 1990. A key space of: 340,282,366,920,938, 000,000,000,000,000,000,000,000 keys.

[3]   *Properly formed key* - This refers to the fact that each character of the key (in the IDEA example 16 characters) has up to 256 possible values. If the user makes use of only a subset of those possible characters (just lower case alpha characters for example), then the strength (security) of the outcome will be reduced accordingly.

[4] *IsEncrypted* - An AccessData Corporation product designed to find files that have been encrypted with specific products - like Word, Excel, Pkzip, etc. - www.accessdata.com.

[5] *Steganography* - the technique of hiding data within other data. For example, using a product such as Invisible Secrets (NeoByte Solutions product) a user could hide an encrypted message within various graphic image files without appreciably affecting the visible quality of the image.

[6] *Nicodemo Scarfo* - Under investigation by the FBI for several months prior to being indited in December 2000. Scarfo used strong encryption to hide his alleged illegal activities. The FBI assumed that he would not cooperate and installed a key logger on his computer that captured his keys and made them available at their (the FBI's) discretion.

[7] *Universal Declaration of Human Rights - Article 12* - No one shall be subjected to arbitrary interference with his privacy, family, home or correspondence, nor to attacks upon his honour and reputation. Everyone has the right to the protection of the law against such interference or attacks. - Adopted and proclaimed by General Assembly *Resolution 217 A (III)* of 10 December 1948.

[8] Casey, Eoghen, *Digital Evidence and Computer Crime*, Academic Press, London, 2000, ISBN: 0-12-162885-X.

[9] Guidance Software, Inc., *EnCase Legal Journal*, Second Edition, South Pasadena, California, October 2001.

[10] Mandia, Kevin, Prosise, Chris, *Incident Response: Investigating Computer Crime*, New York, 2001, ISBN: 0-07-213182-9.

[11] Schneier, Bruce, *Applied Cryptography*; 2nd Edition, New York, John Wiley & Sons, Inc., 1996, ISBN: 0-471-12845-7.

[12] Stephenson, Peter, *Investigating Computer-Related Crime*, Boca Raton, Florida, CRC Press, 1999, ISBN: 0-8493-2218-9.

[13] US Department of Justice, *Electronic Crime Scene Investigation: A Guide for First Responders*, Washington D.C., July 2001, NCJ-187736.

Section 7
Strategic issues

Legal and policy challenges facing electronic commercial marketplaces and trading exchanges

J. Matsuura
University of Dayton School of Law, U.S.A.

Abstract

Electronic marketplaces and exchanges now handle a significant portion of the commercial transactions associated with international e-business. Many different laws and regulations govern those marketplaces and the transactions they process. This paper identifies legal issues that have the greatest impact on the expansion of electronic marketplaces. These key legal issues have the greatest influence on public perception of the integrity of the digital markets. The continued expansion of digital marketplace activity requires widespread public confidence in the integrity of the marketplace. Effective legal oversight of the markets is essential to foster the necessary level of public confidence. Resolution of certain fundamental legal issues associated with electronic markets is vital to the future success of those markets.
Keywords: law, regulation, digital markets.

1 Introduction

This paper examines the key legal issues affecting the perceived integrity of electronic markets. It focuses on: prevention of fraud; transaction security and enforceability; information privacy; antitrust and competition law compliance; and securities regulation. These legal issues have the greatest potential impact on public perception of the integrity of digital markets. These legal concerns have significant impact on public confidence in digital markets because they affect the perceptions of fairness and security that the public holds with respect to the markets. In general, markets are perceived to be of high integrity if they are easily accessible, if the transactions are transparent and enforceable, and if all participants are treated fairly. Continued expansion of use of electronic marketplaces requires continued user confidence in the integrity of those markets. Only the legal system can provide a foundation for that public confidence. In this way, future success of digital markets depends on the effectiveness of the legal system as a means to promote public perception of market integrity.

2 Key digital marketplaces

There are three leading forms of electronic marketplaces: consumer-oriented markets (e.g., eBay); industry trading exchanges (B2B portals, such as Covisint); and securities/commodities exchanges. Each of these marketplaces serves a different set of users and offers a different set of transactions. Consumer marketplaces generally connect individual buyers and sellers, commonly in an auction setting. They process many transactions, and the value of each transaction is relatively low. Industry trading exchanges facilitate transactions between companies. They generally support transactions between businesses and their suppliers or their corporate customers. These digital markets commonly process fewer transactions, but each transaction has a greater dollar value. They establish a network of transactional connections between commercial organizations in a given industry. Online securities exchanges facilitate sale and purchase of financial instruments, including securities and options. These exchanges process a high volume of transactions involving both individual and institutional participants.

3 Demand for market integrity

The public in general and the users of each of these different markets demand integrity in the markets as the price of their support for the markets and their participation in the markets. Users of digital markets expect to be protected by law when they participate in those markets. To the extent that they have confidence that laws are adequate to provide protection and that the laws are fully and fairly enforced, they will believe in the integrity of the markets. Based on that belief, users will continue to participate in the digital marketplace.

For consumer-oriented markets the leading issues of concern as to market integrity are fraud prevention, transaction security, and effective information privacy (FTC [1] and FTC [2]). Consumers look to government authorities to implement and enforce a legal framework that will reduce the risk of fraud in online auction transactions. In the United States, the Federal Trade commission (FTC) at the national level, and state consumer protection agencies have played an active role in fraud control. Globally, consumer protection authorities from many different countries are coordinating their online regulatory efforts, through initiatives such as econsumer.gov (http://www.econsumer.gov) recognizing that consumer protection in digital markets is an international undertaking.

Each consumer also expects secure transactions. Consumers want assurance that payments associated with digital market transactions will be processed securely. Another aspect of secure transactions involves the privacy of personal information. Consumers want to be sure that their personal information is used only for the purposes they intend and only by the parties they authorize. With respect to information privacy, some jurisdictions, the European Community and Canada for example, have adopted specific legal protection for personally identifiable information. The United States has not followed that approach, but information privacy issues have now been brought within the framework of the consumer protection process. Under that approach, information privacy breaches can be treated as unreasonable trade practices, and legal remedies are available.

The integrity of B2B exchanges is most extensively affected by an assessment as to whether the exchanges promote fair competition. Traditional antitrust principles are applied to B2B markets in an effort to preserve market integrity (FTC [3] and Crowell and Moring [4]). There is public concern that the collaboration among businesses necessary to develop and maintain B2B exchanges can evolve into collusion that threatens competition. For this reason, antitrust regulators continue to monitor B2B digital markets carefully.

In online securities and commodities markets, the integrity of the markets is most directly influenced by the perceived integrity of the trading supported by the markets. Among the legal issues of greatest concern in online securities trading are the accuracy and accessibility of market information (SEC [5], SEC [6], Unger [7]). Securities regulators now direct significant attention to online markets and transactions. Electronic markets are now an integral part of the global financial marketplace, largely because user confidence supported their expansion.

4 Digital markets and the law

The legal system and legal institutions play a critical role in the public perception of market integrity. The law establishes the rules associated with the operations of the markets. Legal institutions are the mechanism through which those rules are enforced. Public confidence in digital marketplaces is largely influenced by a belief that legal requirements will be effectively enforced. The law thus performs two important functions in support of digital marketplaces. It maintains order by providing a deterrent for bad conduct and a remedy to redress such conduct when it occurs. The law also builds public confidence in the integrity of the markets. This confidence is what fuels increased participation in the markets. Both of these functions of the law are of vital importance to preservation of healthy and dynamic electronic markets.

The law influences market integrity in at least two ways. At one level, legal institutions directly regulate the structure and operation of some markets. Securities markets, for example, are commonly subject to direct regulation regarding their structure, practices, and procedures. In addition, the law provides a mechanism through which individual private parties can enforce their legal rights in association with market activities. For example, an individual consumer claiming that another party failed to perform its commercial obligations could initiate a private legal action against that party, or could ask the government consumer protection regulator to take action against the party. The law influences the structure and operations of digital markets through direct regulation and by providing the formal mechanism through which private parties can enforce their rights. The existence and effective functioning of both of these legal processes contribute to public confidence in the markets.

Some participants in the digital marketplace advocate significant reliance on self-enforcement of policies to protect market integrity. Under this approach, markets or industries develop their own standards of conduct and practice, and they then self-enforce those requirements. Self-regulation can play an important and helpful role in promoting public confidence in digital markets. It is important, however, that self-regulation is effectively integrated with formal legal oversight of market activities. Although self-regulation can be an effective method to manage market behaviour and practices, self-regulation alone is not likely to provide as a great a level of public confidence in market integrity as will self-regulation coupled with formal legal review. Self-regulation can provide a valuable foundation for management of market behaviour; however, market users are generally more comfortable if that self-regulation is supplemented by regulation involving formal legal institutions, such as the courts and government regulatory agencies.

An example of seemingly effective balancing of private, self-regulation with formal legal oversight involves management of information privacy. In some countries, government has taken the lead in regulation of commercial use of personal consumer information (e.g., the European Community). In other countries (such as the United States), self-regulation through industry organizations and consumer groups has played a leading role. Yet, in both contexts a combination of self-regulation and formal regulation by legal authorities seems to be evolving as the optimal approach to protect public confidence in the commercial marketplace on the issue of information privacy.

Proponents of digital markets should have an interest in effective enforcement of laws applicable to the markets, even if that enforcement at times requires them to incur some additional costs or to limit their conduct. Those short-term costs and constraints can yield long-term benefits if they help to inspire greater public confidence in market integrity, and thus drive greater market participation. Thus developers, operators, and users of digital marketplaces should recognize that effective enforcement of rules of market operation and of user conduct are critically important to the future success of the markets. Digital markets rely on law and legal institutions to win the confidence of users. Digital markets are largely dependent on law for their survival.

5 Conclusions

There are three leading classes of digital marketplaces. Each confronts slightly different legal issues. All of those markets must, however, develop adequate legal oversight to preserve user confidence in the integrity of the markets. Failure to preserve user confidence will threaten the future viability of those markets. Proponents of digital markets should thus welcome regulation of those markets, to the extent that such regulation encourages user confidence in the markets. Although digital market regulation may cause short-term increases in costs and may constrain some market conduct, that may well prove to be a small price to pay for greater future public confidence in the markets and corresponding growth in market participation.

References

[1] Federal Trade Commission (FTC), *Internet Auctions: A Guide for Buyers & Sellers*, 2003, http://www.ftc.gov/bcp/conline/pubs/online/auctions.htm.
[2] FTC, *U.S. Perspectives on Consumer Protection in the Global Electronic Marketplace*, 2000, http://www.ftc.gov/bcp/icpw/lookingahead/electronicmkpl.pdf.
[3] Federal Trade Commission (FTC), *Entering the 21st Century: Competition Policy in the World of B2B Electronic Marketplaces*, 2000, http://www.ftc.gov/os/2000/10/b2breport.pdf.
[4] Crowell & Moring, *EU Competition Law and B2Bs*, 2001, http://www.crowell.com/content/expertise/europeanpractice/publications9/EUlaw.pdf.
[5] Securities and Exchange Commission (SEC), *Examination of Broker-Dealers Offering Online Trading*, 2001, http://www.sec.gov/news/studies/online.htm.
[6] SEC, *Online Investing Complaint Center*, 2003, http://www.investingcomplaints.com.
[7] Unger, L.S., *Online Brokerage: Keeping Apace of Cyberspace*, 1999, http://www.sec.gov/pdf/cybrtrnd.pdf.

Developing competitive advantages through e-business of Lithuania's SMEs

R. Gatautis
Marketing department, Economics and Management Faculty, Kaunas University of Technology, Laisves av. 55, Kaunas LT-3000, Lithuania

Abstract

The dynamics of information technologies stimulate enterprise to look at the business anew. E-business allows for the enterprise not only to increase the size of market and reach new consumers, but also to lower expenses of work, inventory, logistic, communication and others. The introduction of e-business in the activity of the firm is not a simple process, it is related with the existing reorganization of business models and systems.

E-business solutions lead to higher competition between enterprises. The competitive advantages plays a more important role under conditions of intensive competition. Their peculiarities and development mechanism is the essence of the competitiveness. The usage of e-business for the development of competitive advantages requires a systematic and methodological approach.

Based on the theoretical research of M. Porter, M. Parson, B. Ives, P. Learmonth, L. McFarlan, Y. Bakos, E. Brynjolfsson, J. P. Bailey, M. Sarkar, J. Rockart, M. Scott Morton, T. Malone, J. Yates and R. Benjamin, the model for the development of competitive advantages of economic subjects, making use of opportunities of e-business integrating three standpoints toward the use of e-business for the development of competitive advantages (the value added chain, the optimization of interorganizational relations, M.Porter's competition model), is presented.

The theoretical model of the development of competitive advantages was empirically tested between Lithuania's companies providing e-business solutions for Lithuania's enterprises. Based on this research, the main areas of e-business' use for the development of competitive advantages between Lithuania's companies are identified.

1 Introduction

Increase of electronic business, growing more active during last decade, made up new conditions for the business development. Electronic business gave an opportunity to reorganize the process of business and achieve better results because of information technologies. Dynamics of information technologies and possibilities of their application induce enterprises to look at business processes anew. Information technologies create conditions for both internal and external (intranet, extranet) network creation and carrying out effective activity. E-business allows enterprise not only increase its market share or reaching new customers, but also significantly reduce costs of work, inventory, logistics, communication etc. Introduction of e-business in a company activity is not simple process; firstly it is related with reformation of existing business models and organizational systems.

Development of information technologies and their application in business processes induce competition. While competition becoming intensive, the competitive advantages gain bigger and bigger importance for enterprise success. Their features and formation mechanism is the basis of competitiveness assurance.

Wishing to introduce e-business in its activity enterprise has firstly to reorganize activity in parts of business process chain and in relations with partners. Using of e-business is important for enterprise in development of competitive advantages, allowing company to compete successfully in the market.

Scientific problem
Possibilities of e-business using in activity of enterprises give them competitive capabilities. Under modern business conditions information and decisions, based on information received in real time, gain greater and greater importance. Under such conditions using of e-business in development of competitive advantages requires adequate systematic and methodological provisions. Using of e-business for the development of competitive advantages is actual scientific problem. Methods, models and tools for competitive advantages development using e-business would reduce uncertainty while developing competitive advantages.

Despite the fact that influence of e-business on various aspects of enterprise activity is widely considered, many authors studied using of e-business in formation of competitive advantages. Studies of Porter [13], Rockart and Scott Morton [15], Parsons [11], Ives and Learmonth [7], McFarlan and McKenney [9], McLaughlin et al. [10], Bakos [3] are most noticeable in this field.

Variety of authors' opinions shows the importance of e-business in development of competitive advantages.

Problem of study: theoretical and practical aspects of e-business competitive advantages development methods adaptation under conditions of Lithuanian market.

Aim of study: Identification of e-business usage for competitive advantages in Lithuanian enterprises.

Objective of study: Competitive advantages development model adaptation possibilities under the conditions of Lithuania according to the empiric Lithuanian enterprises research.

2 Competitive advantages development model

The first scientific works of Rockart and Scott Morton [15], M. Parsons (1983), Ives and Learmonth [7], McFarlan and McKenney [9], McLaughlin et al. [10], analysing using of IT and e-business in enterprises for gaining competitive advantages. Authors, such as Porter [13], Bailey and Bakos [2], Adelaar [1], Sarkar et al. [16], in their works more critically estimated using of e-business in development of competitive advantages. When analysing opinions of various authors about the influence of e-business on formation of competitive advantages the following three opinions are classified:
- Development of competitive advantages referring to analysis of value added chain;
- Development of competitive advantages referring to analysis of inter-organization relations;
- Development of competitive advantages referring to analysis of M. Porter competition model.

2.1 Value added chain

Rockart and Scott Morton [15] have classified three main ways, by which e-business can be used to form competitive advantages:
- To improve every function adding value,
- To increase costs of customers and suppliers selection,
- To establish new fields of activity.

Ives and Learmonth [7] further developed research started by Rockart and Scott Morton [15]. In their works Ives and Learmonth analysed thirteen stages **resources life cycle model**, in order to define how enterprise can gain competitive advantages. Although in their works the authors did not used term "value-added chain", however the model of resources life cycle used by them is closely related with chain of value-added. In addition it is needed to notice, that analysis of chain of value-added or resources life cycle, intended for achievement of operational productivity and functional effectiveness, is closely related with enterprises activity strategy.

Using e-business enterprise can become competitive in all stages of relations with customer. According to Ives and Learmonth the model of resources life cycle can be applied to enterprise customers, which treat products or services offered by enterprise as the resources necessary for them. Taking into account this circumstance, authors suggest calling the model - **model of customer resources life cycle (CRLC)**. CRLC model allows enterprises not only define when the possibilities of e-business application exist, but also what specific decisions should be implemented.

M. Porter [13] has a notion that that the main mean helping to understand influence of e-business on enterprises and formation of competitive advantages, is chain of value-added, i.e. sequence of actions, by which product is created and provided to customers. Enterprise competing in industry branch carries out many individual, but interrelated actions creating value, such as activity of personnel of provision of resources, production of components or delivery of goods, and these actions relate with actions of suppliers, distribution channels participants and customers. Chain of value-added is scheme intended to identify all these actions and analyse how they influence enterprise costs and value provided to buyers.

2.2 Interorganization relations

E-business stipulates changes of intermediating services. Enterprises, in order to minimize transaction costs, can use various intermediaries. For minimization of transaction costs using e-business four intermediation kinds can be used – direct market, market free of intermediaries, new (virtual) intermediaries and re-intermediaries Sarkar et al. [16].

E-business can be used for possibilities of better coordination. Better-coordinated operations become more effective. Coordination can be reached using e-business by relating functional fields of individual enterprises. For example, in order to reduce resources volumes and time of new orders turnover, it is possible to relate firm production planning system with suppliers system. (Malone et al. [8].)

2.3 M. Porter competition model

Industry competitive advantages are formed taking into account industry competition forces. Referring to Porter model, competition in industry is stipulated by competition among existing competitors, threat of new participants, threat of changeable goods or services, negotiation power of suppliers and negotiation power of customer.

E-business can be used for competitive advantages development in industry for:

- Enforcement of power of negotiation with suppliers and customers,
- Increase of switching costs of customer using information or services based on e-business,
- Reduction of suppliers' switching costs
- Establishment of barriers for new market participants,
- Cooperation with selected competitors through common nets based on e-business.

2.3.1 Increase of negotiation power

Enterprise, increasing customer's switching costs and/or reducing its switching costs, enforces its negotiation power. In many cases, according to the games theory, each part can improve its position, i.e. create competitive advantage, so increasing number of possible alternatives (Bailey and Bakos [2]). Number of

alternative situations is limited by price of search process. Two main factors define alternative search process:
- Capacity of player (enterprise) information processing, how much it is related with its effectiveness while looking for new alternatives,
- Search characteristics, while looking for available alternatives. When looking for alternatives it is important to separate alternatives "ex ante" and "ex poste", when the agreement is reached, because this event can define limits for one or both parts. "Ex ante" possible alternatives are stipulated by unique product features, and "ex poste" such alternatives are impacted by selection costs.

So it is possible to classify three main factors of negotiation power: search process costs, unique features of product and switching costs.

These factors have high importance for enterprise relations with customers and suppliers. Enterprise will enforce its monopolistic power by increasing costs of customers' alternative suppliers, incorporating unique features of its products and by increasing costs of its customer's alternative suppliers. With respect to suppliers enterprise will increase its monopolistic power by reducing price of alternative suppliers search, its own dependence on unique forces or its costs of selection of alternative supply sources.

Enterprise in order to improve its negotiation position with partners has to provide unique and valuable information and services, which are required by customer or supplier organization. Provision of specific information according to the customer needs stipulates increase of costs of conversion to competitors. Information technologies can facilitate providing of unique information or service, which earlier were unavailable or their price was very high. The higher perceptible value of such suggestions and the more complex are relations with customers the higher are costs of customer competitors' selection. It can stated switching costs are function of information.

$$SC = f(I),$$

where: SC – switching costs, I – information.

While information becoming more complex and specific the switching costs increase.

On the other hand, e-business allows enterprise to collect data about its suppliers and alternative suppliers and their offers. In case of need enterprise can suit current systems to new suppliers or simple join them to its systems.

2.3.2 Establishment of barriers for entrance into market

Threat of new market competitors' appearance depends on that how much high are barriers for entrance into market. I.e. losses, which potential novices of the market who wish to act in some market have to adopt. Although Porter states that e-business reduces barriers of entrance into market, enterprises still can enforce barriers to market using cooperation based on e-business. Establishment of common network with competitors for the exchange of certain level information can be treated as "agreement" among enterprises operating in the industry. Such network can be barrier for new entrant, wishing to enter into market because costs of such network creation can be divided among network participants, and possibilities to create own network or to join network can be related with high investments.

2.3.3 Threat of substitutes

E-business gives firms unique opportunities for product innovations. In many industry branches, from automatic electronics to consumer electric goods, information technology is introduced by modifying products in order to increase their consumption value. In other industries, such as banking, insurance and consulting, e-business allows development of servicing. E-business also allows differentiation of existing goods and develop new or unique products.

3 Data collection and results

To define possibilities of competitive advantages development in enterprises' activity we applied collective expert evaluation model. The advantage of this method firstly is the higher accuracy than using individual expert evaluation (Blumberg and Gluschenko [5]). To increase reliability of questioning method it is possible to use quantitative and qualitative methods of experts' selection. In this case the second was chosen – while studying it was focused not the mass character of questionnaire survey, but to the competence of experts, their knowledge of analysed problem. Such selection also was stipulated by problem complexity.

3.1 Method of data collection

Since the goal of study is to clarify notion of experts, the most suitable method of data collection is survey. Survey is carried out by the help of questionnaire. Since the one specialized theme is analysed, the survey can be defined as specialized survey. To facilitate processing of received data and taking into account character of information we will carry out standardized survey, the questionnaire for which is prepared in advance. Survey is carried out directly, personally giving expert the questionnaire and asking him to answer it. This method is far more effective than questioning by post, because the possibility to receive answers is higher in Lithuania.

3.2 Respondents' selection

There are two approaches to requirements for experts. Following the first approach, experts can be specialists, having dealing with analysed subject according their activity type and disposing sufficient experience. However, agreeing with the second approach, this not sufficient condition. First of all, specialist, participating in expert estimation has to have wide outlook and erudition, and the most important – irregular thinking (Pranulis [14]). According to Pranulis the recommended number of experts is from 10 to 100.

15 experts have participated in research – managers of companies providing e-business solutions for enterprises. Selection of experts is based on assumption that companies providing e-business solutions for enterprises know enough well

possibilities of using e-business and benefit which they give to enterprise. In addition, such experience of various business enterprises allows experts to estimate situation from wide perspective than by opinion of one individual enterprise manager.

Estimating results of empiric research have been calculated correlation relation between importance of e-business in development of competitive advantages and importance of e-business in development of competitive advantages in different business fields.

3.3 Results of study

When estimating expert notions unification the Kendal concordance coefficient W=0,62 was calculated. Because Kendal concordance coefficient is more than 0,6 we can say that the notion of experts is unified.

Competitive advantages development through value chain analysis: main activities
To define whether distribution of variables, the relation of which has to be evaluated, is normal, the Smirnov-Kolmogorov test, identifying level of importance, was carried out.

Table 1: Kolmogorov-Smirnov test results.

	Importance of e-business	Input logistics	Production technological operations	Output logistics	Marketing and sales	Customer service
Average	1,87	1,33	1,60	1,60	1,67	2,33
Standard error	0,92	0,49	0,63	0,51	0,49	0,49
Kolmogorov-Smirnov coefficient	1,142	1,624	1,144	1,491	1,624	1,624
Level of importance	0,148	0,010	0,146	0,023	0,010	0,010

Since level of importance is higher than defined importance level (0,148>0,05 0,010>0,05 0,146>0,05 0,023>0,05 0,010>0,05 0,010>0,05) it means that distribution is normal. In order to estimate relation of empiric study variables we can use Pearson, Kendall and Spearmen correlation coefficients.

Pearson, Kendall and Spearmen coefficient, taking into account relation between importance of e-business in development of competitive advantages and importance of e-business in development of competitive advantages in main enterprise activity fields are provided in table.

Table 2: Pearson correlation coefficient.

	Input logistics	Production technological operations	Output logistics	Marketing and sales	Customer service
Pearson correlation coefficient	0,586*	0,888**	0,800**	0,693**	0,267

** Correlation reliability 0,99
* Correlation reliability 0.95

Table 3: Kendall correlation coefficient.

	Input logistics	Production technological operations	Output logistics	Marketing and sales	Customer service
Kendall correlation coefficient	0,571*	0,882**	0,775**	0,671**	0,235

** Correlation reliability 0,99
* Correlation reliability 0.95

Table 4: Spearmen correlation coefficient.

	Input logistics	Production technological operations	Output logistics	Marketing and sales	Customer service
Spearmen correlation coefficient	0,601*	0,932**	0,816**	0,707**	0,247

** Correlation reliability 0,99
* Correlation reliability 0.95

Generalizing results one can say that (if value of coefficient is less than 0,5 - relation is weak, if value of coefficient is between 0,5 and 0,7 - relation is average strong, if value of coefficient is between 0,7 and 1 – strong relation) : input logistics – average relation; production technological operations – strong relation; output logistics – strong relation; marketing and sales – average relation; customer service – weak relation.

Referring to this evaluation we can say that output logistics and production technological operations are the most important fields, in which enterprises can form competitive advantages by introducing information technologies. Input logistics and marketing and sales are also those activity fields, although not so significant as output logistics and production technological operations, in which enterprise can form competitive advantages. Meantime customer service is not that field in which enterprise could reach competitive advantages with help of e-business based on information technologies.

Competitive advantages development through value chain analysis: supporting activity fields
Using the same technique the result was obtained:
Infrastructure maintenance – strong relation (0,7<0,816<1);
Control of human resources – weak relation (0,411<0,5);
Creation of technologies – weak relation (0,299<0,5);
Servicing – strong relation (0,7<0,707<1).

Referring to received results we can say that maintenance and servicing of infrastructure are the main supporting activity fields, in which enterprise can develop competitive advantages using e-business.

Competitive advantage development through optimization of inter-organization relations
Taking into account calculation data, we can say that there is no relation between intermediaries' selection, while minimizing transactions costs, definition of optimal number of intermediaries and using of e-business in development of competitive advantages between Lithuania's enterprises. Therefore we can say that these activities will be not important in development of enterprises competitive advantages in Lithuania.

Evaluation of using of e-business in enforcement of negotiation power against suppliers and buyers, to establish innovations and market barriers in formation of enterprise competitive advantages.
Received results allows saying that the most important fields in which e-business is used in formation of enterprise competitive advantages, are enforcement of negotiation power against customers and protection from substitutes.

4 Conclusions

The current study indicated the main areas of using of e-business for competitive advantages between Lithuania's enterprises. Although theoretical framework identified more possibilities for using e-business in competitive advantages development, Lithuania's companies uses some of them. The lack of knowledge and financial recourses causes such situation.

References

[1] Adelaar T. Electronic Commerce and the Implications for Market Structure. Journal of Computer Mediated Communication, Vol. 5, Issue 3, March 2000.

[2]   Bailey, J. P., Bakos, Y. An exploratory study of the emerging role of electronic intermediaries. International Journal of Electronic Commerce, Vol. 1, Issue 3, 1997.
[3]   Bakos Y. The emerging role of electronic marketplaces on the Internet. Communication of ACM, 41 (8): 35-42, 1998.
[4]   Bakos, J. Y., "A Strategic Analysis of Electronic Market laces", MIS Quarterly, Sep. 1991, pp. 295-309.
[5]   Blumberg A. V., Gluschenko V. F. Теория управления: Учеб. курс /. М.: Вестник, 1982 – p. 332.
[6]   Dapkus, G.; Gatautis, R. Developing competitive advantages in industrial firms. Engineering Economics. Kaunas, Technologija. ISSN 1392-2785. 2001, Nr.3(23). p. 76-79.
[7]   Ives B, Learmonth G. P. "The information system as competitive weapon". Communication of ACM. Vol 27, number 12, December 1984, p. 1193-1201.
[8]   Malone, T., Yates, J., and Benjamin, R. The logic of electronic markets. Harvard Business Review, May-June, 166-172. 1989.
[9]   McFarlan F. W., McKenney J. Corporate Information Systems Management. Richard D. Irwin Inc., Homewood, Illinois, 1983.
[10] McLaughlin M., Howe R. and Cash J. Changing competitive ground rules – the impact of computers and communications in the 1980s. Unpublished working paper. 1984.
[11] Parsons, G. L., "Information Technology: A New Competitive Weapon", Sloan Management Review, Vol. 25, No.1, 1984.
[12] Porter, M., Miller, V., "How Information Gives You Competitive Advantage", Harvard Business Review, July-August 1985.
[13] Porter, M., Strategy and the Internet. Harvard Business Review, December, 2003.
[14] Pranulis V. Marketingo tyrimai. Vilnius, Kronta, 1999.
[15] Rockart J. F., Scott Morton, M. S. Implications of Changes in Information technology for Corporate Strategy. Interfaces, vol. 14, n.1, January-February 1984. p. 84-95.
[16] Sarkar, M.B., Butler, B., Steinfield, C., "Intermediaries and Cybermediaries: A Continuing Role for Mediating Players in the Electronic Marketplace", Journal of Computer Mediated Communication (JCMC), Vol. 1, No.3, 1995.

E-business technology education: a preliminary model

S. Dhanjal & Y. Khmelevsky
*Department of Computing Science,
School of Advanced Technologies & Mathematics,
The University College of the Cariboo (UCC), Canada*

Abstract

In this paper, we describe a preliminary model proposing that the e-business technology (EBT) should be one area of many specialization areas within Computing Science & Information Technology (CS&IT) departments. This paper explores the emerging educational models, methods and technologies that are associated with CS&IT education from the perspective of EBT. To be able to produce the qualified specialists who can overcome the various obstacles that have presented themselves to the new economy throughout recent global economic crises, we have to make appropriate changes to the CS&IT educational model of the Colleges, Technological Educational Institutions and Universities. This paper proposes possible changes, makes appropriate recommendations and describes implementation strategies for several important undergraduate courses (including Database Management Systems (DBMS), Web-based Information Systems, Programming Languages, Operating Systems, Software Engineering, and Computer Networks; taught many times by the authors during the past decade) from the viewpoint of the preliminary model developed in this paper.
　　One of the original contributions of this paper is that the authors have coined two new terms to reflect the latest technological developments and proposed educational changes: the "mobile PC telephone", and the "e-business centric programming".
Keywords: e-business, e-business technology, e-business centric programming, mobile PC telephone, m-business, education model, DBMS, programming languages, operating systems, software engineering, computer networks.

1 Introduction

The objective of this paper is to explore the emerging educational models, methods and technologies that are associated with Computing Science & Information Technology (CS&IT) education from the perspective of EBT and services utilization by consumers, business, Non-Government Organizations (NGOs), and government. Authors are convinced that many of the largest organizations (largest business companies, largest Universities, and educational training centers) are already effectively involved into e-business. In our opinion, the next wave of the e-business development and utilization is predominantly for middle-size and small businesses, small universities, local government institutions and NGOs.

To involve middle-size and small businesses, the post secondary education system should produce a large number of qualified specialists, who should be able to break developments into appropriate categories such as business-to-business (B2B), and business-to-customer (B2C). These specialists should be able to make appropriate electronic business implementations that are not as expensive and complicated, as the solutions developed for the largest organizations.

To produce these qualified specialists, and to overcome the various obstacles that have presented themselves to the new economy throughout recent global economic crises, we have to make appropriate changes to CS&IT educational model of the Colleges, Technological Educational Institutions and Universities. We propose a preliminary model that the EBT should be one area of many specialization areas within CS&IT departments.

The organization of the remainder of this paper is as follows:

The next section of this paper describes the recent developments in e-business & EBT, and develops the rationale for the preliminary model proposed in this paper. It outlines the typical CS&IT courses, which should be modified to emphasize the e-business solutions and technology. This section essentially concentrates on what should be changed, and why?

Section 3 analyzes possible changes for several important undergraduate courses (including Database Management Systems, Web-based Information Systems, Programming Languages, Operating Systems, Software Engineering, and Computer Networks) taught many times by the authors during the past decade. This section addresses the issue: how to change. It makes appropriate recommendations and describes implementation strategies for course changes from the viewpoint of the preliminary model proposed in this paper.

The conclusion summarizes the original contribution of this paper.

2 E-business and e-business technology

E-business a hot topic in the Colleges and Universities and can be defined as "the conduct of business with the assistance of telecommunications and telecommunications-based tools" [1]. This definition covers a broad range of activities, from B2B, to B2C, to intra-organizational commerce [2] and includes some new activities such as customer-to-customer (C2C) activities. E-business also includes e-commerce, and a relatively new area of m-business (mobile business) technology and covers much more than just the selling of goods through Internet and mobile devices. Business departments also teach e-business courses, but from business and management point of view. Whereas the e-business courses taught by the Business departments focus more on the management and business issues [3], the CS&IT courses have to be focused on programming skills, networking, database management systems (DBMS), software (SW) and information systems (IS) engineering and development, Models of Computation, Programming Languages, and Operating Systems (OS). It is important for CS&IT professors to differentiate between what should be taught in a CS&IT e-business course and what should be taught by the professors from business department. In our preliminary model in this paper, we propose that an e-business component as a small part of several important CS&IT courses should teach students EBT elements and how to build an e-business with the existing technologies.

Many professors and academicians believe that we have strong trend towards free and open source technology, and we should be concentrating on middle-size or small-size e-business technology now. Our CS&IT courses should be oriented for specialists, which will work within small and middle-size business companies, especially while we are facing IT crises at present. The famous economist Rinald Coase, who won the economics Nobel Prize in 1991, recognized the basic concepts in the field of e-commerce as early as 1930. G. Sampson [4] presents an observation for business size companies, based on Rinald Coase's works (works for which he is chiefly known and is today most associated with e-commerce) as follows: "Many contemporary firms are smaller than their counterparts of 20 years ago. Outsourcing is encouraged by factors apart from information technology, often as a response to low wage levels in the Third World; but, in many cases, outsourcing exploits information technology to achieve collaboration across firm boundaries over activities previously conducted within a single firm. However, we also see many mergers producing ever-larger companies. Two recent examples in the IT sector are Hewlett-Packard/Compaq and IBM/PricewaterhouseCoopers Consulting." [4]. Moreover we now have only a few enterprise systems within the so-called enterprise resource planning (ERP) systems (such as SAP, PeopleSoft, Baan and Oracle Financials).

It is important to understand the role of the telecommunications and telecommunications-based tools within EBT. Equally important is to understand the opportunities, which can be exploited by utilizing new inventions in the area of telecommunications. The following examples will illustrate the rationale:

1. One of the most significant inventions in personal computers technology has been networking in the last 10 years. The Internet is the most impressive example of the telecommunications and telecommunications-based tools, and has proven to be an easy and efficient way to provide businesses to millions of customers all over the world (or to provide e-business).

2. Another very important technology from the e-business point of view is mobile telephones and mobile computers, which has been growing rapidly to increase the sophistication of the mobile devices. We now have new mobile telephone devices, which include VCR, Digital Camera, mini-keyboard, operating systems with office software integrated in a single mobile telephone unit. The authors of this paper feel that we should change the name of this unit from the "mobile telephone" to the **"mobile PC telephone"** to reflect these technological changes. The number of mobile phone users worldwide reached one billion for the first time in 2002. "At the same time, 136 million people owned a mobile phone in the U.S. In parts of Scandinavia and Southeast Asia, penetration is more than 80%." [5].

3. Whereas the computer hardware (including **mobile PC telephone** industry) has been rapidly growing as described above, the software industry has been facing a number of problems. For example, the "software productivity has been dropping more rapidly than any other industry. The semiconductor industry had the most productivity growth (86%) from 1990 to 1995. In that same period, productivity for the software industry decreased by 10%, indeed, the worst decline of all industries surveyed." [6]. We are facing a big SW development crisis, which can be faster overridden, if we include modifications for some CS&IT courses proposed in this paper. Consequently, we should start teaching our students "e-business and m-business technology component based" SW development in the courses (such as Web-based Information Systems, Programming Languages, Operating Systems, and Computer Networks) in our current CS&IT curricula.

4. Some important new trends in IT sector related to EBT are: Optical Technologies (OT), Quantum Computing (QC), Nanotechnology (NT), Grid Computing (GC), image recognition, speech processing (e.g. text-to-speech capabilities), high speed communications, and mobile computing. Nowadays, for example mobile devices, which combine mobile telephone, web-browser, computer, VCR and Digital Camera, MIDI device are already on the market. The authors firmly believe that we should teach all these new trends in several important CS&IT courses, such as Database Management Systems, Web-based Information Systems, Programming Languages, Operating Systems, SW Engineering, Computer Networks, Image Processing, Models of Computation, Artificial Intelligence and Computer Graphics.

Based on these observations, the possible changes to the first six CS&IT courses mentioned in the above list are proposed in the following section. We believe that the students educated with our proposed modifications will be able to face modern business and SW challenges much more efficiently.

3 Proposed changes for some undergraduate courses

3.1 Database management systems and advanced database systems

An important new tendency in classical DBMS courses is to use relatively new information technologies, e.g. Open Grid Services Architecture (OGSA), to introduce the secure and reliable virtualization and management of distributed data and computing resources [7, 8]. Web-based data infrastructures support discovery, exploration, analysis, integration, and mining of remote and distributed data [9]. Such efforts are pioneering a new generation of distributed data discovery, access, and exploration technologies promising to transform the Internet into a data-integration platform. On it, users will be able to perform sophisticated operations on remote and distributed petascale datasets [10].

Distributed virtual computers (DVC) components should be included into course outlines, because DVC enable applications to view their world as a safe local cluster environment rather than as a hostile, best-effort, open Internet.

Dynamic DVC serves as a single administrative domain with centralized resource control already used for database systems by major DBMS development companies as well as business companies [11].

The voluminous data, especially produced by e-business environment, needs to be managed, analyzed, and fed into the decision-making process. Data warehouses solutions, which provide decision support to organizations with the help of analytical databases and online analytical processing (OLAP) tools should be special part of the DBMS courses. Incorporating OLAP tools into decision models of e-business as a part of decision support systems improves decision making [12, 13].

3.2 Web-based database and information systems

To teach students how to implement e-business, the professors must be knowledgeable about the tools they can use to do so. Some examples of how to modify specific courses for e-business education exist in literature. One of them is [3], which gives an example of one way to teach e-business with a popular technology called Enterprise JavaBeans (EJB), which means distributed components that encapsulate business logic. EJBs allow business to evolve as the environment and the requirements change. How to implement EJBs for a class project, how to select the appropriate tools such as web servers, databases and hardware components, and after this the foundation of Enterprise JavaBeans has been covered including entity beans and session beans deployment by L. Moffitt [3].

Some other technologies for e-business, such as Java Developer (JDeveloper) and Business Components for Java (BC4Java) from Oracle, Extensible Markup Language (XML), Personal Home Page (PHP) tools and MySQL, PL/SQL Server Pages (PSP), Active Server Pages (ASP), Java Server Pages (JSP), list of most popular Application Servers and Internet Portals (e.g. Sybase, SAP/TopTier mySAP Enterprise Portal, Sun Microsystems Application Server, IBM WebSphere, InfoImage Decision Portal, Oracle Application Server and Portal, Computer Associates, Peoplesoft, Microsoft Share Point Portal Server, Epicentric Foundation Server, BEA WebLogic Portal) should be demonstrated for the students and used for their research projects and presentations.

3.3 Programming languages

Most Programming Languages courses traditionally include discussions around four major programming paradigms: Procedural (or Imperative) programming, OOP, Functional (or Applicative) programming, and Logic (or Declarative or Relational) programming. However, it is important to recognize [14, 15] that "the most dynamic area of new programming community growth is the World Wide Web, which is the enabling vehicle for electronic commerce ..." [14]. Consequently, we have coined a new term **"e-business centric programming."** We propose that the Programming Languages course should emphasize more on the **e-business centric programming** and the students should get more exposure to programming languages that support **e-business centric programming**. Several languages have already been mentioned in the previous sub-section. Other languages such as PERL (Practical Extraction & Report Language), TCL/TK (Tool Command Language/Tool Kit), Python, JavaScript, and Visual Basic can also be included.

3.4 Operating systems

Most Operating Systems courses traditionally include discussions around operating systems for mainframes, minicomputers, and microcomputers. Our preliminary model proposes that the Operating Systems course should emphasize more on the mobile operating systems (the operating systems for Tablet computers, Handheld computers (Personal Digital Assistants or PDAs or palmtops), and embedded operating Systems (operating systems for Microcontrollers or Embedded computers or Hidden computers). The mobile devices are small in size, have a small amount of memory, include slow processors and feature small display screens [16]. Network computers (or thin clients), and Internet Appliances (or Information Appliances or Web pads) fall between stand-alone self-sufficient PCs and dumb terminals because of their limited processing capabilities. The operating systems for these devices as well as the operating systems for the **mobile PC telephone** proposed by the authors earlier in this paper also fall under a category different than the traditional operating systems. Consequently, the students should be exposed more and more to the challenges presented by the design of the operating systems of these devices.

3.5 Software engineering

Component-based Software Development (CBSD) technology is an interesting approach in the SW development. Design, retrieval, and assembly in CBSD offer an effective approach to constructing software products. CBSD can help the software industry realize quality and productivity gains similar to those achieved in the hardware and manufacturing industries [17, 18]. As an increasing number of software projects miss schedules, exceed budgets, and deliver defective products, industry experts have turned to component-based solutions to overcome the current software crisis [19]. This subject should be incorporated into modern emerging educational models for SW Engineering courses.

The recent emergence of the Web services model for delivering component-based solutions over the Internet further underscores the importance of CBSD. The CBSD approach seeks to develop the components required to support various functions and processes for a particular domain or area, especially for n-tier Web-based information systems and EBT solutions [20].

3.6 Computer networks

An important subject related to Computer Networks course is the emerging high speed and wireless technologies for e-science and e-business. The past few years have seen 1Gb and 10Gb Ethernet (GigE) technology in research and education networks, and several hundred Mbps for wireless devices. "As 10GigE and Mbps wireless technologies, available in metro areas today, becomes more widely deployed, exponential penetration in the market will likely occur, and prices will drop...Today, a 10Gbps lambda between major cities in North America and across the Atlantic Ocean costs about $120/hour ($1 million per year). A Nationwide, 20-year, multi-10Gbps capability can be built for the cost of a typical university building or two... Government-funded science programs and university research projects can afford to experiment, but these economies are realizable today if, and only if, the communities of e-scientists themselves provide all the services and manage them, as was done at iGrid 2002." [21]. It clearly implies that the high speed and wireless network technologies within iGrid should be incorporated into our Computer Networks courses as soon as possible.

4 Conclusions

The next wave of the e-business and m-business development and utilization is predominantly for middle-size and small businesses, small universities, local government institutions and NGOs.

The post secondary education system should produce a number of qualified specialists, who should be able to break developments into appropriate categories such as B2B and B2C. These specialists should be able to make appropriate electronic business implementations inexpensively.

To overcome the various obstacles that have presented themselves to the new economy throughout recent global economic crises, we should make appropriate changes to Computing Science and Informational Technology (CS&IT) courses of the Colleges, Technological Educational Institutions and Universities. As described in this paper, these changes revolve around e-business and m-business technologies, Web-based Information Systems and Database Systems, XML, Java programming languages (including J2EE, EJB, and BC4J), n-tier information systems, mobile devices and mobile technologies, wireless protocols and operating systems for mobile and wireless devices, GRID systems and database systems, e-business centric programming, and component based SW development.

In our preliminary model in this paper, we propose that an e-business component as a small part of several important CS&IT courses should teach students e-business technology elements and how to build an e-business with the existing technologies. Consequently, the e-business technology (EBT) should be one area of many specialization areas within CS&IT departments. This area of specialization can be used by itself to improve effectiveness of the education as well through distance and remote learning, on-line conferences and seminars, professional chat rooms and list-groups.

We are facing a big SW development crisis, which can be faster overridden, if we include modifications for some CS&IT courses proposed in this paper. We believe that the students educated with our proposed modifications will be able to face modern business and SW challenges much more efficiently.

One of the original contributions of this paper is that the authors have coined two new terms to reflect the latest technological developments and proposed educational changes: the "mobile PC telephone", and the "e-business centric programming".

In this paper, we have described the possible changes to these six CS&IT courses: Database Management Systems, Web-based Information Systems, Programming Languages, Operating Systems, Software Engineering, and Computer Networks. Possible changes to other CS&IT courses will be included in our future papers as we enhance this preliminary model.

References

[1] Clarke, R., Electronic commerce definitions, www.anu.edu.au/people/ Roger.Clarke/EC/ECDefns.html (1999).
[2] Siau, K. and Davis, S., Electronic business curriculum - Evolution and revolution @ the speed of innovation, *Journal of Informatics Education & Research* 2, 1 (2000), pps. 21–28.
[3] Moffitt L. (2002), Teaching E-business with enterprise Javabeans, *The Journal of Computing in Small Colleges*, Vol.18, Issue 2 (December 2002), pps.362 – 363.
[4] Sampson G. (2003), The Myth of Diminishing Firms, *Communications of the ACM*, Vol. 46, No. 11, pps. 25 -28.
[5] Stuart J. Barnes, Sid L. Huff (2003), Rising Sun: iMode and the wireless Internet, *Communications of the ACM*, Vol. 46, No. 11, pps. 79-84.
[6] Donald Anselmo, Henry Ledgard (2003), Measuring productivity in the software industry, *Communications of the ACM*, Vol. 46, No. 11, pps. 121-125
[7] Atkinson, M., Chervenak, A., Kunszt, P., Narang, I., Paton, N., Pearson, D., Shoshani, A., & Watson, P., Data access, integration, and management, In *The Grid: Blueprint for a New Computing Infrastructure*,

2nd Ed., eds. I. Foster & C. Kesselman, Morgan Kaufmann, San Francisco, CA, 2004.
[8] Chervenak, A., Foster, I., Kesselman, C., Salisbury, C., & Tuecke, S., The Data Grid: Towards an architecture for the distributed management and analysis of large scientific datasets, *J. Net. Comput. Applic.* 23, 3 (July 2000), pps. 187–200.
[9] Grossman, R., Hornick M., & Meyer G. (2002), Data Mining Standards Initiatives, *Communications of the ACM*, Vol. 45, No. 8, pps. 59-61.
[10] Ian Foster, Robert L. Grossman (2003), Data Integration in a Bandwidth-Rich World, *Communications of the ACM*, Vol. 46, No. 11, pps. 50-57.
[11] Larry L. Smarr, Andrew A. Chien, Tom DeFanti, Jason Leigh, Philip M. Papadopoulos (2003), The OptIPuter, *Communications of the ACM*, Vol. 46, No. 11, pps. 59-66.
[12] Narasimhaiah Gorla (2003), Features to consider in a data warehousing system, *Communications of the ACM*, Vol. 46, No. 11, pps.111-116
[13] Koutsoukis, N., Mitra, G., & Lucas, C., Adapting on-line analytical processing for decision modelling: The interaction of information and decision technologies, *Decision Support Systems* 26, (1999), pps.1–30.
[14] Tucker, A. & Noonan, R., *Programming Languages – Principles and Paradigms*, McGraw-Hill, 2002.
[15] Deitel, Deitel & Nieto, *e-Business & e-Commerce – How to Program*, Prentice Hall, Upper Saddle River, N.J., 2001.
[16] Silberschatz, Galvin & Gagne, *Operating System Concepts*, John Wiley & Sons, Inc., 6th Ed., 2002.
[17] Brown, A.W., *Large-Scale Component-Based Development*, Prentice Hall, Upper Saddle River, N.J., 2000.
[18] Szyperski, C., *Component Software: Beyond Object-Oriented Programming*, ACM Press, New York, 1998.
[19] Fayad, M.E & Schmidt, D.C., "Object-oriented application frameworks", *Communications of the ACM*, Vol. 40, No. 10 (Oct. 1997), 32–38.
[20] Padmal Vitharana, Fatemah Mariam Zahedi, Hemant Jain (2003), Design, retrieval, and assembly in component-based software development, *Communications of the ACM*, Vol. 46, No. 11, pps. 97-102.
[21] DeFanti Tom, Cees de Laat, Joe Mambretti, Kees Neggers, Bill St. Arnaud (2003), TransLight: a global-scale LambdaGrid for e-science, *Communications of the ACM*, Vol. 46, No. 11, pps. 35-41.

How can the private sector benefit from the public sector's e-procurement experiences?

H. Lindskog
*Department of Management and Economics,
Linköping University, Sweden*

Abstract

The private sector is often highlighted as the forerunner when it comes to adoption of new technologies and new methods of work. However, in the field of procurements including e-procurement through the use of information communication technology (ICT), the public sector is probably well ahead of the private sector. There are several ways that the private sector can benefit from the public sector's e-procurement experiences. A Swedish example is the Single Face to Industry (SFTI), which is an open everybody to everybody industry standard for e-procurement for the public sector on its way to become an international standard. The needs of the public authorities are not much different from the needs of private enterprises and in many cases the results of this work and standards could be used for Business to Business (B2B) e-procurements. Other examples are discussed in the article.

Keywords: public procurement, e-procurement, ICT.

1 Public sector – characteristics

The public sector makes up a big portion in all countries. At one extreme is a welfare state like Sweden where the number of employees in the public sector is some 30% of the total. In the more capitalistic US, the corresponding figure is some 17% [1].

The public sector organizations range from one person to several thousands of employees. Public organizations can be very local as kindergartens or with the responsibility to cover the whole nation as ministries. In most countries the public administration has three levels: central/federal government, regional and local governments. Responsibilities at each level can vary from country to country. However, there seems to be more similarities than differences between different countries' public organization due to similar responsibilities, working areas and citizens' needs.

To provide the best possible service at the lowest possible price is the driving force for the development of the public sector, and not profitability. This means that there is no necessity for competition within the public sector, but scope for openness even if it is not always used. This is not possible within the private sector.

The exchange of experiences between different organizations does not stop at the border. There are many formal and informal ways and fora of cooperation between neighboring countries, other bilateral groups and international fora. It is not difficult for social workers, policemen or local politicians to recognize their own needs, existing problems and possible solutions in a similar organization in another country. It is easy to learn from each other and to use experiences from other countries.

The public sector typically has many contacts with individuals - citizens, companies and other organizations. Some public organizations count all citizens, households or enterprises as their customers. It is quite normal as a citizen to have contact with at least a dozen public organizations in a year's time. These contacts can be daily, weekly, monthly, quarterly, yearly or more infrequently depending on your current situation. Enterprises have obligations towards the public sector and the result is another flow of contacts some regularly and some more sporadic.

The public sector is dealing mainly with service delivery to citizens and enterprises. These services typically involve direct contact with people – e.g. kindergartens, hospitals, police or judge - and cannot be as easily as the production of goods rationalized by replacing humans with machines.

Production of almost all goods has been and still is dominated by private companies. However, since we are moving towards a service economy, more and more private companies are selling services. Their production pattern is becoming more similar to that of the public sector. Today, many services, which earlier typically government provided, have been wholly or partly privatized. In this sense, the distinction between the private and the public sector is becoming more blurred.

The number of customers and the number of contacts between them and the public sector exceed by a large amount that of customers and contacts with private companies. Only big banks and insurance companies may get close. Every citizen and every company have several different contact entrances to the public sector organizations.

Similarities and differences are summarized in table 1.

2 Public sector market share and public procurement

The public sector is the biggest single buyer in any country. It is buying standard goods, complicated equipment, services ranging from cleaning offices to management consulting or mobile telephony, medicines, building of bridges or digging of tunnels and so on. Government consumption makes up slightly less than 20% of GDP in the US, slightly more than 20% in the Eurozone and almost 30% of GDP in Sweden [1].

Table 1: Comparison between public and private sectors characteristics.

		Private	Public
Competition		Yes	No
Size of organizations		1-10.000+	1-10.000+
Geographical dispersion			
	- Local	Yes	Yes
	- Regional	Yes	Yes
	- National	Yes	Yes
	- International	Yes	Yes (few)
Production			
	- Goods	Yes	No
	- Services	Yes	Yes
Profit driven		Yes	No
Openness		No (limited)	Yes
Contacts with customers		Vary	Many

In many cases private companies consider selling to the public sector more tedious, risky and costly than selling to other private companies. They find it difficult to be sure of getting any contracts and profitability is not always ensured. These circumstances make it difficult and almost impossible for small or medium sized enterprises to prepare tenders, especially as there are almost as many ways to prepare "Requests for proposals" and specifying their requirements as there are public organizations. In addition, the buyers' competence and knowledge can be limited. Many organizations depend on external consultants and this expertise must also be procured.

Public procurements have the same goals as private ones. However, public procurements are subject to a different and stricter jurisdiction than private procurements. The purpose is to protect companies from unfair competition and to avoid corruption and bribery. The result is often that the formal requirements become quite extensive and lengthy.

Contacts between buyers and bidders/prospective contract winners must during the procurement process be very limited. This puts high demands on the procuring organization to structure the requirements of the purchased service or equipment because published "Request for proposal" cannot be changed. Consequently, the seller cannot change submitted proposals and only under some special circumstances supplement additional information.

It is seldom customary for private companies to reveal their needs and detailed requirements by publishing them openly visible for everybody. It is more to choose from existing lists in buying staple goods or simpler services. For more complex requirements direct contacts can be taken or a request can be published in order to initiate a dialogue with some selected suppliers. But what mostly characterizes the private market is an active role of sellers that are looking for any opportunities to sell their products or services. Negotiations, changes of terms, prices, requirements, adding extra functionality, reducing the number of licenses etc can be carried out until the last moment of signing a contract. To reveal detailed results such as special terms or prices is not considered to be beneficial to either side.

This makes the public procurement process quite different from the procurement process in the private sector where dialogues and subsequent changes of requirements and proposals are normal procedures. Without understanding and taking into account these differences it can be difficult for private enterprises even to start bidding for governmental contracts.

Framework agreement is seldom used between private companies, but it is a typical way to procure by public administrations in order to concentrate experiences and knowledge from internal experts as well as to get a better outcome by being a single part to sign contracts with suppliers that can be called-off by authorities.

A framework agreement has a number of different manifestations. It can be as loose as a non-binding arrangement with suppliers to call on them when procuring goods, works or services. Alternatively, it can be a binding contract, a "call-off" contract, under which the contracting authority has the right to require the supplier to supply on pre-determined terms and conditions. The current utilities Directives and the proposed consolidating public sector directive, both define a framework agreement as an agreement with a supplier, the purpose of which is to establish the terms governing contracts to be awarded during a given period in particular with regard to price, quality, technical merit and quantity. Put another way, it describes agreements with suppliers setting out the terms and conditions under specific purchases, may, but are not obliged to, be made during the life of the framework agreement. [2]

There is a lack of specific references to framework agreements in the EU Procurement Directives, which is leading to an uncertain situation. However, the European Commission recognizes that, in principle, a framework agreement must itself be awarded in accordance with the procurement rules, but individual contracts awarded under the framework agreement need not follow the procurement rules, as long as all the key terms and conditions are spelled out in the framework agreement in a binding form. UK Office of Government Commerce puts in guidance with following points:

- when calling-off a contract under a framework agreement, there should be no negotiation of key terms (e.g. price)
- fundamental terms should be set out in the framework agreement
- the procurement rules must be followed in awarding the framework agreement. [2]

3 E-procurement – characteristics

E-procurement can be described as the use of Web/Internet-based technology to support key elements of the procurement process such as: requisition, sourcing, contracting, ordering, invoicing, payment or specification of requirement.

Web search engine Google's glossary gives B2B type of definition stating that:

E-procurement is the business-to-business purchase and sale of supplies and services over the Internet. An important part of many B2B sites, e-procurement is also sometimes referred to by other terms, such as supplier exchange. Typically, e-procurement Web sites allow qualified and registered users to look for buyers or sellers of goods and services. Depending on the approach, buyers or sellers may specify prices or invite bids. Transactions can be initiated and completed. Ongoing purchases may qualify customers for volume discounts or special offers. E-procurement software may make it possible to automate some buying and selling. Companies participating expect to be able to control parts inventories more effectively, reduce purchasing agent overhead, and improve manufacturing cycles. E-procurement is expected to be integrated with the trend toward computerized supply chain management. [3]

Searchio techtarget.com website defines e-procurement as *the business-to-business purchase and sale of supplies and services over the Internet. An important part of many B2B sites, e-procurement is also sometimes referred to by other terms, such as supplier exchange. Typically, e-procurement Web sites allow qualified and registered users to look for buyers or sellers of goods and services. Depending on the approach, buyers or sellers may specify prices or invite bids. Transactions can be initiated and completed. Ongoing purchases may qualify customers for volume discounts or special offers.* [4]

The term e-procurement is quite vague and it is used for a variety of elements in the process of purchasing from a simple scanning of invoices to having almost the whole process done electronically. Quite often, as soon as any element of the procurement process is digitalized and done electronically the whole procurement process is called e-procurement.

4 Some examples of introduction, usage and initiatives of e-procurement in Sweden

Sweden is one of the most advanced countries in the usage of Internet in general with one of the top-places in the world in the amount of telephones fixed and mobiles, number of computers and broadband connections. Many contacts between the Swedish citizens and the public administration are now carried out over the Internet.

Overall, 22.5 percent of the respondents indicated that they use a computer everyday, with Sweden (36.7 percent), Denmark (36.6 percent) and the Netherlands (32.2 percent) with the highest figures. Fourteen percent of those surveyed use the computer several times a week; 5.3 percent use it once per week; 2.2 percent use the computer one to three times a month; and 2.4 percent use it less often than that.

The highest proportion of Internet users that were found are the Swedes (66.5 percent), Danes (59.4 percent), the Dutch (53.8 percent) and the Finns (51.4 percent) [5]

Public procurement in Sweden amounts to *40 bn Euro* [6] and approximately 70% is purchasing done by local authorities and county councils. The local authorities are highly self-governing. Their core activities are: schools, care for elderly and children. Swedish local authorities employ 760,000 people and have tight budgets mainly due to the Swedish demographic development with an increasing number of elderly needing care. In this situation, many local authorities have already made assessments on the benefits obtained by e-procurement:

- *improved compliance with framework agreements and thus better prices*
- *increased price awareness when the prices are available electronically*
- *reduced invoice processing times*
- *improved financial control*
- *better and easier available statistics* [7]

One of the projects of the **Swedish Association of Local Authorities** in co-operation with the Swedish Agency for Public Management and the Swedish Federation of County Councils is Single Face To the Industry (SFTI) project. STFI is an open everybody to everybody industry standard for e-procurement for the public sector. *The purpose of SFTI is to establish a single set of specifications for the interchange of electronic commercial transactions with all public operators, whether at governmental, regional (county council) or local community level. To achieve this, a platform of co-operation has been organised where representatives for all three levels meet with representatives for the suppliers to develop a shared view on the public procurement processes and agree common specifications. The purpose in this co-operation is to identify user requirements, agree on standards and have the resulting specifications recognised among the various industries and groups of users.* [8] STFI supports efficient purchasing and invoice processes. The idea of a uniform public interface through SFTI has received strong support.

Other examples of e-procurement of Swedish local authorities include:

The City of Eskilstuna (90,000 inhabitants) order 95 % of all food and receive the invoices electronically. The staff is very positive to the new way of working and does not want to return to the old procedures.

The City of Malmö (265,000 inhabitants) started their e-procurement initiative with food, office materials, energy invoices etc. They notice benefits such as efficient use of resources – better quality for core activities, positive environmental effects (coordination of transports) etc.

The County Council of Dalarna puts 20,000 orders electronically for 4,000 suppliers/buyers and plans within 2 years to implement e-procurement routines in the whole organization. The direct benefits are improved financial control and compliance with framework agreements.

The County Council of Stockholm with approximately 50,000 employees is the biggest local buyer in Sweden. It has a special portal with 800 coordinated contracts including 30,000 articles/items from 150 different business areas such as medical equipment, medicines, food, furniture, telecom- and data-services and many more.

The Swedish central government has approximately 200,000 employees not including defense. In the field of ICT, there is a central purchasing function which is a part of **Statskontoret**'s (The Swedish Agency for Public Management) responsibilities. Statskontoret has as one of the main project the development of 24/7 government. E-procurement is a part of this project. An example of Statskontoret's earlier project is the Swedish government Open Telecommunication system Interconnection Profile (SOTIP). SOTIP is a model that simplifies the procurement of telecommunication equipment and services. Its objectives are:
- *To achieve supplier independent communications based on open system solutions with standardised interfaces between system components,*
- *To simplify the analysis of user needs, the requirement specification of services and equipment with the aid of a generalised model for describing functional user requirements for telecommunications,*
- *To create priorities for standardisation process based on a user perspective, and the possibility to influence product development and the competitive situation.* [9]

The first version of SOTIP was published 1995.

A buyer can simply follow all checklists and in this way avoid making mistakes by forgetting some important requirements. SOTIP has been tested in a few large procurements in Sweden and in the Netherlands. It was also adopted by the European Commission and it is used as a recommendation under the name EOTIP (European Open Telecommunication systems Interconnection Profile). SOTIP is not yet done in an electronic way, but it would be easy to adapt it due to the structured form and strict interfaces.

5 Why should it be easier to introduce e-procurement in the public sector?

There are many advantages with using web-/Internet in procurement process as a whole or for some of the sub-processes. The benefits are similar to those of introducing computer systems for internal routines:
- Orderliness, easier to control, benchmarking and comparing by having all necessary information structured and stored
- Financial/economic control and follow-up is easier for the same reason
- Time savings for transactions such as invoicing process
- Routine administrative processes become simpler after some initial adaptation and training.

This is valid for both the private and public sectors.

A typical procurement process can be illustrated by blocks/sub-processes such as:
- Market investigation
- Analysis of needs
- Request for proposal
- Evaluation of offers and negotiations
- Decision and signing of contract

- Dissemination of the contract
- Orders during the lifetime of the contract
- Payments during the lifetime of the contract
- Updates and upgrades during the lifetime of the contract
- Evaluation and new market investigation

Many blocks can be digitalized and transactions can be done over the Internet. Some sub-processes are recurrent. Typically the introduction of e-procurement starts in recurrent sub-processes of ordering and paying/invoicing. Scanning of invoices is the first step.

The lack of standards hampers the development of e-procurement. This fact makes the entrance threshold high and the risk for investing in wrong products or wrong solutions considerable. Most existing solutions are proprietary. The Swedish project Single Face to the Industry (SFTI) is an example of standardizing e-procurement. Swedish Association of Local Authorities reasons: *The current situation cannot continue with different solutions depending on the buyer or seller. It is too costly and complicated for all parts. Companies cannot be expected to implement different solutions for different buyers nor can the public sector be expected to implement different solutions for different suppliers.* [10]

At the European level there is an awareness of this deficiency. CEN (European Committee for Standardization) and ISSS (Information Society Standardization Systems) e-Invoicing Focus Group have developed a set of recommendations on standards and developments on electronic invoicing. Still, it will take time to have these standards developed, approved and implemented. If a majority of public administrations nationally, or even better internationally, coordinates their requirements on e-procurement standards it will impact the whole market. It is natural for the biggest sector of an economy to be the market leader.

Since the structure is similar from local government to local government in the same country and not so different from country to country, it is possible to use the same approach with some modifications from one authority to another. That would also make it easier for bidders to know what to expect and to reduce time and cost of preparing tenders considerably. This is relevant especially regarding standardization of the formal part of Request for Proposal. It would also help to improve the development of the whole procurement process since the buyers could easier learn from the experience of others and avoid a repeat of old mistakes.

As the jurisdiction is the same all over the European Union, it should many times not take more than a translation to transport experiences from both the seller and buyer sides from one country to another.

The use of framework agreements is especially attractive as a candidate for e-procurement. The call-off contracts have to follow the terms of the framework agreement but are used by several different authorities. It means that several different buyers will use the same type of contract with only marginal changes. This type of contract is almost nonexistent in the private sector.

6 Conclusions and further research questions

In conclusion the public sector could be the leader for e-procurement due to the openness and the non-competitive environment, the repetitive structure of the sector, the common legal framework of the EU, preferences for standards and extensive use of framework agreements.

E-procurement is but a tool. It will not change the essence of procurement neither for the private nor public sector. E-procurement cannot replace professional purchasers, their knowledge of the needs of users and organizations, their experience in judgment of what is mandatory and what is optional, usage of evaluation models to weight different requirements against each other and their negotiating skills. E-procurement will not replace suppliers' sale organizations, sellers or technical support experts. Suppliers will still inform presumptive buyers, including public administration about their new products, possible solutions and technical development and also collect information development trends and needs of the public administration in question.

E-procurement can simplify tedious routine work and keep orderliness and control of records in the procurement process. E-procurement requires training and it will make the purchaser more of an expert Initiatives such as SFTI in Sweden show that it is possible to take a lead and develop standards, which can be beneficial for all parties using e-procurement. What is really needed is a true commitment from the politicians. Models e.g. SOTIP/EOTIP can easily be adapted and e-procurement can simplify their usage.

Still there are many remaining questions to be answered:

Already today, public procurements have stricter codes for contacts with bidders and presumptive contractors. More and more services and equipment procured are complicated and not fully developed. That makes writing technical specifications a difficult task and requires a close cooperation with the supplier after the award of the contract. How can preferences based of experience and old contacts survive?

Will broad availability and standardized forms for published specifications attract many suppliers? Will the process of evaluation take much longer in order to give treat of all bidders fairly? How can delays be avoided?

There is a need of analysis of what should and what should not be done electronically in the procurement process. An interesting twist is that the procurement of IT itself might be the most difficult case for e-procurement.

References

[1] National Accounts 2003
[2] The European Legal Alliance, *Public Procurement and Framework Agreements,* Field Fisher Waterhouse, p 2, 2003
[3] 128.121.222.187/surveys/glossary.htm
[4] searchcio.techtarget.com/sDefinition
[5] Greenspan, Robyn, *Swedes, Danes and Dutch Lead European Usage* www.cyberatlas.internet.com, 2002

[6] Finansdepartementet, *Mera värde för pengarna,* Upphandlingskommittén, SOU 2001:31, 2001
[7] Wiss Holmdahl, Kerstin, *Användning av IT/elektronisk handel till stöd för inköp- och fakturaprocesserna,* Svenska kommunförbundet, 2003
[8] www.eh.svekom.se/english/STFI.htm, 2003
[9] STATTEL-delegationen, *SOTIP Swedish government Open Telecommunication systems Interconnection Profile version 1,*: p 10, 1995
[10] Lindholm, Evert & Wiss Holmdahl, Kerstin, *Single Face To Industry Standard for e-Procurement, used in Sweden by local authorities, county councils and government authorities and their suppliers,* Swedish Association of Local Authorities, presentation at conference in Como, July 7-8, 2003
[11] Arbetsgruppen för elektronisk offentlig upphandling, *Elektronisk offentlig upphandling,* Rapport 2, 2001
[12] Report and recommendations of CEN/ISSS e-Invoicing Focus Group, *Standards and Developments on electronic invoicing relating to VAT Directive 2001/115/EC,* Final report, 2003
[13] Wiss Holmdahl, Kerstin, *E-handel till stor nytta i kommunerna,* Svenska kommunförbundet, 2003
[14] Tonkin, Christine, *E-procurement in the Public Sector: Story, Myth and Legend,* The Policy Institute at Trinity College Dublin, working paper, 2003

E-procurement: 'supporting opportunities'

J. W. ten Berge[1], J. H. R. van Duin[1] & P. H. M. Jacobs[2]
[1]*Department of Transport Policy and Logistics Organisation,
Faculty of Technology, Policy and Management,
Delft University of Technology, The Netherlands*
[2]*Department of Systems Engineering,
Faculty of Technology, Policy and Management,
Delft University of Technology, The Netherlands*

Abstract

A strategic sourcing research project was done within a large multinational in the food industry. The goals of this project were to research and optimise the procurement process for non-strategic items in the packaging materials portfolio. From the findings in the project followed the need for supplier reduction. Several potential wholesale suppliers were selected to supply the bundled non-strategic items portfolio. The research focussed on the packaging portfolios in the Netherlands and the UK. After having selected the potential suppliers and the portfolio set-up, the E-RFP was set up using the Ebreviate tool [1]. The strategic sourcing project realised reasonable potential savings in the total cost price of the articles and through improvements in the total supply process. The web-based E-RFP as set up in this strategic sourcing project has proved its merits when looking at the results in this project. It is difficult to specify which part of the savings can be ascribed to the E-tool and which part followed from the strategic sourcing process itself. In the procurement process advantages of a web based E-tool are numerous, for example in RFP throughput time, data recollection and data availability. In particular efficiency improvements in the procurement processes are realised through e-sourcing.
Keywords: e-sourcing, e-procurement, Request for Proposal, strategic sourcing

1 Introduction

This paper deals with the results of a case study carried out at Delft University of technology. It is a strategic sourcing research within the European Supply

Management (ESM) department of a large multinational in the food industry performed in the Netherlands and the United Kingdom.

The strategic sourcing process was supported by the e-sourcing tool Ebreviate [1] to engage potential suppliers in an E-RFP and to support the sourcing procedure.

The empirical data in this case, both quantitative and qualitative, have been collected through this study in the company. All quantitative data and all processes are mapped in collaboration with representatives of the company.

Section 2 contains information about the steps in the procurement process and the definitions used. The third section will handle the portfolio analysis and the supply process analysis performed in this project. In the fourth section the E-RFP procedure and the Ebreviate tool will be introduced. The project results will be shown in the fifth section and the sixth section will round up with conclusions especially about the influences of the use of e-sourcing tools encountered in this case study.

2 Process steps and definitions

Procurement consists of all those activities that are necessary to acquire goods and services being consistent with user requirements. [2]

Following this very wide definition, the activities involved have to be defined and specified. To define the term supply management, van Weele's definition [3] for the purchasing function can be used as it is considered to be a synonym, with the remark that supply management also involves the responsibility for stock management and transport.

The purchasing function comprises the following activities:
1. Specify what should be purchased
2. Selecting one or more adequate suppliers
3. Establishing a contract with the supplier(s) after having negotiated the terms and conditions of supply
4. Actually ordering the items or services
5. Monitoring the delivery of the items or services ordered
6. Following up on delivery, e.g. taking care of claims, administrative activities, etc.

van Weele's [3] definition of 'sourcing' comprises the market research for possible sources of supply, the responsibility to ensure the continuity of supply, the activity of looking for alternative sources of supply and keeping up-to-date with all relevant knowledge.

This paper focuses on the strategic sourcing research that was done within the Packaging group of the European Supply Management department of the company. In this strategic sourcing process the web-based electronic tool Ebreviate [1] was used to support the Request for Proposal procedure. This E-RFP procedure will be described after the analyses of both the portfolio and the supply processes.

The definition of e-sourcing used in this project is presented by the Aberdeen Group [4]: Sourcing is defined as the task, which involves the identification, evaluation, negotiation and configuration of suppliers, products and services. E-sourcing is defined by the use of web-based applications, decision-support tools and associated services in the sourcing process.

3 Portfolio analyses and supply process analyses

The Electronic tools available for strategic sourcing are support tools, which facilitate the process. First of all insight has to be created into the portfolio of materials to be purchased. Then, the performance indicators of the supply process have to be determined in order to be able to realize process improvements through an improved sourcing strategy. This is part of the *'classic'* steps in the sourcing process:
-identification, evaluation and configuration of potential suppliers and desired products and services- or -the market research for possible sources of supply, the responsibility to ensure the continuity of supply and the activity of looking for alternative sources of supply- The *'e-factor'* is added in paragraph three.

3.1 Packaging materials portfolio

Since 1999 the company has shifted its procurement activities and supply management approach from national coordinated organisations, through Local Supply Management (LSM) departments, towards a centralised organisation, through the European Supply Management (ESM) department. As from 2004 the former LSM departments will be integrated into the ESM department to form one supply management department. This research project aimed to investigate which part of the packaging materials portfolio was still under national responsibility of the LSM departments. Possible development directions were investigated for this portfolio in order to improve the supply processes. Table 1 and 2 show the general figures from this research. The spend (spend = annual turnover) on packaging materials is not shown for confidentiality reasons. An item is defined as a product with a unique distinguishing article number in the ERP-system.

Table 1:   Division ESM/ LSM purchasing contribution for packaging materials in the Netherlands (annual figures 2002).

NL	Spend mln (€)	%	No of items	%	No of suppliers	%
ESM		94	2,600	82	60	43
LSM		6	600	18	80	57
Total	Confidential	100	3,200	100	140	100

Table 2:   Division ESM/ LSM purchasing contribution for packaging materials in the UK (annual figures 2002).

NL	Spend mln (€)	%	No of items	%	No of suppliers	%
ESM		95	2,600	89	60	60
LSM		5	300	11	80	40
Total	Confidential	100	3,200	100	140	100

From these figures it was concluded that:
- ✓ The packaging material portfolio under local supply management responsibility held relatively low-value and/or low-volume articles. (6% spend (spend = annual turnover) on 18% of the items in NL and 5% spend on 11% of the items)
- ✓ The LSM portfolio held a relatively low percentage of the annual spend
- ✓ The LSM portfolio held a relatively high number of suppliers opposite to the ESM managed portfolio.

In general this means that for the larger part (almost 95% in NL and UK) of the items the supply management is organised on a European centralised level. This centralised focus realises more bundled volumes, this can be seen from the figures showing relatively larger volumes/ larger values than the items still managed on a local level; for example 94% of the spend represents 82% of the items.

Furthermore, the portfolio under ESM responsibility has a more consolidated supply base than the locally managed items; for example 94% of the spend representing 82% of the items is sourced from 43% of the total suppliers for the Netherlands.

The supply management responsibility within the company is spread over different material groups where the material managers are responsible for the supply process of these materials for all sourcing units within the company. For the packaging materials these material groups are for instance divided in flexible materials, carton board, corrugated board, glass, etc. These material groups are based on the company's global hierarchy classification. This classification works two ways, the first division is based on the material the product is made of and the second division is based on the form of appearance.

The first development direction for the materials in this LSM portfolio is to transfer the supply management responsibility to the existing material groups under European supply management responsibility where they can be classified according to the global hierarchy classification. The advantage of this development direction is that these materials are then put under the responsibility of the person having the most expertise for the supply process of these materials within the company in Europe. Furthermore, these materials can be sourced with the existing European suppliers and bundled with large existing European volumes in order to realise product rationalisation, volume bundling and supply-base consolidation.

After this step there are still some products left which do not fit within an existing European material managers portfolio. These items can be referred to as non-Strategic items in the Kraljic strategy matrix (1983) [3] shown in figure 1.

Their total supply value is relatively low compared to the entire portfolio and their supply market has a low complexity, which implies that the same or comparable products (substitutes) are offered by a wide variety of market parties (suppliers). The strategic sourcing process within this project focuses on these packaging materials. Table 3 shows the figures of this non-strategic items portfolio for the Netherlands and the UK.

	High		
		Leverag	Strategi
Valu		Non-Strategi	Bottl-neck
	Low		

Low   complexity supply   high

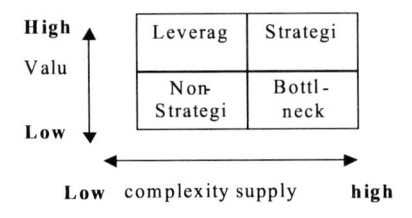

Figure 1: Kraljic strategy matrix (1983).

Table 3: Features non-Strategic items packaging portfolio NL & UK (Annual figures 2002).

	Sum of total spend (€)	No of SUs	No of articles	No of suppliers
NL		4	113	44
UK	*Confidential*	7	67	36

The exact numbers of the sum of total spend (spend= annual turnover), average turnover per supplier and average turnover per article are confidential. They are, however, relatively low compared to the total packaging portfolio.

In order to reduce the complexity in this non-strategic items portfolio and to make the most of buying power in this portfolio the possibilities for product rationalisation, volume bundling and supply-base reduction are investigated. Volume bundling can be realized in three ways. Firstly, volumes within material groups can be bundled, this means for example that all tapes should be bundled and sourced from the same supplier. Secondly volumes across material groups should be bundled as much as possible, so that most or all low-value/ low-volume non-strategic packaging items are sourced from the same supplier. Thirdly the volumes across the different sourcing units per country should be bundled in order to make the most of the buying power of the total organisation within these material groups.

Possibilities to expand the geographic vendor base have been researched. Figure 2 shows the conclusions drawn from this research.

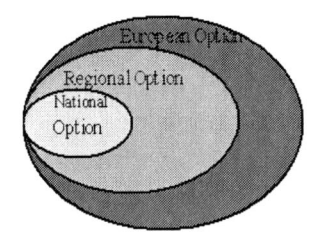

Figure 2: Geographic vendor base for non-strategic items.

A European wholesale supplier, who can supply the combined portfolio of these non-strategic items is currently not present in the market. A regional party, which could supply more countries, could be a possibility in a few specific regions, for example the Benelux. National suppliers are the most established parties in this portfolio range. They have a strong home-market advantage with an established logistic network. This is a situation expected for items with the features in this portfolio. The low-value/ low-volume commodities have a small supply range, because transport costs over longer distances are too high compared to their value. This is an important factor, which is not changed by using e-tools in the sourcing process or other parts of the procurement process. These findings on the possibilities in geographic vendor base are the same the Netherlands and the UK. Although the UK is more isolated or dependent on its own distribution structure, simply because of the 'physical barrier' formed by the North Sea.

3.2 Supply processes

The relatively large number of suppliers in the non-strategic items portfolio, who deliver either low-volumes or items of low-value, indicates possible improvements for the supply process.

The related supply processes involved are mentioned below, they all fall under the name of supply chain processes but not all processes are actually performed by the supply management (purchasing) department:

1) Contract maintenance: Every supplier must have signed a contract before the materials can be entered in the ERP system (SAP R/3) and all materials must be part of a contract. Reduction of the number of contracts and the number of contract lines makes contract maintenance more efficient.
2) Price negotiations: This is a regular activity of the responsible material manager (buyer).
3) Ordering: This is the responsibility of the Sourcing Unit planner, who periodically makes call offs for the required volume of the item. This is based on the stock-level and production planning.
4) Delivery/ goods reception: The ordered items are received and placed in stock in the Sourcing Unit warehouse. This is the responsibility of the sourcing unit warehouse manager.
5) Invoice processing: the financial department processes the invoice
6) Quality assurance: All suppliers of the company should be audited to match the company's quality standards

In these processes a reduction in the points and moments of contact will be realised when supply base consolidation will be applied. Also a reduced supply-base makes it more interesting to invest, by means of e-business support tools, in the supplier relationships and (joint) process improvements. This is the next phase in e-procurement beyond e-sourcing. Elements like web-based forecast communication to replace the order process are thinkable in the near future.

4 E-RFP & E-RFP process

The RFP was set up as a web based e-RFP using the Ebreviate tool from A.T. Kearney [1], which supports the sourcing process. The company had selected this package to support the sourcing process. Ebreviate's Electronic Survey Tool can be deployed to capture data needed to implement effective procurement processes. The technology can be used in many ways throughout the e-Sourcing process to perform, for example Requests for Proposals (RFPs), customer requirement surveys and user and supplier surveys.

4.1 E-RFP

Ebreviate supports the sourcing process by providing a customizable tool, which can be set up and sent out in a protected web environment using the latest SSL (secure socket layer) encryption. The suppliers which where invited to join in the request for proposal phase, received a login name and password to enter the on-line RFP. Furthermore, there is the library functionality to store templates, sections, or best-in-class RFPs for copy and reuse.

The E-RFP was set up to measure two important supplier performance subjects:
1) Pricing table to identify the supplier's material cost-price level:
   - ✓ The Pricing table consisted of the selected items, with their specification and asked for the supplier's current price offer (exc. Works) and their transport costs
2) Performance measurement questions for process improvements, for example:
   - ✓ References of current comparable activities of the potential suppliers
   - ✓ Companies' available resources to support and improve the supply chain processes within company's Sourcing Units
   - ✓ Examples of or suggestions for supply chain improvements

Realizing performance improvement in the supply processes was an important objective in this sourcing research. Therefore it was stressed in the RFP that the business is not necessarily awarded to the lowest bidder, (following the results of the price offers in the pricing table) but overall supply chain performance was just as important.

4.2 The E-RFP process

The RFP process using the Ebreviate e-sourcing tool was first performed in the Netherlands involving four pre-selected potential packaging wholesale suppliers. All suppliers involved received an invitation e-mail with a password and username. The entire RFP cycle from the moment the RFP site went online to the return of all proposals was two weeks. This is half the time spent on former comparable paper-based RFPs.

Two weeks after the RFP was completed in the Netherlands the same steps were performed in the UK. The RFP preparation and set-up for the UK took much less time than the process in the Netherlands. The RFP from the operation in the Netherlands was downloaded from the Ebreviate library and copied. Only the specific details for the UK (dates, locations, product specifications etc.) had to be adjusted, the base text was identical. This saved a lot of time in the preparation. Also in the UK the completed proposals were back within two weeks.

The digital 'uniform' way of receiving the proposals in Ebreviate made them much more easy to process. The entire RFP process was much less time consuming in preparation and it also involved less administration. Every part of the RFP is stored in the Ebreviate tool and that is why there was no large paper-based administration, which was sometimes the case in 'classic' RFPs. Furthermore the web-based data availability made it possible to process the proposals simultaneously both in the UK and in the Netherlands with all the people involved in the RFP process.

5 Project results

The E-RFP as set-up in Ebreviate facilitated a smooth RFP procedure. The RFP was performed faster than comparable paper-based RFP procedures in the past. It also saved time in the strategic sourcing procedure within the supply management department and therefore the procedure put less 'stress' on the resources of the ESM-department.

5.1 Financial results in the cost price of the items

The bundling volumes sourced at a national packaging wholesaler showed a potential direct savings (following the proposals) of 10% - 15% in the cost price of the items purchased. The RFP in the Netherlands as well as the RFP in the UK showed these same saving figures. There are even more opportunities for future savings through product rationalisation and re-specification across all sourcing units.

5.2 Process improvements

There is a huge efficiency potential through supply base consolidation. Supply-base rationalisation realises a reduction in the points and moments of contact in the different steps of the supply management processes. The different steps of: contract maintenance, price negotiations, ordering, delivery/ goods reception and quality assurance all benefit from a reduction of the points and moments of contact.

Combined transport with all items in this non-strategic portfolio coming from one wholesale supplier, can reduce total transport costs. This can lower the price of the products purchased.

The total savings contribution through the process improvements realised in the 6 processes mentioned are estimated at 10-15% of the total non-strategic items portfolio purchasing value. These indirect savings are mainly realised through efficient processing in the physical product flow (goods reception in the warehouses, efficient transporting etc.), the information flow (ordering, contract maintenance, price negotiations, etc.) and the financial flow (processing invoices etc.).

Furthermore, there are opportunities for investing in a supplier relationship, i.e. through new e-business/ e-procurement tools, in order to realise further process efficiency. The opportunities for investing in supplier relationships and process improvements with one larger supplier are far better than with over 40 very small suppliers. For example (Web-based) forecast-communication can in time replace the ordering process.

5.3 Outsourcing opportunities

Introducing a single supplier packaging wholesaler in this non-strategic items portfolio offers opportunities in the direction of outsourcing activities in the supply management processes. A single, larger supplier has better overview of the desires within the company's organisation regarding the supply of the items. Furthermore, following the supplier responses in the submitted proposals, a partnership relation with a packaging wholesaler offers further improvement opportunities in:
- ✓ Dedicated resources from this supplier, locally and centrally
- ✓ Product rationalization across all sourcing units
- ✓ Looking for substitute items with better performance or prices
- ✓ Just in time delivery service
- ✓ Local stockholding
- ✓ Direct line feed
- ✓ Scheduled reporting for stock Management
- ✓ Partnership approach, continual improvement policy on key performance indicators basis
- ✓ Forecast communication
- ✓ Vendor Managed Inventory

All these activities are optimisation opportunities, in which the responsibility for the task is pushed towards the supplier in the direction of outsourcing. All these activities also offer new opportunities for the introduction of e-business tools, which could support these activities very well.

6 Conclusions on the role of the 'e' in this sourcing project

Most of the activities performed in this strategic sourcing project would exist even without the availability of the Internet. However, e-sourcing realises several clearly experienced benefits in:
- ✓ Speed/ shortened sourcing cycles; through efficient processing of information the time required for completion of the RFP was reduced to two weeks.
- ✓ Efficiency in sourcing process; no large paper based archive and work reduction through availability of example RFPs in library
- ✓ Equal information distribution; all suppliers involved in the RFPs had equal access to all on-line information.

- ✓ Scale-ability; it does not take more time to send out the RFP too extra suppliers, it takes just one e-mail address extra and an extra account is made in the on-line RFP.
- ✓ Knowledge distribution; through the available library a knowledge base and proven sourcing methodologies are available company wide

The total financial savings through this (e-)sourcing project were a potential 10-15 % in direct costs through the price of the articles and another 10-15 % savings in indirect costs through process improvements. The process improvements were realised through supply-base consolidation and process improvements with the one wholesale supplier for the total portfolio.

It is difficult to indicate which part of these savings (if any) can be ascribed to the use of the Ebreviate e-sourcing tool. The findings in this project are that the use of this e-sourcing tool realises savings and improves efficiency especially in the sourcing process itself.

For the reason stated in the first sentence of these conclusions it goes too far to say that these savings are only realised through e-sourcing. The normal sourcing activities have a far bigger contribution to the savings than the 'e-influence'.

The 'e' in e-sourcing however does really have its influence in the process efficiency of the sourcing process! One point where the e-sourcing tool can really affect the content of the sourcing process is in its possibility for simple scale-ability. Through the efficient data processing and the relative ease to add extra potential suppliers in the Request for Proposal phase, more suppliers can be involved or contacted for a proposal at almost no extra cost.

And what is even more important, it facilitates the supply management/ purchasing department so that it can work more efficiently. The e-sourcing tool reduces the sourcing process and administration costs. These improvements create the opportunity to apply strategic sourcing to a greater part of the spending, with the same available resources. This is of course a very huge benefit in itself and offers the supply management department to pick up even more opportunities to contribute to the profitability of the entire organisation!

References

[1] A.T. Kearney procurement solutions; www.ebreviate.com
[2] Coyle, J.J., Bardi, E.J., Langley Jr.,C.J.: The management of business logistics; A supply chain Perspective; seventh edition, west publishing company, 2003
[3] Weele, A.J. van: Inkoop in strategisch perspectief; analyse, planning en praktijk (in Dutch). Alphen aan de Rijn Samson, 1997
[4] Aberdeen group: Make e-sourcing strategic; from tactical technology to core business strategy, Sept. 2002
[5] Berge, J.W. ten; Insight in the supply process of packaging materials, Delft University of technology, Aug. 2003.
[6] Seppanen & Suomala: E-business in b-2-b wholesaler's supply chain: effects on costs and activities, 9th annual conference of European operations management association. Copenhagen, Denmark. 2002

Knowledge management in higher education: the business-side performance

L. C. Rodrigues[1] E. A. Maccari[2] & M. I. R. de Almeida[3]
[1]*Regional University of Blumenau, Graduate Studies in Management Program and Post-Doctoral Program in Management, FEA/USP, Brazil*
[2]*University Center Nove de Julho, UNINOVE, Brazil*
[3]*University of São Paulo, USP, Brazil*

Abstract

As a unique case of knowledge production, higher education institutions typically deal with knowledge offering, but seem to lack in using the advantages of knowledge management (KM). The target of this work was to identify KM presence and processes in Higher Education Institutions (HEI) in Brazil. Our research was circumscribed to the five best higher learning institutions, all of which are universities, according to the Student Guide 2001. Results indicated that KM, in the research and the understanding of KM, is still restricted to knowledge production (fundamental research and intellectual publication). There are little, or rare, organizational mechanisms, such as work design, or formal organizational structures, supportive of KM. Our conclusions indicate that the universities researched are still trying to break ground in finding mechanisms and ideas to appropriate tacit, into explicit knowledge, to their best interest.
Keywords: knowledge management, higher education, higher education and knowledge management, knowledge management policy.

1 Introduction

The objectives of a Higher Education Institution are said to be diffuse because of the complex and sophisticated nature of these institutions. In general, the value perceived by society of such an institution depends either on the scientific impact of the knowledge it generates (research), or on its knowledge transfer capabilities (learning), along with the usefulness of the technology it develops. The nature of the challenges that an HEI must face, whether in structuring its internal chain of values or marketing its products and services, is therefore decidedly different from that of a product- based organization.

There exist however, many areas of common interest where both types of organizations can learn from each other, improving their respective managerial capability and overall performance. For example, attitudes towards learning organizations are less present in an HEI than they are in product-based organizations. Their more 'ad-hocratic' management style may have prevented HEIs from building on the principles of a learning organization. Another element is knowledge management itself. The perception that a scientific knowledge center is a sort of mission has instead kept HEI from managing knowledge as a means of increasing both learning and innovation.

In the last decade, knowledge management became a powerful tool for increasing the market value of an organization. Since knowledge management supports the organization's overall capacity to generate innovation, it has an impact on creating alternative solutions designed to improve business and competitiveness. This capacity is an intangible asset, called intellectual capital by Stewart [1], which is responsible for the skyrocketing market value of any organization that uses its people's knowledge to leverage the value of its product.

1.1 Problem and objectives

It seems that teaching the value of knowledge and its contribution to an organization's success was not enough to modify the conventional wisdom and political attitudes about managing knowledge in HEI. These institutions generate knowledge and are charged with the mission of making it available to society. Performance in managing knowledge, however, still does not correspond to the nature of the business of these institutions. Knowledge generation and distribution remain too rooted in HEI function and activities.

The traditionally paradoxical dimensions of an HEI – pedagogical and business – are the cause of most managerial incongruities. The pedagogical dimension signifies the educational mission of an HEI. The paradox arises from the vision of an HEI as held by purists, who argue that education cannot be sold. A more rational view however, is that providing education and increasing the intellectual preparedness of individuals are services just like any other and therefore must be paid for. We do not advocate that the business side of an HEI should win out over the educational side but, nevertheless, the effectiveness of the academic system clearly depends on maintaining equilibrium between these two dimensions.

KM is important to any kind of organization, as pointed out by Stewart [1]. Despite translating competitiveness as the attractiveness of an HEI, developing tools for KM is a factor in organizational effectiveness. While establishing a link between educational functions and business activities in HEI, KM updates the managerial styles and tools employed by HEI managers. Studying KM in an HEI environment thus contributes to the formulation of new insights into the evolution of the state-of-the-art in HEI management.

In our judgment, cultural values prevent members of an HEI from using KM as a tool for formulating business strategies. The perception that the relationship between client/market/product, i.e. student/society/course, is fundamental to the survival of HEI demands new HEI management tools and mechanisms for increasing organizational dynamics. How would HEI be dealing with its practices? Would their focus be on creating/generating knowledge, or would it be on driving forces to increase intellectual ability in individuals and groups to consolidate HEI essential competencies? This paper is the result of research whose main objective was to identify the knowledge management practices in Brazilian HEI that are similar to those in product-based organizations.

1.2 Method

We designed the research under a descriptive method, described in Borg and Gall [2]. Our focus was to pinpoint what KM practices are being used in HEI. The nature of the research was exploratory and qualitative. We intentionally selected the five top HEI in Brazil, according to the Student Guide 2001. The selection focused on a specific audience because of our need, determined by the research design put forth by Sellitz et al. [3], for critical opinions on KM practices in HEI to come from within. In order to guarantee objectivity, we used a structured interview guide. Fig. 1, below, shows the construct for data collection.

Research Objectives	Variables	Items of the Collecting Instrument
To identify the understanding of respondents regarding the concept and function of KM in HEI.	- Meaning of KM - Concept of KM - Function of KM	1 2 3
To determine processes and actions used in the researched HEI regarding KM.	- Building KM - Factors, procedures and actions - First steps toward KM - Other/alternative steps toward KM - Conceptual structure x management of Knowledge	4 5 6 7 8
To identify the characteristics and macro-tendencies of KM in the selected HEI.	- All variables	Interpretation of items 1 through 8.

Figure 1: Research construct.

2 The nature of HEI

The nature of HEI has been widely studied by such well-known researchers as Baldridge [4] and Cohen and March [5]. The specialized literature seems to be in unanimous agreement about the nature of HEI. While the fundamentals of HEI are grounded solidly on the principles and profession of human education, their organization objectives are ample, diffuse and poorly circumscribed. This nature not only differentiates HEI from other organizations, but it also reveals the degree of complexity of both their structure and rationale.

The diversity of objectives in HEI results in two major issues. One is their readiness to conflict. The other is their sensitivity about knowledge, that and the sensitivity of specialized people; the first may be a result of the second. In fact, the need for a diverse group of specialized people permits selfishness on the part of individuals and groups regarding knowledge. The chance to develop power (through specialized knowledge) and exert it within the context of the organization creates space for the emergence of conflicts, as Romero points out [6].

The selfsame heterogeneity of the academic system gives rise to the ability of HEI to adapt and evolve, counters Stankiewicz [7]. From their main areas of conflict: specialist versus generalist knowledge and education, philosophical-scientific or vocational-technological orientation, teaching or research and finally, the polarizing concept of critic or servant of established society, are born both dynamism and institutional innovation. How did HEI manage to adapt and evolve, in order to steer away from conflicts and respond to new demands? Stankiewicz [7] identifies three major paths that HEI followed to face these issues. The first one is *specialization*; the second is internal *diversification* and the third is *hybridization*.

Specialization derives from the classification of scientific knowledge. The rational knowledge that was classified, packed up, stored and transmitted from generation to generation, forced HEI to structure themselves under areas of specialized knowledge, such as biology, chemistry, physics, mathematics and the like, Ben-David asserts [8]. From specialized knowledge came the professions, i.e. mathematicians, chemists, biologists (from natural science) and physicians, lawyers and engineers in the technological-vocational professions, according to Price [9]. The fundamentals of HEI as organizations that are in place today came from viewing HEI as specialized organizations.

Bugliarello [10] points out that the Humboldtian reform of the German university system had, by the mid 19th Century, incorporated research as a major function in the mission of HEI. The idea of institutional differentiation (teaching-research-extension) was used to protect new and innovative mechanisms in HEI from the conservatism of established interests. The new German research university flourished as a model, although in American universities.

The utilitarianism ideally seen in American universities is a successful step forward in the integration of new functions. The perception that the return paid to society through social development also involves economic development requires the new HEI to incorporate the development of technology as one of its basic functions (Ben-David [8]). Thus the integration of technology development in the functions of HEI creates a new source of priority. These days, social development through technology is also part of the mission of HEI. This is the principle behind the hybridization concept of HEI as organizations.

3 Knowledge and HEI

In western culture, cognitive science has been characterized by two important schools of thoughts: rationalism and empiricism. Both are highly defensible, but neither suffices alone. Rationalism, determined by Socratic thinkers, such as Socrates himself, Plato, Descartes, and Kant, for example, advocates that knowledge is a deductive, mental process. For the rationalists, man builds knowledge through rationalizing, thus knowledge is cumulative and conclusive and can be made available.

Empiricism however, originated with Aristotle and his intellectual posterity, men such as Locke, Spinosa and Leibniz, who assert that knowledge is a result of sensory experience; it cannot be transferred as it is. Man learns by memorizing sensations. Thus learning is cumulative, but it cannot be transmitted. While rationalism utilizes deduction as a mechanism for constructing mental concepts, laws and theories, empiricism finds induction to be the means of generating knowledge from sensory experiences, as Nonaka and Takeuchi show [11].

These two schools became the foundations of most modern research into human development and the building of knowledge. The constructivism of Jean Piaget, cited by Coll and Piaget [12], Vygotsky, cited by Veer and Valsiner [13] and, more recently, Gardner's theory of multiple intelligences [14], all use, in one way or another, those same principles.

In the post-war era, Polanyi [15] has committed himself to differentiating between the two traditional schools of thoughts on knowledge generation and transmission. Polanyi [15] established a clear distinction between tacit and explicit knowledge. Tacit knowledge is personal, linked to an experimental context, such as swimming or riding a bicycle. In both cases, as much as the individual might know about the laws and theories of physics, for instance, knowledge of the two events (swimming and riding a bicycle) is can only be incorporated through experience. Explicit knowledge, on the other hand, is objective, and can be systematized and transmitted in a patterned way. Reading and calculating, for instance, are systematized knowledge and therefore are transmissible. Polanyi [15] calls additional attention to the importance of tacit knowledge as a source for the creation of explicit human knowledge.

For organizations, explicit knowledge interests most. It can be counted as an asset. Explicit knowledge however, is a function of tacit knowledge. It directly interests the business of any organization. This is no different from an HEI. In fact, all the structuring, organizing and operating of HEI were conceived on the basis of the Socratic rationale of knowledge creation and transmission. For HEI, managing knowledge is a question of stimulating tacit knowledge to produce explicit knowledge. This task cannot be oversimplified however. KM is a set of processes that require integration of an organization's structure, information technology, work place design and strategic planning, as Davenport et al. point out [16]. This is a major issue.

4 Knowledge management

According to the 1998 Report of Economic Development Cooperation Organization – EDCO, cited by Cavalcanti and Gomes [17], more than 50% of the GNP in developed countries is due to adequate use of knowledge. In the knowledge economy, wealth and development, ordinarily intensive in labor, raw material and capital, shifts to products, process and services technology and becomes knowledge intensive, indicate Cavalcanti and Gomes [17]; Zabot and Silva [18]; Ghoshal [19]. This same report calls attention to data that shows that the average unemployment rate is 10.5% among individuals with elementary education and only 3.8% among individuals with higher education.

Obviously, the search for competence pushes organizations to treat knowledge as an important tool for business success. Additionally, knowledge must be carefully managed, because the competitive advantage enjoyed by an organization remains not in the amount of knowledge created internally, but in the organization's effectiveness in knowledge management.

Knowledge management requires the explicit definition of the objectives and basic mechanisms involved in knowledge creation. The creation of knowledge, according to Nonaka and Takeuchi [11] is reached through the integration of tacit and explicit knowledge, in a four-stage process: socialization (shared knowledge); externalization (concept knowledge); combination (systemic knowledge); and internalization (operating knowledge). This process can be visualized in Figure 2 below.

	Tacit Knowledge	Explicit Knowledge
From Tacit Knowledge into	SOCIALIZATION (shared knowledge)	EXTERNALIZATION (conception knowledge)
From Explicit Knowledge into	INTERNALIZATION (operating knowledge)	COMBINATION (systemic knowledge)

Source: Nonaka and Takeuchi [11], p.81.

Figure 2: Knowledge creation process.

Socialization means conversion of tacit knowledge into tacit knowledge. *Externalization* represents the conversion of tacit knowledge into explicit concepts through spoken and written language. Externalization is the key to creating knowledge because it originates and generates new and explicit concepts developed from tacit knowledge.

Combination is the process of converting explicit into explicit knowledge. In the combination stage, the systematization process of concepts becomes a knowledge system. As we pointed out above, the combination process follows the Socratic school of knowledge. Combination is the format in which knowledge conversion occurs in HEI and other educational institutions.

Finally, *internalization* is the conversion of explicit into tacit knowledge. Internalization is realized by the verbalization and diagramming of knowledge in documents, manuals and oral stories.

In the organizational learning and Knowledge Management process, information technology plays a fundamental role. Senge [20] and Quonian [21] emphasize the importance of the quality of information, not its quantity, and the necessary capacity of the organization for using it, or product-based organizations, the challenge is to select information and to distribute it among those who could make it useful to the organization, notes Rodrigues [22]. For an

HEI, the challenge is to nurture people with knowledge, to find people who can collaborate, and to network through organizational "pull", say Manville and Foote [23].

Nurturing people with knowledge means to balance knowledge learning based on people's interests with knowledge learning based organizational interests. Therefore, it isn't just a question of what people want, but also a question of tapping into the knowledge locked in people's experiences. Finding people who collaborate means to create an environment or motivational culture that initiates the interconnectivity process among people. Finally, after finding people who want to connect, network them through organizational "pull", which means not overloading them with information from a centralized information system. Learning, of course, is an individual responsibility. No organization or manager can require the will to learn from any individual. It is their duty however, to give direction and motivate people to increase and share their knowledge. In HEI, due especially to their nature, the essence of KM is dominion of perception – that knowledge is beneficial to both the individual and the institution – which can be reached through a motivating culture that, in turn, raises the aspirations of people, advise Davenport et al. [16].

5 Research results

5.1 Understanding and function of KM

The three different audiences of the research – Deans of Undergraduate Schools; Deans of Research and Postgraduate Studies; and Financial and Administrative Controllers – pointed to an understanding of KM from divergent perspectives. Controllers see it as a database for managing administrative information. Undergraduate deans see it as the mechanism to ensure better transmission of knowledge to students. Graduate deans see it as the processes involved in strengthening the images of their institutions, which could give their institutions more attractiveness. As we can see, their understanding of KM refers mainly to the institutional infrastructure (data base – mechanisms – processes) that supports managerial actions.

With respect to the functions of KM, the responses did not arrive at the main issue: functions. Instead, respondents divert themselves around tools, mechanisms and systems that could eventually be linked to or support KM. Academic biases about managing research and knowledge generation for the sake of freedom of research were always present. A striking diversion was the understanding of the function of KM as a curbing process on reaching the levels of intellectual production, research and academic productivity necessary for complying with Government standards of excellence.

5.2 Internal procedures and activities

Unanimously, the respondents show attention to human educational qualification as one fundamental element to improve KM. Norms and regulations that compel academia to commit to KM activities relate to the educational standards of excellence determined by the central government, not explicitly to construct and motivate the internal development of KM.

In spite of recognizing the importance of integrating KM into the strategic planning of the institution, respondents did not mention any kind of existing policy towards KM, nor any in the works; neither as a goal nor an explicit objective in strategic planning. As for the steps for building KM in the institution, with one exception, all responses were evasive and focused instead on internal rules that govern academic excellence.

5.3 Administrative, structural and technological mechanisms

Regarding institutional mechanisms – administrative, structural and technological – supporting KM, respondents pointed to local mechanisms and incipient directorships to take care of the subject. In some of the researched institutions there exist rare administrative mechanisms, however, oriented towards restricted activities like patent rights, royalties and directorships.

Specific sectors of the researched institutions displayed only structural mechanisms. In spite of their existence, structural mechanisms are fragmented into feuds and divisions, most of them dealing with institutional controls or regulatory functions within the institution.

Technological mechanisms were the most evident. Nearly all of the institutions exhibited computer networks and databases, used to control academic activities, (student grades and attendance), internal administrative processes, research and teaching. What was also evident was the lack of integration, in the network, of information available to different sectors of the institutions.

6 Conclusion

From the data presented it became clear what the important conclusions were:
1.- The use of KM as a managerial tool in HEI to improve institutional attractiveness is still incipient. HEI still see them selves much more as educating systems with no business needs than as systems reaching out for business objectives.
2.- The researched HEI show poor understanding of the concept, role and function of KM. The understanding of HEI top managers regarding KM was linked much more to information technology infrastructure – computer, physical network, and software – than to the structural and integrative architecture of processes and people, leading to the Nonaka and Takeuchi [11] knowledge spiral: socialization, externalization, combination and internalization of knowledge.
3.- There are no internal formal procedures or activities that directly support KM in the HEI researched. The 'ad-hocratic governance of HEI is not conducive to KM practices. Therefore, all norms and rules are interpreted in terms of compliance with intellectual standards of excellence.

4.- There is an obsessive effort on the part of HEI management to observe the standards of excellence that drive education, as determined by the central government. This effort gives no leeway for HEI to search for alternative patterns of excellence.

5.- Results also show that the HEI researchers demonstrate no knowledge of processes for implementing KM. They are sensitive to the strategic importance of KM, but prove they are not familiar with how to structure and direct a KM system.

6.- As a corollary of the preceding, research results also lead us to conclude that HEI possess no policies for the formal stimulation of KM, either by a direct policy, or through the incorporation of elements into their strategic plan.

7.- There is no administrative or structural mechanism to support KM implementation in the HEI researched. Small wonder that no hint of processes or elements was found of Nonaka and Takeuchi's [11] knowledge spiral.

8.- Technology mechanisms basically relate to physical instruments, such as computers, network and logical systems, not to processes or formal systems.

9 – Lastly, it is important to discuss what should be a trend in KM in Brazilian HEI. Results indicate that the principles of KM used for product-based organizations are neither understood nor practiced in the HEI researched. It is naïve, however, to bet on the ignorance or negligence of HEI in implementing KM. In fact, there is knowledge management within HEI, but in a different way. Understanding of the role and function of KM is still focused on providing faculty with intellectual preparedness, along with intellectual production and publication. As both a major recipient and a knowledge production center, HEI see knowledge management as an end in itself and as a part of its mission, not as a process for increasing organizational effectiveness.

Undoubtedly, knowledge generation does not follow the same pattern of Nonaka & Takeuchi's [11] knowledge creation spiral. In HEI, knowledge production follows its own way and process (basic and applied research). Thus, knowledge management in HEI nurtures the *combination* and *socialization* processes much more than the *internalization* and *externalization* processes.

References

[1] Stewart, T. *Capital Intelectual*. São Paulo: Campus, 1998.
[2] Borg, W. and Gall, M. D. *Educational Research*, New York: Longman, 1983.
[3] Sellitz, W. et al. Métodos da Pesquisa nas Relações Sociais. São Paulo: EPU, 1987.
[4] Baldridge, J. V. *Estruturación de políticas y liderazgo efectivo en la educación superior*. México: Noema Editores, 1982.
[5] Cohen, M. D. & Marsh, J. G. *Leadership and Ambiguity: the American College President*. Boston (MA): Harvard Business School Press, 1986.
[6] Romero J.B. Concepção de Universidades. In: Almeri P. Finger (org.). *Universidade: Organização, Planejamento e Gestão*. Florianópolis: Edufsc, 1988,

[7] Stankiewicz, R. *Academic and Entrepreneurs*. New York: St. Martin's Press, 1986.
[8] Ben-David, J. *The Scientist Role in Society – a comparative study*. New York: Prentice-Hall, 1971.
[9] Price, G.L. Professional tensions in science and technology: the case of the Colleges of Advanced Technology. *R&D Management*, **9(2)**, p.17-24, 1979.
[10] Bugliarello, G. Focusing on the Function of the University. *Proceedings from the First Midland Conference*. Cleveland (OH), p. 18, October, 1979.
[11] Nonaka, I. & Takeuchi, H. *Criação do conhecimento na empresa*. 6ed. Rio de Janeiro: Campus, 1997.
[12] Coll, C. Piaget, O construtivismo e a educação escolar: onde está o fio condutor? *Substratum*: Temas Fundamentais em Psicologia e Educação. v.1(1), p.145-164. Porto Alegre: Artes Médicas, 1997.
[13] Veer, R.Van & Valsiner, J. *Vygotsky: Uma Síntese*. São Paulo: Loyola, 1996.
[14] Gardner, H. *Frames of Mind*. New York: Basic Books, 1985.
[15] Polanyi, M. *The tacit dimension*. New York: Doubleday, 1966.
[16] Davenport, T. H., Thomas, R. J., and Cantrell, S. The Mysterious Art and Science of knowledge-worker Performance. *MIT Sloan Management Review*, 43(1), p.23-30, 2002.
[17] Cavalcanti, M. & Gomes, E. Inteligência empresarial: Um novo modelo de Gestão para a Nova Economia. *Produção*, **10(2)**, p. 53-64, 2001.
[18] Zabot, J.B. & Silva, L.C. Mello da. *Gestão do Conhecimento: aprendizagem e tecnologia – construindo a inteligência coletiva*. SãoPaulo: Atlas, 2002.
[19] Ghoshal, S. A empresa individualizada. *HSM Management*, v.14 (mai-jun), p.20-24,1999.
[20] Senge, P. *A Quinta disciplina*. Rio de Janeiro: Quality Mark, 1997.
[21] Quonian, Luc. Inteligência Competitiva como inteligência de negócio. In: 2º Workshop Brasileiro De Inteligência Competitiva e 3º Seminário Catarinense De Gestão do Conhecimento, 2001, Florianópolis. *Inteligência Competitiva e Gestão do Conhecimento*. Florianópolis: Senai, 05 outubro, 2001.
[22] Rodrigues, L.C. Business intelligence – the management information systems next step. In: *Management Information Systems Third International Conference On Management Information Systems, Incorporating Gis & Remote Sensing*. Halkidiki, 2002. Greece: WIT, p. 269-278, 2002.
[23] Manville, B. & Foote, N. *Strategy as if knowledge mattered*. Available at www.informal.com.br/ artigos/a15032000001.html. Access: 03/07/01.

Author Index

Abu-Hola I. 109
Aedo I. 243
Allegra M. 227
Andrade R. 157

Barba C. 157
Basbas S. 99
Bennedsen J. 61
Biocca F. 195
Bond-Hu D. 131

Chiazzese G. 227
Chifari A. 227
Clawson S. 69
Conely K. 37
Constantinescu N. 177
Cucchiarelli A. 165

Dalibart M. 139
Darabi A. 215
de Almeida M. I. R. 309
Dhanjal S. 279
Díaz P. 243
Doherty L. 3

Fitzgerald H. 195

Gatautis R. 269

Hafich A. 79
Higgins S. 27
Hofer F. 147

Jackson L. A. 195
Jacobs P. H. M. 299
Jansen W. 183

Kellermann R. 157
Khmelevsky Y. 279

Layden M. 3
Lindskog H. 289

Maccari E. A. 309
Mangan P. 3
Matsuura J. 263
Mecca S. 49
Miller J. 27
Morgan K. 89

Neville K. 157
Nuss S. 37

Ottaviano S. 227
Owens J. 79

Packard N. 27
Papaioannou P. 99
Paparrizos K. 205
Pekos G. 235

Riess J. S. 13
Rodrigues L. C. 309

Samaras N. 205
Sanz D. 243
Schwaninger A. 147
Seta L. 227
Sifaleras A. 205
Sorensen H. B. 13, 79, 157
Stavredes T. M. 69
Stephanides G. 177, 235

Taxiltaris C. 99
ten Berge J. W. 299
Tsiakis T. 235

Valenti S. 165
van Duin J. H. R. 299
von Eye A. 195

Wall K. 27
Weeden E. M. 119
Wolfe H. B. 253

Zhao Y. 195

WITPRESS

Data Mining V

Editors: **A. ZANASI**, TEMIS Text Mining Solutions S.A., Italy, **N.F.F. EBECKEN**, COPPE/UFRJ, Federal University of Rio de Janeiro, Brazil and **C.A. BREBBIA**, Wessex Institute of Technology, UK

Yielding substantial knowledge from data primarily gathered for a wide range of quite different applications, data mining is a promising and relatively new area of current research and development. Financial institutions have derived considerable benefits from its application while other industries and disciplines are now applying the methodology to increasing effect.

This book features papers from the Fifth International Conference on Data Mining, Text Mining and Their Business Applications. Sharing state-of-the-art results and practical development experiences, these allow researchers and applications developers from a variety of areas to learn about the many different applications of data mining and how the techniques can help in their own field.

The volume features contributions on: DATA PREPARATION – Data Selection; Preprocessing; Transformation. TECHNIQUES – Neural Networks; Decision Trees; Genetic Algorithms; Information Extraction; Clustering; Categorization. SPECIAL APPLICATIONS – Customer Relationship Management; Competitive Intelligence; Virtual Communities; National Security; Applications in Science and Engineering, Business, Industry and Government, and Health and Medicine.

Series: Management Information Systems, Vol 10

ISBN: 1-85312-729-9   2004   apx 500pp   apx £150.00/US$240.00/€225.00

Text Mining and its Applications

Editor: **A. ZANASI**, TEMIS Text Mining Solutions S.A., Italy

Organisations generate and collect large volumes of textual data, which they use in daily operations. Unfortunately, many companies are unable to capitalize fully on the value of this data because information implicit within it is not easy to discern. In short, most organizations are unsure of how to extract the underlying business or research knowledge contained in their vast deposits of textual information such as articles, web pages and surveys and are unable to integrate it with traditional structured data sources to enrich the overall data mining process.

Primarily intended for business analysts and statisticians across multiple industries such as retail, telecommunications, financial services, government and pharmaceuticals, this book provides an introduction to the types of problems encountered and current available text mining solutions. It will also be suitable for use on undergraduate courses specializing in this area, and on business oriented graduate and postgraduate courses.

Series: Advances in Management Information, Vol 3

ISBN: 1-85312-995-X   2004
apx 300pp+CD-ROM
apx £114.00/US$182.00/€171.00

All prices correct at time of going to press but subject to change.
WIT Press books are available through your bookseller or direct from the publisher.

WITPRESS

Handling Missing Data
Applications to Environmental Analysis

Editors: G. LATINI and G. PASSERINI, Ancona University, Italy

Featuring a wide range of techniques for analysing and filling gaps in time series data, this book contains recent research by the Air Pollution and Environmental Fluid Dynamics Group at Marche University of Technology, Ancona. The contributions may be viewed both as tools to manage practical air pollution problems and as a compendium of theoretical knowledge for a new understanding of lesser-known aspects.

Contents: An Introduction to the Statistical Filling of Environmental Data Time Series; Data Validation and Data Gaps in Environmental Time Series; Statistical Modelling of the Remediation of Environmental Data Time Series; Imputation Techniques for Meteorological and Air Quality Data Filling; Neural Networks and Their Applications to Meteorological and Air Quality Data Filling.

Series: Advances in Management Information, Vol 1

ISBN: 1-85312-992-5   2004   200pp
£91.00/US$145.00/€136.50

Find us at
http://www.witpress.com

Save 10% when you order from our encrypted ordering service on the web using your credit card.

Risk Analysis IV

Editor: C.A. BREBBIA, Wessex Institute of Technology, UK

The analysis and management of risk and the mitigation of hazards is of fundamental importance to planners and researchers around the world.
The papers featured in this book come from the fourth in the popular international conference series on this subject and cover areas such as: Estimation of Risk; Man-Made Risk; Seismic Hazard; External Events - Terrorism and Sabotage; Risk Perception and Philosophy; Landslides and Slope Movements; Data Collection Analysis; Emergency Response; Soil and Water Contamination; and Air Quality Studies.

Series: Management Information Systems, Vol 10

ISBN: 1-85312-736-1   2004   apx 400pp
apx £132.00/US$211.00/€198.00

We are now able to supply you with details of new WIT Press titles via
E-Mail. To subscribe to this free service, or for information on any of our titles, please contact the Marketing Department, WIT Press, Ashurst Lodge, Ashurst, Southampton, SO40 7AA, UK
Tel: +44 (0) 238 029 3223
Fax: +44 (0) 238 029 2853
E-mail: marketing@witpress.com

WITPRESS

Modelling of High Complexity Systems by means of a Personal Computer and Applications

F. STĂNCIULESCU, *Research Institute for Informatics, Bucharest, Romania*

Addressing a wide audience of theoreticians and practitioners including systems analysts, designers, control engineers, informaticians, ecologists, biologists, hydrologists, physicists and chemists, this interdisciplinary research monograph provides new methods, techniques and tools for computer analysis, modelling, simulation and control of complex systems. The author also demonstrates how the theory discussed can be applied to solve aquatic, terrestrial and atmospheric environmental problems.

ISBN: 1-85312-778-7   2004
apx 200pp
apx £81.00/US$129.00/€121.50

WIT eLibrary

Making the latest research accessible to researchers and professionals within academia, industry and government, the WIT eLibrary provides individual papers presented at Wessex Institute of Technology's prestigious international conferences and published in the accompanying WIT Press proceedings.

Access the WIT eLibrary at
http://www.witpress.com

Management Information Systems 2004
Incorporating GIS and Remote Sensing

Editor: C.A. BREBBIA, *Wessex Institute of Technology, UK*

Bringing together contributions from researchers in academia and industry as well as land use planners and technology network managers, this volume features papers presented at the fourth international conference on this topic. Representing the state-of-the-art in MIS, individual contributions reflect the various ways in which this technology plays an active role in linking together economic development and environmental conservation planning. The growing use of MIS in various fields of application is also highlighted.

Series: *Management Information Systems, Vol 8*

ISBN: 1-85312-728-0   2004
apx 400pp
apx £132.00/US$211.00/€198.00

WIT Press is a major publisher of engineering research. The company prides itself on producing books by leading researchers and scientists at the cutting edge of their specialities, thus enabling readers to remain at the forefront of scientific developments. Our list presently includes monographs, edited volumes, books on disk, and software in areas such as: Acoustics, Advanced Computing, Architecture and Structures, Biomedicine, Boundary Elements, Earthquake Engineering, Environmental Engineering, Fluid Mechanics, Fracture Mechanics, Heat Transfer, Marine and Offshore Engineering and Transport Engineering.

WITPRESS

Software Process Assessment and Improvement

Editor: **T. ROUT**, *Software Quality Institute, Griffith University, Australia*

Set apart from other products by its experimental flavour, this CD-ROM presents a wide-ranging view on the conduct and use of software process assessment.
Partial Contents: Software Process Improvement - A Multi-Dimensional Perspective; Software Process Assessment - Benefits and Limitations; Empirical Studies of Software Process Assessment Methods; On Comparing Process Assessment Results - BOOTSTRAP and CMM; An Architecture for Quality Systems in Information Systems Departments.

ISBN: 1-85312-609-8   1998
Book on CD-ROM
£59.00/US$98.00/€88.50

Implementing a Quality Management System

Editor: **D.N. WILSON**, *University of Technology, Australia*

In this CD-ROM the contributors provide advice and document experience in implementing quality management systems.
Partial Contents: Designing Quality Management Systems - A Software Development Metaphor; QMS - Issues for the Smaller Organisation.

ISBN: 1-85312-593-8   1998
Book on CD-ROM
£59.00/US$98.00/€88.50

Computational Finance and Its Applications

Editor: *WESSEX INSTITUTE OF TECHNOLOGY, UK*

Intelligent computational systems have become increasingly important in many financial applications while traditional techniques are constantly being improved and developed as a result of the power of modern computer systems.
Reflecting the considerable interest and ever-increasing amount of development work going on in the field, this book features most of the contributions presented at the First International Conference on Computational Finance and Its Applications. It will be invaluable to both professionals and academics involved with financial modelling and engineering, and computational intelligence in finance.
The papers included focus on current advances within the following areas: Trading Strategies; Risk Management; Credit Risk; Derivatives Pricing; Advanced Computing and Simulation; Expert Systems and Decision Support; Time Series Analysis and Forecasting; and High Frequency Financial Data.

ISBN: 1-85312-709-4   2004   320pp
£90.00/US$144.00/€135.00

WITPress
Ashurst Lodge, Ashurst, Southampton, SO40 7AA, UK.
Tel: 44 (0) 238 029 3223
Fax: 44 (0) 238 029 2853
E-Mail: marketing@witpress.com